Praise for *Against the World*

"Every story in this book is relevant and abs[...] her narrative strands together with such d[...] nothing is out of place."
—Jennifer Szalai, *Ne[...]*

"In this original, ambitious history, Zahra homes in on the early 20th century to show, with a fascinating cast of nationalists, pacifists, and reactionaries, how globalization prompted resistance and genuine suffering from the outset."
—*New York Times Book Review* Editors' Choice

"A thought-provoking contribution. . . . *Against the World* is at its best in recalling the unexpected ways in which the collapse of the imperial world of nineteenth-century trade and bourgeois hegemony played out in the era of mass politics. It sketches a convincing and fresh picture of the torment World War I brought to eastern Europe and of the plight of Europe's Jews, in particular. Zahra also draws out the new forms of mass mobilization that flourished between the wars and the new actors who emerged onto the political scene."   —Mark Mazower, *Foreign Affairs*

"It's impossible in a review of this, or any, length to do justice to the richly layered tapestry Zahra weaves. . . . Reading *Against the World* against the backdrop of the present makes it hard not to conclude that the path forward lies not in more deglobalization—or more globalization—but in more justice."   —Sean T. Byrnes, *Jacobin*

"[A] superb history of the interwar period. . . . Zahra has produced one of the best and most timely works of global history of the past few years."
—Gavin Jacobson, *New Statesman*

"Drawing lessons from current events, Zahra's [*Against the World*] builds its case from Zahra's archival research in seven countries. Using those materials, she shows how anxieties about the perceived and real consequences of globalization fueled wide-ranging efforts to change or slow cross-border flows of people, goods, and capital. The cast of characters includes Benito Mussolini, Mahatma Gandhi, and other famous nationalists, as well as people usually at the margins of power, including migrant women."

—Elizabeth Station, *University of Chicago* magazine

"[Zahra] sets out to examine antiglobalism and nationalist politics between the two world wars. . . . Ms. Zahra believes that, by understanding this period better, we can defuse the unresolved tensions between globalism and democracy in our own time. . . . [V]igorous and informative."

—Tunku Varadarajan, *Wall Street Journal*

"For more than three decades now, globalization has seemed inevitable, unstoppable, and unambiguously beneficial. Resourcefully and coolly detailing a long history of resistance to it, *Against the World* not only alerts us to the central intellectual folly of our age. Splendidly timely, it also explains our bewildering present of war and rancorous mass politics, and outlines both challenges and possibilities in our shared future."

—Pankaj Mishra, author of *Bland Fanatics: Liberals, Race, and Empire*

"Everything Tara Zahra touches turns to gold—and her new masterwork on what happened between the world wars when liberal globalization met mass politics is no exception. This gifted historian's dramatic preoccupation with the Central European epicenter of the revolt and the human characters and consequences make the results impossible to put down. Yet *Against the World* is hardly just history. With so many fascinating parallels to our own age's ongoing revolt against market freedom and moral cosmopolitanism, Zahra's state-of-the-art reconstruction is not merely about our past; it bears on our future too."

—Samuel Moyn, author of *Humane: How the United States Abandoned Peace and Reinvented War*

"*Against the World* is a tour de force: Tara Zahra brings her formidable talents as a writer and scholar to this elegant, consistently surprising, and richly peopled book, which positively brims with relevance for our troubled times. Zahra convinces us that unless the defenders of open societies and open borders address head-on the inequalities at the heart of globalization, those who would put up walls are likely to triumph again."
—Sunil Amrith, author of *Unruly Waters:*
How Mountain Rivers and Monsoons
Have Shaped South Asia's History

"Deeply researched, timely, and erudite, *Against the World* illuminates why, after 1918, the world took an anti-global turn. Interrogating the myriad relationships between nationalism and globalization, Tara Zahra moves deftly between local histories and macro trends, producing a page-turning account that is a must-read for anyone interested in how and why the world's current conditions are not unique."
—Caroline Elkins, Pulitzer Prize–winning author of
Legacy of Violence: A History of the British Empire

"Every day brings another headline about the end of globalization but, as Tara Zahra shows us in her lively and learned new book, we have been here before. The years between the world wars also brought calls to bring the supply chains home and sparked efforts for local food security, domestic manufacturing, and even autarky. Through vivid portraits of contemporaries from Czech shoe baron Tomás Bat'a to Hungarian-born feminist Rosika Schwimmer she reminds us that the politics of separation spawn new conflicts of their own."
—Quinn Slobodian, author of *Globalists:*
The End of Empire and the Birth of Neoliberalism

"Uncovering for the first time the first ever popular revolt against globalism, *Against the World* represents a new and better kind of global history. Unusually rich with the lives and times of ordinary people and

brimming with fresh interpretations and insights, this is the best book about the mass politics of globalization yet written."
—Jonathan Levy, author of *Ages of American Capitalism: A History of the United States*

"Immigrant garment workers in New York, community gardeners seeking food self-sufficiency in Vienna, anti-colonial nationalists in India— Tara Zahra brings to life these and other popular movements in the decades between the two world wars. Zahra shows that the struggle in Europe and beyond was not just between fascism and communism. It also involved conflicts over the inequalities that globalization had wrought, with diverse politics that were both 'right' and 'left.' *Against the World* counterintuitively offers a global history from the perspective of its discontents. Brilliantly conceived and masterfully told."
—Mae Ngai, Bancroft Prize–winning author of *The Chinese Question: The Gold Rushes, Chinese Migration, and Global Politics*

"Discouraging yet important, expertly rendered political history."
—*Kirkus Reviews*

AGAINST
THE WORLD

ALSO BY TARA ZAHRA

Objects of War
(coauthored with Leora Auslander)

The Great Departure

The Lost Children

Kidnapped Souls

AGAINST
THE WORLD

ANTI-GLOBALISM AND MASS POLITICS

BETWEEN THE WORLD WARS

◆

Tara Zahra

W. W. NORTON & COMPANY
Independent Publishers Since 1923

For information about permission to reproduce selections from this book, write to
Permissions, W. W. Norton & Company, Inc., 500 Fifth Avenue, New York, NY 10110

For information about special discounts for bulk purchases, please contact
W. W. Norton Special Sales at specialsales@wwnorton.com or 800-233-4830

Manufacturing by Lakeside Book Company
Book design by Brooke Koven
Production manager: Anna Oler

Library of Congress Cataloging-in-Publication Data

Names: Zahra, Tara, author.
Title: Against the world : anti-globalism and mass politics between the world wars /
Tara Zahra.
Description: First edition. | New York : W. W. Norton & Company, 2023. |
Includes bibliographical references and index.
Identifiers: LCCN 2022047796 | ISBN 9780393651966 (hardcover) |
ISBN 9780393651973 (ebook)
Subjects: LCSH: World politics—1919–1932. | World politics—1933–1945. | Economic
history—1918–1945. | Anti-globalization movement—History—20th century. |
Nationalism—History—20th century. | Isolationism—History—20th century.
Classification: LCC D727 .Z35 2023 | DDC 909.82—dc23/eng/20221108
LC record available at https://lccn.loc.gov/2022047796

ISBN 978-1-324-07520-2 pbk.

W. W. Norton & Company, Inc.
500 Fifth Avenue, New York, N.Y. 10110
www.wwnorton.com

W. W. Norton & Company Ltd.
15 Carlisle Street, London W1D 3BS

1 2 3 4 5 6 7 8 9 0

For Eloisa

CONTENTS

INTRODUCTION

"In a world of falling prices, no stock has dropped more
catastrophically than International Cooperation."
—DOROTHY THOMPSON, 1931[1]

THE ERA OF globalism was over.

Even committed internationalists "have lost faith and join in the
chorus of those who never sympathized with our ideals, and say internationalism has failed," despaired Mary Sheepshanks, a British feminist
and internationalist. Although she was confident that the spirit of internationalism would return once "the fumes cleared from men's brains," it
had been replaced for the moment by "race hatred and national jealousy,
leading to tariffs, militarism, armaments, crushing taxation, restricted
intercourse, mutual butchery, and the ruin of all progress."[2]

The year was 1916. Hundreds of thousands of European boys and
men were already dead, and nearly everyone was penning obituaries for
internationalism. The fumes did not clear quickly. More than twenty-
five years later, the Austrian Jewish writer Stefan Zweig would publish
his memoir, *The World of Yesterday*. It was a nostalgic eulogy for a lost
era of globalism. Zweig, a self-described "citizen of the world," recalled,
"Before 1914, the earth had belonged to all. People went where they
wished and stayed as long as they pleased. There were no permits, no
visas, and it always gives me pleasure to astonish the young by telling
them that before 1914 I travelled from Europe to India and to America without passport and without ever having seen one." After the war,

everything changed. "The world was on the defensive against strangers ... The humiliations which once had been devised with criminals alone in mind now were imposed upon the traveller, before and during every journey. There had to be photographs from right and left, in profile and full face, one's hair had to be cropped sufficiently to make the ears visible; fingerprints were taken ... they asked for the addresses of relatives, for moral and financial guarantees, questionnaires, and forms in triplicate and quadruplicate needed to be filled out, and if only one of this sheath of papers was missing one was lost." He linked these bureaucratic humiliations to a loss of human dignity and the lost dream of a united world. "If I reckon up the many forms I have filled out during these years ... the many examinations and interrogations at frontiers I have been through, then I feel keenly how much human dignity has been lost in this century which, in our youth, we had credulously dreamed as one of freedom, as of the federation of the world."³

In Britain, economist John Maynard Keynes penned his famous obituary for globalization shortly after the war ended. "What an extraordinary episode in the economic progress of man that age was which came to an end in August, 1914!" he wrote. In the golden age before the war, "The inhabitant of London could order by telephone, sipping his morning tea in bed, the various products of the whole earth, in such quantity as he might see fit, and reasonably expect their early delivery upon his doorstep." It was an age in which "the projects of militarism and imperialism, of racial and cultural rivalries, of monopolies, restrictions, and exclusion, which were to play the serpent to this paradise, were little more than the amusements of his daily newspaper." These looming threats "appeared to exercise almost no influence at all on the ordinary course of his social and economic life, the internationalization of which was nearly complete in practice."⁴

Stefan Zweig and John Maynard Keynes remain among the most renowned analysts of the changes brought by the First World War. They both understood these changes in terms of the end of a golden era of globalization, during which people, goods, and capital breezed across international frontiers. But their very nostalgia for a lost world of globalism offers an important clue as to the causes of its downfall. Both men were myopic about the extent to which the freedoms they associated with globalization were the privileges of a narrow elite ("It may be I was too greatly pampered," Zweig speculated . . .). The earth had not belonged to everyone before 1914. It had, however, belonged to people like Keynes and Zweig.

Zweig and Keynes traveled the world unmolested by bureaucrats before the First World War largely because they were wealthy, highly educated, white European men. They traveled freely for business and pleasure, with no concern for their physical safety. Nor did they worry about the meddlesome interference of husbands, fathers, or state authorities.

In steerage, the World of Yesterday looked quite different. Migrants headed toward the United States in the late nineteenth century were already subjected to the poking and prodding of doctors charged with excluding sick, disabled, and mentally ill migrants, along with those deemed "likely to become a public charge" (including most single women). Nonwhite migrants were categorically excluded. Millions of people in the world lived in deep poverty in regions that were denied political sovereignty and exploited economically for the benefit of Europeans and North Americans. While it was true that international trade benefited all parties in the aggregate, it exacerbated inequality between rich countries and poor countries. Likewise, within industrialized countries, globalization did not benefit everyone equally: there were clear winners and losers.[5]

Keynes frankly acknowledged all this. The bounty of globalization was not shared equally. But inequality, he claimed, had been seen as a necessary corollary to progress in the nineteenth century. "The greater part of the population, it is true, worked hard and lived at a low standard of comfort, yet were, to all appearances, reasonably contented with this lot." This was because they believed in the prospect of social mobility. "Escape was possible," he insisted, "for any man of capacity or character at all exceeding the average."[6]

The war shattered those illusions. The magnitude of wartime sacrifices bred popular demands for more immediate justice. Across Europe and the world, workers, women, and colonial subjects took to the streets, demanding sovereignty and greater equality. In Russia the discontent combusted into revolution, which seemed poised to spread westward. The wheels of global integration ground to a halt. This spelled disaster for Europe and the world, Keynes warned. "An inefficient, unemployed, disorganized Europe faces us, torn by internal strife and international hate, fighting, starving, pillaging, and lying."[7]

His warning was prescient. The era of anti-globalism lasted another two decades, punctuated by the greatest global economic crisis in world history, the Great Depression. Nor would the strife be overcome with a new treaty or a peaceful handshake. Rather, as American journalist Dorothy Thompson would observe from Berlin in 1931, "Looking at Europe, from the British Isles to the Balkans, one is forced to the admission that after twelve years of the League of Nations, the International Court... multilateral treaties, Kellogg Pacts, the International Bank and disarmament conferences, the whole world is retreating from the international position and is taking its dolls and going home."[8]

WHY AND how did so many people turn against the world after 1918? And what were the consequences of this anti-global turn? This book attempts to answer these questions. In the process, it reframes the history of interwar Europe not only as a battle between fascism and communism, democracy and dictatorship, but also as a contest over the future of globalization and globalism. The era between the two world wars was defined by attempts to resolve mounting tensions between globalization on the one hand and equality, state sovereignty, and mass politics on the other.

Moving through time and across space, I aim to give voice to the diversity of individuals who participated in this debate, to how it played out in local everyday contexts and at the level of national and international politics. The protagonists include several famous and infamous people—dictators, internationalists, industrialists, and economists— but also many individuals on the margins of history, including migrant women, garment workers, shopkeepers, unemployed veterans, radical gardeners, and disillusioned homesteaders.

There is no doubt about the decline of global mobility and trade in this period.[9] On the one hand, the First World War was a "global" war. It mobilized human and material resources around the world and increased international financial entanglement through a massive web of international debt (especially debts to the United States).[10] But at the same time, the war produced unprecedented supply shocks. The cost of shipping tripled, and inflation soared. Meanwhile, states introduced new tariffs, exchange controls, and other protectionist measures, and sought to cut off supplies to their enemies.[11] Economic historians estimate that global exports declined by 25 percent due to the outbreak of the First World War, recovering to prewar levels only in 1924. There was a brief period of growth in the late 1920s, but all these gains were lost during the Great Depression. By 1933, world trade had declined 30 percent from 1929 levels and was 5 percent lower than it had been in 1913. Trade did not reach pre-1913 rates of growth again until the 1970s.[12]

Transatlantic migration, which reached a peak of 2.1 million in 1913, came to a sputtering halt during the First World War and recovered only briefly after the war ended. Global migration rates remained high in the 1920s, especially within Asia, but the Great Depression radically curbed mobility everywhere in the world. This was partly due to a reduction in demand for migrant labor, but it was also caused by the closing of state borders and new restrictions on migration and mobility. Global communication also slowed down. News that raced via telegraph from Europe to North America and Australia in a single day in 1913 took weeks to arrive in 1920. And the gold standard, the motor of global financial integration, broke down during the First World War and was abandoned by the roadside during the 1930s, first by Great Britain (1931), then the United States (1933), and finally by France and other European powers.[13]

These numbers, and the broader economic histories of globalization and deglobalization between the two world wars, are critically important.[14] But my focus is rather on the grassroots origins and human consequences of the popular revolt against globalism, both for self-professed globalists such as Keynes and Zweig and for individuals who saw globalism as a threat to their aspirations for greater equality and stability. It was this popular confrontation with globalization that ultimately caused its disruption and transformation. Popular anti-globalism arose with accelerating globalization itself in the late nineteenth century, but in the 1920s and 1930s, the demands of anti-global activists were increasingly taken up by political parties and states. Their efforts to render individuals, families, and states more self-sufficient had mixed results, but lasting consequences.

I use the term "anti-globalism" to refer to political, social, and cultural movements that sought to insulate societies from the global economy by mobilizing against policies, people, and institutions associated with globalism and/or internationalism. Sometimes, these movements produced "deglobalization," the actual slowdown or curtailment of the transnational flows of people, ideas, goods, or capital. More often, however, the actors in this book sought to alter the terms on which globalization took place. They aimed to restructure or reorient global flows of people, goods, or capital, rather than to stop them altogether.

The people and movements I write about, however, did not use the term "deglobalization" at the time. They spoke of "freedom" versus dependence on the global economy, "nationalism" versus "internationalism," "sovereignty" and its violation. They promoted "autarky," "self-sufficiency," and "self-containment." My use of the terms "globalization" and "deglobalization" is therefore self-consciously anachronistic and requires some contextualization.

The terms "globalization" and "deglobalization" came into widespread use in the 1990s, at a moment when a certain kind of free-market capitalism and global integration appeared to be the unstoppable victors of history. After the collapse of Communism in Eastern Europe in 1989, many social scientists and journalists began to talk about "globalization" like they once spoke of "modernization." It seemed to be an irrepressible force that moved in only one direction. McDonald's had opened in Moscow, global finance was ascendant, and a new innovation called the World Wide Web was bringing people into ever more constant communication. Many economists in the 1990s and beyond maintained that "globalization" was a "natural economic process," which would accelerate indefinitely if only left unmolested by government intervention. They saw deglobalization, by contrast (including interwar deglobalization) as the product of "unnatural" political interference with that process.[15] But one only needed to look backward to see forward. The history of Europe between 1918 and 1939 reveals very clearly that the history of globalization was punctuated by pauses and (attempted) reversals.

As historian Stefan Link has argued, moreover, the notion that globalization is "natural" and deglobalization "political" radically "underestimates the politics of globalization." There was nothing "natural" or apolitical about the intensification of globalization in the nineteenth century. Nor was it directed by an invisible hand. Imperial states and armies generally guaranteed that their colonies would be hospitable to foreign investments, and that debtors would pay back international loans. Popular support for free trade in Britain was embedded in a popular political culture that had to be sustained through active political campaigning.[16] Even at the moment of globalization's most rapid acceleration, "free trade" was more a British exception than the rule. After a brief period of greater openness in the 1860s and 1870s, tariff walls sprang up again across the European continent. Otto von Bismarck's infamous coalition of wealthy industrialists and landowners demanded protection for iron and rye, and France, Austria-Hungary, and other European states quickly followed with their own tariffs. The United States maintained high protectionist tariffs right up to the eve of the First World War.[17]

There was nothing contradictory about the synchronous rise of globalizing and anti-global policies and politics. While the terms "globalization" and "deglobalization" appear to be binary opposites, globalism and anti-globalism, like internationalism and nationalism, were often flip sides of the same coin. This simultaneity was baked into the foundation of internationalist projects and accelerating global connection in the late nineteenth century. As historian Jürgen Osterhammel has argued, once the era of globalization began, "conflict and cooperation, integration and disengagement were taking place on a global scale. There was simply no escaping one another."[18]

Even between the two world wars, global flows often moved into new channels and morphed into new shapes, rather than rising and falling. The most radical anti-globalists rarely sought (let alone achieved) total isolation from the global economy, or autarky: they sought globalization on their own terms, or at least better terms.[19] And anti-globalists themselves organized in transnational networks, a phenomenon frequently noted by contemporaries. "The only international which seems to be winning these days is the international of the anti-internationalists," quipped Thompson in 1931.[20]

Nor is anti-globalism simply an alias for nationalism, long recognized as a defining political force throughout the world in 1918.[21] Nationalism and anti-globalism were (and remain) closely connected. But there were many contexts in which nationalism and anti-globalism departed company. For example, anti-colonial advocates of economic self-sufficiency in interwar India preached a self-consciously universalist and "globalist" political agenda. They argued that more economic independence would produce a more genuine form of internationalism that was based on cooperation rather than exploitation.[22] Likewise, growing diasporic nationalist movements in the 1920s and 1930s were simultaneously internationalist and nationalist. Many European socialists in the 1920s and 1930s called for political internationalism but also sought to insulate domestic workers and industries from foreign competition. In this book we will meet political internationalists who argued for economic self-sufficiency; nationalists who promoted global trade; imperialists who saw empire as a route to greater self-sufficiency; and individuals whose views on the global economy were simply eclectic or inconsistent.

Even the most ardent globalists sometimes changed their minds. Keynes famously penned an article in 1933 arguing for more national self-sufficiency. It read like a conversion narrative. "I was brought up, like most Englishmen, to respect free trade not only as an economic doctrine which a rational and instructed person could not doubt, but almost as a part of the moral law," he recalled. "I regarded ordinary departures from it as being at the same time an imbecility and an outrage." But in the years after the war, he had changed his view, to the point that he could now identify "with those who would minimise, rather than with those who would maximise, economic entanglement between nations . . . let goods be homespun whenever it is reasonably and conveniently possible; and, above all, let finance be primarily national."[23]

Deprived of his Austrian citizenship by the Nazis, Stefan Zweig was also forced to confront the limits of his identity as a global citizen. He reflected in his memoir, "For all that I had been training my heart for almost half a century to beat as a *citoyen du monde* it was useless. On the day I lost my passport I discovered, at the age of fifty-eight, that losing one's native land implies more than parting with a circumscribed area of soil."[24]

THE REVOLT against globalism was the product of two developments that collided in the nineteenth century: the acceleration of globalization itself, and the rise of mass politics. The world had been "globalizing" for centuries, through colonial conquest, scientific voyages, and expanding trade networks. But the pace and magnitude of integration quickened in the 1880s, thanks largely to new technologies. Trains, steamships, telegraphs, postal services, and press dispatches transported goods, people, information, and diseases at unprecedented speed and in once unfathomable quantities. Scientists, artists, social reformers, and policy makers gathered at great international congresses to exchange ideas. Banking and finance became more international through the gold standard, which greatly facilitated global trade and investment. Ever more remote corners of the world were sucked into the whirlwind of the global economy. Farmworkers and textile workers in Poland were aware of higher wages in Chicago and New York (and prepared to cross the ocean to earn them); shoe factories in Czechoslovakia and Massachusetts competed with shoemakers in Japan. The world became more interdependent, not only for labor and consumer goods but also for basic necessities such as food and energy.[25]

If, as neoclassical economics suggests, global integration produced more wealth overall, this wealth was not distributed equally. While global trade did enable some European consumers to eat cheaper meat and bread, these prices did not necessarily reflect the true costs of a globalized food supply chain, including the impact on labor conditions and the environment.[26] Migration also had real winners and losers. Economists estimate that the era of mass migration in the United States between 1870 and 1910 corresponded to a decline in US wages of about 8 percent. At the city level, a 1 percent increase in the foreign-born population was linked to a 1–1.5 percent drop in wages.[27]

The problem of growing inequality was exacerbated by the gold standard. Adhering to the gold standard was the ticket to entry in the global economy until the 1930s. But it radically constrained the ability of governments to respond to economic crises. In an economic downturn, in order to maintain the value of their currencies pegged to gold, governments were forced to lower wages and cut spending. Tightening the money supply benefited those such as banks and creditors who supplied money, but it hurt workers and those in debt—such as the midwestern farmers who supported the American populist movement at the end of the nineteenth century. When populist presidential candidate William Jennings Bryan famously argued in 1896 that he would not help to "crucify mankind upon a cross of gold," he was arguing in favor of increasing the money supply to help farmers pay off their crushing debts (inflation would make those debts disappear). During the Great Depression, European governments initially responded to the crisis by trying, once again, to cut spending, adhere to the gold standard, and dutifully pay their debts (especially to the United States). A dose of austerity appeared to have cured the global economy in the immediate aftermath of the First World War. A decade later, the same treatment almost killed the patient.[28]

Global integration interfered with states' sovereignty in other ways. After the First World War, international organizations such as the League of Nations attempted to rebuild the global economy by assisting in the economic and financial reconstruction of states—such as Austria—that lay in ruin. But in exchange for loans for reconstruction and development, their governments had to submit to oversight by international institutions. The forms of international economic governance invented between the wars became the foundation for contemporary institutions such as the World Bank and the International Monetary Fund (IMF) that still offer loans and development assistance with long strings attached. But since the beginning of their existence in the 1920s, they have generated popular protest. The cost of "belonging" to the global economy, some argued, was simply too high.[29] Fantasies of escaping this global system altogether or of gaining greater individual and national self-sufficiency within it intensified in this environment.

It would be a mistake to tell this story simply in terms of *economic* winners and losers, however. When people challenged the terms of globalization and globalism in the 1920s and 1930s, many were responding to direct economic threats: lost jobs or wages, farms or homes repossessed. But they were also often responding to cultural and social changes that either resulted from or were conveniently blamed on globalization. Mass immigration transformed the material environment of cities in Europe and North America, bringing new sounds, sights, and smells to the streets.[30] Mass emigration disrupted family ties, separating wives and husbands, parents and children, sometimes permanently. The interference of international institutions such as the League of Nations in "domestic" policies and budgets provoked powerful *feelings* of injustice, especially when the rules were not applied uniformly. Individuals and states feared dependence on foreign powers for essential foods and raw materials, for economic reasons, but also for political, cultural, and existential reasons. Emotions were central to the history of anti-globalism. But the words and actions of globalists and internationalists who believed deeply in the morality and benevolence of their own visions of global integration were no less emotional.

EMOTIONS WERE famously important to the second force behind anti-globalism: the rise of mass politics, what historian Carl Schorske famously called "Politics in a New Key."[31] Mass politics began with the gradual expansion of suffrage itself in the nineteenth century. In 1880, most states in Europe were still monarchies (France and Switzerland were the exceptions). But most had some institutions of self-government as well, such as parliaments, regional legislatures, local village and city councils. France and Germany elected national parliaments with a system of universal manhood suffrage. Britain gave the vote to most men over the age of thirty in 1884. Most other societies started out with more restricted franchise systems. Only men who paid a certain minimum in annual taxes or who had achieved a high level of education enjoyed the right to vote. By the turn of the twentieth century, however, even these restrictive systems were becoming more democratic.

The expansion of suffrage created spaces for new political movements and parties that sought to represent workers, peasants, and lower-middle-class artisans and shopkeepers. These included parties on the left and right, with Socialist, Christian Socialist, populist, and nationalist platforms. As political parties attempted to reach new voters, political life transformed, becoming more of a spectacle and a form of entertainment. Politics happened in the streets and not just in the halls of parliaments, and politicians began to use more radical and extreme rhetoric and tactics to engage voters. They also communicated in new ways, as the range and circulation of newspapers expanded, and sensationalist journalists competed to cater to broader audiences. The First World War further politicized and radicalized workers, women, and colonial subjects. By 1920, massive numbers of new voters (including millions of women) were eligible to cast votes for the first time. There was an immediate connection between democratization, the rise of mass politics, and the revolt against globalism. Increasingly, people negatively affected by global integration had the opportunity to speak back at the ballot box and in the streets.

The rise of mass political parties such as the Social Democrats, Communist Party, and fascist parties such as the National Socialists were central to the rise of anti-globalism in the 1920s and 1930s. But mass mobilization against globalism extended well beyond the realm of organized party politics. Indeed, political parties and states often followed the lead of more grassroots organizers, such as the urban gardeners who took to the streets of Vienna at the end of the First World War. More broadly, political parties and governments—from New Deal Democrats and anti-colonial nationalists to fascists—incorporated many of the demands of popular anti-global movements into their platforms and policies in the 1920s and 1930s. From tariffs and migration restrictions to back-to-the-land campaigns and consumer boycotts, states implemented policies that were intended to restrict the mobility of people, goods, germs, and capital across borders.

Individuals who perceived themselves to be victims of globalization animated the anti-global movements that swept across Europe and beyond. They included women and children who starved during the trade blockades of the First World War because they no longer had access to imported wheat and potatoes; parents who lost their children to emigration; those same young migrants, working in inhumane conditions in foreign factories and mines. They included small shopkeepers and farmers bankrupted by chain stores or foreign competition; colonial subjects for whom globalization was linked to imperial exploitation; and, later on, millions of people whose livelihoods were wiped out by the Great Depression or by other global economic forces beyond their control.

But there were also many victims of anti-globalism, such as the millions of individuals who belonged to national and religious minority groups now persecuted by nation-states that rejected cosmopolitanism. Jews, socialists, feminists, and internationalists were favored scapegoats of anti-globalists, along with businesses and industries owned by minorities or foreigners. Stateless persons and refugees were also among the multitude of anti-globalism's victims, homeless in a world of closed borders.

ANTI-GLOBALISM AND anti-internationalism gained particular purchase in states that had lost the First World War, including Germany, Austria, and Hungary. During the First World War, the Allies had successfully blockaded Germany and Austria-Hungary. The goal was to defeat the Central Powers by preventing critical food and supplies from reaching the population, including civilians. Historians still debate the number that died of starvation—whether it was over 700,000 or closer to 400,000. Regardless, the lesson many Central Europeans learned from the experience was that their countries should never again be dependent on foreign imports for food.[32]

Citizens of these states had sacrificed greatly during the Great War. They lost their fathers, husbands, and sons. They had been forced to stand by as their children cried of hunger. At the end of the war, many citizens across the political spectrum were deeply embittered, not only by the senseless bloodletting but also by what felt like the petty vengeance of the victors. They were particularly angry about their territorial losses, the loss of empire and imperial resources that sustained them. Austria and Hungary each lost nearly two-thirds of their territory, while Germany lost 12.2 percent of its territory and all of its former colonies. This made it even more challenging to grow enough food and mine enough coal to supply calories, heat, and energy to populations and industries recovering from war. The war's losers also felt humiliated by the new international order, embodied by the Paris Peace Treaties and the League of Nations.[33]

Central Europe therefore holds a special place in this story. The Habsburg Empire, which had been the largest free-trade zone in Europe before the war, was often represented as a kind of miniature global economy.[34] The empire's dissolution into warring nation-states, each with policies of extreme economic nationalism, was perceived by many contemporaries as a microcosm of the global economy's implosion. But Central Europe also became a laboratory for the reconstruction and rehabilitation of globalization and internationalism. Historian Natasha Wheatley has compellingly argued that Central Europe was a "Ground Zero" for the creation of a new international order after the First World War.[35] This was not only because the Habsburg successor states were seen as "immature" democracies, in need of international (Western) tutelage, but also because so many new international organizations flocked to East-Central Europe after 1918 to fill the vacuum left by the Habsburg state's collapse.[36]

In recent years, historians have paid a great deal of attention to these new forms of interwar internationalism.[37] Certainly, not *all* the internationalists and globalists simply packed up and went home between 1918 and 1939. There were periods (and pockets) of more or less hope for global or international cooperation. This included a brief period of stability in the mid-1920s when the prospects seemed bright even in Germany, which joined the League of Nations in 1926. In the late 1930s, economists and other experts in the League of Nations recognized the failure of their efforts to revive the global economy through traditional means (such as diplomatic agreements to cut tariffs and stabilize currencies) and developed new and more progressive visions for the future that included tackling global inequality and poverty head-on. They launched programs that anticipated the developmentalist policies of postwar states in the Socialist Bloc and the Global South.

The flourishing of interwar internationalism was therefore deeply entangled with interwar anti-globalism and is central to this book's story. But that does not mean we should forget the depressing sense of failure, futility, and demoralization that set in among many internationalists in the 1930s. "Prime ministers spend half their time on international trains, but not on the route to Geneva," Thompson quipped.[38] It is notable that historians have spent the past several decades combing archives for examples of internationalism and transnational and global connection but largely ignored resistance to globalism and internationalism. This was itself a reflection of the era of globalization between 1989 and 2008, which produced hundreds of books investigating the history of internationalism and the transnational or global movement of people, ideas, goods, and capital. We were all (myself included) looking to "see beyond" the nation-state, because it reflected the world in which we then lived. This book—with its emphasis on the popular politics that animated anti-globalism—is no less a history of the present.

IF CENTRAL EUROPE was an epicenter of anti-globalism, it would be a mistake to assume that anti-globalism found fertile ground *only* in imperial debris or in states that veered toward fascism. One of the most striking things about anti-globalism in the past and present is its political promiscuity. "The outstanding characteristic of Europe's economic life today is the movement everywhere, from England to Turkey, toward what the Germans call *Autarkie*," Thompson wrote. Anti-global movements gained ground across Europe and in the United States and beyond in the 1930s, on the right and the left, in the most resilient democracies, and in the parliaments of small states as well as those of great powers.[39]

To some extent, the overlapping agendas of anti-globalists on the right and left reflected the fact that they were the same people. Several individuals in this book moved across the political spectrum. Benito Mussolini most famously began his political life as a Socialist. Henry Ford might have been taken for the quintessential globalist in the early twentieth century. His automobiles and production methods were exported around the world, earning him millions. At the outset of the First World War, he was a diehard pacifist who embarked on a mission to bring peace to Europe with progressive Jewish feminist and internationalist Rosika Schwimmer. But Ford's pacifism and his objection to involvement in the First World War stemmed precisely from his hostility to international financiers and foreign entanglements. By the 1920s and 1930s, he had moved further to the right, becoming infamous for his anti-Semitism, isolationism, and support for "back to the land" movements that would enable factory workers to grow their own food between shifts. Ideas also moved freely across political lines that were ambiguous to begin with. German lifestyle reformers who advocated "natural" lifestyles, garden cities, and local diets at the turn of the twentieth century inspired left- and right-wing anti-globalists alike after 1918. And populism, a major force behind anti-globalism, has always been politically amorphous, often combining hostility to globalization, big business, and other elites with hostility to foreigners.

Yet another way in which anti-globalism crossed political lines in the 1920s and 1930s was in its focus on family life and gender roles. Both the stories of individual women and the theme of gender have been underrepresented in histories of globalization and global capitalism.[40] Yet women were key objects of and actors in anti-global campaigns on the right and left. Anti-globalism was animated in part by anxieties about the ways in which globalization appeared to radically disrupt gender and family roles.

Many social reformers and government and religious officials closely associated the dangers of globalization with uprooted women and families. Efforts to restabilize gender roles in interwar Europe typically aimed to anchor men and women in spaces and places that represented globality's opposite: the locality, the nation, the soil, and the home. Care work and agricultural and industrial production that had been outsourced to migrants or to foreign production were all supposed to return to the nation and the home. The new era of individual and national "self-sufficiency" typically required a great deal of unpaid labor from women and children.

The fact that right- and left-wing anti-globalists shared common tactics, concerns, and goals does not mean that they were *the same*, however. Rather, anxieties about globalization produced distinctive political movements that competed for popular support. On the right, anti-globalists typically imagined the nation as the primary victim of globalization and internationalism. Their enemies included Jews; Bolshevik internationalists; liberal internationalists; feminist internationalists; migrants and refugees; foreigners and foreign capitalists. Right-wing anti-globalists were often anti-urban. They hoped to prevent working-class "proletarianization" (and politicization) as well as flight from the land by "resettling" racially desirable families in the countryside, where they would produce the food (and babies) necessary to achieve national self-sufficiency.

Their vision was not, however, romantic or backward-looking. It was produced and supported by modern science.[41] Right-wing anti-globalists generally did not want to turn the clock back. Rather, they believed that the Treaty of Versailles and the Great Depression had demonstrated the bankruptcy of political and economic liberalism. "The global economy is broken and will never again exist in its past form," proclaimed Nazi settlement official Johann Wilhelm Ludowici.[42] Far-right anti-globalists tended to see political internationalism and economic globalization as a two-headed monster, often equating the two. Both threatened the sovereignty of the nation. They were allegedly orchestrated by the same people. Nazi propaganda accused Jews of being puppeteers of the liberal international order, Bolshevik internationalism, and global capitalism all at once. This amounted to three different ways of associating Jews with (and blaming them for) globalization.

Left-wing anti-globalists were not necessarily opposed to nationalism, and many were xenophobic even by the standards of their time. But they generally depicted the *worker* rather than the *nation* as the primary victim of globalization. They focused less on purifying the nation than on alleviating the precarity and inequality caused by fluctuations in the global economy. While some demanded immigration restrictions to protect their jobs, they also sought to insulate workers from the shocks of the global economy through economic redistribution. Many progressive anti-globalists also saw rural homesteads and home production as a potential shelter from the vacillations of the business cycle. But they simultaneously demanded land reform to break up large estates or advocated workers' or farmers' cooperatives to counter the power of global enterprises. They were typically less hostile to political internationalism, particularly solidaristic forms of organization (such as international unions, socialist or anarchist movements) that advanced their goals.

In spite of these important differences, right- and left-wing anti-global movements often adapted common tactics and strategies. This is because they were both driven from below by grassroots activism, as farmers, unemployed veterans, hungry workers, and others sought to restore the self-sufficiency and security they believed had been compromised by globalization. Locally, both right- and left-wing critics of globalism occupied farmland, boycotted foreign goods, and marched in streets. They attempted to achieve self-sufficiency in their everyday habits and lives by producing their own goods and eating only local foods.

Anti-globalism reshaped societies both locally and globally. Between the two world wars, significant anti-global movements emerged in the United States, Ireland, India, England, France, Japan, Turkey, Spain, Portugal, Germany, Italy, and the Soviet Union, to name a few examples. This book focuses on only a handful of these cases. I chose them on the basis of the languages I could read, available sources, and in order to highlight the political diversity of anti-global movements: their momentum in countries that had lost or won the First World War, in democracies and in fascist states, in imperial capitals and in countries seeking liberation from colonial rule. I hope that others will deepen our understanding of anti-global politics in these contexts and in the many others that I neglected.

The book's three parts highlight change over time. Anti-globalism did not simply appear out of nowhere in 1914. Part I traces discontent with globalization and internationalism that intensified alongside globalization itself, ending with the First World War. Part II turns to the years immediately after the Great War. As fears of starvation, disease, migrants, refugees, and revolution spread across Europe and the Atlantic, anti-globalism gained a mass following. Part III analyzes the far more radical anti-global movements and state policies that arose after old-world certainties had been deeply shaken by the Great Depression.

IN 1931, Dorothy Thompson remained optimistic that right-wing, anti-global nationalism would exhaust itself. She believed that cutting off global trade would result in a "terrific decline in the standard of living," as closed borders and high tariffs would reduce people to barter and smuggling for food and basic necessities. "For as long as ships sail the seas, airplanes traverse the air, and trains run, human common sense will find some way to overcome impediments to trade. The human race is not yet possessed of sufficient patriotism to condemn itself, for the nation's sake, to starvation," she concluded.[43]

But by 1939, it turned out, many humans were willing to condemn *other people* to starvation "for the nation's sake." Adolf Hitler and Benito Mussolini are remembered for their efforts to conquer the world, not as anti-globalists. But fascists eventually justified their quest for empire in the name of achieving insulation from the global economy and international politics. They went to war to create anti-global empires. If German and Italian peasants and workers could not produce enough wheat, oil, or rubber to secure a high standard of living, the soldiers of those nations would seize those resources through conquest. Hitler famously envied the United States for having built a continental empire vast and rich enough to provide for its population—even at the cost of millions of native lives. This was precisely the kind of empire he would create for Germany, one that would sustain the master race's "self-sufficiency" *and* its standard of living by condemning Germany's neighbors to slavery and starvation.[44]

The legacy of anti-globalism was not only imperial conquest and mass murder, however. For anti-colonial nationalists, economic self-sufficiency was a route to decolonization. Anti-globalism stimulated the creation of new products and synthetic substitutes, such as synthetic fabrics, designed to decrease reliance on scarce goods that could only be acquired through trade. It galvanized efforts to increase agricultural production—including the development of technologies and practices that ultimately made land more productive and decreased global hunger. It transformed the way the global economy itself functioned. The anti-global revolt generated transformative new social programs and policies that aimed to reduce the precarity and pain caused by ups and downs in the business cycle (including the New Deal). It inspired ideals of "development" that aimed to reduce poverty and global inequality and improve standards of living. When the Second World War ended, global leaders renewed their efforts to create more robust and inclusive international institutions to bring about a more stable form of globalism and globalization. Whether or not they succeeded remains to be seen.

AGAINST
THE WORLD

⟨ PART I ⟩

A World Together?

ONE

Victory Lies Just Ahead

BUDAPEST, 1913

In June of 1913, Rosika Schwimmer was at the height of her powers. She had finally succeeded in bringing the annual meeting of the International Women's Suffrage Alliance to her hometown on the Danube. The alliance, founded in 1902 by a coalition of mostly British, American, and German middle-class feminists, had already made the rounds to capital cities in the United States and Northern Europe. But to many delegates, Budapest represented an unfamiliar and possibly unsuitable host city, a place "very far away" in a country "not associated with representative government."

Despite or perhaps because of the exotic locale, the gathering in Budapest was a spectacular success. Two hundred forty delegates from twenty-two countries attended, making the congress the largest in the alliance's history. This was in no small part a result of Schwimmer's efforts. With her Hungarian allies, she drummed up donations from state offices and private donors, selling a record 2,800 tickets to the event. She rounded up a team of English-speaking university students to help attendees cope with the "extreme difficulties" presented by the Hungarian language (Schwimmer herself was fluent in Hungarian, German, English, and French). Between sessions, attendees could make an excursion to Hungary's famous Lake Balaton or tour the State Asylum for Children. The highlight, everyone agreed, was an evening cruise on the Danube, complete with dinner and music, "a happy, congenial party with three hours of exquisite scenery along the shores." Music accompanied the suffragists everywhere.

The opening day of the festivities in Budapest was capped off by a special performance of Mozart's *Abduction from the Seraglio* at the National Opera House, a highly symbolic program. The *Abduction* tells the story of two men attempting to rescue their fiancées from the harem of a despotic Ottoman pasha. The performance would have affirmed Hungary's place on the Western side of the imaginary East-West divide, as well as the alliance's mission to bring "enlightenment" to oppressed women in the patriarchal Orient. It was also a metaphor for enlightenment closer to home. Attendees proudly recalled in 1922 that a group of Hungarian peasant women "with shawls over their heads, having walked fifty miles to attend the Congress," took in Mozart's opera from the galleries; "provision was made for their return home by train."

With Mozart's libretto ringing in their ears, delegates would hear the message of enlightenment and progress driven home in the days that followed. One session posed the question: "How might women still bound by ancient custom, tradition, and prejudice be awakened by the realization that these new times demand new duties and responsibilities?" If no definitive answer emerged that week, alliance leaders were confident that solutions lay just around the corner. In the West, they believed, victory was imminent for the cause of female suffrage; in the past year, suffrage bills had been brought before seventeen national parliaments as well as the legislatures of twenty-nine US states. Since delegates had last gathered in 1911 in Stockholm, "not a backward step has been taken," declared Carrie Chapman Catt, the alliance's president. "On the contrary, a thousand revelations give certain, unchallenged promise that victory for our great cause lies just ahead."

In light of such successes close to home, the suffragists turned their attention to their sisters abroad. "The women of the western world are escaping from the thralldom of the centuries," Chapman Catt declared. "Their liberation is certain; a little more effort, a little more enlightenment and it will come. Out of the richness of our own freedom must we give aid to these sisters of ours in Asia." For Chapman Catt, aid was not a matter of concrete action, however, but of inspiration by example. "Every Western victory will give them encouragement and inspiration, for our victories are their victories and their defeats are our defeats."

Above all, the delegates in Budapest celebrated their own internationalism. Internationalism had a very specific meaning to these feminists: they intended to enlighten and embolden women in every corner of the globe. But the delegates themselves came exclusively from Europe and North America. "It was a disappointment to all that no Asiatic delegate came to Budapest. Asiatic women are unaccustomed to travel alone," organizers lamented. South America was another "unexplored territory so far as our movement is concerned." Indeed, the only country outside of Europe and North America that sent a delegate to Budapest was South Africa.[1] The exclusion of nonwhite women from feminist and international organizations was typical of the time. In response, some women of color created their own organizations, such as the International Council of Women of the Darker Races, founded in 1920.[2]

Chapman Catt nonetheless speculated that in the winter of 1913, "when perpetual darkness shrouded the land of the Midnight Sun, women wrapped in furs, above the Polar Circle, might have been seen gliding over snow covered roads in sleds drawn by reindeer on their way to suffrage meetings. At the same moment, other women, in the midsummer of the southern hemisphere, protected by fans and umbrellas and riding in 'rickshas' were doing the same thing under the fierce rays of a tropical sun." To the imagined "East" of Budapest, she saw hope for the women of the seraglio. "Behind the purdah in India, in the harems of Mohammedanism, behind veils and barred doors and closed sedan chairs there has been rebellion in the hearts of women all down the centuries." Soon, the only remaining frontier for women's rights would lie in outer space: "Like Alexander the Great, we shall soon be looking for other worlds to Conquer!"

This self-congratulatory spirit dominated the convention until the final evening. Typically, an international congress might end with a banquet and a final round of ceremonial toasting. But in Budapest on June 20, 1913, delegates and guests crammed into the convention center's largest banquet hall for a noisy celebration punctuated by bursts of patriotic song, the exchange of addresses, and earnest promises to return in 1915.

Above all, applause rained upon Rosika Schwimmer, celebrated as the "genius" behind the entire affair. As a token of their appreciation, Hungarian feminists presented Schwimmer with a necklace set with jewels. In her acceptance speech, she boasted that her colleagues had accomplished a goal that long eluded Hungarian men. It was the dream of all Hungarians to see Budapest become "the resort of the world." But the suffragists had actually enticed the world to the banks of the Danube. Schwimmer was optimistic that their efforts would pay rich dividends, spreading the spirit of internationalism for years to come. "These ambassadors, who came, to quote the words of Mazzini 'in the name of God and Humanity,' will report to their countries the friendly reception they have met and will surely help the cause of international good feeling."[3]

FOR INTERNATIONALISTS such as Schwimmer, as well as scientists, doctors, industrialists, jurists, and other experts, it was the heyday of the international congress. At least one hundred new international organizations were created in the final decade of the nineteenth century. Their members flocked to conventions and expositions intended to facilitate international exchange (and, for the hosts, to impress the world with a dazzling display of culture, hospitality, and "modernity"). Some, like the International Women's Suffrage Alliance (IWSA), pursued social and political agendas as part of a transatlantic progressive movement. There were also international organizations devoted to pacifism, child welfare, criminal justice, public health and hygiene, and the exchange of scientific expertise. Still others committed themselves explicitly to the work of international cooperation and standardization. Jurists created new international laws to govern war and to define war crimes (resulting

Rosika Schwimmer in 1914.

in The Hague Conventions of 1899 and 1907). At the first World Espe-
ranto conference, held in 1905, globalists promoted the dream of a world
language. The International Bureau of Weights and Measures, founded
in Paris in 1875, aimed to guarantee that a meter was the same distance
everywhere in the world; the Telegraph Union (1865), International
Postal Union (1874), and the International Statistical Institute (1885)
sought to coordinate global communication and information gathering.

Perhaps most ambitious of all was the movement to universalize
time itself. As technology seemed to compress time and space, scientists
and policy makers promoted the unification of clock times and calen-
dars. Self-conscious globalists heralded the international coordination
of time as an essential lubricant to the movement of people and goods
across frontiers. But in a pattern that was emblematic of the rush toward
world unity, the movement to standardize time was not without resistance. Clocks ticking in global synchrony may have been music to the
ears of middle-class internationalists. But as historian Vanessa Ogle has

shown, attempts to impose universal time were often received locally with apathy or hostility, as an assault on local traditions or as a symbol of colonial domination. Resistance to the standardization of time was only one manifestation of a growing suspicion that globalization was not evenhanded in the distribution of its rewards.[4]

By the eve of the First World War, socialists, anti-colonial nationalists, and other reformers were becoming more vocal critics of a form of internationalism that seemed to serve imperial or capitalist interests. Even in Budapest in 1913, many Social Democratic feminists in Budapest saw Schwimmer and her colleagues as hopelessly out of touch. "Rich and wealthy gentlewomen have come from many different parts of the world, who have been able to obtain very pleasant experiences here in Budapest. There were good arrangements, there were many ceremonies, masses, banquets, Danube floodlights, traditional Hungarian knights. . . . But how the vast majority of women—at least 90 percent— live here, the fate of the working-women, the proletarian women, has not been recognized by members of the congress."[5] The Socialist women's movement even organized a counter-congress featuring an appearance by the Austrian Social Democratic feminist Adelheid Popp. The Hungarian newspaper *Népszava* reported, "At this meeting, we did not see lustrous perfumes and jewels, but rather hundreds of women who wither in the unhealthy air of factories and workshops, who grow old in their young age for a few pay slips."[6] Socialist feminists were not anti-globalists or political anti-internationalists. But they challenged the self-congratulatory optimism of many liberal internationalists.

From the beginning, liberal and Socialist forms of internationalism emerged in conversation and competition with one another. Globalization, internationalism, and nationalism likewise depended on one another for meaning, reinforcing rather than replacing one another. A decade after the closing ceremonies in Budapest, Rosika Schwimmer would insist that she had "no nationalistic feeling" but rather a "cosmic consciousness of belonging to the human family." But even among her peers who cruised the Danube in 1913, self-described "world citizens" were a rarity.

More typically, internationalism was premised on the assumption of strong sovereign states and European hegemony. The delegates in Budapest and other world congresses and conventions came together as representatives of nations and empires; more often than not their goal was to further specific national and imperial interests. The era of internationalism and globalization was, not coincidentally, the era of colonial expansion and consolidation. There was a widespread perception in Europe that there was a shortage of space in the world, and that whoever mastered the most space—and with it, population and natural resources—would have a global edge. In 1885, European leaders infamously gathered in Berlin to divvy up Africa; no Africans were present. By 1902, 90 percent of the continent was under European control. In 1916, IWSA leader Emily G. Balch, a Wellesley professor and committed pacifist (and later winner of the Nobel Peace Prize), proposed the creation of an international colonial administration as a means of securing world peace: "The fact that backward territories are more or less openly hanging as prizes for whoever is strong enough or clever enough to grab them is a constant cause of jealousy, suspicion, and trouble in international relations and one main cause of wars and armaments," she argued. The solution, she suggested, was not to end colonialism, but rather to create an international system for parceling out the world to Europeans. The League of Nations mandate system created after the First World War closely resembled her scheme.[7]

It is not surprising, in light of what came after 1913, that so many European internationalists would later look back upon the period before the First World War with nostalgia. "Never had the prospects seemed so favorable for accomplishing its objects; never had the fraternity among the women of the different nations seemed so close," one IWSA delegate recalled a decade after the delegates in Budapest returned home. Her memories were undoubtedly colored by the fact that there would be no reunion in Berlin in 1915, nor any international congress of the International Women's Suffrage Alliance until 1920.

In truth, the suffragists gathered in Budapest had solid grounds for optimism in 1913: long-fought victories were just around the corner for the European and North American suffrage movements, although obstacles to voting remained (and even increased) for nonwhite women

in the United States, in particular. What the suffragists could not predict was that these new rights would not reflect the victory of pacifist
internationalism. Women would instead get the vote in recognition of
their blood sacrifice to the nation in a global war that would pit the
delegates' husbands, brothers, and sons against one another on the bat-
tlefield. The dream of women's suffrage would be realized on internationalism's graveyard: women in Britain, the United States, Germany,
Austria, Poland, Czechoslovakia, and Hungary all demanded and
received the right to vote at the end of the First World War.

TWO

A Way Out

DERAZHYNIA AND NEW YORK, 1913

As Rosika Schwimmer and her allies celebrated their internationalism, seventeen-year-old Raikhel Peisoty prepared to run away from home. Home was Derazhynia, a Jewish ghetto in the western borderland of the Russian Empire. Nine months earlier, she learned that her parents had arranged to marry her off to a neighbor's son without her knowledge or consent. Her younger sister Marishka informed her over breakfast, bursting into laughter and snorting hot cocoa all over the table.

"What's the matter with you?" Raikhel demanded. "Are you crazy, or what?"

"You're getting married!" her sister exclaimed.

"What are you talking about?"

"It's the truth. You're getting married. Dad said so last night."

She didn't believe it at first but soon confirmed that her parents, prosperous Orthodox Jews, planned to offer a respectable dowry to a neighbor, who had just returned from the army. Raikhel remembered him as a "nondescript lad" who had "not been much to look at or listen to four years earlier."

After breakfast, she rushed to meet her fiancé and concluded that the army had not improved him. "A feeling of outrage and revolt against this high-handed plan took possession of me. I determined that come what might no such marriage would take place . . . If I accepted my parents' plans, it would mean my marrying this returned soldier, keeping house, bearing children, and getting lost in the narrow life of a market town, as had most of the girls I knew . . . The idea of such a future appalled me. All day, automatically attending to my tasks, I kept repeating to myself: 'I must find a way out. I must find a way out. I must find a way out . . .' "

Raikhel considered her options. She was active in a democratic circle and was tempted to join her revolutionary heroes, fighting for political reform and social justice; men and women who did not fear exile, death, or prison. But she was not sure the risks were worth it. "If only one could be sure that a life devoted to the revolutionary cause would not be given for nothing. How many thousands had been hanged or imprisoned or sent in chains to the depths of Siberia, and how little actually had been achieved in the name of the revolution that was still to come."

Then she came upon the obvious solution. America! Raikhel's older sister Esther had followed her fiancé to New York a few years earlier. Raikhel knew little about America. She knew it had a democratic government, which "permitted everybody to get ahead in life, everybody who was willing to work hard." And she knew that she wanted to put an ocean between herself and her unwanted fiancé.

Recently, news had trickled back from a neighbor who went to the United States. Israel Seifner had traveled on the same steamship with Raikhel's sister Esther and returned only a year later, a changed man. Before he left, he had been "a person of no consequence, a sleepyhead . . . and a lazy good-for-nothing." Now he was a big shot. "He wore a tailor-made suit, patent-leather shoes, black derby hat, stiff high white collar, and a long, bright-colored necktie." Most impressively, he had a set of brand-new gold teeth. "Youngsters and grown-ups alike would ask him to open his mouth, and he would gladly oblige, so that we could see those jewels in all their glory." When neighbors asked how he had acquired this shining mouth of gold, Israel boasted of huge salaries making men's clothing, enormous skyscrapers, gluttonous meals in fine restaurants. Some people asked him why he had come home if America was so great. Israel confessed he'd been homesick. "Money isn't everything," he admitted.

Raikhel had reasons to be suspicious. The New York that Esther described in her letters was far less glamorous. Esther wrote of deplorable conditions in the factories that employed newly arrived immigrant girls. But she also wrote of participating in mass meetings, walkouts, and strikes as a member of the International Ladies' Garment Workers' Union. It sounded thrilling. Esther, she reasoned, "had escaped the fate that now hung over me. She would understand my dilemma and was in a position to rescue me.... She was my only hope." She ended with a plea of desperation: if Esther refused to help her, she would "take carbolic acid and end it all."

About a month later, Esther's reply arrived in a telltale fat envelope. It contained a second-class steamship ticket. Raikhel's parents were heartbroken. "Are you really so keen on leaving our comfortable home for an unknown place?" they implored. "Wouldn't it be better to stay here in Derazhynia and get married as other girls do, and still be part of the family?" "Haven't we treated you well?" They relented only when Raikhel's grandmother agreed to serve as chaperone. Her father escorted both women to the German border in order to protect Raikhel from the "white slavers" who allegedly trafficked young girls from Eastern Europe to South America and the Orient.[1]

ON THE eve of the First World War, nothing symbolized the growing interconnection of the world more than women such as Raikhel, who made their way across borders, continents, and oceans by the millions; not to attend international conferences like Rosika Schwimmer, but to earn a living, make or escape a marriage. It was not only parents who worried about this exodus of girls and women. It was already clear to many—migrants and reformers—that the gains from free trade, imperial expansion, and mass migration were not shared equally. Inequality—globally and locally—generated radical social and political movements on the right and the left. But in Europe and North America, two groups of migrants were at the forefront of debates about the promise and perils of globalization, and Raikhel Peisoty belonged to both of them: women and Jews.

Women and Jews became lightning rods for the anxieties surrounding globalization, but for different reasons. Women were (and still often are) imagined to be sedentary by nature. They symbolized local and national cultures and traditions, reproduction and stability, homes and homelands. In reality, women had been migrating for centuries, often locally or regionally, in search of work, with or without the company of men. But at the turn of the century, more women than ever were traveling greater distances. In 1900, 37.7 percent of new arrivals to the United States from Europe were women, and 46 percent of the European immigrant population in the United States was female. The percentage of women among Italian immigrants to the United States had increased from 15 percent in the 1880s to about 34 percent on the eve of the First World War.[2] The fate of these mobile women came to symbolize the future of states, families, and national communities in a global age. Was globalization a motor of progress, of liberation from oppressive traditions and governments? Or was it the courier of destruction—of bodies, morals, and cultures; of the authority of fathers and the sovereignty of states?

The "wandering Jew," by contrast, was often depicted as an eternal and ahistorical figure (and threat). As an allegedly "nomadic" people without a national home; as leaders in transnational and transimperial networks of commerce, finance, and trade; and as facilitators of mobility, Jews became emblems of globalization par excellence. They became targets of political and social movements that hoped to restrict, control, or redirect global capitalism and migration. But of course, migrating women and Jews were not only visible as objects and symbols of fears about globalization; they became important actors in their own right, in movements to publicize and reform the inequalities generated by global labor markets.

WHILE STEFAN ZWEIG remembered the era before the First World War as one of unfettered mobility, anxieties about mass migration began well before 1914, inspiring both state-led and social-reform projects that aimed to control and direct global mobility. Gino Speranza was one such reformer. Speranza (whose name means "hope") had been born to middle-class Italian parents in Connecticut in 1872 (his father was a professor at Yale). He eventually attended New York University School of Law and became an attorney and an advisor to the Italian consul general in New York City. Specializing in immigration issues, Speranza worked on behalf of the Italian government to protect the rights of Italian immigrants in the United States.[3]

His position mediating between migrants and governments gave him a unique vantage point. Like many other internationalists in his time, he celebrated globalization as an unstoppable process that was inherently progressive. He described it as "a new spirit" that was changing the world for the better. Speranza identified mass migration and globalization with freedom and progress. "This new spirit is one of greater individual freedom ... freedom to move and see ... freedom of the laborer to try his hand and his craft and to seek his opportunity anywhere ... powerfully aided by immense improvements in international relations and by wonderful facilities for travel and communication."

But Speranza also feared that new individual freedoms created new dangers in the United States. "Wonderful as this new force is ... it does not follow, however, that we should let it carry to our shores on its broad wave all sorts of persons, of all classes and conditions, in every state of development or in any stage of decay. Every great tide carries some refuse and debris."[4] What sort of "debris" concerned him most? At congressional hearings on immigration before the First World War, he advocated social and eugenic criteria for new Americans: "We do not want anybody who may either bring down our physique through physical or moral causes, or anybody who is going to increase the criminality in this country. I think when you sift it all down, it comes largely to that."[5]

Speranza was no traitor to his own nation. He fiercely defended Italian migrants, including southern Italians, who were at the time often considered racially inferior and prone to criminality by nativists. In response to a question from Republican congressman Joseph Hampton Moore about "the racial characteristics of the Southern Italian,"

he replied, "I believe that what might be called an apparent inferiority is really due to four centuries of misgovernment." When pressed
directly, he vouched for the classification of the southern Italian as "a
full-blooded Caucasian."⁶

But Speranza was far less sanguine about migrants like Peisoty. "The
fact is that the Jew, in America as elsewhere, holds tenaciously to his
racial and special culture and, in the last, deepest and profoundly honest analysis of his conscience he realizes that he neither can, nor wants
to, merge it with other cultures," he wrote in his 1925 treatise *Race or
Nation.*⁷ Speranza characterized Jewish difference as a direct threat
to democracy. "Large admixtures of aliens far removed in their history, antecedents and ideals from those of the original dominant stock
unavoidably places too great a strain not only on the assimilative powers of any nation, but on the political, social, and spiritual life of any
democracy. That such a strain is already clearly perceptible on American
institutions and American life seems to me undeniable."⁸

Speranza was clearly not alone in his belief that Jews embodied the
threat of globalism. Fantasies of international Jewish economic and
political conspiracy and power animated anti-Semitic movements in
Europe and beyond in the nineteenth and early twentieth centuries.
Werner Sombart, the German economist and sociologist, penned what
became the most notorious sociological analysis of Jews and capitalism
in the early twentieth century. He represented Jews as quintessential
agents of global capitalism. Migrating Jews first brought capitalism with
them from Southern to Northern Europe, Sombart claimed. And then,
as they migrated beyond Europe, they created new networks of colonial
commerce, capitalizing on their own dispersion. "Jews were scattered all
over the world. . . . One result of these wanderings was that off-shoots
of one and the same family took root in different centers of economic
life and established great world-famed firms with numerous branches in
all parts. . . . What Christian business houses obtained only after much
effort, and even then only to a much less degree, the Jews had at the
very beginning—scattered centers from which to carry on international
commerce and to utilize international credit." Sombart also argued that
Jews benefited from their status as foreigners and "semi-aliens," which

forced them to adapt quickly to new surroundings and innovate in the economic realm.[9]

Although immediately controversial, Sombart's work was not universally seen as anti-Semitic at the time of its publication. Zionists were attracted to some of Sombart's ideas—his insistence on Jewish distinctiveness as a nation, his emphasis on Jewish contributions to world history, as well as the suggestion that there was something stunted about Jewish development that could be fixed by deglobalizing Jews through settlement in Palestine and manual, rural labor.[10]

Yet Sombart's text had an even longer afterlife as a tool of anti-Semites, and he was celebrated and cited by the Nazi Party before his death in 1941. He made his own anti-Semitism and affinity for National Socialist ideals explicit in his 1934 writings on "German Socialism." In response to the question, "Should persons of purely Jewish blood have equal rights, in all respects, with all other citizens of the Reich in holding leading and responsible positions?" his answer was decisively negative. Merely excluding Jews from German society was not sufficient for Sombart. The real challenge, he argued, was that of excising what he called the "Jewish spirit" from German society. This would entail introducing policies to facilitate Germany's deglobalization: economic autarky, domestic (home) production, the re-agrarianization of the German population, and the elimination of foreign influences from German culture.[11]

The *Protocols of the Elders of Zion*, a text forged in 1903 in Russia and translated and disseminated widely around the world after the Bolshevik Revolution in 1917, was a less-academic and far more widely circulated fantasy of a global Jewish conspiracy. The *Protocols* purported to record the deliberations of a committee of Jewish elders bent on achieving world domination. Revealed to be a hoax in 1921 by a British journalist, plagiarized in part from an 1864 French text as well as other sources, the sensational *Protocols* nonetheless lived on. They were subsequently promoted by Henry Ford and the Nazi Party; they continue to be disseminated on the websites of Holocaust deniers and white nationalists.[12]

Jews were indeed disproportionately represented in fields that came to be seen as emblems of globalization at the turn of the twentieth century. This was clearly not because of innate nomadic instincts or aspirations for global domination. Jews migrated en masse in an effort to escape persecution, because they were forcibly expelled from their homelands, or when paths forward had been blocked by discrimination. Building on transnational or transimperial contacts, they facilitated migration as steamship ticket agents, labor brokers, and hotel and tavern owners. Jews could often find work only as peddlers, traders, merchants, and moneylenders, developing skills and connections that would aid them in creating new commercial networks. By the turn of the twentieth century, Jews had developed niches in finance as well as the import and export of colonial produce, diamonds, textiles, and even ostrich feathers. They had also organized international philanthropic organizations to represent Jewish political interests. Contacts with kin, neighbors, and co-religionists overseas facilitated these ventures. But, of course, the vast majority of Jews on the move were not international financiers, philanthropists, or merchants. They were poor immigrants and workers.[13]

In an age of growing nationalism, this did not stop anti-Semites from construing Jewish globalism as a threat and Jewish migrants as unassimilable. Jews became villains in narratives about globalism in part through their role as middlemen who facilitated (and profited from) mass migration and international trade. While some countries such as the United States and Britain worried about and began to restrict immigration, others began to panic about emigration. Jewish travel agents were often the targets of this emigration panic, as they were blamed for seducing ignorant or illiterate peasants into abandoning their homeland.

It was, in reality, not easy to get from Derazhynia to New York. This created a business opportunity for travel agents and smugglers, who earned a living by helping migrants cross increasingly well-sealed borders. Some of these middlemen were honest, others less so. Raikhel was fortunate: Esther had sent her sister a second-class steamship ticket (she herself had traveled in steerage), which meant that she was spared the worst ordeals (including the trip through Ellis Island). But a typical migrant making her way from Russia, Italy, or the Habsburg Empire to New York City encountered innumerable obstacles. In Russia, the government allowed Jews and other unwanted minorities to depart (despite heavily restricting the mobility of more "desirable" subjects), but passports were expensive and difficult to acquire. Those who emigrated legally lost their citizenship and could technically never come back. If they were rejected at Ellis Island, they could end up stateless and stranded in European port cities.[14]

Jewish agents and smugglers were frequently denounced as "parasites" and "human traffickers" for their role in facilitating migration. Broughton Brandenburg, an American writer who posed as an Italian immigrant in 1903 in order to write about mass migration from the "immigrant's perspective," was typical in his insistence that Jews were to blame for the exploitation of fellow migrants (including Jews). "An ignorant Jew possessed of some wealth is almost certain to lose much of it at the hands of unscrupulous Jews who infest principal stations, border towns, etc. There have been cases where poor families even lost their little all to these harpies, ending by becoming charitable charges in England or Belgium."[15]

THE GREATEST perceived threat to mobile young women such as Raikhel Peisoty, however, was not the travel agent or the border police. It was the sex trafficker. Muckraking journalists at the turn of the century frequently emphasized the global reach of the sex industry in sensational reports. They highlighted the supposedly prominent role of East European Jews, who emerged out of the "racial slum of Europe" to lure "the miserable Jewish girl from European civilization into Asia." In an expose in *McClure's Magazine*, George Kibbe Turner focused on Jewish pimps in New York City as part of a global network.

> Once acquainted with the advantages of the foreign trade, the New York dealer immediately entered into competition with the French and Polish traders across the world. There are no boundaries to this business; its travelers go constantly to and fro upon the earth, peering into the new places, especially into spots where men congregate on the golden frontiers . . . they followed the Russian army through

the Russo-Japanese war; they went into Alaska with the gold rush, and into Nevada; and they have camped in scores and hundreds on the banks of the new Panama Canal.

These reports must be taken with a heaping mound of salt. Many women knowingly emigrated to work in the sex trade or were already working as prostitutes before leaving home. Many attempts to "rescue" female migrants from sex traffickers failed when the women concerned insisted that they did not need saving.[16] But they did reflect a broader political and social reality: female migrants were seen as potential victims the moment they left home. A social worker posing as a Bohemian peasant in order to investigate steerage conditions on transatlantic steamship journeys described the experience in a 1909 report to the US Immigration Commission. At every moment of the journey, she described assaults on the dignity and morality of female travelers:

> During these twelve days in the steerage I lived in a disorder and in surroundings that offended every sense. . . . The vile language of the men, the screams of the women defending themselves. . . . Worse than this was the general air of immorality. For fifteen hours each day I witnessed all around me this improper, indecent, and forced mingling of men and women who were total strangers and often did not understand one word of the same language.

Passengers and crew alike, she reported, passed the tedious hours seeking sexual diversion. Several times she interfered. "Do you know you could be deported for immorality if your actions are reported upon landing?" she asked the offenders. But most had been in America before, she lamented, and generally responded: "Immorality is permitted in America if it is anywhere. Everyone can do as he chooses; no one investigates his mode of life, and no account is made or kept of his doings."[17]

Raikhel's second-class journey to the United States was luxurious (and apparently uneventful) by comparison. But she got a glimpse of the conditions in steerage, "where hundreds of third-class passengers were huddled in an atmosphere thick with stench." Years later, she recalled,

"Even now, I feel faint as I recall the misery spread before me. Those people looked tired and worn; many of them were ill; and who wouldn't be, I thought, in this airless place?"[18]

OF EVEN more concern for religious and political authorities were the long-term effects of female mobility on the stability of families, in the new world and the old. In Calabria in southern Italy, where many men had gone abroad and left their wives and children behind, social reformers lamented that "adulteries, infanticides, and vendettas are the order of the day—manifestations of that abnormal social state brought on by emigration and the consequent disequilibrium of the sexes."[19]

Concerns about the breakdown of patriarchal authority were not always unfounded. The migration of husbands, fathers, and brothers sometimes expanded women's opportunities (or burdens) at home. The *New York Times* reported in 1907 on a Hungarian town that had lost its entire male population to emigration. "One by one the male residents of Kerisova felt the call across the water and they emigrated in batches until the Mayor was the only adult male to remain in the village. Finally, he also succumbed to the reports of good wages and golden chances in America sent back by his fellow-townsmen and packing his trunk made his way to the emigrant ship in Fiume. As a result of this exodus of males the women of Kerisova have just elected a young woman to the place of Mayor."[20]

Less dramatically, women took on new responsibilities within their families and communities as well as new economic roles when their husbands emigrated. Men and women learned to read and write so that they would be able to communicate with one another. For better or worse, thanks to emigration, women and children at home worked longer hours for higher salaries, as they replaced men who had gone overseas.[21]

Migration could disrupt gender roles and expectations in other ways as well. Historians (and often, family lore) tend to perpetuate an assumption that migration was a strategy to better the economic lot of family units, and that women, in particular, almost always migrated in order to join family members and unify families. But many women (and

men, for that matter), like Raikhel Peisoty, emigrated to get away from
their families or from arranged marriages. Emma Barruso, an Italian
woman who fled to the United States in the early twentieth century,
recalled of home, "There was nothing for us there. . . . Father used to
scream at us. . . . Over here, I figured, it's more free, you can do anything
you want, there is more money."[22]

For Raikhel, and for thousands of other women and men, globalization offered a chance to break free: from an arranged marriage, family
expectations, or a cloistered religious or village environment. A young
man "sometimes broke with his father over a girl, told him to keep his
old homestead or give it to the next oldest son, and went to America,"
Louis Adamic recalled. Pauline Reimer left Galicia for the United States
at the age of seventeen with similar intentions. "At home they give you
money when you get married. If you got more money, you get a better
husband. You got less money, you know what it is," she recalled. She said
to her parents, "Send me to America. I don't want to be here. You can't
marry me off, and I don't want to get married either." Her mother cried
and objected but eventually let her go.[23]

Sometimes, emigration became a "poor man's divorce." Wives and
children abandoned on one side of the Atlantic or the other could easily
end up destitute. Not infrequently, men formed families on both sides
of the ocean. During his undercover voyage across the Atlantic, Brandenburg recalled meeting an Italian man who had two wives, "one in
Italy and one in America, and did not seem to consider any very great
harm done. He looked at the matter from no standpoint of sentiment,
merely from one that was utterly practical. In investigations since that
time I have found that there are many Italians in America who have
wives and families on both sides of the water."[24]

The National Desertion Bureau, founded in New York City in 1911,
was created for the express purpose of stopping Jewish immigrant men
from abandoning their wives and children. Its goal was to "ferret out the
deserter" and either reunite him with his family or bring him to justice.
Photos of delinquent husbands were published in the "Gallery of Missing Husbands," a weekly feature in the Yiddish newspaper *Forwarts* at
the turn of the twentieth century, and in other immigrant newspapers.

The "Gallery of Missing Husbands," 1912.

The National Desertion Bureau threatened missing husbands with deportation if they refused to meet their financial responsibilities toward their families. Social workers with the bureau were convinced that desertion was not a consequence of economic troubles but was rather evidence of personal flaws and circumstances, including "immorality of husband, of wife, or both," as well as "shiftlessness, intemperance...discrepancy in ages, interference of relatives, differences in nativity, forced marriages, immigration of the husband ahead of the family." Deserters were depicted as inadequate, unmanly men, but the women they deserted were often characterized even more negatively: as dowdy immigrant women, inadequate housekeepers who let themselves go and could not keep their husbands happy or compete with modern American girls.[25]

The bureau rarely made the effort to track down a woman who deserted her husband, but investigations in such cases often turned up stories of severe domestic abuse. In fact, it was through organizations such as the National Desertion Bureau that many cases of domestic violence first came to public light. Before domestic violence received widespread attention, battered wives sometimes turned to the bureau, declaring their intention to "desert" their husbands and request support. Many deserted women, meanwhile, were unenthusiastic about searching for their missing husbands. They resisted, rather than aided, the bureau's efforts to "ferret out the deserter," and they may have welcomed a husband's return to the Old Country.[26]

RUNAWAY HUSBANDS and wives were not the only migrants who responded to the hardships and opportunities created by global migration on their own terms. Other migrants became leaders of radical anarchist, socialist, and trade-union movements that mobilized politically to protest the glaring inequalities generated by the global mobility of capital and labor. Politically, these movements typically promoted internationalism even as they highlighted the exploitation and abuse suffered by migrant workers or the hypocrisy of the image of America as the "land of the free."

In New York City, Raikhel Peisoty became Rose Pesotta, the labor activist. She was among a large number of immigrants (and women) among early union and labor leaders in the United States before the First World War. They knew America was far from a golden land for many immigrants.[27]

For some, this disappointment was immediate and visceral. Marie Ganz arrived in the United States from Austrian Galicia with her mother at the age of five. Her father had come before them, setting up house in a typical tenement building on the Lower East Side. They arrived in the heat of summer and climbed the narrow, airless stairway to their new home. "Flushed with heat and perspiring though he was, my father ushered us in with a great show of joy and enthusiasm. Suddenly his smile gave way to an expression that reflected bitter disappointment and injured pride as he became aware of the disgust which my mother could not conceal. 'So we have crossed half the world for this!' she cried. . . . I can see her now as she stood that moment facing my father, her eyes full of reproach. . . . The look of pain in his face as he saw the impression the place made on her filled me with pity for him, young as I was."[28] Ganz also grew up to be a labor leader.

Social reformer Louise Odencrantz interviewed more than 1,000 Italian migrant women between 1911 and 1913 and reported widespread disillusionment. These women had arrived in America "filled with hope for emancipation" from poverty, "only to find that they were unable to free themselves from their heavy burdens and that in addition they were deprived of the fresh country air and the wide spaces of their native villages. Crowded together story upon story in insanitary tenements, often in only three or four rooms, these women and their families enjoyed none of the 'modern conveniences' that we associate with American city life."[29] Armando Pelizzari, an Italian immigrant and organizer for the United Mine Workers of America, asserted in 1909 that such disillusionment led many migrants to radical politics: "America is a land where demoralization, poverty, and slavery reign in abundance, and where our enchanted dreams from across the ocean become disillusions as soon as we set foot upon this land."[30]

There were many ways to organize. Immigrant women were active as union members, strikers, and speakers, but also as writers, boarding-house managers, and cultivators of the social and cultural spaces and networks in which anarchist and syndicalist movements flourished. The decade before the First World War represented a high point for such activism. The International Ladies' Garment Workers' Union (ILGWU), founded in 1900, had organized 84,000 workers by 1912, gaining steam with a landmark 1909 strike in which about 20,000 (mostly immigrant) shirtwaist factory workers struck for better conditions, including Raikhel Peisoty's sister Esther. In the same month, in Hoboken, New Jersey, Italian women working in the textile industry walked off the job, demanding better conditions and wages. Three months later, 60,000 cloak makers struck for three months and won concessions from their employers.[31] Marie Ganz recalled that these strikes brought great hardship and required great sacrifice. With her own mother out of work because of the strikes, her family's main source of income came from a boarder and from the earnings Marie made in a button factory, where she had begun to work twelve hours a day at the age of thirteen.[32]

Marie herself became an organizer and an anarchist, famous for charging into the Standard Oil Company building in Manhattan and threatening to kill John D. Rockefeller (he happened to be out of the building at the time). She spent sixty days in jail but continued to agitate for workers' rights after her release. Her activism was inspired by a combination of hunger and acute awareness of extreme inequality. She briefly worked for a wealthy dressmaker on Fifth Avenue, where she was exposed to the lives of the wealthiest New Yorkers. Until then, she later recalled, "I had taken the conditions in which we lived as a matter of course. I had thought almost everybody lived in that way. The discovery of how wretched we were as compared with the people in other districts roused the spirit of discontent and a hatred of my lot. I was sorry I had ever gone outside our ghetto. Never did life seem so bitter and hopeless as now."[33]

Upon her own arrival in America, Rose Pesotta (née Raikhel Peisoty) immediately began work in a shirtwaist factory, following in her sister's footsteps. She also followed her sister into the ILGWU and soon became an organizer herself. She recalled that a group of women defied their boss's threats to fire them if they skipped work to participate in a May Day protest. "We answered with a shrug of our shoulders. In the morning we met as agreed in front of the shop and marched in a body to the Jewish Daily Forward Building in Rutgers Square and Stewart Park where the procession was to start." The next day they returned to work as usual and "pledged to walk out again on strike if the boss did any firing. But he only threw side glances at our defiance. The busy season was on, and he needed our output. That day we sang the rousing labor songs of the day before, feeling we were not alone, and invincible."[34]

That May Day, Pesotta and her colleagues marched past the former Triangle Shirtwaist factory on Washington Square. Esther had briefly worked there, along with hundreds of other teenage immigrant girls who labored for twelve hours a day and were locked in the factory each morning to prevent stealing. It was one of the factories where management had successfully resisted a major unionization campaign in 1909. Not long after Esther left her job there, a fire consumed the building, resulting in the deaths of 123 young immigrant women and 23 men, including two women from Derazhynia.

For labor activists, the lot of a shirtwaist factory worker was a symbol not only of the dangers of unregulated industry but also of the dangers faced by women unmoored from their homes—women who found death instead of fortune on the "golden" sidewalks of New York. Rose Schneiderman, another immigrant from Russia who grew up to be a garment industry worker and labor activist, spoke at a mass meeting at the Metropolitan Opera House held the day after the Triangle Shirtwaist fire. "This is not the first time that girls have been burned alive in the city. . . . Every year thousands of us are maimed. The life of men and women is so cheap and property is so sacred. There are so many of us for one job it matters little if 143 of us are burned to death."[35] For Schneiderman, the only answer was a strong working-class movement.

These women acted locally, protesting their workplace conditions, and they certainly did not use the term "globalization." But they were acutely aware of the extent to which their fate was a product of global processes such as mass migration and trade. Autobiographies by these women focused in particular on the struggles their families faced as immigrants, including prejudice, language barriers, and limited opportunities. Labor organizers noted that organization was hampered by language differences and observed that factory owners took advantage of the inability of workers to communicate. "At a mass meeting one had to have at least four interpreters—for Polish, German, Yiddish, and Italian, and sometimes a fifth one for Slovene." While Schneiderman was proud of the solidarity among migrants, she was aware that "the language problem was an asset to employers like the Triangle Waist Company. By hiring newly arrived immigrants from several different countries who not only spoke no English but could not communicate with each other, they protected themselves against the union."[36]

Activists such as Pesotta, Schneiderman, and Ganz were far removed from the anti-migrant activists who wanted to close American gates to "threatening" immigrants. Politically, they were embedded in international anarchist, socialist, and trade-union movements.[37] As migrant Jews, they were targeted by people such as Speranza, who saw them as the "debris" that globalization washed up on American shores. As migrant women, they symbolized the threat globalization seemed to pose to families and traditional gender roles. But this did not mean they shared the optimism of liberal internationalists or globalists, those who believed that more global connection would inevitably lead to more progress, more peace, and more prosperity. These women were authors of a powerful left-wing critique of inequalities exacerbated by globalization, a critique that would grow harder to ignore in years to come.

Far from New York City, however, more immediate threats to globalism were brewing. In July 1914, Rosika Schwimmer foresaw the apocalypse. After her triumph in Budapest in 1913, she moved to London, where she served as the corresponding secretary for the International Women's Suffrage Alliance. At a breakfast meeting with David Lloyd George, she warned that the British were "taking the assassination of the Archduke much too quietly." It had "provoked such a storm throughout the Austrian Empire as she had never witnessed." Unless action was taken immediately "to satisfy and appease resentment, it would certainly result in war with Serbia, with the incalculable consequence which such an operation might precipitate in Europe." Lloyd George concluded that "official reports as came to hand did not seem to justify the alarmist view she took of the situation" and promptly forgot about her.[38]

THREE

We Are Bringing Peace

HOBOKEN, 1915

ON DECEMBER 4, 1915, a crowd of 12,000 people jammed the piers in Hoboken, New Jersey, anticipating a spectacle. They were not disappointed, according to the *Chicago Tribune*, which reported "scenes so extravagantly remarkable as to be almost beyond belief." The occasion was the departure of a ship. The *Oscar II* was about to sail for Europe, with sixty-three pacifists, fifty-four reporters, a delegation of university students, two stowaways, and "four Chicago babies" aboard. A band played "I Didn't Raise My Boy to Be a Soldier"; William Jennings Bryan served as witness to a marriage on deck; a man dove into the icy-cold water from the docks; and doves mingled with a cage of squirrels that had been placed on the gangplank and labeled "To the Good Ship Nutty." At the helm of the mission was an unlikely duo: Rosika Schwimmer and American automaker Henry Ford. Their aim was to bring European boys "out of the trenches by Christmas" and end the First World War.[1]

The idea was Schwimmer's, and convincing Henry Ford to sponsor the mission was her greatest triumph to date. Initially, feminist pacifists, including Schwimmer, hoped that the 1915 International Women's Suffrage Alliance annual meeting, scheduled to take place in Berlin, could be moved to a neutral country. It was not to be. Because Schwimmer was stationed in Great Britain when the war broke out, she faced the prospect of possible internment as an enemy national. Instead of returning to Budapest or heading for Berlin, she set sail for the United States shortly after the outbreak of war, where she planned to continue her campaign for peace.

Not long after her arrival, in September 1914, she managed to secure an interview with Woodrow Wilson, during which she urged the president to call a neutral mediation conference. She claimed to speak on behalf of 1 million women in thirteen countries. Afterward, in interviews, she exaggerated the president's enthusiasm for her mediation plan. Wilson declared reports that he intended to call a peace congress "entirely without foundation." In fact, he had already offered mediation in August 1914 and been rebuffed; afterward, he had decided upon a course of watchful waiting until the warring governments requested mediation.[2]

Schwimmer fared better on the lecture circuit, where she spoke movingly of the suffering of European women and children and linked women's internationalism and pacifism to what she (and many other pacifist feminists at the time) saw as their maternal instinct. "We women of the Old World are united to resist the command to fight. . . . We will not be belligerents. We are united by the motherhood instinct and by the knowledge that the terrible waste of life is unnecessary." Women's stance against war, she insisted, strengthened their moral claim to the vote. Only when women were enfranchised would they be in a position to prevent men from leading the world into senseless wars.[3]

But contrary to Schwimmer's claim to speak on behalf of the women of the "Old World," most European women were not clamoring for peace in the summer of 1914. Internationalism had gone out of style. Women had been swept up in the same nationalist and patriotic fever that induced their husbands and brothers to rush to enlist and crowds to cheer them on. Many women who had been active in the prewar suffrage movement now distanced themselves from internationalism and turned their attention to patriotic war work.[4] In August 1914, the German Union of Women's Associations (*Bund deutscher Frauenverein*;

Gertrud Bäumer, 1930 or earlier.

BDF), an umbrella organization for middle-class German women's organizations that was led by Gertrud Bäumer, began to denounce pacifists and internationalists in their own ranks. Bäumer wrote in *Die Frauenfrage* in 1915, "We cannot make ourselves international! We cannot—we women least of all—cast off the deepest, strongest, warmest experiences that burn within us ... and, theoretical ghosts of ourselves, ascend into an international fourth dimension."[5]

THE FIRST WORLD WAR sent millions of European men and women—as soldiers, nurses, workers, and refugees—out into the world beyond their villages, cities, and countries for the first time. It gave rise to violent forms of transnational contact through wartime occupation and internment, as well as new forms of international humanitarianism. The war also mobilized resources and people from all parts of the globe, and it tied the world together through networks of debt.[6] But war simultaneously shut down many of the globalizing forces that had recently seemed irrepressible.

Indeed, European countries now devoted all of their destructive energy to damming international flows of people, supplies, and intelligence. They stopped exporting the machines and raw materials that they now needed at home for the war effort. They targeted one another's ships, railroads, and telegraph lines in order to break down communications and hinder the transport of supplies and troops. Many concrete measures introduced during wartime for one purpose continued or became models for anti-global policies and politics after the war. In the name of security, for example, states now required travelers to carry passports when they traveled abroad, a new innovation. It was supposed to be temporary, but the requirement was not lifted after the war.

Consumer boycotts also became more widespread as a tool to mobilize populations politically. "With the great expansion of international trade in recent years the number of international boycott movements is increasing," one legal analyst explained in 1916.[7] Boycotts were a flexible instrument. They served diverse political causes and could be directed at states, individuals, or corporations. They could be nationalist or internationalist, imperialist and anti-imperial. In the last two decades of the nineteenth century, there had already been an Indian movement to boycott England to protest the partition of Bengal, a Chinese boycott of the United States because of its exclusion of Chinese immigrants, and a boycott by the Ottoman Empire against the Habsburg Empire to protest the occupation of Bosnia. In the late Habsburg Empire, Polish and Hungarian anti-Semites boycotted Jews, and Czech and German nationalists refused to drink one another's beer. But the boycott really gained traction as a tool of international diplomacy, war, and mass politics during the First World War.[8]

During the war in Allied countries, boycotting German goods became a matter of patriotism. In 1915, the Anti-German League of the United Kingdom issued a call to arms that transformed every purchase into a political and military decision. A full-page ad published in the London *Times* implored citizens not to buy German goods, in order to avenge "the vast army of phantom dead, of the poor breastless women, of the outraged girls, of the little children torn to pieces, of our brave soldiers with their faces beaten to a pulp as they lay wounded."[9] While these boycotts were justified in the name of the war effort, they were often organized by protectionist groups, and many continued after the war. Even during the war, the Anti-German League of the United Kingdom attempted to rally citizens against globalization as well as against Germany. In a 1915 advertisement, the league appealed to British citizens: "Thirty years ago we were miles ahead of all our competitors in manufacturing, in trade, in finance and in labor, but what have we done to maintain that premier position among the great Nations? We have alas permitted foreigners, particularly Germans, to dump their goods at the very gates of our great works, while our men have starved or emigrated. We have, to our lasting disgrace, readily purchased German products to the detriment of our own industries. We have driven our capital and labor abroad in enormous volumes and have left our ships to compete, unaided, against the subsidized vessels of other countries."[10]

Responding to these campaigns, some British advocates of free trade worried that the British were "gradually proceeding towards a boycott of all foreign goods, without discrimination as to country of origin." R. D. Maratray wrote in a letter to the editor of the London *Times*, "Are we all going to shut ourselves up within our respective frontiers by blindly restricting each other's imports . . . ? Instead of that, let us follow a more judicious and more fruitful course by forming with our Allies an economic union, an immense commercial basin with no separate compartments."[11] He was right to be worried. The boycott only spread after 1918. A Google Ngram search shows a dramatic increase in use of the term "boycott" in English, German, and Italian between the wars, peaking around 1920 and 1934.

In neutral countries such as the United States, there was still more tolerance for internationalism and pacifism in 1914–1915, which is why Schwimmer set her hopes on the American public and president. She published a pamphlet directed to "All Men, Women, and Organizations Who Want to Stop the International Massacre at the Earliest Possible Moment." Because belligerent governments would not ask for mediation (this would be tantamount to admitting defeat), she insisted that it was up to neutral states, especially the United States, to form an "International Watching Committee" to intervene. Schwimmer drew on the ideas of Julia Grace Wales, a Canadian feminist and instructor at the University of Wisconsin, whose proposal for "continuous mediation" by neutral powers was officially adopted by the Women's US Peace Party, founded in January 1915.

But internationalism, pacifism, and globalism had hit rock bottom. Even many of Schwimmer's pacifist colleagues rejected pacifism and internationalism. A group of Dutch women led by Aletta Jacobs did ultimately convene a peace conference at The Hague in April 1915. The Hague Peace Conference of 1915 brought 1,100 women from the Netherlands, the United States, Canada, Denmark, Great Britain, Austria-Hungary, Sweden, Germany, Norway, and Italy together. "All of the delegates openly declared that they did not represent the sentiment of the majority of women in their fatherlands, but only small, radical groups," reported American journalist Mary Chamberlain.[12] The French and Russian governments prohibited their citizens from attending. Gertrud Bäumer denounced the conference as "superfluous," "untimely," "impossible," and "tactless." The German Union of Women's Associations declared that attendance was "incompatible with the patriotic sentiments and national duties of the German Women's movement."[13]

American pacifist and social reformer Jane Addams, who chaired The Hague Peace Conference, described a climate in which "the individual, through his own overwhelming patriotism, fairly merges his own personal welfare, his convictions, almost his sense of identity, into the national consciousness. It is a precious moment in human experience, almost worth the price of war, but it made the journey of the women leaving home to attend the Congress little short of an act of heroism." She speculated that it was perhaps necessary for pacifists and internationalists to bend to the spirit of the times, to appeal to "emotion and deep-set racial impulses."[14]

In spite of this hostile environment, the conference represented a significant accomplishment. In addition to continuing the fight for female suffrage, delegates passed resolutions demanding self-determination for all people, parliamentary democracy, disarmament, and free trade. Several of these resolutions were incorporated into President Wilson's Fourteen Points. They adopted the Women's US Peace Party goal of "continuous mediation" by neutral powers. And finally, under Schwimmer's influence, delegates resolved to visit European diplomats and leaders personally in order to deliver by hand their resolutions and plea for mediation. The delegates succeeded in securing meetings with prime ministers and foreign ministers in London, Berlin, Paris, Vienna, and St. Petersburg, as well as with leaders in neutral states. In her own account of conversations with European leaders, Jane Addams affirmed that the delegations were well received. Although no European leader would actually request mediation, they generally agreed that if respected neutral powers should "study the situation seriously and make propositions, over and over again if necessary, something might be found upon which negotiations might begin."[15]

But who would provide this essential mediation service? Neutral powers in Europe were willing to mediate, but only if the United States led the way. Schwimmer hoped that American pacifists could put enough pressure on Wilson that he would call or at least participate in a mediation conference. American pacifists Louis Lochner and David Starr Jordan managed to secure a meeting with Wilson on November 12, 1915, where they urged him again to intervene in Europe. While Wilson listened sympathetically, he demurred when asked directly about whether he would act. Lochner, the 28-year-old director of the Central West section of the American Peace Society, was now convinced that "official action would not be forthcoming unless, indeed, American public opinion was so aroused and expressed as to compel some decisive step by the President."[16]

"AROUSING PUBLIC OPINION" therefore became the pacifists' foremost goal. The problem was that generating publicity cost money. The movement needed a patron. And increasingly, US pacifists set their hopes upon one patron in particular: Henry Ford, a man who had already proven himself capable of arousing public opinion. In the past two years, Ford's status had risen from auto manufacturer to American folk hero. In January 1914, he had announced that he would pay his workers $5 a day for an eight-hour shift, doubling the standard rate for unskilled labor. His own publicity office relentlessly promoted a humanitarian image, solidifying his reputation as the champion of the working man, the industrialist who proved that profit-sharing could be profitable (his profits in 1914 amounted to more than $48 million).[17]

Ford had the public relations skills and the money, and he had recently declared himself to be a committed pacifist. In April 1915, the *New York Times* published an interview with Ford in which he denounced "moneylenders," "commercialists," "militarists," and munitions makers for leading Europe to war. "Why do vast masses of mankind allow themselves to be marched off to the slaughter when in their hearts they know that when they die it will be in no good cause, but will be merely to satisfy the ambition of some greedy individuals?"[18] Then in August 1915, Ford gave an interview with the *Detroit Free Press* that contained an even more sensational promise: headlines blazed with the announcement that Ford was prepared to devote his "Life and Fortune to Combat Spirit of Militarism Now Rampant."[19]

The interview, widely publicized throughout the United States, generated hope among pacifists that they had found their benefactor. Ford was however closely guarded by his staff, particularly the anti-Semite Ernst Liebold, and he evaded persistent attempts by peace activists to sit down with him. But Liebold had met his match in Rosika Schwimmer, who was nothing if not tenacious. She managed to dine with the elusive tycoon by mid-November 1915. Even after a discouraging lunch, during which Ford blamed German Jewish bankers for the war, she remained undeterred. During a second meeting, Schwimmer and Louis Lochner together gained the sympathy of the Fords. Conversations continued over the next few days until they struck upon the idea of sending a "Peace Ship" to The Hague in order to generate support for a mediation conference. The idea of a sea voyage immediately captured Ford's imagination. Feeling triumphant, Schwimmer sent a celebratory telegram to her feminist colleagues in Budapest. "Dreams realized. Ford couple fully supportive of me. No further obstacles to our efforts. We are bringing Peace."[20]

The plan was hammered out in only a few weeks: Ford's "Peace Ship" would sail to Europe's neutral capitals—Norway, Sweden, Denmark, and Holland (at The Hague they hoped to meet with delegates from Switzerland and Spain)—and invite delegates from each country to join the expedition. If the mission failed to convince any government to act, the delegates would themselves form an unofficial neutral conference. The conference would study the problem, draft a peace plan, submit it to all of the belligerent governments simultaneously, and then revise it until "the warring factions declare themselves ready to enter into direct peace negotiations with each other."[21]

From the Biltmore Hotel in New York, Ford sent out invitations, which declared that the "time has come for a few men and women with courage and energy, irrespective of the cost in personal inconvenience, money, sacrifice, and criticism, to free the goodwill of Europe that it may assert itself for peace and justice." The slogan of the *Oscar II*, he announced to the press, would be "Out of the trenches before Christmas, never to return."[22]

The Peace Ship was quick to generate publicity. But it was not the sort of publicity that Schwimmer and Ford had in mind. The spirit of internationalism and pacifism was now waning in the United States. "Great War to End Christmas Day. Ford to Stop It," reported the *New York Times*. Ford's hubris, alongside his lack of concrete knowledge of European affairs, made the mission vulnerable to ridicule from the outset. Ford quickly secured his own interview with Wilson, where the two men exchanged jokes but Wilson rebuffed (once again) the request to call or participate in a mediation conference. The press, meanwhile, began to mock the ship as a "traveling asylum" and a "ship of fools." It did not help that Thomas Edison, John Wanamaker, and William Jennings Bryan all declined invitations to join the mission. As a going-away present, Wanamaker gave Lochner and Ford a copy of *Pollyanna*. He publicly declared that Ford had a "mission, a generous heart, and a fat pocketbook, but he has no plan to stop the war." Jane Addams committed to sail with Ford but worried that "the offer of a crusading journey to Europe with all expenses paid could but attract many fanatical and impecunious reformers." Friends attempted to dissuade her from participating, but she remained steadfast. "It became clearer every day that whoever became associated with the ship would be in for much ridicule and social opprobrium," she later recalled, "but that of course seemed a small price to pay to protest against war." At the last minute, in what was probably a stroke of good fortune, she was taken ill and remained in the hospital in Chicago the day *Oscar II* set sail.[23]

The mission was also greeted with skepticism by other pacifist leaders. Henry La Fontaine, the Belgian president of the International Peace Bureau (and winner of the 1913 Nobel Peace Prize), warned Louis Lochner that Ford's plan was misguided. "It is true that the populations of the belligerent peoples are sick of the war," he wrote. "But it is not true that they want the peace. They want their peace."[24]

Meanwhile, a cloud of suspicion surrounded Schwimmer. She was targeted as a woman, as a Jew, and as a citizen of Austria-Hungary. "Crusade Not Ford's Idea," the *New York Times* reported in a front-page headline on November 26. "First Proposed by Mme Schwimmer and Indorsed [sic] by Pro-Germans."[25] Others speculated that the Peace Ship was a giant advertising stunt intended to expand Ford's European markets.[26] Several of Ford's own advisors—including his wife—urged him to reconsider the mission.[27]

Ford was not deterred. "Among other things which Mr. Ford had gained from his wide experience was an overwhelming belief in the value of advertising: even derision was better than no 'story' at all," Jane Addams later reflected.[28] But the Peace Ship was above all a public relations stunt. Intended to create positive publicity and pressure that would force neutral states (particularly Wilson) to initiate mediation, it would succeed or fail on the basis of the kind of publicity it generated. And regardless of what actually happened aboard, the Peace Ship disproved the notion that all publicity was good publicity. Instead of the story Ford imagined—the heroic American industrialist bringing peace to Europe—journalists wrote about an alleged mutiny aboard; invented headlines ("Ford a Prisoner in His Cabin; Chained to Bed by Secretary"); and depicted Schwimmer as an autocratic Jewish German agent who was squandering Ford's fortune.[29]

By the time the Peace Ship arrived in Christiania (Oslo), Ford's own faith was shaken. The piers were almost empty the morning the ship finally pulled into its first port. Journalist Burnet Hershey recalled that "when the delegates eagerly disembarked, they were met with no more interest than some local group coming back from a day's fishing excursion."[30] Ford, meanwhile, had come down with the flu and holed up in his cabin with advisors who encouraged him to cut his losses. In his last interview with Norwegian journalists, he rambled about the potential of the tractor to rebuild Europe after the war. Then, on December 23, he snuck off the ship in the middle of the night and sailed home.[31]

The mission continued, but the damage was done; the press's ridicule was even more relentless after Ford abandoned the mission. Schwimmer and her colleagues attempted to remain in contact with Ford and reassure him that everything was going as planned. Their mission, they concluded, was "a wonderful and complete success."[32] But this was not the message that reached the American public. At the end of January 1916, William C. Bullitt of the *Philadelphia Public Ledger* sent a scathing dispatch from The Hague, widely republished, in which he reported that the mission had descended into lunacy, thanks to the "strange actions of the Hungarian high priestess of the pilgrimage, Frau Rozsika Schwimmer," speculated to be "a member of the German-Austrian secret service, toying with Mr. Ford on behalf of the Teutonic powers."[33]

Having failed to convince any neutral state to sponsor an official peace conference, the Peace Ship pilgrimage officially disbanded after electing delegates to an "unofficial" neutral mediation conference. That conference took place as planned in Stockholm in the winter of 1916, without Rosika Schwimmer, who had resigned "both because her status as a subject of a belligerent government was a source of embarrassment and because serious differences had arisen between herself and some of the delegates."[34] Ford continued to pay the bills. The delegates in Stockholm appealed once again to the neutral powers to offer mediation; their governments replied again that they would only act with the leadership of the United States. The delegates also produced a peace proposal that they sent to all of the belligerent powers. It insisted on the "right of nations to decide their own fate," parliamentary control of foreign policy, the creation of a new international organization to mediate international disputes, disarmament, a World Congress, freedom of the seas, and a guarantee that "economic activity of all peoples should be afforded development on equal terms." The proposal was well publicized and bears a resemblance to work later undertaken by the League of Nations. But none of the warring powers were ready to negotiate for peace in 1916, and Schwimmer and her colleagues would never get much credit for their efforts.[35]

By the winter of 1916, Ford himself had experienced a change of heart about the war. "Like many another pacifist, who does not believe in war as such," Ford was "nevertheless making an exception of 'this war,'" Jane Addams lamented. He withdrew his support for the mediation conference to occur in Stockholm in March 1916. He ran for the US Senate in 1917 on the platform that he would not pocket a penny in profits from the war (and ceremoniously returned $130,000 to the US government) but narrowly lost the campaign. He ultimately earned an estimated war profit of $925,000, the remainder of which he did not return.[36]

After resigning from the mediation conference, Schwimmer returned to the United States and attempted with characteristic persistence to get back in touch with the Fords. She sent three wireless telegrams and two letters to Ford's home. She received no response. "I thought after all the trouble you took that you ought to be informed that nothing was wasted in vain. Just as the Peace Expedition fulfilled its mission in Europe in spite of its misrepresentation in America, so the Conference will ultimately also carry out its plans in spite of all the stupid and wicked steps taken to spoil it," she wrote in an open letter published in the *Detroit Free Press*.[37]

A reply arrived from Clara Ford. "The way Mr. Ford's name and money was used was shameful. And you were the leader. . . . You and your followers cared not if he died, just so long as he went along to lend his name and provide money to be squandered." She accused Schwimmer of "many other underhanded, secret doings" that were un-American in character. "We Americans are honest and open, and do not have to do things in secret." Finally, she vowed that her husband would never see Schwimmer or give her money again.[38] That promise was kept.

The pacifists aboard the Peace Ship championed ideas that would

"By Wireless from the Peace Ship," *Minneapolis Daily News*, 1915.

"Tug of Peace," *Punch*, December 15, 1915.

be revived by the League of Nations, but it was their failures, more than their visionary proposals, that foreshadowed the peace to come. Neither Ford nor Schwimmer ever recovered their prewar reputations (though Ford's bottom line did not suffer). There is ample reason to blame their respective personality flaws and the sensationalist press reports flowing from the ship. But they (and the Peace Ship itself) were also casualties of the rising tide of anti-globalism. The battlefields of the First World War were graveyards not only for millions of young men in their prime but also for the confident internationalism of the turn of the twentieth century. As the *Oscar II* crossed the Atlantic, the sea shifted beneath it. Schwimmer's brand of internationalism and pacifism, celebrated in Budapest in 1913, was an easy target of ridicule and suspicion by 1915. Even Henry Ford's patronage could not save it.

FOUR

The Hunger Offensive

VIENNA AND BERLIN, 1917

UNTIL THE MID-NINETEENTH CENTURY, most Europeans subsisted largely on the products of local soil. While large empires such as Britain imported massive quantities of tea, sugar, and rice from their colonies, high transit costs prevented the large-scale import and export of perishable foods. That all changed with the revolution in transportation and communication in the mid- to late-nineteenth century. The same railways and steamships that enabled migrants to crisscross the globe also transported wheat, meat, fruits, and vegetables. Advances in refrigeration enabled Europeans to eat meat from Argentina beginning in 1876.[1]

Britain led the way in outsourcing its food production, importing eight times as much food in 1910 as in 1850. By that time, the majority of bread eaten by British consumers was made from imported wheat. British citizens also consumed a huge percentage of the overall food traded on the world market, including, by 1930, 99 percent of the world's exported ham and bacon, 59 percent of its beef, and 46 percent of its cheese.[2] Germany was not far behind. The country rapidly industrialized and urbanized in the late nineteenth century and began to import most of its food even without the benefit of a global empire. By the eve of the First World War, Germany dominated the European market in chemicals and the global market in electronics. It became one of the largest industrial exporters in the world.[3] But at the same time, Germany imported five times as much food in 1913 as it had in 1880. German farms could no longer feed the German population.[4]

Even before the First World War, the rise of this global food economy was a source of great anxiety among economists and policy makers in Central Europe. They worried about what would happen if access to international food imports was blocked; for example, in the event of a war. Large landowners and industrialists meanwhile lobbied against competition from foreign imports. In 1879, Otto von Bismarck imposed tariffs on iron and rye in order to protect large German landowners and industrialists from cheap imported goods, and other European states followed suit. An escalating tariff war in Europe was yet another sign that the era of unfettered globalization was coming to an end, well before Europe's armies mobilized against one another. Even in the United Kingdom, where the ideal of free trade had been sacrosanct, the stronghold of the free-trade movement was weakening. Joseph Chamberlain's Tariff Reform League had attracted 250,000 members by 1914, arguing for higher tariffs and the creation of a protectionist imperial trade bloc.[5]

Economists were not the only ones worried about Germany's dependence on foreign food. They joined forces with so-called *Lebensreform* ("life reform") movements, which were concerned about the social, cultural, and political consequences of flight from the land. Life-reformers had diverse (and sometimes conflicting) agendas, from promoting organic diets, to countering urbanization, to erecting a bulwark against Polish settlement in the east. Some of these interests came together in campaigns for "internal colonization." Beginning in the 1880s, state and private associations mobilized to resettle German peasants from overcrowded land in the west to the more sparsely populated provinces of eastern Prussia and Posen.[6] These efforts to colonize the German east represented early fantasies of independence from (or mastery over) globalization. In 1893, for example, agronomist Max Sering wrote a treatise in which he upheld western colonization in the United States as a model for the German settlement of the east. State-sponsored settlement programs were to reverse the dispersion of Germans around the globe, prevent a Slavic invasion of Germany's eastern territories, and feed the German nation.[7] By 1912, Sering was warning anyone who would listen about the perils of German dependence on foreign imports, insisting that "we must not only provide food for our population, but also maintain wherever possible the basis for self-sufficiency. That includes insuring that our agriculture can provide the greater part of life's necessities from our own land."[8]

NEITHER BISMARCK'S tariffs nor Sering's warnings decreased Germany's appetite for foreign calories. As of 1914, Germany relied on imports for about one-third of its total food supply, including one-third of its wheat, 42 percent of fats, and much of its fertilizer. But where tariffs failed, war succeeded. Beginning in 1914, Britain used its formidable naval power to blockade the Central Powers, preventing food and military supplies from reaching its enemies, including civilians.

On the eve of the First World War, statesmen and jurists disagreed about the ethics of starving civilians. In fact, justifying the blockade required a fair amount of legal gymnastics by British statesmen, who were concerned that their actions at least appear to conform to international norms. Germany had attempted to cut off British supplies through its U-boat campaign, so the British first framed the blockade of Germany as a "reprisal." On November 2, 1914, Britain declared the entire North Sea a "war zone," stretching the definition of the term, as it was such an immense area and no actual combat was taking place there. Britain set another precedent by its order in March 1915 targeting exports from as well as imports into Germany, even those going through neutral ports on neutral ships.[9]

Blockading the enemy was a very old military strategy, but the rise of a global food economy in the nineteenth century amplified the consequences. Between 1913 and 1918, imports into Germany declined by an estimated 60 percent. Domestic harvests also suffered catastrophically, as agricultural workers were called up for military service, transport and storage networks were disrupted, and poor weather devastated potato harvests. During the so-called turnip winter of 1916–17, food prices in Berlin rose to 800 times the prewar level. According to German government estimates, the German population was reduced to 1,100 calories a day by the summer of 1917; during the turnip winter, some urban consumers subsisted on 700–900 calories a day.[10]

Austria-Hungary, the largest free-trade bloc on the European continent, had actually been largely self-sufficient when it came to food production before the outbreak of the war. The blockade should therefore not have been nearly so catastrophic. But as in Germany, domestic food production declined dramatically. From 1913 to 1918, agricultural output in Austria decreased by 48 percent and in Hungary by 34 percent. A confluence of events contributed to the meager harvest. When Galicia and the Bukovina were occupied by Russian troops in the summer of 1914, farmers took flight, and their farms were looted. As in Germany, soldiers called up to serve in the army abandoned their farms (imagining they'd be back in time for the harvest). Trade also broke down between provinces of the empire. Viennese workers depended on food from nearby Hungarian farms, but in Hungary, the harvest had also suffered, and Hungarian officials needed what little they had for their own population and the army. Ties between the two halves of the empire frayed as Viennese citizens imagined Hungarians feasting on schnitzel and Sacher torte while they starved. In Vienna, where the situation was most dire, consumers were allocated only 830 calories a day by the end of the war.[11]

As calories declined, the search for scapegoats intensified. Germans and Austrians alike blamed Jewish black marketeers and war profiteers, state authorities, shopkeepers, farmers, and refugees. Food shortages turned neighbors against one another and eroded citizens' faith in their rulers, ultimately contributing to the Habsburg state's collapse. "To obey the food laws is equivalent to suicide," concluded Anna Eisenmenger, a middle-class Viennese woman. In October 1918 she wrote in her diary, "For a long time we have only been getting a part of the food due to us on our ration cards. The doctors have discovered that, even if we got the whole of our ration, this would only be sufficient to meet one-fourth of the food requirements of an adult person weighing 11 stone."[12]

Dwindling food supplies corroded citizens' faith in the fairness and reliability of markets and the global economy. Many consumers demanded more state intervention and regulation of food supplies. As the war dragged on, governments seized greater control of the economy, setting the stage for a postwar economic order based on far more government regulation of the market.[13] This regulatory state would be crucial in creating interwar "national economies" that aimed for greater economic self-sufficiency.

Initially, the state's activity entailed mostly moral persuasion— exhorting housewives to scrimp and sacrifice for the war effort, with "war cookbooks" that touted the health benefits of stale bread and vegetarian diets.[14] But more serious measures were necessary. In Austria, rationing was introduced for flour and bread in April 1915. Over the course of the war, milk, lard, sugar, coffee, potatoes, marmalade, and meat were added to the list. In Germany, the government began to requisition grain in January 1915 and soon introduced ration cards for bread and other essential foodstuffs, including potatoes, meat, fish, eggs, milk, butter, and sugar.[15]

Waiting in line became a full-time occupation in urban centers, with women and children often standing in line from 10:00 p.m. until 7:00 a.m. in order to guarantee that they got a share of elusive goods when the shops opened. Manès Sperber was ten years old when he arrived in Vienna in 1916 as a refugee from Galicia. He recalled long nights of queuing:

> Badly dressed, inadequately protected against cold and wet, people had to spend hours upon hours outdoors: lining up in the morning and at all times of the day, of course. But now, the lines often formed before morning and, eventually, in the middle of the night. Everyone wanted to be at least relatively certain that there would still be something left when it was his turn to buy. For it often happened that after a night of waiting, the "Sold-out" sign would be put up just as you finally managed to reach the threshold of the shop.[16]

In both Austria and Germany, customers confronted with the "soldout" signs took matters into their own hands, rioting, hijacking food carts, or even "self-provisioning" by breaking shop windows and plundering anything edible. Protests began in Germany with the bread shortages of 1914. In February 1915, police in Berlin described mob scenes in which women trampled over one another and ripped potatoes from each other's arms. Scavenging became commonplace in the countryside around major cities. On the outskirts of Pilsen in Habsburg Bohemia, Antonín Nedvěd, a Social Democratic writer, observed crowded trains transporting convoys of hungry plunderers toward the countryside, where they stole whatever food they could find. "All had visible signs of malnutrition and great suffering," he recalled. "They dragged bags remade to be worn on their backs filled with 50 to 80 kilograms of potatoes. One could only see the bags and, under them, bent over tiny humans like wretched shadows." Viennese authorities were forced to concede that without this scavenging, citizens would "die a slow, miserable death of starvation."[17]

Initially dismissed by authorities as "irrational" outbursts by women and children, these protests were increasingly understood to be explicitly political. In July 1917, one police officer in Berlin reported, "The market halls are daily stormed by hundreds of women . . . it often comes to wild rows, lootings, and even to blows." In January 1918, up to 4 million Germans went on strike, demanding bread and peace. Police began to sympathize with the protesters and were reluctant to intervene. Particularly in the aftermath of the Bolshevik Revolution in 1917, revolution seemed imminent.[18]

THE EFFECTS of the blockade on civilian mortality have been disputed since the end of the war. This is partly because it is so difficult to measure the exact contribution of malnutrition to disease and death. But by the end of the war, Central Europeans blamed their reliance on imports for both their devastating military defeat and the death of millions of civilians. In 1918, the German government attributed 762,796 deaths to the blockade. In Vienna, physicians estimated that starvation was the direct cause of 7–11 percent of civilian deaths during the war. The German Food Ministry denounced the blockade in 1919 as a biolog-

"Hunger Map of Europe," US Food Administration, 1918.

ical weapon, "intended by its very nature to strike the bodies and lives of the entire civilian population—women, children, and the unarmed— and to lead to the extinction of the German race."[19]

Although there has been disagreement over the number of casualties, belligerents on both sides agreed that the blockade contributed to Allied victory. British prime minister David Lloyd George concluded after the war that "Germany has been broken almost as much by the blockade as by military methods."[20] German naval officer Friedrich Lützow agreed in 1921: "On November 2, 1914 . . . The hunger offensive against the women, children, and elderly of Germany began. . . . It alone succeeded in exhausting the German people in 1918."[21]

The importance of food security had been seared into the bodies of hungry citizens. This hunger (or fear of hunger) prompted many Central Europeans to turn against the processes of urbanization, industrialization, and globalization that had rendered them dependent on foreign imports. Max Sering, now a government advisor, clearly felt vindicated when he spoke in the Reichsrat on October 27, 1915: "For many years, we were dazzled by urban culture and the development of wealth and inclined to undervalue land management and the rural population," he declared. "Only the clear light of the current war has made the plain truth once again apparent to the general public. Our own stomachs have taught even those who once denied it—that the cultivation of our native land is the foundation of a secure national economy and therefore also of the nation's existence."

Sering was confident in 1915 that Germany would triumph in the war, that the Wehrmacht's conquest of vast expanses of "exceedingly fertile lands" in the east would secure the nation's food supply. But that did not mean that Germans could rest easy. Previous decades of globalization and industrialization had upset a precarious balance between town and country. Railroads and steamships had induced the "greatest mass migration that human history has known." The revolution in transit had led to mass abandonment of the countryside, emigration abroad, and the replacement of German peasants by "foreign migratory laborers of a lower culture." All of these processes had to be reversed. Sering advocated the creation of new self-sufficient family farms and the settlement of disabled war veterans and widows on the "empty" lands of the east. These settlements, he believed, would be key to regaining German self-sufficiency in food production. In 1919, his proposal to the Weimar government to support the creation of new agricultural settlements was largely adopted in the form of a new Settlement Law.[22]

Sering was far from the only German voice in the debate over land, settlement, and internal colonization after the war. Settlement had long been a profoundly elastic ideal in Germany and beyond, mobilized for an extraordinary range of political and social causes.[23] Baron Magnus von Braun, the minster for food and agriculture from 1932 to 1933 (himself a conservative Prussian estate owner), admitted as much in a radio speech in July 1932: "Agricultural settlement is an idea that like cut crystal can appear to have the most different colors depending on the perspective and desires of the onlookers."[24] In the early years after the First World War in Central Europe, the term "settlement" could evoke anything from ramshackle allotment gardens on city parklands to the full-blown colonization of Germany's eastern frontiers, and it found support across the political spectrum.

The interwar settlement movement built on a deep grassroots urban-gardening movement in Germany that dated back to the nineteenth century. This was a solidly left-wing tradition. Workers who had recently migrated from the countryside to German cities sought to escape crowded urban tenements and to supplement their meager diets. They created small gardens in and around the peripheries of growing cities. Over time, these gardeners organized into associations or colonies that pressured city and provincial governments for greater support.[25]

Many urban gardeners and settlement advocates in the early twentieth century were inspired by the international garden city movement, founded by British urban planner Ebenezer Howard. Howard's influential 1898 book, *The Garden Cities of Tomorrow*, outlined a vision of self-sufficient communities that would combine industry, agriculture, and small dwellings, surrounded by "greenbelts." These communities generally aspired to reconnect working-class people with the land as an antidote to the moral, social, and biological dangers of life in crowded and unsanitary urban centers. They combined a progressive critique of capitalism with anxieties about the insalubrious impact of city life on both the individual and the nation.[26]

During the hunger crisis of the First World War, a grassroots urban-gardening movement flourished, as city dwellers literally tried to feed themselves from grass and roots. Wealthy Berliners razed their flower gardens to make space for chicken coops and war gardens, while working-class urbanites raised goats on tenement balconies. They also appropriated plots of land near railway tracks and in public parks, where they grew potatoes and other vegetables. In Vienna, so-called wild settlements appeared around the city before the war ended, as unemployed workers and returning soldiers squatted on unoccupied land, built dwellings out of wood planks, waste material, and dirt, and ate what they could grow.[27] Quaker humanitarian worker Francesca Wilson, who was stationed in Vienna for several years after the war, noticed these settlers immediately upon arriving in Vienna. "The movement grew out of the need for food. On every scrap of available soil, the Viennese had their allotment gardens, and so acute was the housing shortage after the war, that people built out of packing cases, petrol tins and old iron, little shacks where they lived in the winter as well as the summer," she recalled.[28]

After the war, many Central European cities, often governed by Social Democrats, responded to these initiatives by establishing government offices to support gardeners. In cities such as Vienna, Berlin, Leipzig, and Frankfurt, city governments made unused land available to gardening associations. In 1921, popular garden associations across Germany banded together to form the *Reichsverband der Kleingartenvereine Deutschland* (RKGD), which had 300,000 members by 1924.[29]

The tradition of urban gardening competed and coexisted with plans for the rural resettlement of workers or peasants on small, self-sufficient family farms.[30] Here too, there was a left-wing vision for internal colonization. Franz Oppenheimer, a doctor turned economist and social theorist on the left, hoped to use settlement to break up large landed estates in eastern Germany, for example. Oppenheimer, who also advised Zionist settlement projects for Palestine, proposed the creation of agricultural cooperatives out of these estates. Landowners would rent their land to groups of workers, who would receive a share of the profits in addition to land and living space.[31]

But Germany's new Weimar government, composed of a coalition of Social Democrats, liberals, and Catholic centrists, supported Sering's more conservative vision of rural settlement over Oppenheimer's more radical vision. The 1919 Settlement Law provided funds to establish self-sufficient family farms, either through the purchase of new land or the expansion of existing holdings. There was some concession to advocates of land reform: regions dominated by large estates were required to reallocate some land to settlers. This reform was supposed to free up 5 million hectares for the creation of new small and medium-sized farms.[32] The most ambitious plans entailed the cultivation of large areas of so-called wasteland and the mass relocation of families from city to country or from one part of Germany to another. Experts such as Sering hoped to cultivate up to 3.5 million hectares and to resettle 200,000–300,000 families.[33]

There remained a great deal of latitude for interpretation of the 1919 Settlement Law, with ongoing conflicts between right- and left-wing advocates of gardening and settlement. But the lines between left- and right-wing visions of settlement remained blurry. On all sides, eugenic arguments were powerful. A "return to the land" was supposed to improve the biological health and social welfare of the German population. These green spaces were to offer an escape from crowded, polluted, and unhealthful tenement housing and unsavory leisure activities. While there were many divisions between Left and Right when it came to the ideal *form* of settlement, there was general consensus regarding the use of settlements as a bulwark against the global food economy. Urban gardens and rural settlements were intended to deglobalize the dinner table.

LEBERECHT MIGGE, a German landscape architect, was among the leaders of the Weimar settlement movement. His trajectory reflects the political ambiguity of the settlement ideal and the turn toward anti-globalism among settlement advocates. Migge was a passionate proponent of small urban allotments on which workers could grow their own food. "No future German should be denied the opportunity to be close to the land from which he is descended," he insisted in 1917. His thinking was shaped by a politically eclectic set of reformers. These included Ebenezer Howard, as well as Germany's own Schreber garden or allotment garden movement, named after Daniel Schreber, a doctor in Leipzig who promoted the benefits of urban gardening in the mid-nineteenth century. Other influences included the anarchist Peter Kropotkin, the nationalist land reformer Adolf Damaschke, and Franz Oppenheimer.[34]

In 1913, Migge wrote *Garden Culture of the Twentieth Century*, outlining his vision for the German garden city. His orientation at that time was simultaneously nationalist and internationalist. The German gardening movement was to contribute to the nation's international prestige. "Now in the era of global exchange of all goods, an achievement can only be considered to be of national significance when it has the capacity to have an international effect," he argued. "In this sense, the new gardening belongs to one of the greatest national endeavors that I can imagine." He also insisted that "something more than merely a desire to be self-sufficient will incite us to take in hand this important, promising area within the world economy."[35]

But with the outbreak of the war, and especially in its aftermath, Leberecht's thinking took a sharp anti-global turn. He began to emphasize the need for autarky. In 1917, Migge estimated that 15 million Germans lived in cities. If only one-third were given small plots of land to cultivate, he calculated, the nation would save 50 million German marks on vegetables that were currently imported. In Saxony during the war, 50,000 "otherwise unemployed" people had farmed 5.5 million square meters of "otherwise unused land for the production of human foodstuffs" that did not have to be imported. "The value of the allotment garden to the national economy can no longer be disputed," he concluded.[36]

The First World War had transformed "self-provisioning" into both a survival mechanism and a way of life. In 1918, Migge's own commitment to the rural settlement movement became more personal and more political. Against the wishes of his wife, Andrea, he moved his family of seven children to a settlement in lower Saxony. The children were homeschooled and worked on the farm, while Migge promoted the ideal of self-sufficiency and helped run a settler's school.[37] That same year, he published *Jedermann Selbstversorger!* (Everyone a Self-Provider!) outlining his vision for internal colonization after the war.

The war had taught Germans that "as a nation, we must provide for ourselves," the pamphlet declared. This meant changing how Germans ate, consuming only what could be grown locally. Migge promoted a reformed German diet that would eschew meat and fats in favor of fruits and vegetables grown on small allotment gardens. *Jedermann Selbstversorger!* was reprinted in 1919 and translated into several languages; it became influential in the settlement movement in Vienna after the war as well as among Zionists, whose own vision of self-sufficiency on the land flourished during the interwar years.[38]

Six years later, Migge's *Green Manifesto* made the choice between globalization and deglobalization starker. "Now, citizens, we must emigrate! Not to drudgery in foreign lands and colonies. No, to our own country, to the old, eternal, young, native soil." While emigration abroad would always be an "act of desperation" that "no one undertook voluntarily," internal colonization would regenerate the German nation. The "fast cities of the nineteenth century," produced by globalization and industrialization, were a thing of the past. In abandoning these cities, he insisted, "we leave behind only piles of stones, from which we cannot live, and which we cannot love. And which are completely hopeless without the global economy." Reversing globalization, going back to the land, did not mean going backward in time. It was the German nation's only hope for the future.[39]

PART II

A World Apart

FIVE

Disease Binds the Human Race

NEW YORK, 1918

WELL BEFORE 1918, public health experts had identified contagious disease as one of the deadliest by-products of globalization. In an 1895 essay titled "The Microbe as Social Leveller," New York City commissioner of health Cyrus Edson observed, "Disease binds the human race together as with an unbreakable chain. More than this, the industrial development of the world has enlarged this chain until all nations are embraced within its band." To illustrate the point, he recalled the flu pandemic of 1889, which had ravaged Russia and then "journeyed along the travelled roads of commerce to Germany, France, and England, until it at last reached the United States."[1]

Edson did not live to experience the 1918 flu pandemic, but he might have predicted it. While the death toll has been notoriously difficult to estimate, the "Spanish flu" (which did not originate in Spain) reached six continents, penetrating isolated mountain villages as well as remote islands. The calculation of casualties is complicated by incomplete reporting and by the challenge of assigning a cause of death in populations weakened by wartime and postwar hunger. But historians have estimated that between 24 and 39 million people died, with staggeringly high death tolls in Asia (19–33 million) and Africa (1.9–2.3 million). By comparison, an estimated 550,000 Americans and 2.3 million Europeans succumbed to the disease. Still, more US servicemen died of the Spanish flu than were killed in combat.[2]

The economic toll was also enormous. Economists estimate that the 1918 pandemic resulted in an 18 percent decrease in manufacturing.[3] Railroads and hotels were hit especially hard, along with retailers, mines, restaurants, bars, and theaters—any business that depended on assembling a crowd. The flu was most deadly to adults in their prime, which meant an incalculable loss to family members—including thousands of children who lost their parents and breadwinners.[4]

The disease's rapid advance around the world shadowed and showcased the war's global reach. It spread with soldiers, sailors, and refugees as they crowded into barracks and camps and crossed oceans and state frontiers on steamships and trains. Homer Folks, the director of the Department of Civil Affairs of the American Red Cross, reflected in *Harper's Magazine*, "The constant streams of prisoners, wounded soldiers, new recruits, refugees, and laborers from every part of the world to and from the seats of war easily account for the speed which influenza traveled east and west around the world."[5] Ships transporting soldiers and sailors in the summer and autumn of 1918 carried the virus from Boston to Brest, from Plymouth to Freetown, from Manila to Guam, from London to Australia, and from Marseilles to Reunion.[6]

Underlying the flu's global transmission was globalization itself. People and germs moved so quickly in 1918 that the death rate peaked simultaneously in Paris, Berlin, Zurich, and New York during the week ending on October 26.[7] Public health authorities in New York believed that the flu had entered the city via its ports in August 1918, with steamships carrying the virus that month alone from Christiania (Norway), Liverpool (United Kingdom), Rotterdam (Holland), Bordeaux (France), and Port Said (Egypt). By the end of October 1918, 48 percent of the personnel at Ellis Island had contracted the disease.[8]

In the United Kingdom, health officials linked the pandemic's "conquest" of the world to a deadly coalition of global mobility and global conflict. "If anywhere in the world there be large collections of men, whether through war or economic strife ... herded together *en masse*, there will be opportunities for other modifications of the *materies morbi* which renders it apt to conquer the world. No sanitary cordon, no quarantine, will shield from this danger." Germs were clearly indifferent to borders and thrived on misery and conflict. For these British officials, that meant the only viable weapon against them was international cooperation. "To realize that the material well-being of the inhabitants of a foreign—perhaps even a hostile—country is a pressing concern of ours is very hard. Yet the teaching of this pandemic is that it is a hard truth. Any supra-national organization for the control of epidemics will need to face it."[9]

In the immediate aftermath of the pandemic, many internationalists and public health officials took this advice to heart, creating a global system for exchanging information and combating contagious diseases. The League of Nations' new Health Organization built on international health initiatives that predated the First World War, such as the International Office of Public Hygiene (1905) and the Pan-American Sanitary Bureau (1902). Philanthropic organizations such as the Rockefeller Foundation also invested heavily in global public health. These organizations reflected the view that the mass mobility of people and goods around the world also meant the global spread of disease, which required a coordinated international response. An account of the Health Organization's activities explained, "The world has shrunk so much in size that a case of smallpox in the Chaco may mean an outbreak in New Orleans. Or a plague infected rat aboard a ship in China or India may infect the rats in an American port."[10]

But even as the influenza pandemic of 1918 generated new forms of international cooperation, it also exacerbated anti-globalism, as individuals, states, and international organizations all sought to erect barriers against contagion. The global transmission of information about the path of epidemic diseases expanded, thanks to the work of internationalists in the league's Health Organization and the Rockefeller Foundation.[11] But this exchange of information simultaneously became a tool used to stop the movement of people. While these measures were justified in the name of public health, the pandemic of 1918 provided a new pretext for states to reinforce their borders even once the immediate threat of contagion had passed. The Spanish flu helped to launch a state of "quarantine" from which the world would emerge only decades later.

THE FIRST wave of the flu struck during the spring and summer of 1918. It was so mild that many people didn't take it seriously. One survivor's account, widely published in the American press under the headline "Get 'Flu' and Be Happy," recommended that readers stay clear of imported Castilian soap, but reassured them, "This new Spanish 'enza is not at all serious, excepting that it is causing a great many holidays in munition plants and government offices." Soldiers, the author reported, "seem to be immune." For most people, it amounted to a few unpleasant days. The author confessed that he wouldn't mind contracting this "jolly little disease" a second time.[12]

When the flu returned in the autumn of 1918, having mutated to become more deadly, fear set in. This fear was directed toward foreign people and places now identified as sources of infection. In Central Europe, there was widespread concern that soldiers returning from Eastern Europe—along with migrants and refugees—would bring diseases (as well as revolutionary ideas) with them. Meanwhile, in the United States, public health officials, journalists, and nurses blamed immigrants for the epidemic's spread. An association between germs, disease, and migrants had been well-established before the First World War but intensified in the context of the 1918 pandemic, justifying new restrictions on mobility. Anti-globalism spread globally on the virus's heels.

Lillian Wald, a nurse by profession, was on the front lines in the battle against the influenza pandemic and in the care of sick immigrants. At the Henry Street Settlement, she had launched a pioneering visiting nurses' program, enabling many immigrants on the Lower East Side of New York to receive health care in their homes. In the first four days of October 1918, the flu pushed these nurses to their limits. They were overwhelmed with cases of influenza and pneumonia, and 31 out of 171 nurses were ill themselves. On October 10 at 4:00 p.m., Wald was summoned to attend an emergency meeting of the Atlantic Division of the Red Cross "to consider ways and means for mobilizing the nursing power, actual and potential, to combat the epidemic then already gaining alarming headway throughout this section of the country." There was a desperate need for more nurses, more doctors, and more supplies. Wald was appointed head of the Nurses Emergency Council, charged with recruiting volunteers and providing home care to sick New Yorkers.

Her first task was to assemble the troops. The First World War had accustomed women to service. Like the war, the Spanish flu required the mobilization of thousands of women as unpaid workers. Wald set the presses running through the night, printing flyers that advertised "A Stern Task for Stern Women." "There is nothing in the epidemic of SPANISH INFLUENZA to inspire panic—There is everything to inspire coolness and courage and sacrifice on the part of American women." The next day, "well-heeled" and "discerning" women stood at the entrances to Tiffany's and Altman's on Fifth Avenue "accosting passersby" with the flyers to recruit volunteers.[13] Thanks in part to Wald's nurses, and a strong response from public health authorities (which did not include closing schools), New York City's death toll was the lowest on the Eastern Seaboard, at 452 per 100,000 individuals (147,000 registered cases and 20,608 deaths).

Wald came from a middle-class German Jewish family in Cincinnati. While training and working in New York City in her twenties, she discovered the Lower East Side, where many of New York's newly arrived immigrants first landed. She was teaching a course on home nursing in the neighborhood when a frantic child interrupted her lesson on bed making and begged her to attend to her sick mother. What Wald saw that day changed her life. "The child led me over broken roadways . . . over dirty mattresses and heaps of refuse—between tall, reeking houses . . . The rain added to the dismal appearance of the streets and to the discomfort of the crowds which thronged them, intensifying the odors which assailed me from every side." Upon arrival, she was led "up into a rear tenement, by slimy steps whose accumulated dirt was augmented that day by the mud of the streets, and finally into the sickroom."

Wald was quick to insist that what she found in that room did not reflect the personal defects of the immigrants. "The family to which the child led me was neither criminal nor vicious," she assured readers. "Although the sick woman lay on a wretched, unclean bed, soiled with a hemorrhage two days old, they were not degraded human beings, judged by any measure of moral values."[14] Moved by this encounter, she took on a mission that was emblematic of the relationship—in both the United States and Western Europe—between middle-class, "assimilated" Jews and newly immigrated Jews from Eastern Europe. Motivated by a combination of benevolent solidarity and less benevolent anxiety that newcomers would stoke anti-Semitism, these reformers sought to "civilize" and "assimilate" newcomers into the national community.[15]

Wald was a vocal opponent of immigration restriction, convinced that "the immigrant brings in a steady stream of new life and new blood to the nation." She possessed the optimism of a progressive internationalist reformer, firm in her belief that "few, if any of the men and women who have had extended opportunity for social contact with the foreigner favor a further restriction of immigration."[16] But even as she sat by the bedside of sick migrants, she reinforced what was already a widespread association between migrants and disease.

In the United States, the first restriction on immigration targeting a specific racial or national group was animated by fears of disease. During a smallpox epidemic in San Francisco in 1876, San Francisco public health officials blamed the spread of the disease on "unscrupulous, lying and treacherous Chinamen" whose "willful and diabolic disregard for our sanitary laws" had transformed Chinatown into a "laboratory of infection."[17] Only a few years later, the Chinese Exclusion Act of 1882 banned immigrants from China altogether.

Throughout the early twentieth century, the percentage of immigrants from Asia who arrived at Angel Island in San Francisco and were barred from entry was much larger than the percentage denied entry among immigrants who arrived at Ellis Island, the primary port for Europeans.[18] Disease was also used as a pretense for repressive policing in immigrant neighborhoods. In 1900, officials in San Francisco responded to an outbreak of plague in Chinatown by quarantining the entire neighborhood. Amid talk of burning Chinatown down, they ordered that every home in the city be inspected and that residents be forcibly inoculated with a vaccine that had painful side effects. The mobility of Chinese and Chinese Americans was also sharply curtailed, as railroads were forbidden to sell them tickets, and officials were stationed at the state's borders. Representatives of the Chinese community successfully challenged these discriminatory measures in the courts, but the stigma remained.[19]

European immigrants, particularly Eastern European Jews, were also widely viewed as couriers of infection. With far less empathy than Lillian Wald, the Sanitary Aid Society of New York referred to its charges as "human maggots" and "festering masses" who resided in "filthy homes and pestilential rookeries." When typhus and cholera outbreaks hit the city in 1892, the association between immigrants, dirt, and disease further intensified.[20] The United States halted immigration altogether for several months. Nativists used the threat of contagious disease to argue for more permanent restrictions on immigration. Even once the cholera epidemic had passed, an editorial in the *New York Times* insisted that immigrants represented "a positive menace to the health of the country. Even should they pass the quarantine officials, their mode of life when they settle down makes them always a source of danger. Cholera, it must be remembered, originates in the homes of human riffraff."[21] Migrants did not have to be infected to be considered infectious. Jacob Riis, who famously documented and sensationalized conditions in New York City's tenements, claimed that contagious diseases such as typhus and smallpox were endemic to the Jewish Lower East Side, where "they sprout naturally among the hordes that bring the germs with them across the sea."[22]

THE IMAGINED link between migrants and infectious disease was not limited to the flu or to the United States. Shortly before the First World War, bacteriologists had identified body lice as the cause of typhus. On the Eastern Front, German soldiers imagined themselves as heroic combatants not just against Russian soldiers but against Slavic and Jewish lice, disease, and dirt. Military officials adopted harsh measures, searching homes for signs of dirt and disease, forcibly vaccinating people, and driving them from their homes to "delousing stations," where they were subjected to brutal and invasive disinfection procedures.[23]

In September 1918, a Viennese newspaper speculated that all of Europe had an interest in peace in order to stem the tide of refugees from Russia "given how often the most dangerous infectious diseases are imported from the East."[24] As the war ended, the panic amplified. There was particular concern in Germany and Austria about prisoners of war and troops returning from Russia. The German government planned elaborate procedures to disinfect, delouse, and quarantine returning soldiers. But the reality of demobilization was anarchic. Soldiers and their families saw the required sanitary procedures as an unnecessary delay to their long-awaited homecoming. In 1919, health officials conceded that the effort to prevent the spread of epidemics during demobilization had failed completely because of popular resistance. "It is well known that the voluntary fulfillment of sanitary regulations in the general population continuously decreased."[25] Once demobilization was complete, anxiety refocused on migrants and refugees from the east, especially Russian refugees, Eastern European Jews, and Polish workers. A Viennese newspaper reported, "The Russian border states and Poland are in the greatest danger of being overwhelmed by excessive migration, against which no cordon can help. Cholera and Plague are knocking on all of Europe's open doors."[26]

The governments of Germany and Austria erected medical inspection, delousing, and quarantine stations all along their eastern frontiers, in an attempt to prevent more "undesirable elements" from importing diseases onto German soil. Austrian border officials used medical inspections on its borders to discriminate between "German" refugees and Jews. Health experts endorsed the use of Zyklon poisonous gas to eradicate lice.[27] The image of the diseased Eastern European Jew became a self-fulfilling prophecy. German police and border authorities used the threat of disease as an excuse to round up Jewish migrants and detain them in former prisoner-of-war camps, where bedbugs, rotten food, and atrocious sanitary conditions actually made them sick. Similar "delousing" stations on the Polish border, divided into "dirty" sections for arriving refugees and "clean" sections for disinfected refugees, also made healthy migrants sick, as the "dirty" sections were not kept clean.[28]

There was a slippery slope from identifying diseased people to identifying an entire people as a disease. Under the Nazi regime, propaganda would compare Jews to parasites, lice, or rats that fed off and infected the German national body. It is not coincidental, historian Paul Weindling has argued, that the regime chose to disguise gas chambers as showers. "The Nazi transformation of cleansing into killing exploited expectations of delousing as a routine and widespread medical procedure for migrants. The modern rituals of hygiene facilitated the destruction of persons stigmatized as parasites on an unprecedented scale."[29]

THE INFLUENZA pandemic of 1918 killed millions more people in Europe than did typhus or cholera imported from Russia. So why was so much attention focused on a danger from the east, rather than the possibility of another flu pandemic at home? In part, as Weindling has argued, typhus became a pretext for Allied intervention in Eastern Europe. Focusing on a disease associated with Eastern European migrants and Jews also enabled Europeans and Americans to displace their fear of pandemics onto a foreign enemy.

But the Spanish flu did generate its own forms of xenophobia. The flu circulated under the name of many other scapegoats, such as the "Naples soldier," the "Hun flu," the "German plague," the "Bolshevik disease," and the "Turco-Germanic bacterial criminal enterprise." In the United States, rumors circulated that the flu was a German conspiracy, spread by German spies.[30] The list of afflicted luminaries included Kaiser Wilhelm II, David Lloyd George, Woodrow Wilson, and Franklin D. Roosevelt, as well as many soldiers returning home, but public health officials and journalists in the United States often blamed ignorant foreigners for the spread of influenza in 1918.

In Colorado, the secretary of the state Board of Health claimed that the large number of deaths in the state was the fault of the "large foreign population." Containment efforts, he maintained, were hindered by their "insanitary ways of living, poor ventilation and crowding. . . .

Many of the foreign population cannot be made to understand the necessity for adopting sanitary rules."[31] An article in the *Denver Post* elaborated, "When one member of an Italian family gets ill of influenza, all his relatives—two or three dozen or more—crowd into the house and visit the sick man, woman, or child. And this crowding around a sick person is the best way in the world to become infected with the influenza germ."[32]

It was not migrants, but rather authorities' refusal to cancel a Liberty Loan parade attended by 200,000 people in late September 1918 that made Philadelphia one of America's hardest-hit cities. About 12,000 people died in four weeks. The appalling conditions in the city's emergency wards and homes were documented by the many Catholic sisters who constituted the volunteer nursing force. From the hub of Philadelphia, the contagion undoubtedly spread through the state. In Pottsville, a mining town in eastern Pennsylvania, conditions were dire. Arriving at one hospital, the sisters were informed that three-quarters of the patients would die imminently. Half were foreigners, and many could not speak English. There was little they could do but send for priests. "The Slavish and Lithuanian priests were sick in bed. However, the sisters reached a Greek priest in New Philadelphia, who came, and prepared twenty men for death between the hours of 11PM and 4AM." Among the (barely) living, the sisters reported:

> So many foreigners were among the sick, one pitied them all the more. . . . Some were so far gone that worms were crawling out of their mouths. One morning when I was combing a woman's hair, she coughed, and putting in her hand pulled out a worm that seemed to me a yard long; nor were worms the only kind of vermin crawling about. And the poor babies! One could not tell at first whether they were black or white: one woman refused her baby when it was taken to her, not recognizing it after it had been washed."[33]

These accounts emphasized the extent to which the Catholic sisters' care generated interfaith solidarity, countering anti-Catholic prejudice (and perhaps gaining some converts). "With the exception of two Mexicans, all the patients were most eager to be waited on by the Sisters, and were also very grateful to them. Even the Jews and Protestants would repeat, like children, the prayers and aspirations suggested by the Sisters." In one parish, "the Sisters have been subjected to all sorts of indignities for many years. They could scarcely leave the convent without encountering Jews, who openly insulted them; even the very children spat at them, threw mud at them, or (what was much more deplorable) called such epithets as 'Jesus-girls.'" Now, as a result of the sisters' care, "those people who formerly despised openly the habit of the religious, now openly manifest towards it marks of reverence and respect."[34]

Sympathy and pity could easily be combined with scapegoating. Newspapers reported that immigrants refused to go to the hospital when they were ill, not mentioning that they might have been concerned about the cost of treatment. "They seem to fear that if they go to a hospital it means that they are beyond help."[35] In Lowell, Massachusetts, observers linked the spread of the epidemic to immigrants' failure to learn enough English to understand public health guidelines.[36] And the traditional scapegoating of Asians as a source of disease returned in force in the context of the flu epidemic. One US Army Medical Corps captain claimed that the Spanish flu was actually a plague imported from China to Europe "by the 200,000 Chinese coolies imported into France as laborers last year." He elaborated, "Solid trainloads of them were transported across the United States on their way to France."[37] Newspaper readers in Oregon were informed that "influenza epidemics nearly always have originated in the East and traveled toward the West," because "the inhabitants of the Far East are most gregarious and least enlightened as to matters of sanitation."[38] And during the flu epidemic, the *San Francisco Chronicle* featured an image of the "Beggar Class Type of Manchurians Who Live in a Condition of Frightful Uncleanliness and Facilitate the Spread of Every Epidemic."[39]

The worst was over by December 1918. Lillian Wald returned to her work at Henry Street Settlement, but not without mourning the loss of 207 Red Cross nurses who died that fall.[40] It had been an immensely challenging time for her, but also energizing. At the height of the epidemic, she wrote, "Strange to say I have worked more hours steadily

IT MADE THE WORLD A BETTER PLACE TO LIVE IN

"Deadly Germs Destroyed in 1919," *Denver Post*, November 17, 1918.

than I remember ever to have worked before . . . many times I have been as much as twenty hours in the day in motion. And yet I feel very well."[41]

Like many of her generation of social reformers, Wald identified thoroughly as an internationalist. "We on Henry Street have become internationalists, not through the written word or through abstract theses, but because we have found that the problems of one set of people are essentially the problems of all," she explained. She wrote these words in 1934, hardly a high point for internationalist or universalist ideals. "We have found that the things which make men alike are finer and stronger than the things which make them different, and that the vision which long since proclaimed the interdependence and the kinship of mankind was farsighted and is true."[42]

But for many people on both sides of the Atlantic, the encounter with global pandemics did not strengthen universalist or internationalist ideals. The Spanish flu was only one among many factors that contributed to immigration restrictions and anti-globalism in the 1920s and 1930s. In Europe, its impact was greatly overshadowed by memories of the First World War. But the rapidity with which the disease "conquered the world" in 1918 reinforced popular and official anxieties about the biological as well as the social, political, and economic dangers of global mobility and trade.

Quarantine is a medical procedure to prevent contagion by isolating potentially infectious people. A quarantine is conventionally temporary, two weeks. But in the history of anti-globalism, quarantine serves as a useful metaphor. The period from 1918 to 1939 represented a quarantine era. It was a time when anti-globalists and deglobalizers sought to isolate individuals and nations from what were perceived to be infectious global agents, including people, goods, and diseases. While the Spanish flu had mostly passed by 1921, the quarantine continued.

SIX

Reduced and Impoverished

PARIS, 1919

In June 1919, John Maynard Keynes resigned from the British peace delegation in Paris, where the treaties that would end the war were being hammered out. "I ought to let you know that on Saturday I am slipping away from this scene of nightmare," he informed David Lloyd George. "I can do no more good here. I've gone on hoping even through these last dreadful weeks that you'd find some way to make of the Treaty a just and expedient document. But now it's apparently too late. The battle is lost."[1] Keynes was among the most vocal critics of the peace settlement, and in the autumn of 1919, he penned an apocalyptic polemic about its consequences. At the time, Keynes was in the minority among his countrymen. But he spoke for millions of disillusioned citizens of Central Europe.

Many Germans, Austrians, and Hungarians initially had high hopes for a peace that would be based on Woodrow Wilson's Fourteen Points and the ideal of "self-determination." But those hopes were dashed in the suburbs of Paris in 1918–1919, and with them a great deal of faith in liberal internationalism. If internationalists such as Keynes came out of the peace negotiations disillusioned, the reaction was more severe on the Far Left and Far Right, where anti-global and anti-international visions for postwar survival nourished revolutionary and counterrevolutionary violence.

The losers' rage in 1919 was not necessarily directed against globalization or internationalism per se, however. Rather, it revolved around exclusion from Keynes's global promised land. Citizens in Berlin and Vienna were still hungry in 1919, as the Allies continued the blockade in order to force their leaders to accept the terms of the Paris Peace Treaties. These treaties, the losers believed, offered no promise of relief. There were two ways in which industrialized states could get access to food and natural resources in the early twentieth century: trade or imperial conquest. The Paris Peace Treaties, they claimed, deprived them of both, ejecting them from the global economy and excluding them from the club of European colonial powers. Having allegedly been "banished" from the global economy, many Germans and Austrians claimed that they had no choice but to become more self-sufficient. They pursued autarky in the name of self-defense, claiming it was their only hope for survival.

Officially, the diplomats gathered in Paris drew Europe's new borders in the name of the Wilsonian principles of national self-determination and democracy, reinforced by armies of geographers and ethnographic "experts" who attempted (in vain) to match the borders of states to the outlines of "nations." Less officially, Europe's new borders were determined by politics, including the desire to create a buffer zone of states loyal to the Allies between Germany and Bolshevik Russia; by French insistence on punishing the Central Powers; and by the efforts of armies on the ground to seize as much territory as possible, creating a fait accompli. The new map of Europe, many critics believed, was a puzzle with far too many pieces.

The Allies eventually created (or recognized) several new states in the east (the three Baltic states and Poland, Czechoslovakia, Yugoslavia), rewarded others (Italy, Romania), and punished Germany and Austria-Hungary. Rosika Schwimmer's homeland, Hungary, was the biggest loser, shedding two-thirds of its prewar territory and population; Cisleithanian Austria lost about 60 percent of its former territory and three-quarters of its population, including its industrial

heartland in Bohemia and its precious oil and grain fields in Galicia. Vienna and Budapest became imperial capitals without empires.
"Vienna itself with its population of nearly two million was like a
colossal brain with a child's body to support it," one commentator
noted.[2]

Germany was stripped of its overseas colonies and forced to return
Alsace and Lorraine to France, give up small territories to Belgium and
Denmark, and relinquish a large chunk of land in the east to Poland.
Much of this territory had been essential to Germany's prewar and wartime agricultural and industrial production. Germany lost "the vegetable garden of upper and lower Alsace," as well as the vineyards of Alsace
and the Rhine valley and the fertile "bread basket" of the east; this
amounted to 12.5 percent of the rural population, 15 percent of grain
production, 18 percent of potato fields, and 20 percent of the sugar beet
crop. Germany also lost the resources it had extracted from its prewar
colonies, including palm oil, copper, coffee, peanuts, and cotton.[3]

The extent to which the terms of the Treaty of Versailles between the
Allies and Germany were "fair" has been subject to intense debate since
its inception.[4] But regardless, many Germans, Austrians, and Hungarians clearly *felt* that the Paris Peace Treaties were deeply unjust and vin-
dictive. The vanquished framed their anti-global policies as a self-defense
mechanism in the face of involuntary isolation and countless losses: of
land, territory, food supplies, raw materials, population, colonies, and
racial and civilizational status.

At first, the losers focused on winning the war of public opinion,
appealing for justice to the Allies and the world. But as efforts to revise
the Paris Peace Treaties failed, German commentators began to warn
of dire consequences. They claimed that the treaties amounted to a sentence to perpetual hunger, reducing Germans and Austrians to a semi-
colonial and semi-feudal status not fit for Europeans. In a letter to the
Paris Peace Conference in May 1919, German foreign minister Ulrich
Brockdorff-Rantzau declared that the Treaty of Versailles condemned
the German people to "perpetual slave labor," as they would be forced
to work for generations to pay off their reparations debt. He resigned
rather than sign it.[5]

Germany's exclusion from the global economy was a central theme of German protests. Brockdorff-Rantzau elaborated that during the previous two generations, Germany had transformed from an agricultural to an industrial state, but this had only been possible by importing food. In 1913, about 12 million tons of goods had been imported to Germany, and 15 million people made a living through foreign commerce and navigation. Now, Germany was to be deprived of its overseas colonies and the infrastructure that had facilitated its globalization. The German navy was reduced to a fleet of six small battleships and six cruisers, insufficient for transoceanic trade. German property, businesses, and interests in Allied states, including private property, were confiscated as a form of reparations. The Allies also forced Germany to relinquish its concessions, private or public, in other foreign countries, along with all of its international telegraph lines. Germany was forbidden from boycotting or limiting imports of Allied goods or exports to Allied states, and German waterways, including ports and rivers, were to be controlled by an international commission. Finally, Germany was indefinitely shut out of the League of Nations, excommunicated from the club of great powers.

For many Germans, Brockdorff-Rantzau insisted, the only hope for survival would be emigration. But Germans were not welcome anywhere as migrants. In short order, he speculated, Germany's involuntary deglobalization would result in millions of deaths by starvation. Agronomist Max Sering believed that the Allies knew what they were doing. Their very aim, he argued, was "the destruction of Germany's global economic standing, its exclusion not only as an equal competitor to America and Britain on the world market, but as a self-standing member of the global economy at all."[6] The German reply to the Treaty of Versailles echoed these accusations, insisting that Germany's exclusion from the global economy would backfire. "The economic prosperity of the world is . . . dependent on the total sum of the produced goods," the delegation argued. "The entire elimination of Germany from the world's trade may, to be sure, oust an obnoxious competitor," however, "as a result of the economic breakdown of Germany, the world as a whole must become infinitely poorer." Instead of exclusion and isolation, "What the world is in need of is international cooperation in all fields. . . . The fact that this is an age in which economic relations are on a world scale requires the political organization of the civilized world."[7] But these pleas were ignored.

AUSTRIANS AND Hungarians expressed similar concerns about the loss of food, natural resources, and opportunities for regional and global trade. German-speaking deputies in the Viennese parliament created a Provisional National Assembly and proclaimed the Republic of German-Austria on November 12, 1918. Karl Renner, a Social Democrat, was named chancellor, and a governing coalition of Christian Socialists and German nationalists took control. Renner believed that First World War had been waged "between two imperialisms, that of the Allies, and that of the Central Powers, for domination of the global economy." But the global economy itself had been defeated. "As a consequence of the war we not only have no free trade, but protective tariffs in every country, direct barriers against foreign goods in every country, and often against foreign people as well. In place of the freedom of all nations, for the first time in history we have a situation in which entire nations are in debt slavery to others, and these nations will have to gather and pay out millions for an entire generation."[8]

The Austrian government claimed chunks of Bohemia, Moravia, and Silesia that were populated by many German speakers, as well as the German-speaking South Tyrol, and demanded annexation (*Anschluss*) to Germany. Anschluss was supported by an unlikely coalition, including socialists attracted by Germany's left-leaning republic and pan-German nationalists, united in the belief that Austria, deprived of its hinterland and regional trade, simply could not feed itself.

The Allies rejected these demands, however, not wanting to strengthen or reward Germany or Austria. Already suffering from the effects of wartime hunger, many Austrians responded with outrage and despair. In Graz, German nationalists addressed a telegram to Woodrow Wilson in which they insisted that the terms of the Treaty of St. Germain "will make us a nation of slaves, deprive us of every possible means of making a living and strike a blow to the face to the most basic human rights."⁹

In Hungary, protests against the Treaty of Trianon hammered home the same message. Count Albert Apponyi, who led the Hungarian delegation in Paris, called the Treaty of Trianon a "death sentence" for the Hungarian people, as the loss of two-thirds of territory and population would create a "reduced and impoverished rump" incapable of survival. The terms of the Treaty of Trianon would deprive Hungary of "almost all her woodland, pasture grounds, iron ore, salt, oil, bituminous gas, water-power, of the greater part of her manufacturing establishment and her coal-mines." It would destroy "the natural economic interdependence of the lowland and the mountainous border districts and the whole system of communications based on it." While forcing the Hungarian state to subsist on agriculture alone, he continued, the Treaty of Trianon "deprives her agriculture of the only source of prosperity left to her, of every chance of progress, of maintaining its present standard—by cutting it off, as we have seen, from all its raw materials and from all its natural markets."¹⁰

If trade would not provide access to wheat and oil, empire was the other alternative. Although, or perhaps because the prewar German Empire was small compared to the empires of Britain and France, Germans were particularly indignant about the loss of colonies. Germany did not only claim to need colonies to feed its population, however. Equally important, the possession and development of colonies signified a nation's global and civilizational standing. A petition submitted to the German government and National Assembly on February 2, 1919, declared, "As a great cultured-state [*Kulturstaat*] Germany has a moral entitlement to continue to participate in the world-historical task of the peaceful development of undeveloped lands and the uplift of their peoples."¹¹ Another petition, created by the *Reichsverband der Kolonialdeutschen*, was signed by 3,865,549 Germans. In addition to the standard economic arguments, signatories demanded the return of Germany's colonies "because every nation has a right to a share of the undeveloped lands of the Earth corresponding to its vitality, the size of its population, and its abilities." Petitioners warned, "The violent exclusion of a nation from the exercise of this right endangers the peace of the world."[12]

The German minister for the colonies, Johannes Bell, made an appeal for empire directly to Americans. As the United States expanded its own global power, he called upon Americans to empathize with the German predicament. "We are defeated, hungry, and impoverished," he pleaded. "We demand the inviolable and holy right to life. We demand space [*Raum*] to breathe and to work. We can find no space in Europe and therefore we must seek it out across the sea." How would Americans respond, he asked, if the entire American population was "confined to the state of Texas?"[13] Under the Nazi regime, these demands for "living space" (*Lebensraum*) would find their expression in the violent conquest of Eastern Europe and the pillaging of its resources.

Austria-Hungary had not possessed overseas colonial territories before the war (though there had been a growing colonial movement), but Austrians did protest their loss of status as a European and global power, claiming that they had been reduced to a form of colonial subservience. A petition from the Lower Austrian Trade Association warned that the Austrian rump state would be "not only economically unviable but also perpetually subservient," reduced to the status of a semi-colonial "vassal" or "slave colony."[14] A telegram issued by a gathering of members of the Austrian Christian Social Party and right-wing German Freedom Party in May 1919 warned that war would be the inevitable result of the "dictated peace." "We will not allow ourselves with our wives and children to be sentenced to death or eternal economic slavery, but demand fairness, humanity, and justice."[15]

The constant invocation of "slavery" in these mass protests was not coincidental. In part, Central Europeans were playing to their audience: Woodrow Wilson liked to compare himself to Abraham Lincoln, a modern-day "emancipator" of the "slaves" of Eastern Europe—supposedly in bondage to their Habsburg and Ottoman rulers for centuries, and still unripe for democracy (but not quite as unripe as the peoples of the former Ottoman Empire or subjects of existing British and French colonies).[16] But the protesters were also objecting to the ways in which the diplomats in Paris failed to treat the Habsburg successor states as civilizational equals—as fully "white" or "European" nations, capable of self-government. The Habsburg successor states were ultimately reduced to second-class citizens in the new international order; an "in-between" status that hardened the animosity of many Central Europeans toward internationalism and globalism.

In particular, the hypocrisy of the great powers was not lost on the citizens of the new Central and Eastern European nation-states. Before the war ended, a Viennese newspaper speculated that the Allies would be as eager as the Central Powers for peace, given their own "minority problems," writing, "The Irish and Indian questions plague the British global empire no less than the Czech and South Slav questions plague us."[17] But when Lithuania in 1922 proposed that all member states of the League of Nations adopt universal standards of minority protection for all members, a French delegate responded, "France has no minorities." Armed with an ethnographic map, a Romanian delegate contested this claim, only to receive the reply: "Minorities only exist where there is a Treaty."[18]

According to contemporary logic, members of minority groups in Western Europe or the United States did not need protection because those societies were fully civilized and fully democratized. Eastern Europeans, by contrast, could not be fully trusted. One of the most influential players at Versailles, Jan Smuts, president of South Africa, argued, "The peoples left behind by the decomposition of Russia, Austria, and Turkey are mostly untrained politically; many of them are either incapable or deficient in the power of self-government."[19]

WHAT WOULD be the consequences of the Paris Peace Treaties on globalism? The British journalist Stephen Miles Bouton, writing in Berlin, concluded that the Paris Peace Treaties failed to create the conditions for world peace precisely because of their deglobalizing effects. The Treaty of St. Germain, he argued, has "Balkanized Europe: it has to a large degree reestablished the multiplicity of territorial sovereignties that handicapped progress and caused continuous strife more than a century ago; it has revived smoldering race-antagonisms which were in a fair way to be extinguished; it has created a dozen new irredentas, new breeding-places of war; it has liberated thousands from foreign domination but placed tens of thousands under the yoke of other foreign domination, and has tried to insure the permanency not only of their subjection, but of other subject races which have for centuries been struggling for independence."[20]

Keynes, the greatest pessimist, predicted revolution. "In continental Europe the earth heaves and no one is aware of the rumblings," he warned.[21] It all came back to food, and the fact that the peace settlement would destroy the networks of regional and global trade created in the decades before the war. "In relation to other continents Europe is not self-sufficient; in particular it cannot feed itself," he explained. "The danger confronting us, therefore, is the rapid depression of the standard of life of the European populations to a point which will mean actual starvation for some. . . . Men will not always die quietly. For starvation, which brings to some lethargy and a helpless despair, drives other temperaments to the nervous instability of hysteria and to a mad despair."[22]

We should not take Keynes's rhetoric at face value, of course. In reality, recent scholarship has shown that there was far more continuity than one might expect between prewar and postwar economic relations. For example, in Romania, many Transylvanian elites adapted well to the new circumstances, and even prospered. Members of the German and Jewish minorities maintained positions of power within business and industrial circles. And trade relations between the Habsburg successor states were partly reestablished in the 1920s before being disrupted once again by the Great Depression.[23]

But there were serious causes for alarm in the early 1920s. In 1923, Harry Graf Kessler, a prominent German liberal who had served on the Western Front and as an ambassador to Poland in the early Weimar Republic, gave a series of lectures in the United States. The handcuffing of the global economy, he worried aloud, posed a major threat to global peace and security. Before the war, "Every growing nation had to face the question, how to secure its necessary supplies of food and raw materials against the equally pressing demands of other growing nations." After the war, the blockade, and the postwar settlement, these existential concerns were even more pressing. He hoped that a strengthened League of Nations could improve and mediate economic competition but was concerned about the rise of left- and right-wing violence and radicalism. In Germany, fortunately, he did not yet see a Lenin or a Mussolini on the horizon. "A rather reassuring feature is . . . that neither opposition movement [on the left or right] has, up to date, developed any great outstanding figure, either in the Reichstag or without," he concluded. "Hitler, of whom much is heard in the newspapers, is merely . . . a local agitator endowed with some sort of magnetism for Bavarians."[24]

SEVEN

The Victors Have Kept None of Their Promises

FIUME, 1919

On September 12, 1919, the Italian nationalist poet Gabriele D'Annunzio led hundreds of mutinous Italian troops into the contested port city of Fiume, a commercial hub with a multilingual population of Italian, Croatian, Hungarian, and dialect speakers. They encountered no resistance. D'Annunzio was already a celebrity and a war hero, and his cause—taking Fiume for Italy, against the decisions of the diplomats at Versailles—was popular in Italy and in Fiume.[1]

It was not D'Annunzio's first political stunt. He spent the entire war engaged in nationalist performance art, attracting press attention with fiery oratory and military hijinks. In August 1918, he led an air raid of Vienna, consisting of eleven airplanes adorned with the Lion of St. Mark, the symbol of the city of Venice. Instead of bombs, the planes showered the city with propaganda leaflets urging the Viennese to capitulate. In a poem published the same year, he coined the phrase "mutilated victory" to describe the outcome of the First World War for Italy. It caught on quickly among Italians who were bitter and angry about the outcome of the war, including Fascists such as Benito Mussolini.

Italy was on the winning side of the war and was rewarded in Paris with significant territorial gains. The Italians hung on to the piece of

Austria they took called the South Tyrol, with a population of close to 300,000 German speakers, and also seized most of the Adriatic coast, including Trieste. But these gains did not placate Italian nationalists, who felt they had been deprived of their rightful spoils of war. In 1915, the British and French had concluded a secret treaty with Italy (the London Pact), promising even more territorial rewards to persuade Italy to join forces against its former allies, Germany and Austria-Hungary. The pact had promised Italy territory in the north and domination of the Adriatic, alongside other potential colonial prizes. After the war, Italian leaders expected to cash in on these promises. But the Americans, who had not been privy to the deal in 1915, were aghast by the secret treaty. They refused to cede Fiume, in particular, to the Italian state. Wilson's priority was to support the new state of Yugoslavia, which also claimed the city.

In Italy, it was not only nationalists or protofascists such as D'Annunzio who felt that the Paris Peace Treaties were a raw deal. Francesco Nitti, a left-liberal (Radical Party) economist and Italian prime minister between 1919 and 1920, considered the Paris Peace Treaties to be a hypocritical betrayal of the promises laid out in Wilson's Fourteen Points. He wrote in 1923, "The victors have kept none of the promises which they made in their hour of danger, but have on the other hand, belied the principles of freedom, democracy, and self-determination of peoples which they pretended to guard."[2] Socialist Gaetano Salvemini, one of Wilson's supporters and a distinguished historian, was just as offended by the selective application of "self-determination." In response to Wilson's refusal to grant Fiume to Italy, he protested:

> Why does he want to impose what he considers absolute justice on the Italian people alone? Why does he not first issue a message to the English people to deny it the German colonies and ask that they all be entrusted to the League? Why does he not send a message to the French people, denying it the right to violate the principle of nationality in the Saar basin? ... Why does he not send a message to the American people, to explain that the Monroe doctrine cannot be reconciled with a League of Nations that claims to insure equal-

ity of rights to all civilized nations? . . . It is against this discrimination in treatment that Italy has revolted.[3]

Like German colonial advocates, Italian protestors continually emphasized Italy's alleged *need* for empire on the basis of its large population. This need, they claimed, was particularly urgent given the new limits on international migration, as emigration abroad had been Italy's long-standing solution to the endemic problems of overpopulation and underemployment. To Italian nationalists, therefore, Fiume thus represented more than a small Adriatic port city in a nation of many ports. It became symbolic of the territorial and imperial ambitions that had been thwarted by Wilson and the peacemakers in Paris. "Italy is big, and wants to get bigger," D'Annunzio insisted in a 1919 editorial. That meant control of all of the Adriatic coast.[4]

D'Annunzio's occupation of Fiume, in turn, was one of the boldest acts of defiance against the new liberal international order created in Paris. "Our delegates had left the gaming-table where they had remained seated from the very first day with the spirit of beaten men. But the Italian people had risen; the national will at last had spoken," D'Annunzio wrote.[5]

The occupation was also an act of defiance against the liberal Italian government. As much as Italian officials wanted Fiume, they were hesitant to defy Britain, France, and particularly the United States, upon which Italy was dependent for credit and food. The Italian government therefore rejected D'Annunzio's grand gesture and threatened to blockade the city. D'Annunzio responded by declaring Fiume an independent city-state, which he called the "Regency of Carnaro."[6]

D'Annunzio's aspirations were spiritual and political more than economic—returning Italy to its greatness under the Roman Empire, reviving its "vitality," and establishing a culture that would shake off the corruption, weakness, and degeneracy he associated with liberal politics. He was neither a globalist nor an anti-globalist. But for many nationalists, Italy's insistence on mastery over the Adriatic was simultaneously a bid for global economic power. Adriatic port cities were gateways to the eastern Mediterranean, India, and the Far East, as well as to the Central European hinterland. For nationalist critics, the refusal of Western diplomats to recognize Italy's claim to Fiume reflected an international capitalist conspiracy against the Italian nation. The Fascist newspaper *il Popolo* proclaimed in October 1919 that the rights of Fiume had been "trampled upon in the interests of international banking concerns, trusts, and navigation companies like the Cunard Line, and plutocratic coalitions. The League of Nations reveals itself a society for business on a large scale."[7]

The story of Fiume and D'Annunzio has been told time and again as a prelude to Fascism. D'Annunzio, to be sure, inspired Mussolini and provided the Fascist movement with many of its signature aesthetics: the straight-arm salute, the black uniforms, the military pageantry, and the rhapsodic glorification of the nation, violence, and death. But contrary to myth and legend, the people of Fiume did not support D'Annunzio (and hold out against the dictates of the international community for more than a year) because they were all rabid Italian nationalists. Rather, they were responding to the threat of being cast out of the global economy and saw annexation to Italy as their best chance of maintaining the status and autonomy they had enjoyed under Habsburg rule. As historian Dominique Reill has argued, they demanded what they saw as the benefits of belonging to a powerful *empire*. Italy, which at least had a seat at the table of the great powers, seemed like a better bet than Yugoslavia in terms of retaining the privileges and prosperity associated with empire.[8]

Before the First World War, Fiume had lived off globalization. Its bread and butter was emigration, steamships, the oil trade, and agricultural exports. One factory in Fiume processed 400,000 bags of Indian rice a year and distributed them throughout Hungary; another produced and exported thousands of naval torpedoes to the United Kingdom, South America, Japan, and the United States. Hungarian sugar, extracted from sugar beets in the town of Hatvan, shipped out from Fiume to Smyrna, Aden, Bombay, Calcutta, Karachi, Singapore, Shanghai, and Yokohama. The city was Hungary's primary point of access to the sea and the world and the tenth busiest port in Europe as of 1914. It was also Hungary's third richest city.[9]

In the eyes of merchants and business elites, that global position was threatened by annexation to Yugoslavia, a new state with an uncertain future. Andrea Ossinack, who represented Fiume in Paris in 1919, was also a member of one of Fiume's most important financial families. He insisted that the economic interests of Fiume lay firmly with annexation to Italy. "As for the alleged ruin of Fiume if it were united with Italy, I must say only that the trade of Yugoslavia is an insignificant factor in the movement of the port. The port of Fiume is the natural outlet of Hungary and Hungary will be able to secure this outlet only if it is Italian and not Yugoslav."[10] Based in part on economic realities, and in part on cultural chauvinism, Ossinack and other city elites saw Italy as a recognized global power that would attract foreign investment and (they believed) invest more in the city's future.[11]

Likewise, in another former Habsburg port, Trieste, economic elites and merchants pushed for annexation to Italy rather than Yugoslavia.[12] This is also often interpreted as a story of nationalism triumphing over economic interests, but in fact, the merchants of Trieste were not simply blinded by nationalism. They made the same bet as their counterparts in Fiume: Italy was a global power, while Yugoslavia was a new state, seen as "backward" and "immature." Elites in Trieste assumed that they would have the same special status as a "free port city" in Italy that they had enjoyed in Habsburg Austria, and that the Italian government would invest heavily in the port.

They made the wrong bet. In 1920, the Italian newspaper *Il Piccolo* described an atmosphere "of unease, anxiety, and uncertainty" in Trieste, blaming the Italian government for its failure to achieve "a return of commerce to its former vigor." The volume of goods shipping in and out of Trieste declined by more than 50 percent between 1913 and 1921, and the volume of goods transported by railway from Trieste to the Central European hinterland dropped by more than two-thirds. The city was ultimately reduced from a global hub to a minor provincial port.[13]

WHILE DELEGATES were stamping their feet in Paris, and D'Annunzio ruled over Fiume, social protests about food, land, and sacri-

"The Flight of D'Annunzio over Trieste," *La Domenica del Corriere*, August 1915.

fice escalated at home. These protests began toward the war's end and only escalated after the armistice. They were not simply violent clashes between Socialists and Fascists. They also revolved around Italy's relationship to the global economy and the crises created by new restrictions on migration.

The food situation in Italy during the war had never been as dire as in Austria-Hungary or Germany, partly due to supplies and credit from the Allies. But local and regional shortages and distribution problems generated serious unrest as the war dragged on. Once again, reliance on imported foods was partly to blame. Italian diets were based almost entirely on carbohydrates, and in 1911–1913, wheat imports had doubled. The war immediately cut off these essential wheat supplies from Romania and Russia; it also cut off remittances from emigrants, which declined by three-quarters between 1913 and 1918. Once Italy entered the war, the situation got worse, with local and regional shortages and a 50 percent increase in prices in the war's first year. Imports declined by

40 percent.[14] To the outrage of consumers, the liberal government was reluctant to intervene in the market or set limits on prices. Price controls and requisitions were only introduced in 1916–1917, once inflation had already spiraled out of control.[15]

Mass protests, often led by women (as in other parts of Europe), became bolder and more violent as the situation deteriorated in the final years of war. In Turin in August 1917, women led a protest over rationing that expanded into a general strike, with workers erecting barricades in the streets. The strike ended brutally when the army intervened and killed dozens of workers. Discontent was also widespread in the Italian countryside, where women took the lead in organizing strikes and land occupations. The occupiers demanded the end of the war and return of their men as well as land and food.[16]

When the war ended, little changed. Prices got higher and food shortages more severe. Protests spread across Italy, led by newly organized peasant leagues and the growing ranks of Socialists, anarchists, and Communists. As Italian leaders negotiated the "mutilated peace" in Paris, Italy teetered on the verge of revolution. In the countryside, returning veterans and women were angry that they had not received land they felt they had been promised in exchange for wartime sacrifices, and they began to seize it for themselves. Land occupations were particularly widespread in Lazio and Sicily, where a few large landowners owned vast estates, but by September 1919, land occupations had spread to Calabria, Campania, Puglia, Abruzzo, Molise, Basilicata, and Sardinia.

During these so-called Red Years, many government officials feared a Socialist revolution—which they associated with the total breakdown of law and order. One prefect reported, "The demands of the peasants have almost no limits; they invade or threaten to invade not only uncultivated land and pastures, but cultivated land and olive groves, causing damages to the owners and the general economy of the countryside."[17] Peasants justified these occupations, the prefect reported, with the "pretext of unemployment, claiming the urgent necessity of increasing production," and were becoming "increasingly less tolerant of any delay and deaf to any objection." As of August 1919, there had been land occupations in 40 out of 228 communes of the province of Rome.[18]

The threat of revolution on the left generated a counterrevolutionary reaction on the right. Benito Mussolini founded the first Fasci Italiani di Combattimento in March 1919. Mussolini, himself a former Socialist, espoused a program that was both radically nationalist and anti-global. In January 1921, he wrote, "Today we are economically slaves of those who give us coal, slaves of those who give us wheat."[19] Italians would have understood that he meant "slaves" of the United States, which supplied Italy with more than 1.5 million tons of coal and 60 million bushels of wheat in 1921.[20] Mussolini's Fascist squads were composed mainly of unemployed veterans, who spent their time roaming the countryside and terrorizing Socialists, Communists, and anarchists. Landowners and industrialists, fearful of revolution, often supported their activities.

In his 1930 account, Fascist minister of agriculture Arrigo Serpieri insisted that the left-wing protests of 1919–1920 took place "in the complete absence of any government authority," retrospectively justifying the violence with which Fascists had crushed the protests. "During the strikes, violence and crimes against people and things, thefts, pillaging, arson, the destruction of harvests, the abuse of animals, the siege of homes and the threats to owners who resisted . . . injuries, murders—all were incredibly frequent." He described land occupations, in particular, as assaults on the ideal of private property, against which authorities were powerless (or even sympathetic). "In vast territories," he claimed, 1919–1920 "represented a situation . . . of civil war and anarchy."[21] In fact, contemporary reports from prefects in the provinces afflicted by land occupations in 1919–1920 indicate that government officials did their best to maintain order. Land invasions mostly took place without violence, unless the state responded violently. In September 1920, for example, the Socialist newspaper *Avanti* called for the occupation of "all land that is non-cultivated or badly cultivated," but recommended that "no violence be used against people or things."[22]

And yet many liberals, as well as Fascists, were deeply shaken by the disorder of the Red Years. Economist and journalist Luigi Einaudi, a liberal anti-Fascist and the future president of the Italian Republic, described the situation in Forlì, Italy, in July 1919 in the *Corriere della Serra*. "Tumult in the markets, overturned vegetable and fruit stands and baskets, workshops assaulted and emptied of all goods, crowds that divide the spoils and take them home . . . in brief, a portrait of the events that are taking place in all parts of Italy."[23]

Protests continued throughout Italy in 1920–1921, revolving around access to food and land, as peasants and workers demanded the resources necessary to feed and house their families. In Albenga in December 1921, a group of 400 women carrying children invaded a municipal government building yelling, "We are hungry, we want bread!"[24] In Civitella, a local castle was occupied by unemployed families. A report from the village explained that the commune was suffering greatly because many Italians, frustrated by new American immigration restrictions, were returning to Italy from the United States. These returning families ended up homeless or living in "impossible hovels that offend the most basic norms of hygiene and morality."[25]

Protesters and officials saw deglobalization as a major source of the hunger and civil unrest afflicting Italy. In particular they focused on new migration restrictions that closed off opportunities for emigration, along with Italy's lack of colonies and access to raw materials. But Fascists and Socialists alike proposed more deglobalization as the solution: land reform, settlement, and intensified agricultural production, all of which would employ people at home and enable Italy to produce more food. In Rovigo, a prefect explained, "It is common knowledge that the land . . . cannot absorb all of the unemployed labor here. It cannot absorb it today just as it has never been able to absorb it. Emigration has always been the great safety valve for this province and the source of non-negligible well-being." Now, however, after the war, "emigration is completely closed off." There was no money for public works, and the land still could not provide enough work or food. As a solution, he proposed a project of settlement on the Adriatic island of Donzella. The project was supposed to simultaneously employ people, create new land for agricultural production, and liberate a vast expanse of land from malaria.[26] The liberal prefect had just outlined the plan that Mussolini would embrace on a vast and monumental scale.

The prefect's local vision of autarky centered around an island. It was an apt metaphor for a self-sufficient nation: difficult to invade, flourishing in isolation, an ideal site for social and political experimentation. Islands have long been objects of social and political fantasies of regeneration. In 1918–1921, deglobalization was likewise a powerful fantasy, compelling across political divides, even as Italian Socialists and Fascists violently clashed in the streets and on the fields.

BACK IN FIUME, D'Annunzio's 1919 occupation only heightened tensions between Italian statesmen, Wilson, and nationalist advocates of expansion in Italy. The Italian government wanted to acquire Fiume legally, not through the actions of a renegade poet. D'Annunzio transformed the government's pressure on the people of Fiume into a public relations fiasco. The closing of the port, the withdrawal of credit and food aid meant that shops and markets were soon empty; people were hungry.

D'Annunzio turned to piracy for provisions. In one stunt, legionnaires stole fifty draft horses from the Italian military. After threats of severe reprisals, D'Annunzio promised to return them, but instead returned fifty malnourished horses that were incapable of any work. There was also an organized "children's crusade," when hundreds of children from Fiume were sent to host families on the mainland so that they wouldn't starve, a mission that the Italian government attempted to block because it was so embarrassing.[27]

But the people of Fiume were gradually worn down by the instability and the privation. In December 1919, the Italian government offered a *modus vivendi*. This compromise would have preserved Fiume's status as a free port city (no annexation to Italy or Yugoslavia), but with more Italian investment in the city's financial reconstruction, the re-opening of the port, and recognition of the city's aspirations to eventually join Italy. In a fiery speech, D'Annunzio urged the people of Fiume to reject this compromise and called for a plebiscite. But when the plebiscite took place, the people of Fiume voted to accept the government's offer. D'Annunzio promptly nullified the results of his own plebiscite and rejected the modus vivendi anyway.

In the wake of this fiasco, he attempted to bolster his cause yet again by claiming to represent a global coalition of oppressed peoples. "From the dauntless Sinn FEIN of Ireland to the Red Banner which in Egypt unites the Crescent and the Cross, all the insurrections of the spirit against the devourers of raw flesh and against the exploiters of weapon-less peoples, will catch flame anew from our sparks which fly afar," he wrote (with his signature combination of grandiosity and wordiness).[28] The League of Fiume was dubbed the "anti-League of Nations," and D'Annunzio promoted it as a launching pad for global revolutionary movements. But there was no hiding the fact that Italy's bid for territorial aggrandizement was rooted in its self-interest.[29]

D'Annunzio hung on to Fiume for fifteen months. Finally, the Treaty of Rapallo established Fiume as an independent city-state in November 1920. D'Annunzio rejected the treaty and responded by declaring war on Italy. He had notified his nationalist followers in Italy to prepare for an uprising; his plan was to "set out like Garibaldi and march through the country, turning the troops sent against him into followers of his crusade." The *New York Times* surmised, "When D'Annunzio from his despotat of Fiume declares war, not against Jugoslavia, but against Italy, the natural inclination is to suppose that the man has gone crazy."[30] By this point, many Italians may have agreed with this assessment. In any event, the uprising failed to occur. D'Annunzio's legionnaires were defeated in one week, between Christmas Eve and New Year's Eve, when D'Annunzio flew away from Fiume in an airplane, declaring "Italy is not worth dying for."[31]

EIGHT

Tinder for the Bolshevist Spark

BUDAPEST AND MUNICH, 1919

ROSIKA SCHWIMMER HAD exactly one thing in common with Gabriele D'Annunzio: her frustration with the borders drawn in Paris. In March 1920, as Budapest was gripped by violence, she cursed the diplomats who had decided Hungary's fate. "They blindfolded themselves, there in Paris and with knives in their hands they played at drawing a map. The new Europe, result of this blind game, is in a shape which cannot be maintained," she wrote in a letter to American suffragist Lola Maverick Lloyd in 1920. Unlike D'Annunzio, however, Schwimmer did not have the luxury of an airplane—or even a passport—to escape, as her passport was confiscated by the Bolsheviks and then kept by the counterrevolutionaries. Her personal trajectory—from citizen of the world to stateless refugee—was in several ways emblematic of the fate of internationalism in interwar Europe.

The postwar era began well enough for Schwimmer. She returned to Budapest in 1918 and was named ambassador to Switzerland for the new liberal republic led by Mihály Károlyi. She was the world's first woman to serve in the role of ambassador. But Károlyi's regime was short-lived and Schwimmer's term as ambassador even shorter. Stymied by the sexism and anti-Semitism of colleagues who flat-out refused to work with her (and falsely accused her of being a Bolshevik), Schwimmer was recalled in January 1919.[1] The Hungarian Democratic Republic lasted only two months longer and then fell to a Bolshevik revolution in March 1919. Many Hungarians saw the Communists as their best hope for defending Hungary against the invasion of Romanian and Czechoslovak armies. The Bolshevik army promptly turned the tables and attempted to take back the Slovak and Transylvanian territory that had been lost at the end of the war.

Although on the left, Schwimmer was no fan of Bolshevism. "Communism, as it was practiced here, was nothing more than a raging, tyrannical, brutal application of the principle that the world and everything it has to offer belongs to whoever commands the rifles and canons," she lamented to a friend in the United States. "Public hangings on Budapest's large squares, attended by tens of thousands of people . . . house-searches, a militarism lubricated with all the ointments of the old system, women going wild and serving unquestioningly, and all of that in the name of the most noble, beautiful axioms of humanity!" After spending much of her life fighting for women's suffrage, she was not eligible to cast a vote in the first election in which women were enfranchised, because she was not a member of the Communist Party.

As Schwimmer was to experience, Communist internationalism had itself been somewhat deglobalized. This was true in the Soviet Union as well as Budapest. Over the course of the 1920s and 1930s, the Soviet regime tightened border security, denounced "cosmopolitanism," and sought to insulate itself from the global economy through more autarkic economic policies.[2] In Budapest, Bolsheviks refused to give Schwimmer a passport to travel abroad, a hardship for someone who earned a living as an international speaker.

As much as Schwimmer despised Bolshevism, what came next was even worse. When Romanian troops defeated the Hungarians on June 30, a counterrevolutionary movement seized power and unleashed a reign of terror on its enemies. "Liberals, radicals, and even socialists are hunted like wild game," Schwimmer reported. "Literally wild game, being shot down by the hundreds. And first the feminists and pacifists! It is no empty phrase when I say that one's life is in danger." Jews in particular were targeted and blamed for the Communist takeover. "Being of Jewish origin," Schwimmer lamented, "I can no longer call myself a Hungarian according to today's terminology." Schwimmer sank into a deep depression. She spent the months of the White Terror in fear for her life, selling off her belongings and scavenging for food, wood, and medicine, her idealism exhausted. "I am so tired of life and so utterly hopeless, that I consider everything useless, every effort to better the world in vain," she despaired.[3]

Although she was not a Socialist and had not supported the Communists, the new right-wing government also refused to allow her to exit the country. "It is the irony of fate," Schwimmer wrote in December 1919, "that during Bolshevism I was denied a passport because I was anti-Bolshevist, and—as I was openly told today—they were afraid 'that my grand eloquence will send their little Soviet Republic to hell' and now I shall stay home, because I was an agitator. If things had not such tragic aspects one could but smile."[4] Schwimmer was trapped. Without saying goodbye to her family, she eventually snuck out of Budapest in the middle of the night in January 1920, wearing a disguise and carrying a forged passport. She landed in a sanatorium in Vienna, where she began to plan for her eventual emigration to the United States.

AS IN ITALY, the threat (and reality) of revolutionary and counterrevolutionary violence was omnipresent in Central Europe after the war. The Russian Revolution had demonstrated the frightening possibilities. Revolutionary and counterrevolutionary violence followed similar patterns in Hungary and Germany. Indeed, the violence was facilitated by transnational contact between radical movements across national borders.[5] At stake was not simply the future of nation-states and nationalist movements, but the relationship of postwar states to globalism (in both real and imagined forms) and to a new international order.

In all of these contexts, it was difficult to tell when the war ended and the postwar violence began. In Germany, many (including Adolf Hitler himself, who cried into his pillow in Munich upon hearing that the war had been lost) responded to defeat with shock and disbelief and refused

to accept Germany's new republican government. This is not to say that
the Weimar Republic was doomed from the start. In January 1919, more
than three out of four Germans cast their votes for the parties that were
firmly behind the republic: the mainstream Socialists, the Catholic
Center Party, and the liberal German Democratic Party. But some disenchanted Germans, including demobilized soldiers and youth who felt
they had "missed out" on the glory of the war, organized into paramili-
tary troops, the so-called Freikorps, and joined anti-Communist forces
in Latvia. They were lured there in part by the promise of free land to
settle and farm. These soldiers, along with many on the German Far
Right, believed that Germany had only lost the war because it had been
"stabbed in the back" by a fifth column within Germany, composed of
Jews, international war profiteers, and Bolsheviks. They exacted revenge
through a lawless assault on Bolsheviks in the east.[6]

The German Left, meanwhile, grew impatient with the pragmatic
reformism of the Weimar government. Friedrich Ebert's Socialist government had no taste for revolution. German Social Democracy instead
reaffirmed its commitment to parliamentary democracy and to improving the living and working conditions of Germans through cooperation
between industry and labor. The Social Democrats were promptly challenged on the left by the Spartacists, led by Rosa Luxemburg and Karl
Liebknecht. The Spartacists consisted of a union of the two parties to
the left of the Socialists, the USPD (Union of Democratic Socialists)
and the KPD (Communist Party of Germany). Their rivalry escalated
into a bloodbath that would permanently scar the republic.

When a navy revolt erupted in November 1918, Ebert called in the
army against his left-wing challengers. Then, in January 1919, fearing
imminent revolution, Ebert and his military advisor Gustav Noske took
a more fatal step: they recruited the right-wing Freikorps to violently
suppress the Spartacists. The reckoning that followed permanently
divided and weakened the German Left. The Freikorps marched into
Berlin believing that they had free reign to assault, torture, and murder
suspected Bolsheviks. Liebknecht and Luxemburg were brutally murdered and their bodies tossed into the Landwehr canal.

Revolutionary and counterrevolutionary violence raged in Munich as well. After the Bavarian king was ousted in November 1918, a Socialist Council of Workers, Peasants, and Soldiers seized power, led by Kurt Eisner of the USPD. His government was defeated at the ballot box, but he was assassinated as he walked into parliament to submit his resignation. Next came a government led by Johannes Hoffmann of the SPD, which was overthrown in turn by a Bavarian Soviet Republic in April 1919.[7]

Victor Klemperer, the linguist and diarist most famed for his account of the Nazi era, was a recently demobilized soldier in Munich in 1919. He was employed teaching other veterans at the Ludwig Maximilian University and wrote for the *Leipziger Neueste Nachrichten*. A staunch liberal, Klemperer was no fan of the revolutionaries. In fact, he had a hard time taking them seriously. "Ridiculousness was one of the main characteristics I associated with the Council Republic [the Bavarian Soviet Republic], such abject and utter ridiculousness that for the longest time I thought it was highly unlikely the pathetic affair would come to a truly bloody end."

He was wrong, as he soon discovered. When the bloody end came, Jews bore the brunt of it. The anti-Bolshevik movement in Munich, he observed, "expressed itself neither beautifully nor cleverly, but anti-Semitically." When the establishment of Munich "began to realize that the council Republican game . . . could actually mean something worse for them than just a wild, carnivalistic, performance, how did they demonstrate their awakening to resistance? Through spontaneous anti-Semitism. 'Jewish pigs!' ranted individuals in front of the posters on the wall, 'Jewish pigs!' roared the occasional small chorus, and flyers appeared blaming the Jews entirely for the Council Republic, for the revolution itself, for inciting the war, for its disastrous outcome."[8] In a civil war that began May 1, at least 600 people were killed, many summarily executed, before the Council Republic was defeated.

The alarming spread of revolutionary violence in Germany convinced many outside observers that there was truth to the view that Germany could not feed itself. British journalist Stephen Miles Bouton observed in the winter of 1919, "The working people, hungry and miserable, waiting vainly week after week for the food which they believed had been promised them, were tinder for the Bolshevist spark."[9] Yet the Allies had maintained their naval blockade of Germany throughout the revolutionary winter and spring of 1919, in order to "motivate" Germany to sign the Treaty of Versailles. Woodrow Wilson, in a message to Congress in January 1919, warned that "Bolshevism is steadily advancing westward. . . . It cannot be stopped by force, but it can be stopped by food." Yet in the same appeal, Wilson was quick to specify that not a single US dollar would go to feeding a German child. "The money will not be spent for food in Germany itself, because Germany can buy its food, but it will be spent for financing the movement of food to our real friends in Poland and to the people of the liberated units of the Austro-Hungarian Empire and to our associates in the Balkans."[10] Some Allied leaders, such as Winston Churchill, even insisted that hunger was a useful tool in the peace negotiations. "Germany is still an enemy country, it would be inadvisable to remove the menace of starvation by a too sudden and abundant supply of foodstuffs. This menace is a powerful lever for negotiation at an important moment."[11]

In a remarkable about-face, however, once Germany signed the Treaty of Versailles, Germans were transformed almost instantly from the world's most threatening enemies to its most deserving victims. The apparent threat of Bolshevik revolution in Germany now propelled a massive American relief mission. Herbert Hoover's European Children's Fund explicitly promoted food relief in Germany as a means of securing world peace and Western "civilization" against the onslaught of Bolshevism from the east. Germans ultimately received 1,215,000 tons of food aid from the United States after the war, more than any other country, including Austria and Russia, which objectively faced more severe famines.[12]

Hoover's feeding programs represented a new form of internationalism aimed at preventing the spread of what was seen as a more threatening form of internationalism, namely Bolshevism. It also reflected a tacit consensus within and beyond Central Europe that the defeated powers were not capable of feeding themselves, and that if the international community failed to provide relief, it was practically inviting revolution.

These countries were reliant on a global food system and would need imports, whether acquired through charity, trade, debt, or conquest.

ALTHOUGH THE European counterrevolution was anti-global in its ideology, it generated both transnational momentum and an international humanitarian response. In Hungary, counterrevolutionary violence against the "global" threats of Judaism and Bolshevism was propelled by events in both Russia and Germany. The counterrevolutionary assault on Jews in Hungary was particularly vicious and continued several years after the war. Joseph Marcus of the American Jewish Joint Distribution Committee (JDC), a newly created organization that aimed to provide relief to European Jews, traveled to Hungary in the spring of 1921. In 130 unflinching pages he described countless atrocities, stories that were difficult to extract from the victims, who feared for their lives and the lives of their family members if they spoke out. About twelve to thirteen corpses were fished out of the Danube each day, Marcus reported:

> Many of them have the hands or feet tied with wires; many bear the marks of torture or bullet wounds. The police is [sic] forced to issue a statement that the deceased had committed suicide. And when a newspaper dares to question the possibility of persons committing suicide with their hands and feet tied, or by first filling their abdomen with rags, or similar acts, the paper is punished by the Minister of Interior.

Many corpses were buried without being identified. The wife of Eugen Schwartz, a Jewish merchant from the small town of Orkény, appeared before Budapest police on May 30, 1921. She showed the police an anonymous letter received a week earlier, in which her family was threatened with violence. "Jew! The entire community despises you. If you and your family do not leave for Palestine in three days, we cannot guarantee the safety of your lives." Local gendarmes did nothing. On May 29 her husband disappeared for good. Other Jews were arbitrarily interned in camps. Marcus visited a camp in Zalaegerszag that housed more than 1,100 men, women, and children. He found prisoners naked and starving, and heard many stories of arbitrary beatings, torture, and rape. An estimated 1,500–2,000 people died in the counterrevolution.[13]

Anti-Jewish violence spread rapidly throughout Central Europe in 1918–1921. Anti-Semitism was nothing new, nor were many of the factors driving this wave of pogroms: local economic tensions; rumors and propaganda. But anti-Semitic violence in Central Europe in 1918 was also a violent manifestation of anti-globalism. Jews were targeted as symbols of international finance, unchecked migration, cosmopolitanism, and national disloyalty. Even if they were long-standing citizens, they were scapegoated as "foreigners" who controlled the local and global economy. Jewish refugees were accused of being freeloaders and criminals who consumed all-too scarce resources, including housing and food.

In spite of its reputation as the most "democratic" and cosmopolitan state in Central Europe for Jews, assaults on Jewish property and people were also widespread in Czechoslovakia in the fall of 1918. Beating up Jews and destroying or looting their property became a common way to assert Czechoslovakia's newfound national sovereignty. Here Jews were seen as foreign invaders or nationally unreliable allies of Germans or Hungarians.[14]

In Slovakia, a JDC official found 40,000 Slovak Jews in a state of total destitution after the armistice, exacerbated by the fact that they were "being actively boycotted by the non-Jewish population." Large numbers of Jewish refugees who arrived in Slovakia during the war were expelled afterward. Ongoing violence and population displacement in the region meant that Czechoslovakia continued to attract new waves of refugees after the armistice. Local Slovaks, including government authorities, depicted these refugees as welfare parasites. The exasperated chief of police in the Slovak border town of Bardejov complained, "They are Orthodox, not one family makes a living doing productive work, they are all only hawkers, racketeering, smuggling across the border to Poland. The town is in an impoverished state because of them; all business is in their hands."[15]

In what is now Poland and Ukraine, pogroms were even more rampant after the First World War. The death toll is disputed, but historians conservatively estimate that between 40,000 and 100,000 Jews died as a result of anti-Semitic violence between 1918 and 1921, more than 600,000 were displaced, and millions of homes and businesses burned, destroyed, or looted.[16] The most infamous outbreak of anti-Semitic violence occurred in Lviv/Lemberg/L'vov in 1919, during the war between Poland and Ukraine to determine Poland's postwar borders. The large Jewish population of the city was caught in the middle of the violent struggle between Polish and Ukrainian nationalists. Local Poles saw Jewish neutrality and Jewish self-defense as support for Ukrainians and killed at least seventy-three Jews in a gruesome three-day pogrom in the city between November 21 and 23, 1918; 7,000 Jewish families were victimized by the violence, with 2,000 left homeless and more than 500 shops and businesses destroyed.[17] Jews were also murdered and assaulted in Kielce, Pinsk, Lida, Wilna, Kolbuszowa, Czestochowa, and Minsk.[18]

Sir Stuart Samuel, sent by the British government to investigate anti-Jewish persecution in Poland, linked this persecution directly to a perception of Jews as foreigners and agents of globalism. He reported a "severe private, social and commercial boycott of Jews" encouraged by the Polish press. The boycott was intended to transfer into Polish hands sectors of the economy that were perceived to be dominated by Jews, including foreign trade. Samuels disputed the "fallacious idea . . . that it is possible to transfer a large percentage of business carried on by the Jews to other hands," and warned that "if the social boycott were successful in securing a large emigration of Jews, it would result in a very large decrease in the productive powers of Poland. As the future of the Republic depends largely upon its exports the future of the state itself might be imperiled."[19]

The Polish government disagreed. It made about 1,300 arrests of pogromists, but simultaneously urged Polish Jews to emigrate, directly and indirectly.[20] Like Hungary, Poland attempted to impose a limit on the number of Jews who could enroll in universities in 1923, but backed down under pressure from the League of Nations. Local anti-Semitic violence and boycott movements continued anyway. An anonymous anti-Semitic pamphlet distributed in Prussian Poland in 1921 urged merchants, artisans, and workers not to sell their products or labor to Jews, and landlords to refuse to rent to them. "Poles! You must know that no country in the world wants to have these Jewish parasites. Why then should the poorest of them all, our unfortunate Poland, have to suffer them and to maintain millions of them. Let us get busy without delay and protect ourselves ... LET US GET BUSY ON THE JOB WITH OUR OWN FORCES! Let our motto be: AWAY WITH THE JEWS!"[21]

Under these circumstances, many Jews were desperate to get away. From Vienna, Rosika Schwimmer wrote to a friend, "We are now the real, eternal Jews who have to wander homeless from place to place. I have been here as a political refugee for four weeks now, but should something reactionary happen in Austria, I would have to keep on fleeing."[22] She eventually did flee to the United States, arriving in August 1921, thanks to her connections in the international feminist movement. She applied for United States citizenship in 1924.

However, in keeping with her diehard pacifism, Schwimmer refused to pledge to bear arms in defense of her new country. She testified at her hearing that she had "no nationalistic feeling," other than a "cosmic consciousness of belonging to a human family." It was not a good moment to belong to the human family. As a fifty-year-old woman who suffered from diabetes, Schwimmer would never have been asked to take up arms in defense of the United States. Her application was denied anyway, in a decision that was upheld by the US Supreme Court in May 1929. That decision, delivered by Justice Pierce Butler, explained, "One who is without any sense of nationalism is not well bound or held by the ties of affection to any nation or government. Such persons are liable to be incapable of attachment for and devotion to the principles of our constitution that are required of aliens seeking naturalization." Nationalism, he argued, was essentially a requirement for citizenship.

Justice Oliver Wendell Holmes Jr. dissented. He famously argued that the Constitution was meant to protect free thought not only "for those who agree with us, but freedom for the thought that we hate."

Schwimmer entered into a correspondence with Holmes for the rest of his life, grateful that his decision "did justice to my motives for seeking American citizenship. And also because it saved me from feeling a perfect fool." She explained, "A person born into the wrong family—and *choosing* another wrong one when chance permits the selection of a new family—that seemed to be my foolish position. You and your dissenting colleagues' statements reassured me that my conception of the ideal standards of the new family I was seeking, was justified."[23]

NINE

No Chestnut Without a Visa

SALZBURG, 1922

WHILE ROSIKA SCHWIMMER plotted her escape from Central Europe, another Austrian globalist planned to return home. "From the standpoint of reason," Stefan Zweig recalled, "the most foolish thing I could do after the collapse of the German and Austrian armies was to go back to Austria, that Austria which showed fairly faintly on the map of Europe as the vague, grey, and inert shadow of the former Imperial Monarchy." Before returning from Switzerland (where he had spent the last year of the war) to Salzburg in March 1919, Zweig prepared himself as though "for an Arctic expedition." He loaded his bags with warm clothes because there was no heat, with chocolate because there was no food, and with well-soled boots because there were no shoes. Then he insured it all to the maximum, assuming his luggage would be looted (and, remarkably, that insurance companies would pay). At the frontier station where he changed trains, Zweig hesitated. "It might be wiser to go back," he speculated. "I felt that I was at a turning point in my life. I concluded in favor of the difficult way and boarded the train again."

His doubts were intensified by the sight of a special luxury train rolling through the station on its way out of Austria. Peering into the glass windows, he was surprised to recognize the passengers as the Habsburg

Emperor Charles and his wife, Empress Zita. "All of those who stood about sensed history, world history, in this tragic sight," Zweig recalled. "It was the moment in which the almost millenary monarchy really ended. I knew it was a different Austria, a different world, to which I was returning."[1]

In its prime and its afterlife, the Habsburg Empire was often seen as a microcosm of the world itself. Its dissolution was also synonymous with the end of a certain vision of the world and of globalism as a positive ideal. The *World of Yesterday* mourned by Zweig was the cosmopolitan world of the imperial capital. "The genius of Vienna—a specifically musical one—is that it harmonized all the national and lingual contrasts. . . . Its culture was a synthesis of all Western cultures. Whoever lived there and worked there felt himself free of all confinement and prejudice. Nowhere was it easier to be a European."[2] The "Austrian Idea" for which Zweig was famously nostalgic had been propagated by the Habsburg dynasty, scientists, and state builders since the early nineteenth century. This was the notion that Austria was united precisely by its multinational, multilingual, and geographic diversity.[3] For its adherents, the Austrian Idea was a model for global peace. In Robert Musil's *Man Without Qualities*, the Austrian patriot Diotima proclaimed, "True Austria was the whole world," insisting that "The World . . . would find no peace until its peoples learned to live together on a higher plane, like the Austrian people in their fatherland." She called this ideal "Global Austria."[4]

This vision of unity in diversity applied to Austria's economy and natural resources as well as its population and languages.[5] Austrian scientists and politicians imagined the empire as a world in miniature precisely because of its capacity for autarky. "If it were economically beneficial to free oneself from all trade with foreign countries, Austria would be in a position above all other countries to become independent and self-sufficient," proclaimed politician and journalist Ernst von Schwarzer in 1853. In 1841, the economist Friedrich List had made the case that the most highly developed states possessed precisely this capacity for autarky, combining manufacturing, agriculture, and commerce. "In the economical development of nations, it is necessary to distinguish the following principal stages: the savage state, the pastoral state, the agricultural state, the agricultural and manufacturing state, and finally, the agricultural, manufacturing, and commercial state," List wrote. Austria, von Schwarzer argued, had reached this pinnacle of development: "Austria has no specific economic vocation. It is simultaneously an agricultural, manufacturing, and commercial state."[6]

Still another notion of "Global Austria" centered on Austria's global presence and power. While the empire participated in global trade via its ports in Trieste and Fiume, and aspired to great power status, the state lacked the formal colonies that gave Britain and France their global stature at the turn of the century. But for advocates of Global Austria, it was precisely the lack of formal colonies that made Austria so well suited to become a peaceful agent of influence beyond its borders, especially through its trade.[7]

WHEN THE Austrian Empire collapsed in 1918, all of these visions of Austria—in the World and *as* the World, dissolved with it. The situation was well encapsulated in a scene from Joseph Roth's *The Emperor's Tomb*. In that scene, a Polish count bemoans the fate of a simple chestnut seller after the First World War. "He is only a chestnut roaster, but he is quite symbolic. Symbolic for the old Monarchy. This gentleman once sold his chestnuts everywhere, through half of Europe one might say. And everywhere where his roasted chestnuts were eaten, was Austria, and the Emperor Franz Joseph reigned. Now there is no chestnut without a visa."[8]

Real-life Austrian traveling salesman H. R. Fleischmann reflected on the challenges he faced in 1919. The First World War had virtually eliminated international travel and his business. Now it was unclear whether he would ever regain his livelihood, thanks to the "arbitrarily-drawn borders of the micro-states which are serving the world economy by bringing our export industries to ruin." In addition to the "enmity of neighboring countries," he had to deal with new currencies and exchange rates, tariffs and trade laws, passport and visa requirements.

Not to mention the need to learn new languages, as no one wanted to buy from a salesman speaking German.[9]

Postwar Austria was an epicenter and microcosm of deglobalization. The language of dissolution, dismemberment, and fragmentation dominated postwar discussion of the state's fate. At the heart of the problem was a paradox: on the one hand, the logic of national "self-determination" seemed to require the creation of "small states" between Germany and Russia. At the same time, tariff walls, economic nationalism, and migration restrictions made the survival of these small states seem impossible.

Before the First World War, the Habsburg Empire had been the largest free-trade zone in Europe. The Paris Peace Treaties divided that single zone into six warring economic units. Hungary increased tariffs up to 50 percent for finished goods; Yugoslavia up to 170 percent. Trade between Austria and what was now Czechoslovakia, regions once tightly linked, decreased 50 percent.[10] In 1924, Arthur Salter of the League of Nations reiterated what many Austrians had been saying since 1918: "Of the fragments into which the old empire was divided Austria was by far the most miserable.... The new Austria produced less than one-third of her food supplies and few raw materials. She was hemmed in by new political frontiers, which became also for a time almost impassable economic barriers. These barriers separated the urban populations from the food, without which they could not live, and the main industries both from their raw materials and from their market."[11]

The Austria that Zweig returned to was thus defined precisely by its *lack* of self-sufficiency, its lack of an Idea, and its lack of any will to even exist. "According to all human previsions it was impossible for the country—an entity artificially created by the victors—to exist independently, and, in the unanimous opinion of all parties, Socialist, Clerical, and Nationalist, it had no wish to exist independently. It was the first instance in history, as far as I know, in which a country was saddled with an independence which it exasperatedly resisted," Zweig noted.[12]

Yet, as the Czech historian František Palacký famously suggested in 1848, "If the Austrian State had not existed for ages, it would have been in the interests of Europe and indeed of humanity to endeavor to create it as soon as possible."[13] Once the dust of empire settled, internationalists descended upon East-Central Europe to begin this reinvention. The shards of Global Austria were simply too dangerous to leave scattered across the crossroads of Europe. International organizations appeared on the scene and collected fragments, attempting to piece them back together.[14] This was not simply a lurch back toward globalism, however. The interwar successor states to the Habsburg Empire became *simultaneous* epicenters of globalization and deglobalization, nationalism and internationalism.[15]

Many Central Europeans sought salvation in new political forms, such as federation, that would facilitate more economic cooperation between former Habsburg lands. Hans Schober, the head of the Vienna City Police and briefly chancellor of Austria, was among these advocates of federalism. He insisted that Austria would only be able to live independently if Central and Southeast Europe were reconstructed as an economic unity. "Nobody need fear that the political system existing before the war will reappear; that is absolutely impossible today; but the absurd economic barriers raised between countries economically dependent on each other for their welfare must be removed."[16]

Oskar Jászi, the minister of nationalities under the short-lived Károlyi regime in Hungary, meanwhile called for a "United States of the Danube" with free trade between its members and a shared foreign and military policy. Visions of a Danube Federation had circulated since 1848. His model was something like the United States or Switzerland. Such a union would possess "such a wealth of natural, climatological, and ethnographic resources" that autarky, which he claimed was "an intrinsic test of a viable polity," would be attainable to a greater extent there than in almost any other state in world history. For Jászi, the choices were clear: "Federation or war! . . . Only the complete freedom of economic circulation is capable of . . . creating lasting peace."[17]

In Austria, economist and diplomat Richard Riedl also sought to reintegrate Austria into regional and global economies. Riedl's vision of federation, however, remained tied to aspirations for annexation to Germany. In 1915, he had drafted a memorandum calling for a postwar customs union between Germany and Austria.[18] When Austrian demands for annexation were rejected after the First World War, Riedl reimagined this German-Austrian union as a regional trade bloc including the former states of the Habsburg Empire. He denounced the "endeavours of the new States in Eastern and Southern Europe to develop as extensively as possible their home production and to become self-supporting through shutting out foreign competition."[19]

Other Austrians reimagined Habsburg economic integration on a far broader scale. Aristocrat Richard N. Coudenhove-Kalergi, founder of the pan-Europe movement, promoted a free-trade union that extended well beyond Central Europe, to include Africa. It was intended to revive trade relations within Europe and to put Europe on a more equal footing with the United States, which many Europeans (including Hitler) envied and feared precisely because of its vast hinterland, its capacity for self-sufficiency. Coudenhove warned that in the absence of such a federation, Europe was doomed to become an "economic colony of America," and that European workers would be "enslaved by American capital."[20]

To newly empowered leaders in Belgrade, Bucharest, and Prague, however, these visions of federation sounded too much like the former Habsburg Empire. They had no interest in resuscitating it.[21] But

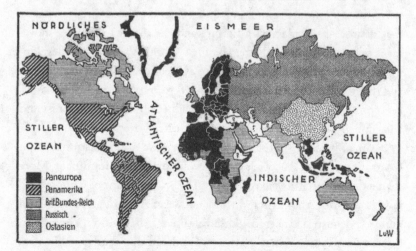

Paneuropa, as envisioned by Richard N. Coudenhove-Kalergi, 1925.

while formal federalist schemes enjoyed limited success, other efforts were more successful. Behind the scenes, trade relations between the Habsburg successor states gradually picked up again in the 1920s. Austria bought coal from Czechoslovakia and Poland; Viennese trading houses handled Czech and Polish exports, and by 1929, at least 25 percent of Austrian trade was flowing to or from Czechoslovakia, Hungary, and Poland. This was in part thanks to the regional and international connections and outlook of Viennese bankers and entrepreneurs, who remained connected to one another and invested in economic cooperation.[22]

International organizations and humanitarian activists meanwhile arrived in droves after 1918, in order to reconnect ties that had been broken by the Paris Peace Treaties. Many of these efforts responded to problems created by anti-globalism. The International Save the Children Fund sought to feed children who were starving because of the Allied naval blockade. The Near East Relief Committee, the League of Nations' Refugee Commission and its Nansen passports, and the American Jewish Joint Distribution Committee all mobilized to assist the vast number of refugees and stateless people created by closed borders. The challenges of economic deglobalization in Central Europe also produced new ideas. In the realm of trade and economic policy, historian Quinn Slobodian has argued, Austrian economists responded to the collapse of the Habsburg Empire and the threat to the free movement of goods and capital after the First World War with the development of what are now often referred to as "neoliberal" economic policies and institutions. These "globalists" hoped to "protect" or insulate markets from democratic politics, and especially from the protectionist and anti-globalist policies of democratically elected governments.[23]

Fears of Bolshevism fueled the postwar wave of internationalism in Central Europe. In Austria in 1922, revolution seemed imminent. More than a decade later, Zweig reflected, "To this day I cannot comprehend how it was that the revolution did not seize Austria.... A couple of hundred determined men could have gained mastery over Vienna and the whole of Austria then."[24] Zweig speculated that Austrians' "innate conciliatoriness" prevented a revolt, but while "conciliatory" actions of leading political parties certainly helped, the international community was also determined to stabilize the country. Many believed that a revolution in Austria (following those in Russia, Germany, and Hungary) would bring the rest of the world down with it.

Ignaz Seipel, Austria's chancellor, played on these fears of revolution in his appeals to the Allies and the League of Nations for assistance. In a speech to the league's General Assembly in 1922, he warned that if the international community did not take action, "it would mean the creation of a vacuum in the middle of Europe, a vacuum with monstrous suction that would pull in Austria's neighbors and would disrupt the balance of power among them that had only been established with great skill."[25] That year the League of Nations Economic and Financial Committee stepped in to bail Austria out of its financial abyss with a package of loans.

The league's program to reconstruct Austria's finances called for the government to stop printing money and to undertake reforms to balance the government's budget within two years. In exchange, it received about $130 million in loans to meet its deficits from 1922 to 1924. The loans came at a high cost, however. The league required the Austrian government to open its books to a league commissioner and to implement austerity measures according to the dictates of outside auditors, including cutting social spending, raising taxes, and firing almost 100,000 civil servants. This kind of external financial control had previously been attempted only in colonial or semi-colonial contexts. This humiliation was not lost on league officials or on Austrians.[26]

Social Democratic opponents of Seipel and of the Christian Social Party wasted no time blaming the Christian Socialists for having invited foreign powers and bankers to dismantle Austrian sovereignty. The editors of the *Tagblatt* (Linz) insisted, "No people in the world are subjected to such servitude. . . . England just recently signed a treaty with Iraq which also guarantees the financial rehabilitation of the country, but there is no trace of such undignified conditions. The Irish are heroically fighting . . . to remove the last remnants of foreign rule; the Turks have shaken off the yoke of foreign rule by force of arms." Austria's bourgeois political parties alone "beg for complete enslavement, nonchalantly toss away national freedom and dignity."[27]

In August 1923, leading up to parliamentary elections in October, the Social Democratic Party likewise denounced Seipel and the Christian Social Party for having "sacrificed Austria's national self-determination," bringing "the General Commissioner of international high finance to Vienna as the true replacement for the Emperor." The stabilization of the currency had come not only at the cost of sovereignty but also on the backs of workers and their families. In addition to loss of jobs, the government had closed hospitals, schools, and scientific institutions, sacrificing "happiness, health, and national culture" to pay for the economy's rehabilitation.[28]

While League of Nations officials later remembered the Austrian reconstruction mission as a great success story, other countries disagreed. They increasingly declined the league's offers of financial assistance, repelled by the odor of colonialism. Portugal, Liberia, Poland, Mexico, India, and China all refused the league's loans. In Portugal, Minister of Finance Sinel de Cordes actually sought the league's assistance and was promptly removed from office for the betrayal. He was replaced by António de Oliveira Salazar, who imposed exactly the kind of austerity measures that the league might have requested, earning him high marks from bankers, landowners, and the league alike. Salazar eventually ruled the country as a dictatorship until 1968. To many Europeans, the loss of democracy was preferable to the loss of sovereignty.[29]

International missions dedicated to feeding Austrians also brought imperialist prejudices alongside humanitarian assistance. In the face of famine conditions, Herbert Hoover's American Relief Administration (ARA) and the International Save the Children Fund, both founded in 1919, emerged among the most important efforts to combat hunger in Central Europe. The ARA penetrated the tiniest villages of Central and Eastern Europe through a network of committees and soup kitchens. While theoretically focused solely on feeding starving children, Hoover's mission embraced an anti-Communist motivation from the outset. Its representatives hoped that along with surplus wheat and corn, recipients would learn to appreciate "American" values such as self-help and cross-class solidarity.[30]

Humanitarian workers depicted the region and its people as inherently backward, violent, and corrupt—in contrast to American modernity and efficiency.[31] Orientalist chauvinism undercut their stated goals of facilitating self-help and reinforced the status of the Habsburg successor states as semi-colonial protectorates. One Save the Children Fund fieldworker reported that in Sub-Carpathian Rus in Czechoslovakia in 1920, "The squalor is almost beyond belief. Six or seven people—if one can call them people—in one stuffy room, and a half-dozen hens or rabbits besides. . . . Idiots and cretins abound."[32]

MANY INTERNATIONAL projects to reconstruct Austria and revive internationalism in Central Europe perpetuated a view of Central and Eastern Europeans as backward, uncivilized, and incapable of self-government. They also represented a model for the forms of supranational intervention into the finances of a sovereign state that would later be adapted by the International Monetary Fund (IMF). In many ways, the League of Nations and other international institutions perpetuated the imperial power of the British Empire between the wars.[33] Yet the legacy of the league and other international and humanitarian organizations in East-Central Europe cannot be reduced solely to maintaining or establishing imperial power. Nor did these internationalists simply attempt to reestablish the globalized World of Yesterday. The league also assisted in the construction of new nation-states and forms of national infrastructure and helped in some cases to reinforce national sovereignty rather than undermine it. In several cases, internationalists attempted to create a new architecture for internationalism and globalism that would be sustainable in a world of sovereign nation-states.

League of Nations agencies were staffed and sometimes run by Central Europeans with their own state-building agendas. Ludwik Rajchmann, the chief of the league's Health Organization (himself a Polish Jew), sought to use league resources along with those of the Rockefeller Foundation to strengthen the public health infrastructure of the new

Polish state, by building new hospitals, sanitary stations, and child welfare clinics, and by fortifying the state's borders.[34]

As the chaos of the immediate postwar years subsided, meanwhile, several agencies of the League of Nations gave up on earlier ambitions to return to a pre-1914 world of globalization. League experts instead settled on creating new regulatory frameworks that would facilitate migration and trade within new constraints. For example, during the First World War, European states had introduced a labyrinthine and cumbersome ad-hoc passport system. The rules for travel were constantly changing, and information was not easy to come by. Individuals were sometimes forced to acquire visas from different state offices for each individual journey, for exit, transit, and entry, in a process that was costly, time-consuming, and bewildering. Initially, the league hoped to abolish these passports and visas altogether, to return to the prewar system of relatively open borders to facilitate commercial and leisure travel. That proved unrealistic. League officials gradually abandoned this hope and instead sought to standardize the passport regime within Europe.[35]

In the case of foreign investment and business, internationalists also shifted their goalposts. After the First World War, many states around the world created or strengthened regulations that prevented foreigners from owning property or businesses in their country and from employment in particular professions. For example, only Czechoslovak citizens could practice as physicians, surgeons, dentists, veterinarians, barristers, notaries, chemists, druggists, civil engineers, patent agents, manufacturers or importers of telegraphic and telephonic apparatuses, or purveyors or manufacturers of alcohol. These restrictions were typical of the Habsburg successor states.[36] The League of Nations hoped to ease economic discrimination against foreigners and foreign businesses in the interest of reviving global trade and migration. But league officials ultimately gave up on their effort to create a multilateral framework or convention to achieve this goal.

In June 1925, the league's Economic Committee conceded, "Every state naturally regards itself as being in the last resort the judge of its own vital interests, and it is impossible to lay down international rules of universal application except of the most general character. All we can do is to emphasize that a broad liberal policy in these matters has, generally speaking, been more to the interest, both of the country concerned and of the world generally, than a policy of exaggerated nationalism." The committee instead encouraged bilateral treaties between states, admitting that these might be formed on the basis of considerations including "national and racial affinities, intimate political friendships or treaty relations, or even mere geographical propinquity."[37]

Sometimes international organizations even worked to limit forms of mobility and trade that were deemed undesirable. The emergence of international policing in Central Europe between the two world wars is an important example of this kind of "illiberal internationalism." Alongside the League of Nations Section on Social Questions, a new international policing organization, Interpol, aimed to curb the "wrong" kinds of global mobility. Through greater international cooperation, surveillance, and border control, these organizations sought to limit the transnational circulation of drugs, counterfeit currency, prostitutes, and criminals.[38]

As STEFAN ZWEIG'S train puffed toward Salzburg, the journey itself drove home Austria's dissolution and isolation. "That the train moved at all was a miracle. . . . Distances which used to take an hour now took four or five, and when dusk set in we remained in darkness." Train and telegraph lines had been ripped up, money was worthless, and news traveled slowly, if at all. With his wife and stepdaughters, Zweig settled into a manor house perched on a hill that was inaccessible to cars. Going into town required descending (and then climbing) more than one hundred stairs. No one made deliveries, and the telephone didn't work. As money was worthless, "mankind . . . now dissolved the thousand-year-old convention of money and reverted to primitive barter. . . . There were those who had to take their wedding ring from their finger or the leather belt off their body merely to keep that body alive."[39]

But in sleepy Salzburg, Zweig paradoxically rediscovered some of the hope that he had lost after the war. He had chosen Salzburg as a place to live both because of its remoteness and its proximity to other places. "At

Austria's edge, I could get to Munich in two and a half hours by train, to Vienna in five, to Zurich or Venice in ten and to Paris in twenty; it was thus the right springboard to Europe."⁴⁰ After a few years, he recalled, "We ate our fill again. We sat undisturbed at our desks. . . . Why not once more test the pleasure of one's youth, and travel?" Italy was close by. "I took a chance and, one day at noon, crossed the frontier."⁴¹

In the decade that followed, Zweig recovered his cosmopolitan identity. "Never did people travel as much as in those years," he recalled. Buoyed by his own growing wealth and fame, he was "able to agitate with greater sweep and better effect for the idea, which, over the years, has become central to my life: the intellectual unification of Europe." The world—or at least the transatlantic world of European intellectuals that Zweig identified with—meanwhile came to Salzburg. By the early 1930s, the once provincial town "had become the summer artistic capital, not only of Europe, but of the whole world," thanks to the world-renowned Salzburg Festival, which was founded in 1920 and embodied a spirit of what historian Michael Steinberg calls "nationalist cosmopolitanism."⁴² Zweig reflected, "All at once the Salzburg Festival plays became a world attraction, a modern Olympics of art at which all nations contended to exhibit their best, as it were. . . . Thus I found myself in my own town at the centre of Europe. Fate had again granted a wish of mine which I had hardly dared dream, and our house on the Kapuzinerberg had become a European house." Zweig had re-created Global Austria in Salzburg.

Zweig would look back nostalgically on the happy evenings he spent with his guests, "looking out from the terrace into the beautiful and peaceful countryside without suspecting that on the Berchtesgaden mountain, directly opposite, sat the one man who was to destroy all this!" He later reflected, "As much as Hitler later took from me, the satisfaction of having lived the life of a European for at least one decade according to my own free will and with complete interior freedom, this satisfaction not even he was able to confiscate or destroy."⁴³

TEN

The Defense of Americanism

ELLIS ISLAND, 1924

NEW JERSEY WAS so close you could almost touch it. At 4:30 p.m. on the afternoon of September 14, 1924, there was a light westerly wind, and the water in the New York Harbor appeared calm. Seven men dove into the water in a bid for freedom. The fugitives included two Spaniards, one Italian, a Portuguese, a Russian, a Mexican, and "another whose nationality was in doubt"—all immigrants who had been detained on Ellis Island. Their goal was to reach Liberty Port, on the shores of New Jersey. But several of the men underestimated the distance between themselves and Liberty or overestimated their swimming abilities. Only one-third of the way across, the Portuguese man and one of the Spaniards gave up and started frantically waving for help. James Ferra, a 22-year-old Italian and a very strong swimmer, rescued them both, conveying them one by one back to Ellis Island. He then turned around and swam on, reaching a pier on the Jersey shore along with the Russian, the other Spaniard, and the Mexican. Their liberty did not last long: all four were spotted by a watchman, caught, locked up, and deported. One man, the one with no nationality, was presumed drowned.[1]

In the new era of anti-globalism, Ellis Island had been repurposed.

After the Johnson-Reed Act went into effect in 1924, there were so few immigrants entering the United States each year that the massive center in the New York Harbor was no longer needed to process immigrants. Immigrants were mostly processed by consuls in their country of origin. Ellis Island instead became a detention and deportation center, designed to hold a new category of migrant created by deglobalization: the "illegal alien."[2]

As a detention center, Ellis Island quickly transformed from a place to get through to a place to escape from. There were 2,400 migrants typically detained in the facility, designed to house 1,200, and only 350 beds, all reserved for women and children. For everyone else, there were "bunks in wire cages ... arranged in double tiers, without mattresses, and crowded into a room with unsatisfactory ventilation." In a 1924 letter to the editor of the *New York Times*, a reader begged New Yorkers to turn their attention to "the temporary home of those whose misfortune it is to be sent to Ellis Island pending a hearing." The writer had visited the island four times. "What I saw is not likely to be soon forgotten," he reported. "The living conditions are abominable and the sanitary arrangements are beyond description." Officials charged with caring for the migrants "have not yet heard of the words civility or courtesy. They would make much better attendants in the lion house at Bronx Park." He compared Ellis Island to Dante's *Inferno*, "situated, paradoxically enough, at the very door of the richest and most wonderful city in the world and right under the arm of the Statue of Liberty."[3]

Restrictions on migration in the United States had been increasing since the end of the nineteenth century. Yet at the height of the mass migration before the First World War, only 1.7 percent of incoming migrants were actually turned away.[4] All that changed at the end of the First World War. Whereas it had once been relatively uncomplicated for individuals fleeing poverty, war, or persecution to find refuge, closed borders now left millions in permanent limbo. An epidemic of statelessness was one of the most tragic consequences of postwar deglobalization (even as stateless refugees also seemed to symbolize the perils of global migration).

Transatlantic passenger travel had already come to a virtual halt during the war. In 1914, there were 1,218,480 new arrivals to the United States. By 1918, there was one-tenth that number. After the war, hundreds of thousands of migrants hoped that they might finally have a chance to see their husbands, wives, and children again. There was a brief surge in migration, with 805,228 arrivals in 1921. But new legislation quickly put an end to the family reunions. The long-standing ban on Chinese migrants had already been expanded in 1917 to include people from almost all of Asia and the Pacific (Japan and the Philippines were excluded from the ban), plus a eugenic list of "undesirables": all immigrants over the age of sixteen who failed to pass a literacy test, "idiots, imbeciles, feeble-minded persons, epileptics, insane persons," alcoholics, paupers, and vagrants. Then, in 1924, the Johnson-Reed Act instituted "national" quotas, radically limiting migration from Southern and Eastern Europe. While more than 100,000 Poles per year requested emigration visas to the United States in the early 1920s, the Polish quota in 1924 was only 25,800. In 1914, 283,738 Italians had landed on US shores; in 1924, the quota was 3,845.[5]

In 1927, the Austrian writer Joseph Roth imagined the thoughts of a Jewish migrant detained at Ellis Island. "The medical examination in the European port was bad enough. Now there is a still-more-rigorous one. And something turns out to be not quite right with your papers. The papers are genuine, and very hard to obtain too, but they still look somehow not quite right. Possible too that some vermin has got into the Jew's shirt during the crossing. Everything is possible. And so the Jew winds up in a kind of prison that goes by the name of "quarantine" or some such. A high fence protects America from him. Through the bars of his prison, he sees the Statue of Liberty, and he doesn't know whether it's himself or Liberty that has been incarcerated."[6]

IT WAS a peculiar moment for Americans to turn against globalism, and in many ways, they didn't. By entering the First World War, and especially by financing it, the United States had come of age as a global power. As of February 1922, Allies in Europe owed the United States more than $10 billion. With Europe's fields and factories in ruins, meanwhile, American exports doubled between 1921 and 1925. The United States was arguably the only country in a position to reestablish some kind of economic and political equilibrium in Europe. Woodrow Wilson, meanwhile, clearly had an ambitious vision for American leadership in the world.[7]

But in the face of Europe's overwhelming need, the United States ultimately buried its head in the sand. Wilson's vision of America's global leadership was defeated when the US Senate refused to ratify the Treaty of Versailles in 1919—in order to avoid joining the League of Nations. The United States also refused to forgive any of the massive war debt owed by the Allies (which meant, in turn, that the Allies could show no mercy to Germany, which borrowed from the United States to pay its own debts, in a vicious circle). European governments responded to the crushing weight of debt by instituting deflationary measures and by cutting social spending, a move that emboldened and radicalized European political movements on the Far Right and Far Left.[8]

Meanwhile, two new tariff laws in 1921–1922 significantly raised tariffs on wheat, meat, sugar, and wool in order to protect domestic farmers. The Red Scare targeted "internationalists," "Bolsheviks," and "cosmopolitans" with new zeal and violence. Prohibition became the law of the land in 1919, thanks in part to the success of temperance activists in linking the vice of alcohol consumption to Catholic immigrants.[9] The Ku Klux Klan was also on the rise in the 1920s, resurging in the form of a "100% American" social club that organized fairs and picnics and turned a profit by selling membership cards ($10 each) and official robes and hoods ($6.50) to its 4 million members.[10]

Americans targeted by the rise in racism and xenophobia did not respond passively to these developments. Their responses often reflected the complicated entanglement of nationalism and internationalism in the early twentieth century. W. E. B. Du Bois, who founded the National Association for the Advancement of Colored People (NAACP) in 1909, encouraged Black Americans to see themselves as a part of and in solidarity with a global African diaspora, while continuing the struggle against segregation and for equal civil and economic rights in the

United States.[11] Marcus Garvey, born in Jamaica in 1887, founded the Universal Negro Improvement Association (UNIA) in Jamaica in 1914. He emigrated to the United States during the war, where the UNIA flourished. After the First World War, Garvey was part of a coalition of Black Americans behind the International League of Darker Peoples, established to lobby the Paris Peace Conference on behalf of colonized people around the world.[12] In the early 1920s, his organization became a global mass movement, with hundreds of local branches in North America, Central and South America, the Caribbean, and Africa. Garveyism's diasporic nationalism was explicitly global in its organizational aspirations and solidarity with other oppressed peoples.

In August 1920, at the first UNIA Convention in New York's Liberty Hall, Garvey linked Black demands for self-determination to those of other colonized people around the world. "We are here because this is the age when all peoples are striking out for freedom, for liberty, and for democracy. We have entered this age of struggle for liberty at the same time with the people of Ireland, the people of Egypt, of India, and the people of the Eastern states of Europe." But Garvey also believed that the long-term future of the Black diaspora was in Africa. "Considering all the circumstances and environments that surround the Negro in Western civilization, we of the U.N.I.A. believe that the best thing for the Negro to do is to consolidate his racial force in building his own motherland, Africa. We believe that any progress, any advancement made by the Negro in Western alien civilization is a progress, is an advancement that is insecure, because at any time the alien forces desire to destroy the progress and development of the Negro—the advancement of the Negro—they can do so."

Garvey's goals, like those of other anti-colonial nationalists worldwide, included greater economic self-sufficiency and self-reliance. The UNIA pursued these goals by creating its own shipping company, the Black Star Line, as well as the Negro Factories Corporation to support black-owned businesses. The Black Star Line, while short-lived, was of particular significance because shipping lines were the blood vessels of globalization; Garvey's goal was to create a line financed by Black

investment in order to transport goods produced by Black-owned businesses to and from Africa. It would put at least some of the profits of
globalization in Black hands.[13]

In June 1922, Garvey met with the Imperial Grand Wizard of the Ku
Klux Klan in Atlanta, Georgia. By then he was convinced of the futility
of integrationist efforts, and this meeting affirmed his belief in racial
separatism. He reported back to his followers: "Let me tell you this:
that the Ku Klux Klan is really the invisible government of the United
States of America, and that there are more people identified with the
Klan than you think." His advice was not to fight the Klan on US soil
(provoking violent retaliation and more suffering) but rather to recognize that the Klan's domination made the position of Blacks "hopeless"
in America. And to recognize their common interests. "The Universal
Negro Improvement Association is carrying out just what the Ku Klux
Klan is carrying out—the purity of the white race down South—and we
are going to carry out the purity of the black race not only down South,
but all through the world."[14]

True to Garvey's words, the "second Klan" continued to grow, as did
its invisible and visible influence in government. It was now as much a
northern and midwestern as a southern institution and owed its revival
to the expansion of its mission: in addition to terrorizing Blacks, the
Klan of the 1920s targeted Catholics, Jews, and immigrants. As an article in *The Kourier*, the newspaper of the Indiana Klan, put it, "Those who
favor inter-nationalism and who would make of the United States of
America a Polygot nation and still keep it American, are trying to do the
impossible. . . . Added to this the advocates of internationalism would
force upon us both non-assimilable Asiatics and Americans. . . . The
Klan is the protest of America against the injection of non-American
elements into our government."[15]

The passage of the Johnson-Reed Act, sponsored by Klansman
Albert Johnson, a member of the US House of Representatives from
the state of Washington, was among the greatest self-described victories of the KKK. H. W. Evans, the Grand Wizard of the revived Klan,
explained, "Every Klansman knows how there is a conspiracy of alien
races and religions to overwhelm and destroy America by hordes of

invaders who are hostile to our every thought and purpose and unas-similable to our society. . . . The defense against this alien invasion has been one of the chief duties of the Klan so far, and the enactment of protective laws, the erection of fortifications for the defense of Ameri-canism, has been our greatest triumph." But simply enacting restrictive legislation was "not enough." The Klan's next duty was to "send home every unfit alien." Evans elaborated, "We must get rid of the undesir-able aliens, of the foreign criminals, degenerates, paupers and unfit of all kinds who are an open sore on our body politic, a social cancer, one of the worst evils from which the nation suffers."[16]

He would have been pleased to know that deportation rates increased significantly during the 1920s. In 1920, 2,762 immigrants were deported; by 1930, that number had multiplied more than sixfold.[17] He would have been even more thrilled by the massive wave of illegal deportations that began with the Great Depression. More than 1 million Mexicans, including many American-born children who had never been south of the border, were rounded up and forcibly sent to Mexico as Americans panicked that Mexicans were taking "their" jobs.[18]

In addition to immigration officials, US consuls abroad became enterprising enforcers of America's new immigration restrictions. When it came to excluding the eugenically "unfit," for example, it did not matter if the migrant in question happened to be the spouse or child of a naturalized US citizen or the mother or father of an Amer-ican child. Social worker Cecilia Razovsky, working with the National Council of Jewish Women's Department of Immigrant Aid, concluded, "no one can gainsay the fact that the present legislation operates to sep-arate families."[19]

For Razovsky, the separation of families was the obvious effect of the new migration restrictions, even if it had not been its intent. In theory, wives and children of US citizens were supposed to receive preferential treatment in the form of non-quota visas. In practice, things worked out differently. Kenneth Rich and Mary Brant of the Immigrants Protective League in Chicago lamented that the new laws had caused nothing less than family breakdown. "A large part of the break-down might have been prevented if Quota Legislation in the United States had made proper provision for the reunion of families, without delay and the obstacles which have blocked their path. There is an inexorable recurrence of the same obstacles in case after case, driving husbands and wives apart, and bringing family ruin." They blamed the new US laws for problems including "estrangement, suspicion, accusation, desertion, non-support, illegitimacy, adultery, bigamy," and divorce.[20]

Becoming a US citizen could expedite the paperwork, but there was an ugly Catch-22: the naturalization bureau had been instructed "that no citizenship papers be granted to applicants here whose wives and children are abroad." The result was a "vicious circle: denying citizenship to men whose families are abroad and refusing visas to women abroad because their husbands in this country are not citizens."[21] The number of migrants who gave up and simply returned home to Europe spiked. But often, families were separated for years. As of 1927, an estimated 173,192 wives and children of US citizens were on a waiting list for visas, according to the US House Committee on Immigration and the Department of State. There were 16,000 wives and children of Italian Americans alone waiting in Italy to join their families. At the rate at which visas were processed, it would take seven years for these families to be reunited."[22]

THE WIVES, husbands, and children waiting in lines in front of consuls' offices across Europe were joined in the 1920s by a new kind of migrant: the refugee. Approximately 9.5 million people in Europe were classified as refugees by 1926. The League of Nations' High Commission for Refugees, under the leadership of diplomat and Arctic explorer Fridtjof Nansen, was established in 1921 to contend with the crisis. The Nansen system provided stateless refugees with documents, so-called Nansen passports, as passports were now critical to the establishment of a legal identity and the right to cross national frontiers.[23]

Most of these refugees hailed from large multinational and multiconfessional empires—the Ottoman Empire, the Romanov Empire, and the Habsburg Empire. Russians fleeing civil war and Armenian victims of genocide were the first to qualify for the Nansen passports. After the war, the new nation-states all sought to create ethnically homogeneous populations, often by persecuting, murdering, or expelling members of minority groups deemed undesirable (such as Armenians and Jews). In the process of creating new borders and states, they also created countless stateless persons and refugees. These refugees became symbols of an unwanted form of global mobility.[24]

The peacemakers in Paris tried to prevent statelessness in interwar Central Europe through Article 80 of the 1919 Treaty of St. Germain, the so-called Option Clause. This clause enabled citizens of the former Habsburg Empire who differed "by race and language" from the majority population in the state where they lived to "opt" for citizenship in a different successor state, so long as that state was populated by "persons speaking the same language and having the same race." In practice, Germans were most likely to take advantage of the clause. Approximately 180,000 German-speaking families (totaling 540,000 people) from all provinces of the former Habsburg Empire opted to become citizens of the Austrian Republic.

But not everyone who tried to opt for citizenship in another state was successful. Some people neglected to apply for citizenship before the deadlines established by the treaty, perhaps not even understanding that their status had changed. All of the successor states rejected applicants considered undesirable, including Jews, national minorities, Communists, the poor, the disabled, and the elderly. The problem was so great that in 1922, Italy convened in Rome a Conference of the Successor States, where delegates agreed that in cases of contested citizenship, applicants should have the right to appeal to a Court of Arbitration. If no decision was reached, the place of birth or last place of domicile would be decisive. But the convention was only adopted by Italy and Austria, and never enforced. The problem was exacerbated by the fact that the successor states, building on former Austrian laws regulating citizenship, often required lengthy residence and extensive documentation to be naturalized (ten years in Austria, twenty in Czechoslovakia, according to a law passed in July 1926).

In some cases, stateless individuals were actually deported back and forth across state borders, leaving them in a permanent state of limbo and illegality. A fourteen-year-old stateless orphan who arrived in Austria with his father in 1914 was picked up peddling on the street and deported to Czechoslovakia in the 1920s. He was caught there, imprisoned, sent back to Austria, and then sent back to Czechoslovakia again by Austrian authorities.

Transnational marriage, meanwhile, left women vulnerable to statelessness. Mathilde Herschkowitz, a Jewish seamstress from Szatamar, in interwar Romania, had lived in Hungary for fifteen years with her husband, a Hungarian tailor. When her husband died she was deported to Romania, because the Hungarian government considered her to be a Romanian citizen. The Romanian government, however, viewed her as a Hungarian because of her marriage, and deported her back to Budapest. She lived there illegally with her three children in fear of being caught and deported again. A social worker familiar with her case concluded, "She can only be saved if a Hungarian citizen would marry her."[25]

Unsurprisingly, a large number of the stateless after the First World War were Jews—either refugees from the war or from postwar pogroms and counterrevolutions. The status of Jewish refugees was particularly precarious in Vienna. At the end of the war, Viennese police estimated that 100,000 refugees from the war remained in the city. Most were Jewish and had fled Russian troops occupying their homes in Galicia and Bukovina, which were then provinces of the Habsburg Empire, but were now part of Poland or Ukraine. An American Jewish Joint Distribution Committee (JDC) official traveling through Vienna in 1919 reported, "I have just left Vienna which harbors (but that is too rich a word) over 20,000 wretched Galicians, Bukovinians, and Palestinian refugees [Jewish refugees trying to get to Palestine] . . . seventeen and eighteen people are crowded into one small room. . . . The houses have rotten and broken roofs into which the rain pours. . . . One house called the Beehive, has 700 people in it, who die so rapidly that one room is kept as a morgue."[26]

Almost immediately after the establishment of the new Austrian Republic, state officials sought to expel these refugees from Austria's territory. The writer Joseph Roth later reflected, "The war caused a lot of refugees to come to Vienna. For as long as their homelands were occupied, they were entitled to 'support.' Not that the money was sent to them where they were. They had to stand in line for it, on the coldest winter days, and into the night. All of them: old people, invalids, women, and children. . . . They took to smuggling. . . . They made life easier for the Viennese. They were locked up for it. When the war was over, they were repatriated, sometimes forcibly. A Social Democratic provincial governor had them thrown out. To Christian Socialists, they were Jews. To German nationalists, they are Semitic. To Social Democrats, they are unproductive elements."[27]

On September 10, 1919, the Interior Ministry issued a decree stipulating that "foreign" refugees were to clear out of Austria within ten days. Police plastered the city of Vienna with posters declaring that refugees who ignored the decree would be subject to criminal proceedings and deportation. In practice, transport and financial difficulties meant that the threat was rarely carried out. Poland was not eager to have its Jewish citizens return home and refused to issue the visas and travel documents necessary for repatriation. Because Austria refused to naturalize them and Poland refused to take them back, these Jews also ended up stateless.[28]

Thousands of Jews from what was now Polish territory, typically German-speaking, with a right to Austrian citizenship, meanwhile attempted to opt for it at the end of the war. But Austrian authorities created so many obstacles that this right was illusory in practice. Applicants for Austrian citizenship were required to produce countless documents, such as birth certificates for all of their family members and school report cards. These documents had often been destroyed during the Russian occupation of Galicia and were impossible to acquire.[29] Austrian authorities meanwhile insisted that they were entitled to expel Jewish refugees on legal and humanitarian grounds. They specifically blamed Jewish refugees for the ongoing hunger and housing crisis in Vienna. Because of the refugees, "the meagre food rations, which are scarcely sufficient for the native population, must again be reduced, in order to feed thousands of foreigners. The housing accommodation which is insufficient, and in the majority of cases, of a deplorable nature, is largely monopolised by immigrants, so that the Austrians themselves are reduced to living in the most abject hovels," the Austrian government claimed. "It is above all the humanitarian duty of Government . . . to protect its suffering people against an increase of their misery."[30]

In 1921, the Supreme Administrative Court of Austria heard the case of a Jew from Galicia, Moses Lym, who considered himself German and had applied for Austrian citizenship on the basis of the Option Clause. Lym could prove his German linguistic capabilities and that he had been educated in German. But the Interior Ministry rejected his application. Lym appealed the decision all the way to the Supreme Administrative Court of Austria, which rejected Lym's appeal, insisting that he had not adequately proven that he belonged to the German-Austrian "race." In its decision the court officially defined race as an "inborn, inherent, physically and psychically determined quality," that "cannot be removed at will or changed according to preference."[31] The League of Nations Minority Council ultimately affirmed Austria's right to expel Jews who were denied Austrian citizenship, but with the caveat that "this right of expulsion should be exercised with such moderation as is dictated by feelings of humanity."[32]

In Hungary, likewise, alongside the rampage of violence directed at Jews during the counterrevolution, the right-wing Horthy government issued an edict directed at Galician, Russian, and Polish Jews who had arrived in Hungary as refugees during the war. In March 1921, Joseph Marcus found several hundred of these "foreign" Jews waiting for deportation in abominable conditions in the Piliscsaba internment camp. At least one man, born in Hungary, had been arbitrarily interned simply because he had a beard and was therefore assumed to be a Jew.[33]

In an attempt to facilitate international cooperation where it had broken down, the International Labor Organization (ILO) was established in 1919 to promote (non-Bolshevik) international cooperation on labor and migration issues. Its first session, held in Washington in 1919, was devoted to migration. A 1922 report by the ILO's emigration commission reported that in the aftermath of the war, "Countries both of emigration and immigration appeared to fear that, in the troubles and confusion of the post-war period, large movements of the population might compromise their national future, and severely restrictive measures were adopted."[34]

Within Europe, France—with its low birthrate and a need for workers—was the only country that continued to recruit large numbers of migrant workers between the wars, at least until the Great Depression. In the new nation-states of East-Central Europe, meanwhile, many officials mobilized against *emigration*, viewing it as a symptom of economic and social backwardness that now had to be overcome. They attempted to deglobalize their own nation-states by encouraging return migration and preventing emigration. In 1923 Leopold Caro, a Polish economist and lawyer, declared, "We should not permit emigration, especially permanent emigration, from our country. When, before the Great War, masses of our peasants were forced to emigrate to other parts of the world and place their labor at the disposal of foreign countries— this was the shame of our people."[35]

Interwar migration policies reflected new demographic priorities. An unprecedented number of citizens had been slaughtered in battle during the First World War, and hundreds of thousands more had been lost to starvation or disease as the Spanish flu ravaged populations after the war. These biological losses, along with the pressing need for labor to reconstruct war-damaged societies, transformed human beings into what one emigration expert called the nation's "most valuable commodity," regardless of unemployment at home.[36] The International Labor Organization explained in 1922, "The emigrant is now considered as part and parcel of the human capital of the nation, and governments desire to use this capital in the interests of the nation, and for purposes which have no direct connection with the interests of the emigrant himself."[37]

The Habsburg successor states all introduced restrictive emigration laws. In 1927, Fascist Italy also began to restrict emigration in favor of formal colonial expansion, while Spain adopted an anti-emigration policy with Francisco Franco's victory in the Spanish Civil War. The goal, in every case, was to keep the "right" people in and the "wrong" people out, in order to create more homogeneous nation-states. Anti-globalism meant less mobility for everyone.[38]

These attempts to manage migration after the First World War were intended to reinforce national sovereignty and control over a nation's frontiers. In reality, however, they underscored sovereignty's limits. The only real winners were smugglers, who promised to help desperate migrants subvert the new rules. The losers, of course, were far more numerous: stateless people such as Rosika Schwimmer; migrants separated from family members by restrictive quotas; and those migrants interned at Ellis Island who never made it to Liberty Port.

PART III

The Unsettled World

ELEVEN

Colonies in the Homeland

VIENNA, 1926

IN THE AUTUMN of 1926, the settlers came partly on foot and partly on truck, armed with hoes and hacksaws. Josef Wagner and Franz Reichert led the convoy of unemployed workers and war veterans from Vienna to an abandoned tract of marshy land in the Oberau region of Lower Austria. They called their movement "Colonies in the Homeland." Their members had been hungry since the First World War, and they were determined to feed themselves.

Wagner and his followers had applied to a state fund for veterans for money to purchase 853 acres of land to settle 120 people. Their goal was to farm the abandoned land and grow enough to feed and support their families. When their application was rejected, they took matters into their own hands, storming the swamp. In the days and nights that followed the occupation, more colonists joined them. They began cutting down trees and making demands: they would evacuate only if they were given a large plot of land to farm close to Vienna. While the occupation was under way, hundreds of supporters rallied in front of the Rathaus in Vienna.[1]

The Oberau occupation succeeded in attracting the attention of the nation's leaders. Otto Bauer, the leader of the Austrian Social Demo-

cratic Party, came to the defense of the colonists, demanding the "introduction of a planned settlement action for unemployed rural workers."[2]
But the standoff continued for twenty-nine days, until the Agriculture
Ministry finally gave in. About sixty families each received 2.8 acres
elsewhere, in the Lobau region outside Vienna. Members of Colonies
in the Homeland and its offshoots ultimately created five different
settlements.[3]

The success of the Oberau occupiers inspired copycats and competitors. Requests for support for other settlement projects soon flooded
government offices. Many invoked the consequences of the loss of empire
("our once large economic territory") to justify their demands. Petitioners explicitly compared their plans for "inner colonization" favorably to
schemes for overseas settlement. While overseas emigration entailed the
"departure of the most valuable part of the population, an irreplaceable
loss for the economy and a lasting weakening of our national power,"
inner colonization would preserve these valuable human resources. The
petitioners promised that their movement would increase agricultural
production, decrease imports, shrink unemployment, and mitigate the
housing crisis. "The simple fact that thousands of families would be able
to feed themselves through the natural economy would justify the settlement project," they reasoned. But there were also critical "national
and social reasons" to support the cause. "The immigration of Slovak
workers, who take bread and work from our German agricultural workers, will be contained, and the native-born peasants' sons will have their
own ground and land."[4]

Bureaucrats were skeptical, on practical grounds. Officials contested
the claim that hundreds of thousands of acres of fertile farmland lay
barren. Much of the unsettled land was high in the rocky Alps or perpetually flooded. Building settlements cost money, and there was no
guarantee that settlers would ever be able to repay state-supported loans.
Unemployed urban workers did not necessarily make successful farmers. "The desire for and love of nature is not sufficient to be a settler. One
must be suited to it in character, spiritually, and physically," noted one
dubious bureaucrat.[5]

But the project of internal colonization had immense imaginative and political appeal in interwar Austria, and its grassroots support only continued to grow in the aftermath of the 1929 economic crisis. The movement was politically promiscuous from the start. While some settlers were simply desperate for food, pragmatists mixed with returning veterans, socialists, anarchists, life-reformers, and those who saw the settlements as an alternative to capitalist society. Across the political spectrum, however, the settlement movement was linked to dreams of self-sufficiency at the individual and national levels. Hans Kampffmeyer, one of the founders of the German garden city movement and cofounder of the Austrian Association for Settlement and Small Gardens, put it simply in his 1926 book: "The less food Austria has to get from abroad, the better it is for its national economy."[6]

Allotment gardens, garden cities, and visions of internal colonization were springing up across Europe. These movements were discrete but sometimes connected to one another, as in the case of the Austrian Association for Settlement and Small Gardens. They also exchanged ideas across national borders, as many international conferences devoted to small gardening and settlement occurred in the 1920s and 1930s. The movement was supported by the International Labor Organization itself.[7] But humanitarian worker Francesca Wilson noticed that in contrast to other garden city movements, the Austrian movement truly emerged from below, from popular mobilization. "In many of the settlements round Vienna the amount of voluntary, unpaid work far exceeded the paid," she recalled, as Austrians set about constructing their own homes with their own labor.[8]

From the beginning, the settlement movement was animated by widespread popular protests. In one of the largest demonstrations in March 1921, 200,000 settlers and gardeners marched on the Ringstrasse of Vienna. The protesters shouted, "Whatever you give to settlers, you will save on unemployment payments!" and "Settler's cooperatives instead of emigration!"[9] Popular pressure finally culminated in the creation of a special Settlement Office in the Viennese city government in 1921, a new Federal Housing and Settlement Fund, and a state-financed building cooperative, the GESIBA (Public Utility Settlement and Building Material Corporation) to design and fund settlements.

This early settlement movement had strong ties to Social Democracy. Vienna's first Social Democratic mayor, Jakob Reumann, was a critical ally. In 1920, Otto Neurath, the Vienna Circle philosopher (also a Social Democrat), cofounded the Austrian Association for Settlement and Small Gardens with Kampffmeyer. The association created an annual exhibition for settlement and gardening on the Rathausplatz, attended by 400,000 people a week in 1923. The exhibit featured prize fruits and vegetables, live animals, and model settlers' homes. The association also created a settler school in 1921 and recruited renowned Austrian architects including Adolf Loos, Josef Frank, and Margarete Schütte-Lihotzky to design settlers' homes and train settlers.

Loos, appointed chief architect of Vienna's Municipal Settlement Office in 1922, believed that the settlement movement was nothing less than revolutionary. In 1921 he wrote, "This new movement, which has infested all of the residents of the city like a fever, the settlement movement, demands new humans." His vision, like that of the settlement movement more broadly, was based on autarkic ideals. The new human in the new Austria required a new way of living and eating. "One often used to speak of Austrian cuisine," he wrote. "Only today we have realized that this cuisine was only possible because there was a state-form called the Austro-Hungarian Monarchy.... Moravia, Poland, and Hungary sent the flour, Southern Moravia and Bohemia plums, Bohemia and Moravia sugar ... we have now lost everything that nourished us. And that means reeducation. We need to create our own national cuisine. The Bohemian dumpling, the Moravian Buchtel, the Italian schnitzel, all the things that were an unshakable part of Viennese cuisine for centuries must now be replaced by local foods."[10]

These "local foods" would be cooked in the ideal working-class settlers' homes designed by architects such as Loos and Schütte-Lihotzky. They were, in theory, to be filled with light and air and a rational organization of space, equipped with large gardens designed for self-provisioning. The homes were generally unadorned, with separate sleeping and living spaces and a combined kitchen and living/dining room. The modern, built-in kitchens Schütte-Lihotzky designed for the first settlement homes in the Lainzer Tiergarten (a public wildlife preserve

The Frankfurt kitchen.

on the outskirts of Vienna) were a prototype for the tiny and efficient Frankfurt kitchen, for which she later became most famous.[11]

The designs of these experts were however not always popular with settlers. Loos's wife, Elsie Altmann, recalled the first public tour through a settler's home designed by Loos. The couple had staged the home with items and décor from their own household. Elsie sat at the door and listened. The prospective residents were not enthralled by the modern design, by the small rooms and tiny efficient kitchens. "The women said, 'No, I won't live there, how are you supposed to cook?' In the proletarian houses several families shared a common toilet and faucet in the hallway. But the women said, 'So, what then, in order to get water I have to go out of the house?' And another man yelled, "Well how am I supposed to fit my double wardrobe in this bedroom? My double wardrobe is bigger than the entire house!" Later they discovered that the guests had stolen their vases and ashtrays.

The settlement movement—and the broader movement for autarky—was actually spartan in practice, based on principles of austerity and sacrifice for the greater good. Loos insisted that settlers' homes should not have indoor bathrooms, and most had no gas, electricity, or indoor toilets in the 1930s. Max Ermers, a leader of the settlement movement, argued that autarky should be supported by draconian taxes on luxury goods, including alcohol and tobacco, as well as automobiles, wine-bars, hotels, cafés, coffee, tea, and postcards. Another settlement advocate and life-reformer suggested that settlers should trade meat and potatoes for a local diet consisting solely of chestnuts, goat's milk, and apples.[12]

WHILE PROGRESSIVE urban reformers and architects endorsed settlers' ambitions, Vienna's Socialist city government began to distance itself from the settlement movement by the mid-1920s. Instead of designing suburban settlements and single-family homes with gardens, the architects and city planners of Red Vienna turned toward creating housing for the masses in large-scale, urban apartment complexes. It was a more efficient way of resolving the pressing housing crisis, and it was also easier to connect workers to city services. The city government made a decisive turn toward the mass apartment complex in 1927.[13] Francesca Wilson saw it as a matter of pragmatism. "Though some thousands of cottages were built in these land settlements, and though with their gardens and livestock they contributed to food production and the health of a number of people, they could not solve Vienna's housing problem . . . so the city built into the sky what it could not build along the ground."[14] But politics clearly played a role as well. Increasingly, the settler's movement shifted toward an anti-urban and anti-Socialist message. In 1930, settlement advocate Roderich Müller Guttenbrunn linked the movement to "the rejection of life in the big cities, the rejection of civilization and then, after the war in the bitter hunger years, the rediscovery of the good, generous soil."[15]

When the Socialists abandoned the settlement movement, it was enmeshed in a contentious debate between advocates of the single-family home (what was called the *Eigenheim*) and apartment housing for workers. Architect Josef Frank, a Social Democratic opponent of Red Vienna's mass housing complexes, wrote a 1926 article called "The

The Karl-Marx Hof in 2017.

People's Apartment Palace," in which he outlined the advantages of the single-family home over the monumental "palaces" now favored by the government of Red Vienna. "Even the best, most healthy form of housing in an apartment building is a surrogate. For the moral force (apart from every comfort) of a piece of land with a house on it . . . cannot be replaced by anything." The most superior workers' housing was therefore not a "monumental building, reproduced on the outside like old palaces. A small house, two windows, at the most, above each other; what one has termed a shack up to now is the palace of the future!"[16]

Frank insisted that the single-family home was compatible with collectivist values and politics. But for many Austrians, the allure of the single-family home was precisely that it represented masculine independence and individualism. The settlers' magazine *Baustein* published an article in 1930 with the title "Why I Want a Single-Family Home" in which the authors explained, "Our hearts ache for the feeling of freedom and independence, at least in our leisure time." They compared the noise and chaos of rental apartments with the peace and quiet of the single-family home, which was also an emblem of masculine sovereignty. "We are the masters of our homes, no one can tell us what to do inside, we move and act according to our own discretion and judgment. Our neighbors are separated from us by gardens and fences and do not try to disturb us. The joy of doing-it-yourself in the home and garden unites the entire family in beautiful harmony and allows many of the irritations of the outside world to fade away." For these settlement advocates, the single-family home was a symbol of individual independence and self-sufficiency, as well as health and happiness. "I wish for my own home, because it makes me economically stronger and more independent, and also because it improves the health of my body and soul, because it gives me what my heart seeks most: a little happiness in life."[17]

But Red Vienna's shift toward the mass housing complex was animated precisely by the concern that workers who spent too much of their free time raising chickens would have less time for political meetings, less commitment to community life. In other words, Socialists feared that a self-sufficient lifestyle would also mean isolation from politics. On the right, meanwhile, many supporters promoted suburban or rural settlements precisely because they seemed to reduce the threat of working-class agitation and to restore "traditional" gender and family roles. Albert Gessmann, who cofounded the right-wing, populist Christian Social Party with Vienna's infamously anti-Semitic mayor, Karl Lueger, became a strong supporter of the settlement movement in the 1930s. In 1932, Gessmann argued that "inner colonization is the most important task of the coming decades." He was convinced that settlement would bridge the political and cultural gap between urban and rural Austria and improve family life as well as facilitate greater self-sufficiency in the food supply. He was also happy about the way in which settlement promised to restore traditional gender roles. In particular, he praised female and child labor on settlements for freeing up jobs for men and for its purported benefits to family life. "The work of the children by the mother's side will have beneficial effects on the education of the children and give new meaning to the family life of the worker," Gessmann claimed.[18]

*   *   *

BY THE late 1920s, Austrian Social Democrats had largely turned away from settlement projects. But the Great Depression and mass unemployment prompted another change of heart. The global economic crisis increased enthusiasm for autarky and settlement on the right and left, and across Europe. For Austria, a small, land-locked country, internal colonization and an increase in agricultural production now appeared to offer a last hope for independence from the free-falling global economy. Austrian political scientist Leo Tartakower wrote in 1934, "the friends of autarky have recognized that participation in the global economy for its own sake leads to the downfall of national productive forces, the destruction of the national community."[19] Franz Egert, leader of the Chamber for Trade, Industry, and Business in Innsbruck, penned a 1934 treatise in which he concurred that the global economic collapse necessitated "the fundamental recognition of the primacy of the nation over the global economy." Egert advocated policies including limitations on travel abroad (and the export of foreign currency) and intensive internal colonization. Immigration to Austria was also to be constrained. The pursuit of "an autarkic economic policy requires the conscious regulation—under certain circumstances the complete elimination—of population growth through immigration," he insisted.[20]

In the early 1930s, many saw settlement as a form of employment of last resort for Austria's army of unemployed men and women. Settlement "offers a possibility to give work to unemployed hands, bread to hungry people," explained the Settlement Division of the Austrian Kuratorium für Wirtschaftlichkeit in 1933. Settlement advocates simultaneously demanded that Austrians limit consumption of foreign luxury goods (or really any luxury goods) in favor of homegrown products, associating globalization with frivolous luxury. The Kuratorium explained, "From a purely material perspective, internal colonization . . . means a certain decline [in consumption] through voluntary sacrifice."[21]

Austrian settlement advocate Julius Wilhelm agreed in a 1935 essay that the economic crisis was leading all states to seek to make themselves "as independent as possible." The large city, he insisted, had become "a mass grave" and a "symptom of disease" that could only be cured through internal colonization in the countryside. But this would require a temporary decline in consumption of luxury products. Settlers would naturally consume less meat and alcohol, and more fruit, vegetables, and dairy products, he claimed. While he was not trying to make Austrians into "vegetarians and teetotalers," he explained, "a liter of beer and a goulash at 10 AM is not a life-necessity."[22]

A guide for teachers published in Austria in 1934 echoed the theme of sacrifice in service to national self-sufficiency, urging teachers to promote autarkic consumption in the classroom. Ignorance caused Austrians to neglect many local products, the guide claimed. "Anyone here, every woman, can live from head to toe from local products, and... everyone can build a tasteful home out of local building materials." Girls and women, in particular, needed an education on the value of autarkic homemaking. "The woman determines the way money is spent, she also determines if money will stay in this country or if it will migrate abroad. Therefore, above all every woman, every girl in Austria, must take care to purchase only Austrian goods."[23]

During the Great Depression, settlement activists continued to link the necessity of autarky and internal colonization to the consequences and experience of the First World War, as well as to the immediate economic crisis. One official explained that after the war, the settlement movement had been animated precisely by "the fresh experience of the wartime blockade and postwar deprivation, and on the basis of this experience, a deep mistrust of the reliability of undisturbed trade in a world economy based on the division of labor." Now, in the context of the total collapse of the global economy, the same lesson resonated. Urban workers turned to rural settlement because "there is no other way out of their extreme material and spiritual distress."[24]

As the economic crisis deepened, even Vienna's Socialist city government began to once again support settlement schemes. As of 1932, 162,500 Viennese citizens were unemployed. The city sponsored Vienna's first so-called *Stadtrandsiedlung* that year, allocating land for 800 new settlements, and choosing settlers based partly on their membership and loyalty to the Socialist Party.[25] The president of the Republic, Socialist Karl Renner, had declared his support in 1931. "As the child of a village and son of a farmer, I have great understanding for all efforts

Newly built settlement on the outskirts of Vienna, 1935.

to bring people closer to the earth and its blessings," he announced in a speech at the Viennese trade fair.[26]

Then, under the authoritarian Dollfuss regime (beginning in 1932), Interior Minister Franz Bachinger of the Austrian Landbund continued to promote settlement as a way out of the economic abyss. Bachinger wrote, "In the context of the great economic difficulties of the present... urban circles have made a discovery that is inborn to those of us in the countryside: a nation must ultimately live from what its own land produces."[27] Bachinger drafted a new settlement law that never reached parliament because of the attempted Nazi putsch and dissolution of the Austrian parliament in March 1934.

Not everyone got on the settlement bandwagon, of course. Well before the Nazi Party had taken power in Germany, Hitler's ideas, including the ideal of autarky, crossed the border into Austria via the German press and radio. Editors of the liberal *Österreichische Volkswirt* jabbed in 1932, "It is difficult to imagine something more absurd than aspirations for autarky in such an exceptionally interdependent country like Austria . . . and even though this fashionable slogan was brought to Austria by the Nazis, our Social Democrats don't seem to shy away from indulging it in various economic plans."[28]

The liberal Austrian economist Ludwig von Mises was more emphatic. "An economic policy that strives for autarky would mean the downfall of European culture." In an article for the *Berliner Tagblatt* in 1932, he argued that the growing trend of governments in Europe to seek isolation and self-sufficiency was an anathema, in light of the world's increasing interconnectedness through technology. "Today the means of transportation allow anyone to travel. Any important words, spoken anywhere in the world, are known in a few hours via the radio and press. The technical requirements for the mutual understanding of nations have been developed to the greatest extent. And yet nations have never been more estranged from one another. The new mercantilist spirit has filled interstate relations with mistrust."[29]

But von Mises was also a virulent anti-Socialist and apologist for Fascist violence and economic policies. In 1927, he excused the "deeds of the Fascists" as "emotional reflex actions evoked by indignation at the deeds of the Bolsheviks and Communists." The Fascists would become more moderate, he claimed, with the passage of time. In the 1930s, he served as an economic advisor for the Austro-fascist Engelbert Doll-fuss. While he opposed the illiberal and anti-global tendencies of Fascist economic policies, he conceded, "It cannot be denied that Fascism and similar movements aiming at the establishment of dictatorships are full of the best intentions and that their intervention has, for the moment, saved European civilization."[30] In 1940, von Mises emigrated to the United States.

IN AUSTRIA, the results of the settlement movement were modest at best. The percentage of workers engaged in agriculture continued to decline during the interwar period, and the resettlement law of 1919 increased the percentage of land used for farming in Austria by a meager 0.03 percent.[31] Despite sustained efforts to increase agricultural production, Austrians in 1932 still imported a third of their vegetables, more

Leopoldau settlement, 1935.

Flooded streets in a settlement on the outskirts of Vienna, 1930.

than half of their fruit, and a third of their eggs.[32] And for many, the reality of settler life was sober and disappointing. According to recollections, settlers led a pitiable existence. In the 1930s, settlers in Leopoldau on the outskirts of Vienna had no schools, doctors, public transit, gas, electricity, sewage, or stores. Kids had to walk an hour to school, and the streets flooded every time it rained. Settlers recalled hunger and bone-chilling cold due to a lack of real heating in the winter. There was never any food left to sell, and alcohol abuse was epidemic.[33]

Female settlers often had a particularly rough life, working thirteen- or fourteen-hour days. The success of settlements was dependent on the unpaid labor of both women and children. A 1933 study of settlers in Germany noted that the status of women seemed to sink when they became settlers. "Even women who in Hanover once went together with their husbands to assemblies and political events submit themselves to the new social order of the settler's village."[34] Some women, however, praised settlements as the solution to what they called the "new female question." In 1932, Klara Friedländer, vice president of the Austrian Women's Party, commended settlers' wives for giving up paid work in order to work the land, leaving their jobs free for men. "Among settlers, marriage recovers its old meaning: a union of equals founded to raise the next generation under the best possible conditions," she claimed.[35]

Ultimately, the autarky and settlement movements of the 1920s and 1930s transformed into the more aggressive imperial campaigns of the 1940s. The term "inner colonization" makes sense only in relationship to outer colonization. In the 1930s, inner colonization and settlement were already imagined as substitutes—but also possible preludes—to colonial expansion. In 1932, the *Kronenzeitung*, one of Austria's most popular newspapers, introduced a weekly supplement called "My Little Piece of Land" devoted to gardening and animal husbandry. The supplement's first feature was an article called "What Is Inner Colonization?" It began, "Inner colonization is pure colonial politics. The only difference is that it does not involve the colonization of some foreign land, but rather the colonization of our own homeland."[36]

In April 1938, *Der Siedler*, the publication of the Austrian Association for Settlement and Small Gardens, celebrated Austria's *Anschluss* with Germany with a portrait of Adolf Hitler on its cover, proclaiming Hitler "the liberator of his homeland." The organization declared its joy at being integrated into the Third Reich, which "has greatly supported settlers and small gardeners." Wilhelm Bolek wrote that while the Austrian government had never done enough for settlers, the Third Reich was already coming through. "The first days of this victory without precedent have hardly passed, and the powerful Reich is already extending a helping hand to settlers in Austria. Not grand words and promises, but immediate help, practical acts are being put into place. Millions have already been approved for the goal of settlement and the economic development of Austria in the four-year plan is creating the conditions for ambitious settlement activity in our homeland."[37]

Building materials and labor were scarce, given the priority given to rearmament, but by March 1939, Nazi authorities had created 2,759 new rural settlements in Austria.[38] The Reichskommissar for the Reunion of Austria with the German Reich issued guidelines for the creation of new settlements in 1939. District Nazi Party leaders were to select settlers who demonstrated a "strong determination to create a family with children." Only politically reliable families with "German or similar blood" need apply. Settlers were instructed that their homes should be made out of local materials and adhere to local architectural styles and forms.[39]

Support for the settlement movement and the removal of Jews and Slavs from annexed territories went hand in hand. It would be difficult to evaluate the full progress of the settlement movement on the border between Austria and southern Moravia, one official reported, "until the full effects of the removal of the Czechs and Jews is determined." In the fall and winter of 1939, Nazi housing and settlement authorities appealed to their bosses to speed up the deportation of Jews in order to free up space for settlers and to "solve" the problem of the housing shortage in Vienna and its suburbs. A report from October 1939 noted that 300,000–400,000 Austrian Jews would be deported to Poland over the next few years. "At the same time the most urgent housing shortages in Vienna will finally be eliminated," the report anticipated.[40] For the Nazis, moreover, the settler's movement represented the antithesis of the cosmopolitan globalism they had set out to defeat: "Whoever is oriented internationally has no appreciation of home, of the homeland, or for attachment to the land and therefore to the fatherland," declared one Nazi official responsible for coordinating Austria's annexation to Germany. One could not be an internationalist and a settler at the same time.[41]

By 1939, the settlement movement in Austria—and the fantasies of deglobalization that propelled it, had traveled far from its origins. Late in her own life, Margarete Schütte-Lihotzky reflected on the fate of her dream: providing Austrian workers with simple homes and gardens that would reconnect them to the land and enable them to become more self-sufficient. It had begun "as a progressive movement, which helped people not only to achieve better material conditions, but also gave them the feeling of being part of a larger community that offered them help and support in life," she recalled. "But what was once progressive can today be retrogressive, or even become a menace."[42]

TWELVE

One Foot on the Land

IRON MOUNTAIN, 1931

> Next year, every man with a family who is employed at the
> plant will be required to have a garden of sufficient size to
> supply his family with at least part of its winter vegetables.
> Those who do not comply with the rule will be discharged.
> The man too lazy to work in a garden during his leisure
> time does not deserve a job.
>
> —DIRECTIVE TO FORD EMPLOYEES, 1931

NINETEEN THIRTY-ONE WAS the year of the "shotgun garden" in
Iron Mountain, Michigan. The order to plant gardens came directly
from the top. Henry Ford was convinced that a little rugged self-sufficiency (and a heavy dose of paternalism) could ease the entire nation's
growing economic crisis, much more than the expansion of the welfare
state ever would. "When the people of our country learn to help themselves they will be benefited far greater than they would be by employment insurance. . . . If our agricultural plan is adopted throughout the
country, the dole need never be thought of," he declared.[1]

Workers had little choice but to comply. Iron Mountain was a company town. The Ford Motor Company ran the town's sanitation facili-

ties, schools, power supply, and churches. Shortly after the First World War ended, Ford began to buy up hundreds of thousands of acres of timberland on Michigan's Upper Peninsula, with the goal of sourcing his own lumber. A state-of-the-art sawmill powered by a hydroelectric plant soon employed most residents of the town. Over the course of the next several decades, he added nineteen other "village industries" around Michigan to his portfolio. In places such as Milan, Ypsilanti, Plymouth, and Dundee, Ford employed local farmers and workers, sometimes stopping his car along the side of the road to recruit men directly from the fields. The factories typically produced a single part such as valves or carburetors. Employees at these rural plants were encouraged (and sometimes required) to be both workers and farmers, in many cases given plots of land by Ford. In the Detroit area alone, Ford sponsored 50,000 subsistence gardens.[2]

It was all part of a broader vision for the US economy and society, as well as for the Ford Motor Company. Ford was convinced that the "decentralization" of industry—moving large factories out of urban centers and breaking them up into smaller units—was not simply a "design for good living." It was good business. In Michigan's rural villages he found a labor supply that was both stable and flexible. His worker-farmers would weather the ups and downs of the business cycle by producing their own food, minimizing their need for cash income and welfare assistance. "By linking the soil with the factory, we are forming an alliance capable of resisting every onslaught," he boasted.[3]

Not every logger in Iron Mountain was eager to take up gardening. But Ford's dream was shared by hundreds of thousands of Americans in the 1930s. Some were attracted "back to the land" by idealism or ideological conviction, but many more were pulled there by the Great Depression. Droves of unemployed men, women, and families retreated to the land to survive the global economic crisis. They went to live with relatives when they couldn't pay their rent. They squatted on abandoned farms or shacks. Some hoped to farm for a living, while others just wanted to ward off starvation. A *Wall Street Journal* ad urged readers to "buy an abandoned farm and live on trout and applejack until the upturn!"[4] In 1932, the net gain in the farm population was 1,001,000, the largest since 1920, and movement from city to country exceeded movement from country to city by 533,000 (up from 214,000 in 1931). Urbanization, alongside globalization, had been temporarily reversed.[5]

Albert Risch of Milan, Michigan, was a model of worker-farmer Ford hoped to create. He woke at dawn, when he set out to tend to his cows, pigs, and chickens. He returned from the barn to find his "blond wife, Jane, and a stair-step arrangement of five blond little Risches waiting for him at a well-loaded breakfast table," to which he contributed a bucket of freshly extracted milk. Then Risch traded his farmer's overalls for shop clothes, pinned on a security badge, and drove his Ford to a nearby Ford plant, where he put in eight hours as an electrician. Risch worked hard but was contented by his well-rounded life, according to a profile in the *Saturday Evening Post*. In addition to a happy family, one hundred productive acres, and a good job, he had "achieved his long ambition to follow the advice of his employer—to have 'one foot in industry and another on the land.'"[6]

Not every Ford employee was so fulfilled. In 1934, Helen Bell, age twelve, of Lincoln Park, Michigan, appealed personally to Eleanor Roosevelt for a small plot of land for her own family. (The First Lady received 300,000 pieces of mail in her first year in office, many requesting material assistance.)[7] Her father had been laid off from a Ford plant. "My loving Mrs. Roosevelt," she wrote. "I am writing a few words thinking maybe it would help us some. There is seven of us children in the family, and Pa is working for CWA digging ditches. He makes 12 dollars a week, and he can't pay rent, buy clothes, and grocerys [sic] out of that. I heard that government was going to send some people on small farms. I wish we could get one of them, so we could make a garden and have a cow, pigs, and chickens. We had a little farm before but Pa could not pay for it so they chased us out. Pa had a job at Fords but they laid him off, and never called him back."[8]

Eleanor Roosevelt was not able to help Helen, but neither did Ford, in spite of the family's desire to go back to the land. Ford laid off 91,000 workers between March 1929 and August 1931, claiming it was a temporary measure. We do not know if Helen's Pa was among the several thousand unemployed workers who marched in protest to Ford's River

Rouge Plant on March 7, 1932, demanding "jobs for all laid-off Ford workers." That demonstration escalated into a bloodbath when Dearborn police officers and Ford security guards fired on the unarmed protesters, using at least one submachine gun. Four people were killed and two dozen injured. "Before it was over Dearborn pavements were stained with blood, streets were littered with broken glass and the wreckage of bullet-riddled automobiles and nearly every window in the Ford plant's employment office had been broken," reported the *New York Times*. Gardens were not enough. The massacre came to be known as the "Ford Hunger March."[9]

By MANY standards, Henry Ford could be counted among the foremost globalizers of his time. Fordism itself—the mode of production and managerial practices—is considered one of the United States' most important exports of the twentieth century. By shipping millions of Model T's and Model A's abroad, and sharing his technology with foreign industrialists, Ford did more than almost anyone in the 1920s and 1930s to sustain global trade, and made a fortune in the process. As of 1926, Ford had built plants across Europe, in South America, Japan, Australia, and South Africa.[10] Nor was he opposed to doing business with his ideological enemies. In 1929 alone, 72,000 Ford automobiles arrived in the Soviet Union.[11] Ford boasted in 1931, "Model T has penetrated to every corner of the earth," and announced that Ford would be expanding production and selling stock in Europe, "not primarily for our own benefit but because we believe we have an industrial method of bringing more comfort and more opportunity to people in the old lands."[12] "Taking the methods overseas," he claimed in 1931, was a humanitarian venture, aimed not at "making American business greater at the expense of other nations, but to help make other people more prosperous by the aid of American business."[13]

Ford also relied heavily on immigrant labor. As of 1917, more than half of his employees were foreign-born. The promise of high wages had drawn hundreds of thousands of men from the gates of Ellis Island to the gates of Ford's plants. These workers were targeted for "Americanization" by the Ford Motor Company's infamous Sociological Department. Immigrant workers were required to attend English-language classes and to move out of ethnic neighborhoods in Detroit. "Our one great aim is to impress these men that they are, or should be, Americans, and that former racial, national, and linguistic differences are to be forgotten," explained Rev. Samuel Marquis, who led Ford's employee relations offices. The famous graduation ceremony from Ford's English School was staged on a baseball field and conducted by the school principal, dressed as Uncle Sam. The "graduates" arrived in national costumes and sang songs from their homelands as they climbed a ladder into a giant papier-mâché "melting pot." They emerged from the other side as "Americans," dressed in derby hats and polka-dot ties and singing the "Star-Spangled Banner." Ford also hired African Americans, but they faced discrimination in Ford's workplace and were typically relegated to the worst jobs. The Sociological Department made no effort to move African American workers into nonsegregated neighborhoods of Detroit.[14]

HENRY FORD profited greatly from global trade and immigrant labor; he was also a highly idiosyncratic individual. But he was simultaneously at the vanguard of the anti-global turn. His anti-globalism was most famously directed at Jews, associated in his mind with his other archenemy: global finance. "For centuries, with marvelous forethought, certain hereditary groups have manipulated a large part of the gold of the world, not all of it, but a controlling margin, especially in Europe, where they have used their power to make war or peace," Ford wrote in 1926. These professional financiers, along with professional reformers, he insisted, "are in control of Europe and are responsible for its poverty. The League of Nations and all its adjuncts, are in their control, and under no system which they devise do the people have a chance."[15] Journalists often blamed Rosika Schwimmer for Ford's anti-Semitism. But in reality, his anti-Semitism, populism, and anti-cosmopolitanism were already explicit in 1915, when he blamed the First World War on Jewish bankers and international financiers. By the 1920s, Ford was using his pulpit to spread anti-Semitic propaganda, publishing in his newspaper, the *Dearborn Independent* (circulation: 700,000), not only the *Protocols of the Elders of Zion* but also dozens of other anti-Semitic screeds (ghost-written, but published under his name and with his approval). These articles were gathered together and republished in a four-volume series titled *The International Jew*, translated into multiple languages (including German) and widely distributed in Europe and the United States.

Ford and Fordism appealed to anti-globalists in other ways as well. Fordism may be associated with "Americanization" in popular memory, but his business practices were highly appealing to interwar anti-liberal regimes, including Nazi Germany and the Soviet Union. As historian Stefan Link has shown, they hoped to use Ford's methods and technical know-how to develop their own automobile industries and become more self-sufficient. Transnational technology transfer in the short run was supposed to lead to greater autarky in the long run.[16]

Between 1919 and 1921, the Ford Motor Company itself had been reorganized along autarkic lines. In 1919, Ford acquired all minority shares of the company; it was the only corporation of its size that did not trade shares publicly on the New York Stock Exchange and was not accountable to shareholders. In 1920, the company adopted a strategy of vertical integration, establishing facilities (like the one in Iron Mountain) that produced the raw materials and parts needed for production, including steel, glass, and lumber. Ford even attempted to create his own city in Brazil, called Fordlandia, to produce the rubber that he needed for millions of tires back in Michigan.[17] These strategies made the Ford Motor Company into a model for deglobalizing states, which also sought to "vertically integrate" their economies by producing the food and raw materials necessary to feed their people and sustain industrial production.[18]

Ford's vision of "growing automobiles on farms" emerged from his biography, ideology, and business sense. He had grown up on a farm in Dearborn, and he never stopped extolling the virtues of rural life or shook off his populist dislike for cities. In the nineteenth century, industrialization and urbanization had gone hand in hand, as growing industries attracted workers from farms to factories. But in the twentieth century, the automobile would do more than any other invention in history to decouple industrialization and urbanization, a separation that Ford enthusiastically supported. "The modern city has done its work and change is coming. The city has taught us much, but the overhead expense of living in such places is becoming unbearable. The cities are getting top-heavy and are about doomed," he insisted in a 1924 interview.[19] A return to part-time agriculture, he believed, aided by modern technology, would shield workers from the upheavals of the business cycles and insulate his factories from the threat of unionization. Workers in his "village industries" would earn a city wage but pay country prices for housing and food. They would enjoy shorter commutes. They would thrive on the moral and physical benefits of healthy farm life. And they would drive everywhere in their Ford automobiles.[20]

Ford elucidated his agrarian-industrial ideal in his essays for the *Dearborn Independent* and in books written with the assistance of journalist Samuel Crowther. Crowther, a journalist, spent most of his career writing with or about American industrialists and cooperated with Ford as a ghostwriter on three books. But he also authored an antiglobal manifesto of his own. In *America Self-Contained*, published at the height of the Great Depression, Crowther claimed that the United States possessed a unique gift by virtue of its natural resources: the ability to be self-sufficient in food production. Like deglobalizers in Europe (but departing from Ford), he argued that complete independence from world trade was the key to freedom, as "no nation is free if its daily bread can be given or withheld in war or in peace according to the needs or the pleasure of some other nation." Like other anti-globalists, Crowther also believed that isolation from the global economy did not represent a step backward, but forward; the Great Depression was conclusive evidence of the bankruptcy of global capitalism. "The choice," he claimed, "is between becoming a leader in a new and unselfish rearrangement of the world and becoming a pawn in an attempted revival of that old system of world economy which has been thoroughly tried and which has thoroughly failed." Becoming "self-contained" was a matter of guarding America's borders from cheap imported labor as well as cheap imported goods. "We must choose whether we shall take what we have and, making our isolation more complete, shape our own destinies, or whether we shall break down our isolation, abandon the principles of the founders and accept a standard of life fixed by the lowest common denominator of the world's standards."[21]

As CROWTHER'S text suggests, there was plenty of disagreement among back-to-the-landers, even among erstwhile allies. Ford was part of a movement of "decentralists"—individuals hoping to decentralize America's cities—that had diverse origins and an eclectic group of followers in the United States as in Europe.[22] A US Department of Agriculture report concluded in 1942, "The men and organizations that rallied behind the back-to-the-land movement were in many respects as strangely assorted as any ever found working in a common cause."[23] Agrarianism itself had deep roots in the United States. Thomas Jefferson believed that self-sufficient family farmers were the "chosen people of God" and the foundation for a virtuous republic. The "mobs of great cities," by contrast, "add just so much to the support of pure government as sores do to the strength of the human body."[24]

In the 1930s, a group of writers called the Southern Agrarians anointed themselves heirs of the Jeffersonian tradition, publishing a collective manifesto called *I'll Take My Stand*. Poet John Crowe Ransom, a leader of the circle, lamented the ways in which modern life metaphorically and literally uprooted people from the soil. "Deracination in our Western life is the strange discipline which individuals turn upon themselves, enticed by the blandishments of such fine words as Progressive, Liberal, and Forward-looking. The progressivist says in effect: do not allow yourself to feel homesick; form no such powerful attachments that you will feel pain in cutting them loose; prepare your spirit to be always on the move." Ransom served up his nostalgia for the "rootedness" of the Old South with an apology for slavery, which he called "a feature monstrous enough in theory, but, more often than not, humane in practice."[25]

But as in Europe, there was also a progressive march back to the land. There were reformers and city planners who wanted to build garden communities and save the working class from slum life. There were countercultural types, who advocated healthier, "natural," lifestyles and sought an alternative to consumer society; and there were religious supporters of back-to-the-land projects who promoted rural lifestyles as an antidote to the moral pitfalls of urbanization and industrialization.

Ralph Borsodi was among the most prominent life-reformers. He was the son of William Borsodi, an associate of Bolton Hall, who founded the back-to-the-land movement in the United States in the early twentieth century (Hall was a Progressive). Ralph Borsodi himself was a city boy by origin: he grew up in New York City and worked briefly in advertising until he decided to abandon what he called the "ugly civilization" of the city for a farm in upstate New York.[26] In 1933, Borsodi published a how-to guide for homesteaders called *Flight from the City: An Experiment in Creative Living on the Land*. In the midst of the Great Depression, it struck a chord. By returning to home production, aided by modern technological advances, Borsodi claimed that a family could feed, clothe, and support itself more cheaply than by wage labor. Americans could escape not only the unhealthful effects of city life but also the unsettling fluctuations of the business cycle. His ideal was not commercial farming, but rather a form of subsistence agriculture that would provide refuge from "the rise and fall of the prices in volatile produce markets" due to fluctuations in the national and global economy.[27]

On his farm in Suffern, New York, Borsodi, his wife, and two children produced almost everything they needed. "We weave suitings, blankets, carpets, and draperies, we make some of our own clothing; we do all our own laundry work; we grind flour, corn meal, and breakfast cereals; we have our own workshops, including a printing plant, and we have a swimming pool, tennis court, and even a billiard-room." Their diet consisted almost entirely of local foods they grew themselves, as they shunned "predigested breakfast foods, white bread, factory-made biscuits and crackers and cakes, polished rice, and white sugar." In this way they had also escaped the precarity that plagued wage workers in a global economy. "Through no fault of their own, other millions of cogs in our industrialized world and interdependent economic system find themselves periodically without the income which will enable them to buy the necessities of life." No social program or government intervention, Borsodi claimed, could "furnish . . . a cure for the fundamental defect in our present economic system—the excessive dependence of individual men and women for their livelihoods on nation-wide and even international economic activities." The only sensible solution was for families to liberate themselves from this dependence by producing all the necessities of life on their own homesteads.[28]

There was an individualist core to the ideal of homesteading championed by both Borsodi and Ford. Rugged self-sufficiency, they believed, was the best safeguard against the seismic quaking of the global economy. They said very little (or outright rejected) the possibility of regulating the economy itself or of providing a safety net for individuals afflicted by unemployment or poverty. Indeed, Ford insisted that his village industries represented the antithesis of the New Deal welfare state. "No unemployment insurance can be compared to an alliance between a man and a plot of land. . . . With one foot in the land, human society is firmly balanced against most economic uncertainties. With a job to supply him with cash, and a plot of land to guarantee him support, the individual is doubly secure. Stocks may fail, but seedtime and harvest do not fail."[29]

GIVEN HIS hostility to unemployment insurance (as well as unions and any other form of government interference in his business), it is not surprising that Henry Ford had few kind words for the Roosevelt administration or the New Deal. He backed Herbert Hoover against Roosevelt in Hoover's reelection bid in 1932, famously refused to cooperate with the National Recovery Administration, violently resisted the unionization of his factories, and endorsed Alf Landon in his run against Roosevelt in 1936. In that endorsement, he claimed that Roosevelt and the New Deal were "under the control of international financiers" ("Jewish" left implied).[30]

And yet, the back-to-the-land ideal attracted support in high places in the midst of the Great Depression, uniting (if begrudgingly) ideological and political opponents. Roosevelt and Ford actually shared several ideas, including the notion that "redistributing" the US population away from large cities and "decentralizing" industry could serve as a hedge against the business cycle. Economist Rexford Tugwell, who became an important figure in the first Roosevelt administration, wrote in 1926 that Ford's ideas about merging farming and industry were "of first-rate importance" and "well worth listening to."[31]

Roosevelt, in contrast to Ford, never saw farming as a substitute for unemployment insurance. He knew too well (as did America's farmers) that "seedtime and harvest" often failed. But he did see the redistribution of population as a means of addressing the vulnerability of urban workers to cyclical depression. In a 1931 address before the American Country Life Conference, Roosevelt argued, "The condition of the typical city worker is one of speculative living, with practically no safeguards against the disaster of unemployment that has now fallen on so many of his class. I believe our ingenuity ought to be equal to finding a way by which that condition could be swapped for one of stabilized living in a real home in the country."[32] In his New Year's address to the New York State Legislature, he declared more boldly that the "economics of America, and indeed of the whole world, are out of joint." There would be an "immediate gain ... if as many people as possible can return closer to the sources of the agricultural food supply."[33]

Upon taking office, Roosevelt put these ideals into practice. He created a Department of Subsistence Homesteads under Harold Ickes's Department of the Interior, which received $25 million in funding under the National Industrial Recovery Act of June 1933. Milburn L. Wilson, an agricultural expert with experience in agricultural extension work in Montana, led the division. It was a relatively small operation (and appropriation), intended to fund projects of an experimental nature. The Department of Subsistence Homesteads was interested in developing communities of 25–300 homesteads, which would be sold "on liberal terms" to families with incomes under $1,200 a year ($23,300 in 2019 dollars) on payments of $12.65 ($245 2019 dollars) a month. These homesteaders were not to be full-time farmers or to farm for profit. Unlike the back-to-the-land or resettlement projects of interwar Austria, Italy, and

Germany, the goal was not to increase agricultural production, because the United States was facing an epic crisis of agricultural *overproduction*. Indeed, one of the first New Deal initiatives was the Agricultural Adjustment Act, which paid farmers *not* to grow crops or raise animals including wheat, corn, and pigs. Rather, like Albert Risch, the homesteaders were supposed to produce fruit, vegetables, and dairy products for their own consumption, while working elsewhere for wages.

The project also aimed to assist what were called "stranded" workers, those left unemployed by the closing down or exhaustion of industries. These included former miners in the bituminous coal fields of West Virginia and loggers on the Pacific coast, as well as workers considered "over-age" (over forty!) and unlikely to find employment again. Upon announcement of plans for a settlement in West Virginia for former coal miners, a pet project of Eleanor Roosevelt, Harold Ickes declared that the settlement would "return to usefulness, security, and to a high degree of self-sufficiency a group of men and their families who are victims of the period of planlessness and helter-skelter development and misuse of natural resources which I hope we are leaving behind." The former miners were to grow their own food and work in a government-owned factory that produced machinery for the Post Office.[34]

But these plans for subsistence homesteads drew ridicule from the outset. "Hardly a week goes by but some new leader of public opinion discovers the space between cities as a God-given dump for the unemployed," writer Russell Lord quipped in 1933.[35] Fiorello H. La Guardia, then a member of the US House of Representatives from New York, argued that "a cow, a chicken, a sack of flour, a bit of charity, and perhaps an exploiting landlord" was no substitute for unemployment insurance.[36] Others warned that it was unrealistic to expect former urban workers to transform into farmers overnight. Some of the fiercest opponents of the homestead communities were actual farmers, weary of competition and increasing agricultural surpluses. Phares Horstman wrote to Eleonor Roosevelt in 1934, "We are very sad to witness in our community a great community garden rising close to the farms being paid not to produce. This is a gross error of judgment, based on a false sense of sentimentality. Instead of paying farmers NOT to produce, use this same money to purchase from them the surplus needed for the needy. . . . Must we sit on our fences this summer, receive our government bonus for idle land, and watch the other fellow raise our produce?"[37]

The Department of Subsistence Homesteads responded that the point of the homesteads was to render the poor "self-sufficient," rather than giving them a handout. This dream of "self-sufficiency," with its moral overtones, was clearly among the most alluring aspects of the homestead ideal for both policy makers and settlers. When the department had issued its call for proposals, the response was overwhelming: it received proposals for projects that would have taken up to $4 billion to fund. They included plans for community gardens, housing projects, the enlargement of company towns, and fully cooperative farms and communities. Although it was "soon evident to the more sober-minded that the movement was attracting even more than the usual share of cultists, faddists, and crackpots," the Department of Agriculture later reflected, "the great majority of those supporting the movement were idealists and humanitarians, many of them practical and effective men as well."[38]

The number of individuals who dreamt of a new life on a subsistence farm far overwhelmed the limited scope of the project. More than 300,000 individual men, women, and children wrote to the Department of Subsistence Homesteads pleading for a chance at a home and land. Not surprisingly, these letters rarely talked about "decentralization," the distribution of population, or the global economy. But they did talk about subsistence, dignity, and self-sufficiency. Edgar Adams of Philadelphia, a 46-year-old veteran, wrote that he had been out of work for two years, "and in that time have hardly been able to keep body and soul together and at times had nothing to eat. . . . I thought that I could possibly get some land in Penna or New Jersey where I could raise some livestock and produce and in the meanwhile get some sort of job and from the revenue obtained be able to pay back to the Government their investment in me, and at the same time feel as if I have the right to live."[39]

Most took pains to insist that they did not want a handout. Edith Atkinson, mother and sole supporter of five children, had lost her home and job in 1930. Appealing for a homestead in 1935, she wanted to get her kids out of the city where they had "nothing more to do than mingle with other children and between them all eventually find some mischief to get into." If only she could get a small parcel of land, "enough to allow us to grow our own garden, keep a cow, and raise fowl, that surely would occupy their minds and excess energy." Above all she wanted off relief. "Of course we are not at present starving but how wonderful it would be to feel you were not dependent on a public welfare or relief of some kind as far ahead as you could see."⁴⁰

A great number of prospective homesteaders sent appeals directly to the president or to Eleonor Roosevelt. W. F. Berry, a former cotton farmer, wrote to FDR, "The reason I had to leave the farm is that cotton went down to such a low price I could not make it. I could not pay my debts and I lost all my tools, ploughs, and stock. In other words I was cleaned out. I have depended on the C.W.A. for my livelihood for the past two years and I don't like it. Could you please tell me how I could get back on the farm?"⁴¹

The vast majority of these writers were to be disappointed. As of 1937, there were 122 subsistence homestead projects under way, housing only 14,000 families. The Department of Subsistence Homesteads was not able to assist individuals, who were only eligible to apply for programs in their own states. The homestead communities were also segregated, and only a single community was ever built for Blacks, in Newport News, Virginia. Blacks generally benefited less than white Americans from New Deal programs, and the subsistence homesteads program was no exception. Blanche Hooey of Austin, Texas, had read about a nearby homestead project for 340 families in her local newspaper. She had been deserted by her husband of twenty-seven years and had four children to support. "We love orderliness, beauty, and work and long for a place to raise truck and chickens. . . . I'm facing old age with no home," she appealed. "Please investigate and consider my family for one of the homes to be built in Beaumont." She received a reply informing her that there were not yet any subsistence homestead projects "for colored people in Texas."⁴²

Another anonymous letter writer expressed enthusiasm for the back-to-the-land ideal but warned that it would appeal to Blacks only if they could own their own small farms. "Majority of people that is on relief in the cities are people reared on farms and a lot of them like farming as an occupation. But they would rather stay in the city and starve than come back to the farm, and work under the system that these plantations are operated under now."⁴³ The Department of Subsistence Homesteads searched for, but never found, a site on which to create an integrated homestead community. Still worse, some Blacks were actually forced out of their homes to make way for white settlers. In Cahaba, Alabama, forty Black families lived on land that had been purchased but not developed by the Department of Subsistence Homesteads. One day they received notice that they had a week to clear out. Families were forcibly evicted and their homes burned to the ground. They were relocated to shacks and shanties on a nearby plot of inferior land, while white tenants settled into brand-new, modern homes on their former land.⁴⁴

AS IN EUROPE, economic protectionism and restrictions on immigration were generally the US government's first responses to the Great Depression. The Tariff Act of 1930 (or Smoot-Hawley tariff) increased tariffs on more than 20,000 imported goods, including both agricultural products and manufactured goods. But as the United States remained a net exporter of agricultural commodities such as wheat, cotton, and corn, farmers did not gain much from these tariffs (except ill-will and retaliation from foreign trading partners). At the time, 96 percent of manufactured goods consumed by Americans were also produced in American factories, and a healthy surplus was exported abroad.⁴⁵

But there were also some important differences between the dreams of self-sufficiency and the back-to-the-land projects promoted by Mussolini and Hitler and those of the New Deal. With the exception of fairly marginal figures such as Crowther, there was little talk of increasing agricultural production or of autarky at a national level in the United States. This may have been because, as Crowther himself argued (and as Hitler jealously observed), the United States was one of few countries in the world already capable of feeding itself without significant imports in the 1930s.⁴⁶

There were also ideological differences between the homesteading movements in Europe and the United States. Although the US government did undertake massive public works during the Great Depression, including spending for homesteaders, there was an important branch of the movement (represented by Ford) that was strongly anti-government. The land reclamation and resettlement programs initiated by Mussolini and Hitler were, by contrast, intended to be monuments to Fascism and state power, emblems of the regime's conquest and control of natural resources and people.

Nonetheless, the ideas for city and rural planning that inspired these projects circulated transnationally among experts and planners who self-consciously imitated one another. One of the architects who designed a "New City" in Fascist Italy, for example, was reportedly inspired by Frank Lloyd Wright's designs for Broadacre City.[47] Even at the popular level, Americans were inspired by Mussolini's example. In Chicago, a "believer in subsistence farms" wrote anonymously to FDR and enclosed a newspaper clipping about Mussolini's swamp-clearance efforts. "If this is true and can be done by another nation it seems the vast empire of space from Lake Okeechobee south in Florida could be redeveloped into subsistence farms capable of sustaining at least several millions of people quite easily. I hope this will appeal to you and that you will have someone look into such possibilities," he advised.[48]

Another feature of the homesteading movement that transcended the Atlantic was an emphasis on restoring traditional gender roles. In the Depression-era United States, as in Italy, Austria, and Germany, settling families on farms was supposed to restore the gender roles that had (in observers' eyes) been painfully disrupted by the global economic crisis. As a way to make a living, subsistence homesteading was the very opposite of global labor migration, with its destructive effects on family life. There was an implicit and explicit aim to "resettle" (on the land) the gender roles that had become "unsettled" by globalization.

As we saw in Austria, the back-to-the-land movement relied extensively on the unpaid labor of women—but this work was in traditionally female domains: raising children, caring for small animals, canning, cooking, preserving, gardening, mending, and sewing. In the United States, likewise, when a man applied for a homestead, his wife was auditioning for the role of farm wife and homemaker (single men and couples without children need not apply). The Department of Subsistence Homesteads explained, "Regardless of how favorable the husband's attitude may be, the wife must demonstrate to the satisfaction of the committee that she is fully convinced of the advantages of the plan. Her aptitude in such wifely duties as canning, sewing or gardening are described as largely adding to the applicant's eligibility."[49]

For inspiration, settler women could turn to Myrtle Mae Borsodi herself, Ralph Borsodi's wife. She became a public voice in her own right in the 1930s. In February 1937, she penned a feature for *Scribner's Magazine* with the provocative title, "The New Woman Goes Home." In it, she reinforced the link between the return to the land and a return to traditional gender roles. "Without questioning the desirability of our having won the right to engage in all of these new activities [voting, employment, owning property] and even abandon homemaking, if we wish, I not only deny the wisdom of this change (except for the minority of women who are by temperament and training unfit for wifehood and motherhood), but I challenge the economic validity of the change," she argued. "Money-making, for the overwhelming majority of women, does not pay. . . . It pays neither them, their families, nor society."

Mrs. Borsodi went on to rehearse the claim that domestic production was economically more efficient than industrial production. For example, she insisted that the cost of preparing nine pints of baked beans with salt pork at home, including depreciation on the stove, labor, ingredients, and "kitchen overhead," was significantly less than the price of purchasing the same quantity of canned beans in a store. The article made an important case for recognizing the economic value of women's household labor. But her insistence that women should abandon paid employment in favor of full-time bean production also rested on underlying assumptions about essential gender differences. "Men and women are biologically so different that there must be a difference in the economic activities in which they engage, if their contribution is to prove of equal value financially. The mere fact that the majority of us must be mothers handicaps us in any kind of work outside the home. If we are to prove our equality, we will do it not by competing with men in the task of earning money, but by dividing between the two sexes the various tasks which need to be done." In other words, while rejecting a global division of economic labor, Borsodi's ideal self-sufficient homestead depended on a gendered division of household labor.[50]

As several critics pointed out, her argument also rested on poor math. In a rejoinder to Borsodi's article, Dorothy Van Doren challenged the economics of the Borsodi plan, pointing out that it required, at minimum, an electric range, a large electric refrigerator, an electric mixer, a pressure cooker, a washing machine, and an electric sewing machine, start-up costs that totaled at least $500. For the vast majority of families, "the cost of the Borsodi equipment is prohibitive," and women worked because it was a "grim necessity." Homesteading also required a lot of skills, none of which were biologically given. Most ordinary women lacked Mrs. Borsodi's domestic talents.[51] In a critical review of Ralph Borsodi's *Flight from the City*, public housing advocate Catherine Bauer likewise concluded that in order to achieve the "self-sufficiency" prescribed by the Borsodis, "You must have a husky wife with a positive taste for domestic production, no desire to do anything else with her time, and a gift for home education as well."[52]

WITH THE support of the Department of Subsistence Homesteads and its successors, at least 14,000 families acquired ground beneath their feet. Their fates were mixed. The project itself changed hands and leadership several times, and in 1935, responsibility for the subsistence homesteads program was transferred to the new Resettlement Administration, which was under the leadership of Rexford Tugwell, one of the members of FDR's "brain trust." Tugwell was more interested in creating so-called greenbelt communities around the edges of existing urban centers than in homesteading. Out of twenty such planned communities, only three were actually built. Then Tugwell himself, tarnished unfairly as a Communist, was forced out, and in 1937 the management of the subsistence homesteads program was transferred to the Farm Security Administration.[53]

In several cases, the more radical and utopian ideals that motivated the original homestead projects were cast aside. Jersey Homesteads, a subsistence homestead community designated for Jewish garment workers from New York City, was initially envisioned as a completely self-sufficient cooperative community. The project had roots well beyond the New Deal, in a global movement to "productivize" Jews by resettling them in agricultural communities—and to disassociate them from the evils of global capitalism and urban life. The ideal of "regenerating" Jewish life through rural settlement inspired many Zionists as well as other rural resettlement projects in the United States and beyond, from Birobidzhan (in the Soviet Union) to the Dominican Republic (a planned haven for Jewish refugees). Two men who were instrumental in the creation of Jersey Homesteads, M. L. Wilson, chief of the Department of Subsistence Homesteads, and Benjamin Brown, who proposed the Jersey Homesteads settlement, had actually met on a trip to Birobidzhan, where they both served as agricultural consultants.[54]

Brown envisioned Jersey Homesteads as a Jewish cooperative homestead on 1,000 acres of land near Hightstown, New Jersey. It was to include a cooperative clothing factory, farm, dairy, and stores. Subsistence gardens were to provide the workers' families with many necessities. Eight hundred families from the Bronx and Brooklyn applied, and almost all of the 200 male "heads of household" selected were immigrants from Eastern Europe. "All knew or sensed the insecurity of the Jewish people in the modern world," the Department of Agriculture reported. "The future of these workers consisted of nothing that was certain except more work, more unemployment, more job seeking, more planning to meet the next seasonal slack." Each family was required to invest $500 in the project. Many families borrowed money from family members, cashed in insurance policies, and sold personal items to raise funds for the down payment.[55]

It took more than two years to get the homes and factory built, thanks to continual delays and conflicts among the organizers.[56] Residents of the surrounding community of Hightstown also began to petition against the arrival of what they called an "undesirable element" of "slum dwellers."[57] In one such letter, John Hayes of New Brunswick, New Jersey, wrote, "I have several reasons for moving to the country, and one of the principal ones is to get as far away from Jewish contact as possible."[58]

The homesteaders responded to these attacks by organizing what they called a "demonstration of Americanism" in Hightstown and Jersey Homesteads on May 17, 1936. Approximately 800 prospective settlers and their families formed a caravan of ten Manhattan Line buses, which passed demonstratively through Hightstown en route to Jersey Homesteads. Each homesteader wore an American flag pinned to his or her lapel, and their children carried tiny flags. Young people between the age of seventeen and twenty-six formed a Jersey Homesteads "Junior League" and led the homesteaders in a procession behind a large American flag. Even Henry Ford's Sociological Department might have approved of the demonstration.[59]

Two months later, the first seven families arrived by truck from Brooklyn and the Bronx and moved into their new homes.[60] Spirits were high at a party to celebrate the pioneers' arrival, but relationships between the town and Jersey Homesteads remained tense. Leo Libove recalled decades later, "Hightstown was anti-Jersey Homesteads and also anti-Jews. But I think that once the buying power of this community became apparent in Hightstown, opinions changed and they began to tolerate us. . . . But in general we were the communists, the kikes, and the Jews. The people called this Jewtown."[61]

The cooperative factory and farm opened to great fanfare but struggled to stay afloat. The factory suffered heavy losses in each of its first three years. Many men ended up commuting to jobs in other towns in New Jersey or even back to New York City. Thousands of coats, suits, and hats were produced and delivered to retail outlets on consignment—and then returned unsold. By 1939, the cooperative factory had gone bankrupt.[62]

The cooperative farm and the gardens didn't fare much better. The tailors in the factory were supposed to work on the farm in their off season, but many did not have the fitness, ability, or desire to pick potatoes for 25 cents an hour. One homesteader recalled, "The tailors were all out there ready to pick. And they picked for a couple hours, but they're not used to that kind of work. You had to bend your back, stand on your knees and harvest potatoes. After a few hours, the sun was pretty warm. They had a union meeting on the field. They decided it was too hot to pick potatoes. Somebody made a motion to leave and the potatoes were left lying in the sun." The farm was divided up and sold in 1939.[63]

Only a minority of the families even made use of their gardens. They claimed it didn't pay: they could buy vegetables for the same price that they could grow them, if they accounted for the cost of their labor. Some enjoyed gardening, but as a leisure activity, a symbol of suburban living, rather than as a means of subsistence.[64] As it turns out, the Great Depression was not the beginning of a permanent return to the land or to farming in America. But it may have accelerated the shift of populations toward suburbs. It didn't take much time for the subsistence gardens and poultry sheds envisioned by the Jersey Homesteads planners to be transformed into flower gardens and green backyards with swing sets and barbecues.

And yet the community was a success in other ways. Many of the residents were happy to be there, formed a close community, and stayed for life. One man recalled years later, "When we came here in 1937 we found a vibrant Jewish life, in all ways—from the religious element, towards the socialist, even to the communist and Zionist. . . . And although we were a very small unit . . . these sixty families carried on a life like it was a big city. . . . It was beautiful."[65]

For Ralph Borsodi, the creation of the Department of Subsistence Homesteads must have initially seemed like a validation of his life's work. Borsodi was recruited in 1933 to lead a community-organized homestead project in Dayton, Ohio, where unemployed families were allocated three-acre plots. The project, with Borsodi's name and credentials attached to it, was the very first to receive sponsorship from the Department of Subsistence Homesteads. By June 1934, twenty families had already moved into their homes.

But progress on the Dayton settlement was disrupted when plans were announced to build an adjacent settlement for African American families. Hundreds of residents of Jefferson Township, where the homestead was to be located, signed a petition in which they rallied against the "arbitrary injection of a colony of thirty-five or more families of colored people with lower standards of living" in their vicinity.[66] Borsodi meanwhile lost the support of many homesteaders, who saw him as autocratic. Some residents reported that they were forced to purchase looms for weaving by hand, a task they had no intention of taking up; many residents wanted to continue working in the city rather than devote themselves wholly to farming. Borsodi also clashed with what he saw as overly meddlesome federal authorities. From the beginning he had advocated local autonomy and local control of homesteads, which was also the initial philosophy of M. L. Wilson and the Department of Subsistence Homesteads. But by May 1934, Wilson had left, and the Department of the Interior under Harold Ickes had changed course, bringing the subsistence homesteads program under greater federal control. At odds with both residents of the community and New Deal authorities, Borsodi resigned and retreated to his own homestead in New York.[67]

Disenchanted by his experience in Dayton, Borsodi renounced the New Deal itself. Like Ford, he began to represent homesteading as the

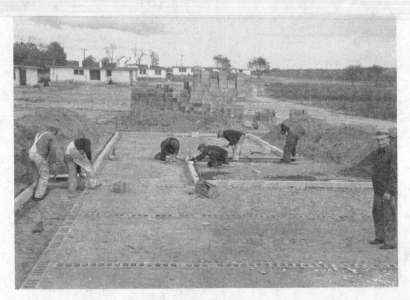

Building Jersey Homesteads, 1936.

Scene at Jersey Homesteads, 1936.

Workers in garment factory, Jersey Homesteads, 1936.

antithesis of government intervention—a bootstraps enterprise that rejected "dependency" and government support in favor of rugged individualism and self-sufficiency. "While the masses of people are frantically calling upon Washington for old age pensions, unemployment compensation and other forms of security from the cradle to the grave, we are providing for our own, as most self-respecting Americans used to do until the gospel of depending upon the government for support began to be substituted for the gospel of independence by the proponents of the New Deal," he boasted.

With the onset of the Cold War, Borsodi's writings took on a darker tone. "Sensible people will begin establishing themselves on the land now," he advised, "before inflation and the loss of their savings, the collapse of the post-war boom, followed by unemployment, or World War III with atomic bombing, make it too late for them to do so."[68] The homesteads of the Cold War era would not merely provide sanctuary from the collapse of the global economy. They were also to become strongholds against government interference, and against the world itself; shelters in which to hunker down and prepare for the apocalypse.

THIRTEEN

Freedom Through the Spinning Wheel

LANCASHIRE, 1931

IT WAS CLOSE to midnight on September 25, 1931, when Mahatma Gandhi's train arrived at Spring Vale station, in the heart of Lancashire's textile industry. A throng of local villagers had stayed up long past their usual bedtimes to catch a glimpse of Gandhi and to cheer him on as he made his way to his temporary home in the village. This warm welcome was not entirely expected.

Lancashire was suffering deeply in the midst of the Great Depression, with more than one-third of textile workers on the dole. In 1929, the Indian National Congress had called a boycott on cloth imported to India, and many cotton mill owners and workers believed that the boycott was responsible for the dismal state of Lancashire's industry. In reality, before the boycott, India had represented at best 15 percent of Lancashire's export trade. The global economic crisis, competition from Japan and America, and the failure of the industry in Lancashire to modernize were at the root of the region's decline. But animosity toward Gandhi was widespread enough that in response to reports of his planned visit, Alderman William Forrest, a cotton manufacturer in Blackburn, declared frankly, "We don't want him here.... There are 71 mills in Blackburn and is it likely that anybody who has been instrumental in stopping those 71 mills will be received with open arms and will be made a fuss of by the people? Isn't it more likely that he stands a chance of being mobbed?"[1]

Gandhi was not mobbed, though he was heavily protected by the police. As it turned out, many workers and officials in Lancashire welcomed Gandhi's visit. They hoped that once he saw their misery with his own eyes, he would be moved to call off the boycott. The morning after his arrival, Gandhi was officially welcomed by Darwen's mayor, who expressed the community's hope that "as the result of your visit to Lancashire and the intimate talks you intend to have with people connected with the cotton trade there will be a resumption of the happy relations which formerly existed between our country and your country, and so alleviate the acute distress which is felt in Lancashire at present." In response, according to one newspaper account, "The Mahatma nodded and smiled, but said nothing."[2]

Over the course of the following days, Gandhi toured mills, met with workers and officials, posed for photos, and gave interviews. But he did not agree to suspend India's boycott of foreign cloth. Rather, he actually appealed to the unemployed workers of Lancashire to boycott the textiles they produced. As far as poverty was concerned, he had seen worse. "I would be a false friend if I were not frank with you," he explained to a group of unemployed workers. "Even in your misery you are comparatively happy. I do not grudge you that happiness. I wish well to you, but do not think of prospering on the tombs of the poor millions of India. I do not want for India an isolated life for all, but I do not want to depend on any country for my food and clothing."[3]

And yet Gandhi insisted that the Indian boycott was not, as many English saw it, a matter of narrow nationalism. Rather he believed that increasing India's self-sufficiency, self-determination, and prosperity would serve humanity at large. "I am pained at the unemployment here. But there is no starvation or semi-starvation. In India we have both. If you went to the villages of India, you would find utter despair in the eyes of the villages, you would find half-starved skeletons, living corpses. If India could revive them by putting life and food into them in the shape of work India would help the world."[4]

The Indian nationalist movement for self-rule (*swaraj*) through *swadeshi* (products "of one's country") made of *khaddar*, also known as *khadi*—a hand-spun and handwoven textile—was a powerful expression of anti-colonial nationalism in the early twentieth century. In several ways, the movement had a great deal in common with other attempts to achieve greater national self-sufficiency in the 1920s and 1930s. But it differed in a crucial respect: Gandhi and his followers insisted that economic deglobalization was not an end unto itself, but instead a means to a more authentic form of globalism that was rooted in mutual interest and universal humanity rather than colonial domination. Deglobalization was an essential step toward decolonization.

The swadeshi movement had begun before the First World War, in Bengal in the first decade of the twentieth century. In 1920, the Indian National Congress formally passed the Non-Cooperation Resolution. The boycott on foreign goods, especially textiles, was one of the movement's fundamental ideals. "India cannot be free so long as India voluntarily encourages or tolerates the economic drain which has been going on for the past century and a half. Boycott of foreign goods means no more and no less than boycott of foreign cloth."[5]

By 1921, bonfires raged across India. Thousands of people gathered to declare their independence from Britain by burning foreign cloth. To a crowd in Bombay in July 1921, a sea of men, women, and children dressed in khadi, Gandhi declared, "I regard this day as sacred for Bombay. We are removing today a pollution from our bodies. We are purifying ourselves by discarding foreign cloth which is the badge of our slavery." The bonfire was piled with foreign-made hats, coats, vests, silks, and umbrellas. Gandhi lit the pyre, and flames leapt to the sky, symbolizing India's independence.[6]

Many nationally conscious Indians pledged to completely boycott foreign cloth. Better still, they would spin cloth and make clothing themselves at home. This campaign was not only about national independence, however. It also linked spirituality and morality to handicrafts. "Our freedom will be won through the spinning-wheel," Gandhi declared. "The revival of hand-spinning is the least penance we must do for the sin of our forefathers in having succumbed to the satanic influences of the foreign manufacturer."[7] Crucially, Gandhi urged Indians to forsake *all* foreign textiles, not only British. "We do not want other people's domination after getting rid of British rule."[8]

Three national institutions supported the movement from the 1920s to independence. The Satyagraha Ashram (founded in 1917) served as a spiritual community and a school whose members were devoted to cultivating swadeshi. Members of the ashram were required to renounce manufactured goods and to spin 140 threads each day. The community was intended to embody the values of anti-materialism, self-sacrifice, and self-sufficiency through their lifestyle and the production of handmade goods. The All-India Khaddar Board (founded in 1921) was responsible for promoting khadi at the local level by establishing schools and promoting production and sales through marketing, publicity, and the investigation of consumers' needs and desires. For example, the board tried to adapt khadi to regional preferences through the use of local and regional patterns and colors. Finally, the All-India Spinners' Association (founded in 1924) regulated the production and sale of khadi at the national level.[9]

Gandhi's critique of dependence on foreign manufactured goods resembled other campaigns to achieve independence from the global economy in the interwar era. But in the case of India, deglobalization was understood as a step toward the paramount goal of decolonization. While many of his supporters did not necessarily object to trade in and of itself, they saw the subordinate place of India within the global economy as an artifact of imperial domination. Hence, unlike many other autarkic movements, Gandhi's swadeshi movement did not require independence from the political ideals of globalism or internationalism. In Lancashire, Gandhi's aim was conversely to rally local and international support for his mission in India. He made an appeal to conscience that was cosmopolitan and universalist. Elsewhere in speeches and in print, Gandhi frequently insisted that he welcomed partnership and collaboration with other countries, including England—so long as it was on equal terms. "Isolated independence is not the goal of the world States. It is voluntary interdependence," he wrote shortly before his visit to England.[10] He frequently appealed to the people of Britain to support

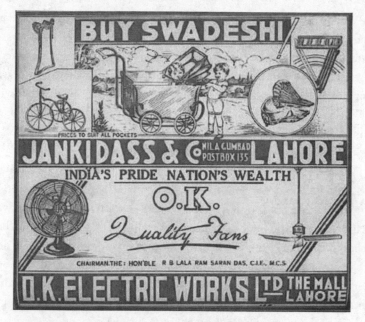

"Buy Swadeshi," date unknown.

Gandhi in Lancashire, 1931.

the Indian boycott and forged ties with other anti-colonial movements around the world. In these appeals, he framed his mission in universalist terms, insisting that Indian nationalism posed no threat to others. "I want Englishmen now to join us in our work of serving the poor. . . . Our nationalism can be no peril to other nations, inasmuch as we will exploit none just as we will allow none to exploit us. Through Swaraj we will serve the whole world."[11]

NOT EVERYONE was immediately impressed. Anna Varki was born in 1921 in Calcutta and moved to Bombay at the age of four. She was inculcated with the value of swadeshi at a young age. One morning, her father informed the family that they would be going shopping, but not in the usual department stores downtown. Instead they would be shopping at the Khadi Bandar, a store that sold only products made in India. Anna was disappointed with the goods on offer, which she found "ugly and rough." But she chose a dress anyway. "I don't remember ever wearing it. It just lay in a box."

Later she came to better appreciate the meaning of the store and the rough cloth, its role in the everyday social life of the nationalist movement. At the time, she recalled, "Gandhi's call to take the Swadeshi pledge, that is never to buy foreign goods, inspired many people to take spinning very seriously." Even small children learned to spin, and women took their spinning on social visits. Anna also recalled the bonfires. "People made heaps of all their foreign garments and set them on fire all over the country. I loathed the idea of throwing my pretty silk frocks on the fire. My father was not very keen on it either. But his elder brother George Joseph, an ardent follower of Gandhi, swore by and urged everyone to do it."[12] The demand for khadi goods was so high in many areas in the early 1920s that foreign manufacturers and local dealers even produced counterfeits. According to a report of the All-India Conference's Civil Disobedience Committee in 1922, this was especially commonplace in stores that sold khadi in large cities "as the demand on them is so great and the sources of supply are limited."[13]

Gandhi prescribed daily spinning for all Indians, male and female, across divisions of class, caste, religion, or region. Briefly, in 1924, the Indian National Congress even instituted a "spinning franchise," which required every member to contribute 2,000 yards of "evenly spun yarn" each month in order to vote. But spinning was always seen as a particularly suitable form of political participation for women. It would ostensibly protect their virtue by enabling them to make a living in the disastrous case of widowhood. Gandhi also envisioned khadi as a strategy for controlling male sexual desire, exhorting women, "If you want to play your part in world affairs, you must refuse to decorate yourselves for pleasing man."[14]

During his visit to Lancashire, London's *Daily Herald* published an essay in which Gandhi reflected on the role of women in Indian society. "Yes, I believe in complete equality for women and, in the India I seek to build, they would have it," he insisted. "But I most sincerely hope that woman will retain and exercise her ancient prerogative as queen of the household. . . . I cannot, for instance, imagine a really happy home in which the wife is a typist and scarcely ever in it." In most cases, he believed, men should be breadwinners. Women were to stay at home, care for their children, and in their "leisure" hours work at the spinning wheel—all tasks that would serve the nation at large.[15]

Like other movements focused on self-sufficiency, Indian advocates of khadi tended to downplay the nonmonetary costs of their goods—particularly the cost of women's time and labor. Indeed, for Gandhi, the labor that went into hand-spinning was not a negative "cost" at all: it was precisely the point. In a report on the village of Kanoor, he wrote in 1925, "Spinning occupies, during the cotton season, and for some time after, all the leisure hours of the women at home." He claimed that most families were saving considerable amounts of money as well. This was not because the cloth was less expensive to purchase but because of the "new simplicity in living which Khaddar brought in its wake. . . . The exclusion of wasteful luxury is in itself no small gain. But a much greater gain than that is the increasing amount of labor at home and the filling of idle hours."[16]

Yet readers frequently wrote to Gandhi or to his publication *Young India* to raise issues with the production and purchase of khaddar, including the unrecognized tax on their time. Khadi was laborious to produce and more expensive than manufactured cloth. It got dirty easily and was hard to clean (which took even more time). It was rough, it came in fewer designs and colors than manufactured cloth, and it was heavy and hot to wear. Gandhi's response to these complaints reflected his ethos of self-sacrifice. "The incentive to use Khaddar must be national for the middle-class people, and they are expected to put themselves to inconvenience in order to popularize it," he insisted. "If Khaddar is dear, freedom is dearer still."[17] One writer complained that in his own village, "The rich people do not like to wear this cloth as it does not satisfy their tastes, while the poor cannot afford to wear it considering its price, washing charges, and other expenses." Gandhi replied, "If we desire *swaraj* we must be prepared to work and give up luxurious tastes at least for the time-being. India, if it cannot part with the soft and cheap calico in favor of rough khadi, will certainly not get *swaraj*."[18]

Swadeshi was a nationalist symbol, a symbol of self-sufficiency, and also central to a campaign for spiritual and moral uplift, framed in universalist terms. And yet, the swadeshi movement struggled against several of the same obstacles that plagued other attempts at deglobalization. Specifically, it asked people to pay more and work harder for the sake of the greater good.

Even among leaders of India's anti-colonial movement, there was no clear consensus about the path toward economic independence. Future prime minister Jawaharlal Nehru believed that there was no way around participation in the global economy—the question was rather on what terms India would participate. In a 1928 speech he proclaimed, "The world has become internationalized; production is international, markets are international and transport is international, only men's ideas continue to be governed by a dogma which has no real meaning today. No nation is really independent, they are all interdependent." India could not afford to isolate itself from the world, nor could it forego industrialization.[19]

Nehru advocated greater industrialization for India alongside the development of village industries as a strategy to alleviate rural poverty. He insisted that there was no real conflict between encouraging the development of village industries and large-scale industrialization. He praised Gandhi's focus on khadi for forcing India "to grasp the fundamental fact that the true test of progress in India did not lie in the creation of a number of millionaires or prosperous lawyers and the like, or in the setting up of councils and assemblies, but in the change in the status and conditions of the life of the peasant." At the same time, Nehru insisted that India had no choice but to industrialize. "An attempt to build up a country's economy largely on the basis of cottage and small-scale industries is doomed to failure. It will not solve the basic problems of the country or maintain freedom, nor will it fit in with the world framework, except as a colonial appendage."[20] Where the two men agreed was that their efforts had universalist and globalist ends. Only an arrogant man would declare himself entirely self-sufficient, Gandhi insisted. The same went for nations. "Through realization of freedom of India I hope to realize and carry on the mission of the brotherhood of man. . . . The conception of my patriotism is nothing if it is not always, in every case without exception, consistent with the broadest good of humanity at large."[21]

INDIA'S BID for national self-determination echoed around the world, and particularly in other states striving to break free from imperial or postimperial economic relationships. In 1920, for example, nationalist and future Irish president Eamon de Valera appealed to Irish Americans to support the Indian cause. He linked India's fate directly to the bid for Irish independence. "We of Irish blood ought to have no difficulty in seeing through the pretenses of the British government when it is unwilling to do right. We ought to have no difficulty in understanding the troubles of the people of India, and they, in their turn, should have no difficulty in understanding those of the people of Ireland," he reasoned. In particular, he sought to expose the hypocrisy behind British claims to be agents of a "civilizing mission" in India. "The people of India, we are told by the British apologists, are backward and ignorant, lazy and unable to rule themselves. They have made exactly the same pretense about Ireland at other times. The Indians are 'mere' Asiatics, we are told. We were the 'mere' Irish."[22]

Arthur Griffith, the founder of Sinn Féin ("Ourselves alone"), was inspired by economist Friedrich List to promote the ideal of greater autarky for Ireland well before the First World War. The party's goal at that time was to end economic dependence on Britain and further develop native Irish industries through protectionist measures. In the 1920s, however, the newly independent state took a more pragmatic stance, and Britain continued to be Ireland's primary economic partner. In 1929, Britain received 92 percent of Irish exports, and 78 percent of all imported goods to Ireland came from Britain.[23]

In 1925, de Valera founded the Fianna Fáil party, which took a more absolutist stance toward Irish economic independence. The party entered parliament in 1927 and soon articulated a call for greater economic self-sufficiency in the production of food, clothing, and shelter. "I have said repeatedly that our guiding principle will be to make Ireland as self-contained and as self-supporting as possible," de Valera emphasized in a speech in Dublin. "That is the only basis on which we can prosper materially. It is the only basis on which we can build up a spirited, self-reliant people."[24]

In parliament in 1928, de Valera further outlined some of the main principles of his economic policy, beginning with a critique of emigration, through which Ireland was losing "the producing part of the population—the young people, the able-bodied people." Ireland was spending more than £4 million a year on education "for the benefit of foreign countries." In order to keep these young people at home, they needed jobs, which they would find only through the protection of native industries. But de Valera, like Gandhi, was honest with his constituents: the cost of self-sufficiency in the long run would be self-sacrifice in the short run. He framed it as a choice between being the debased servant of a lord in a large mansion or a dignified self-employed man living in his own simple cottage. If the servant wanted freedom, he had to be willing to give up the luxurious furnishings and fine foods in the lord's mansion. "He had to forgo these in order to get the liberty of living his life in his own way in simpler surroundings. If a man makes up his mind to go out into a cottage, he must remember that he cannot have in the cottage the luxuries around him which he had when he was bearing the kicks of the master."[25]

Here too, the emphasis was not so much on political anti-globalism or anti-internationalism as on the development of self-sufficient industries and agriculture. But the rhetoric and strategies for inculcating self-sufficiency were familiar. "If we cannot have silk shirts, let us have homespun," de Valera urged Irish nationalists.[26] The week before Saint Patrick's Day was designated "Irish week," an initiative sponsored by the Gaelic League's Industrial Development Commission. Across Ireland, Irish products were supposed to be proudly displayed by local shopkeepers.

As usual, women were expected to do the spinning and the purchasing. "Mothers! Wake up and put your baby in an Irish pram with which we can supply you at a price to support every pocket!" one firm advertised. Another focused on the value of local foods. "We are no advocate of a narrow self-sufficient plan for any nation. BUT we do advocate the wisdom of growing our own food as far as we can, for we realize the obvious fact that home-grown food is best for everybody. For us in the northerly temperate zone there is no food so suitable, so valuable, as the home-grown WAFER OATS."[27]

IRISH WOMEN were often leaders in the effort to nationalize the economy. In 1938, for example, Bridget Loftus of Dublin, a member of de Valera's Fianna Fáil party, sought to be nominated as a member of the Irish Senate, citing her business activities in support of Irish industry. "At all times a firm adherent of the policy in support of Irish industry I can authoritatively claim the rare privilege of being the first and still the only manufacturer of brown bread made exclusively from Irish grown wheat."[28]

Food was at the heart of the Irish campaign for self-sufficiency. The issue was not so much the need to increase production in what was already a predominately agricultural country, but the question of who would enjoy the cream of the crop. A broadsheet in support of de Valera's protectionist policies in the 1930s imagined the following dialogue between a mother and her son:

> PADRAIG: "What's for supper, mother?"
> BEAN A TIGHE: "Paper, Padraig: paper. English ten-shilling notes. We have a box full of them, but there's no other food."
> PADRAIG: "But where are the potatoes I grew?"
> BEAN A TIGHE: "Oh your father sold them to that English firm because the price was good, and he was afraid it might fall."

After establishing that the oats, hens, and pigs had also been sold off, Padraig resigns himself to eating paper and asks if he can have a glass of milk to wash it down.

> BEAN A TIGHE: "You can, today; but tomorrow he's going to sell the cow, because he's afraid the English may prohibit the export of cows and the price may fall. He's always looking to what the English will do before he decides what he will do to help himself."
> PADRAIG: "God help him! I don't believe the men of '98 sold their good stuff cheap to the enemy and fed their families on foreign trash."

The moral was that Irish farmers should create cooperative farms and industries, which "would not be making huge profits for foreign capitalists at the expense of Irish workers."[29]

After the Fianna Fáil party took power in 1932, Ireland raised tariffs until in 1937 they were the fourth highest in the world. De Valera launched an economic war with Britain, refusing to pay land annuities that were owed to the British government. In retaliation, Britain imposed a 20 percent tariff on Irish agricultural imports, and Ireland, in turn, set the same duties on British industrial exports.[30]

This campaign for national self-sufficiency was not only supposed to help Ireland consolidate its independence from Britain but also to sustain the preservation of Catholic, rural values. De Valera's brand of socially conservative, Catholic nationalism was at the time (and still is) often seen as anti-modern or backward looking, particularly with respect to family policy. For example, the regime banned the advertisement and importation of all forms of birth control in 1935.[31] But with respect to ideals of rural self-sufficiency, Ireland was in the European mainstream. De Valera served as leader of the Fianna Fáil party for thirty-three years and was the state's effective leader from 1932 until 1948. Speculating on his success, Keith Hutchinson wrote in *The Nation* in 1942 that de Valera's pursuit of economic self-sufficiency had "brought Ireland few, if any, material gains on balance, and at times Mr. de Valera has appeared to be cutting off his country's nose to spite the faces of his enemies. Yet it must be admitted that from his own point of view and from that of the majority of people whom he leads he has had a large measure of success. For his primary aim has not been prosperity but freedom, and he has been encouraged rather than deterred by the realization that poverty is often the reward of virtue."[32]

WHILE THE Indians were burning foreign cloth and the Irish were boycotting British sweets and beer, another anti-global movement was gaining steam in the British Empire. From the mid-nineteenth century until the First World War, "free trade" had been a civic religion in Britain. As historian Frank Trentmann has shown, the ideal of free trade was grounded not simply in the theories of economists or the interests of businesses but in a popular culture that linked free trade to fair prices and freedom from hunger. But this consensus around free trade gradually eroded during and after the First World War. In political terms, it was the Conservative Party, and Joseph Chamberlain's tariff reform movement, that led the charge, linking protectionism to the interests of the empire.[33] In the place of global free trade, Chamberlain and his followers promoted a policy of "Empire Free Trade," or "Imperial Preference," which would encourage trade within the empire but erect barriers against products from outside. The most important products competing with imperial goods at the time were foodstuffs. Wheat, meat, and produce from Canada and Australia competed with imports from the United States, Russia, and South America. But the policy of Imperial Preference was politically risky. It not only faced opposition from within the government but also threatened the well-entrenched ideal (and expectation) of cheap food for British workers. Even when the Conservative Party reigned from 1924 to 1929, it did not enact any tariffs, instead focusing on persuasion through organs such as the Empire Marketing Board.[34]

The Empire Marketing Board, founded in 1926, famously promoted the cause of "Empire shopping" with the most sophisticated forms of modern propaganda and advertising available, including posters and cutting-edge documentary films that dramatized the production of Canadian timber and insisted on the superiority of Indian tea.[35] In England, Canada, Australia, New Zealand, and South Africa, women were urged to "buy Empire products," to shop at "Empire stores," and to cook "Empire foods" as a means of strengthening the British Empire.

In Birmingham, the British Women's Patriotic League encouraged shopkeepers to transform their storefronts into miniature imperial exhibitions. These "non-political" events would "stimulate pride in the Empire and emphasize the superiority of British goods," organizers explained.[36] To be clear, however, when the Women's Patriotic League demanded that consumers "Buy British," they did not mean that the ladies of Birmingham should adorn themselves in khadi. The Empire shopping campaign was intended above all to support white farmers in the Dominions.

The swadeshi movement and Empire Free Trade had opposing political aims with respect to empire. In India, the boycott of foreign cloth was to end imperial forms of economic dependence and domination. In Britain, Empire shopping was intended to reinforce these same imperial relationships, to make the empire as a whole more self-sufficient. As one advertisement for Empire Shopping Week put it, the campaign was to "direct attention to the fact that most all human needs can be met by the resources of Britain and her dependencies" and to encourage British citizens to "think British" before "buying foreign."[37] But Empire Free Trade and the swadeshi movement were actually flip sides of the same coin. The two movements shared the goal of greater self-sufficiency for the state. The dispute concerned that state's geographic boundaries. For advocates of Empire shopping, it was the British Empire in its entirety that needed to achieve greater self-sufficiency. Anti-colonial nationalists, by contrast, aspired to economic self-containment for an independent, sovereign India.

The ideal of Empire Free Trade also reflected the ways in which empires themselves transformed during and after the First World War. In the nineteenth century, states generally pursued empires as a way to extend their global political and economic influence and prestige. Of course, they wanted to acquire cheap raw materials and expand their export markets, but the ultimate goal was to enhance global power and influence. Empires competed with one another, but imperial states also traded extensively with other imperial states. The age of imperial expansion in the nineteenth century was simultaneously an age of accelerating globalization.

But during and after the First World War, while the naval blockade remained in effect, it was not lost on hungry Central Europeans that England did not suffer from the shortages that had crippled their own bodies and morale. Food appeared on the tables of British citizens in the metropole at the expense of colonial subjects, as massive supplies of rice, wheat, and legumes grown in India were diverted to London. While prices skyrocketed and people starved in Calcutta, there was no rationing in Britain until 1918.[38] To prevent starvation and defeat in the next war, many Europeans concluded, an empire was essential. Meanwhile, Indian nationalists and other anti-colonial nationalists reached the opposite conclusion. In light of wartime and postwar food shortages, it was more urgent than ever to break free of a system that allowed Indians to starve even as they were conscripted for military service and disproportionately died for the empire.[39]

In Britain, the Empire Marketing Board worked to replace the consensus surrounding free trade with a racialized, imperialist moral economy in support of "Buying British."[40] This fact was not lost on Indian critics of Empire Free Trade. In one of critique of Imperial Preference, Indian nationalist D. R. Gadgil observed that "in the first instance, the

Empire Marketing Board
propaganda poster, 1926–1934.

strong sentiment in its favor is based primarily on racial and cultural affinity. Such a sentiment on the part of the English-speaking Dominions and Great Britain can very well be appreciated. It is obvious, however, that the sentimental support to Imperial Preference is, to say the least, weak in India and will ever continue to be so."[41]

The propaganda of the Empire Marketing Board circulated far and wide. In 1930, the board distributed 2 million leaflets and organized sixty-six Empire shopping weeks as well as exhibitions, cooking demonstrations, and film showings.[42] The following year, a "Buy British" campaign began with a speech from the prince of Wales and was advertised with an enormous electric sign on Trafalgar Square. "Within a few days the Board's Message 'Buy British, from the Empire at Home and Overseas' was a familiar phrase in every quarter of the Kingdom, from the Scillies to the Shetlands," boasted the board. Empire shops were also created in Birmingham, Blackpool, and Liverpool.[43]

Whether these campaigns significantly altered consumer behavior is another question, however. Before the General Tariff went into effect, empire products were still often more expensive than other foreign products, and shopkeepers surveyed by the Empire Marketing Board reported that few customers could afford (or desired) to pay a higher price for empire goods. Meanwhile, in the Dominions, local producers and governments were often more interested in persuading customers to buy Canadian or Australian products than imperial goods. As in India and Ireland, they did not want to be reduced to a source of raw materials for England, but wanted to encourage local industry and manufacturing (as well as agriculture) in the interests of their own national self-sufficiency.[44]

As long as free trade remained a sacrosanct policy, persuasion was the only tool readily available to anti-global imperialists. But the Great Depression changed the United Kingdom's course. To the world's great shock, England abandoned the gold standard on September 19, 1931. Then in February 1932, the government enacted a General Tariff. The 1932 Ottawa Agreement transformed "Imperial Preference" into government policy. For British Conservative member of Parliament Leo Amery, it was the end of an era. "The reign of Free Trade was over . . . and the principle which had dominated our national policy since the Repeal of the Corn Laws was now to be abandoned; abandoned, we all knew, irrevocably."[45]

FOURTEEN

The Air Is Our Ocean

ZLÍN, 1931

IN THE WINTER of 1931, Indian "self-sufficiency" found an unexpected champion in a Czech shoe tycoon. That December, the "King of Shoes" took off on what the *New York Times* called a spectacular "aerial raid on the Depression." Piloting his own three-motor airplane, Tomáš Bat'a departed from his hometown of Zlín, Czechoslovakia, accompanied by two pilots, several sales managers, a telegraph operator, and a cargo of shoes. He flew more than 20,000 miles across Europe, the Middle East, and Asia, destined for Calcutta.[1] Bat'a proclaimed that his mission was to bring "cheap shoes" to the unshod people of India. In an interview he explained, "In India there are 350,000,000 people, but only around 10,000,000 of them have the possibility to wear shoes. 340,000,000 people go barefoot. It's true that they don't have snow like we do, but they do have an even worse enemy of human feet, namely the hot sun, which heats the stones in the summer months so much that you could bake bread on them. It is a greater torment for a person to walk on these hot stones with bare feet than it is to walk barefoot on ice."[2]

Along the flight path, Bat'a's plane made pit stops in Tunis, Cairo, Damascus, Jerusalem, Tel Aviv, Baghdad, Tehran, Bangkok, and Singapore. On each layover, he refueled and planned for his shoe empire's expansion. In 1930, there were seven Bat'a shoe stores in Egypt; by 1939 there were thirty. In Indonesia, thirty-one new stores opened in 1932 alone. Iraq had ten new stores by 1939, and in Palestine, twelve new stores opened in 1932. Bat'a shoe factories meanwhile sprung up in Beirut (1933), Baghdad (1934), Alexandria (1938), and Jakarta (1938). By the end of the 1930s, there were Bat'a shoe stores in fifty-six countries around the world.

Tomáš Bat'a saw India as the biggest prize, however, and that is where he made the biggest investment. During his visit there he purchased a former oil refinery in Konnagar, near Calcutta, and transformed it into a shoe factory. It was followed quickly by a second factory and a company town modeled after the town of Zlín. The town was named Bat'anagar for Bat'a. By 1937, Bat'a's Indian factories employed 2,800 people (including 70 Czechs) and produced more than 8 million pairs of shoes per year, sold in the 668 Bat'a stores spread throughout India.[3]

The King of Shoes did not live to see the full extent of his kingdom's global expansion, however. In July 1932, only six months after his return from India, Bat'a insisted on taking off for Switzerland in foggy conditions. His plane crashed into one of his own factory chimneys, killing him and his pilot. The globalization of his company continued under the stewardship of his successors, his half-brother, Jan Bat'a, and his young son, Thomas Bat'a. In the 1930s, the Bat'a firm built new factories in Yugoslavia, Germany, Poland, Switzerland, France, the United Kingdom, Iraq, the Netherlands, Lebanon, Indonesia, Egypt, Canada, and the United States.[4]

All around him, states reeling from the effects of the Great Depression responded by seeking greater self-sufficiency and erecting tariff walls. Bat'a flew over these walls. In his speeches and public pronouncements, Tomáš Bat'a also defied the nationalist gravity of the moment. After his first trip to India in 1925, he returned home and defended the importance of international trade for the progress of humankind. "Just as any industrial enterprise cannot exist without suppliers and customers, not a single State, not even a continent, on this planet can call itself self-sufficient," he insisted. "Britons, Americans, French, Dutch and all progressive nations today know this great law of exchange—that is the secret of their progress." With the disappearance of international trade, Bat'a warned, "the whole of mankind will vanish" because trade was "the basis that enables mankind to live, to grow, and to prosper."[5]

Tomáš Bat'a was an unapologetic globalist in an era of anti-globalism. He fashioned himself as a maverick who could see no national boundaries from his high perch in the clouds. After his 1931 flight around the world, Bat'a claimed that aviation itself had transformed him into an internationalist. "Aviation is well suited to cure men of exaggerated nationalist feelings and the petty hatred that results from it that we confront these days," he explained. Planes were often forced to make emergency landings, wherever they happened to be. "Far from the borders of the homeland, one is dependent on the help of foreign people." Bat'a planned to pay these good samaritans back in shoes.[6]

But of course, there was more to the story of Bat'a's globalization than the grand vision of a maverick industrialist. As historian Zachary Doleshal has shown, Bat'a's globalization was a largely rational response to deglobalization. In the face of rising economic nationalism and tariffs in the 1930s, Bat'a began to produce his shoes abroad rather than exporting them from Czechoslovakia.[7] The case of Bat'a demonstrates that interwar policies intended to control and restrict global trade and mobility did not simply shut globalization down. Rather, these policies stimulated the expansion of new forms of global interconnection, including the rise of multinational firms and the export of technology and factories, while constraining others, such as the mobility of people and finished goods.

The man crowned the King of Shoes did not begin life a prince. Born in the small town of Zlín in the Austrian Empire, Bat'a's family had been making shoes for seven generations. In 1894, when Tomáš was eighteen, he took over the family business with two of his siblings and established a shoemaking workshop. They enjoyed their first big success in 1897 with the production of an inexpensive canvas shoe that was so popular it became known as the *batovka*. In 1904, Tomáš spent six months in the United States. He came home inspired, with a selective and idealized view of American manufacturing. In particular he was impressed by the strict moral codes, the temperance movement, and the gendered division of labor that governed the shoe factories of Lynn, Massachusetts. He was also enamored by the rationalization of American production. Determined to modernize, he built a new three-story factory modeled after those he had seen in the United States.[8]

The company grew rapidly, exporting its shoes to Germany beginning in 1913 and opening a first store abroad in Belgrade in 1919. Business got another major boost when Bat'a began to produce boots for the Habsburg army during the First World War. Its workforce grew from 500 at the outset of the war to 6,000 employees by 1918. As soon as the war ended, Tomáš traveled again to the United States. This time he paid a visit to his hero Henry Ford as well as the American shoe manufacturer Endicott-Johnson. During that trip he laid the groundwork for his first factory abroad, in Massachusetts (it was sold only a few years later), and began creating sister companies in Europe.[9]

The new state of Czechoslovakia was in an enviable position economically compared to other Habsburg successor states. It had inherited 40 percent of the GDP and two-thirds of the industrial capacity of the former Habsburg Empire and was one of the fifteen strongest economies in the world. It had almost 100 percent literacy. It was also the darling of the Allies, as it was seen as the most "Western" and "modern" of the new Eastern European states. Czechoslovakia—and with it Bat'a— was well situated to advance its global economic and political standing.

Still, there were significant obstacles to overcome in the years immediately after the war. The fact that Czechoslovakia had such a highly developed industrial economy and a relatively small population meant that it was dependent on exports. Bat'a's capacity to make shoes had increased tremendously during the war years, as the firm supplied the army of a large empire. Factories in Zlín could produce up to 45,000 shoes a day. But after 1918, the firm could expect to sell only 50,000 shoes a week to its shrunken domestic base of customers in Czechoslovakia. This only increased the pressure to increase sales abroad.[10]

Nationalist activists also lamented that Czechoslovakia found itself "situated at the very center of Europe without an outlet to the sea" and "surrounded on three sides by countries that are still enemy countries, namely Germany and German Austria." Equally lamentable, according to the Bohemian National Alliance of America, was the new Prohibition law in the United States, which meant that there would be "no more Pilsen beer for the thirsty throats of the epicures of America." Before the war, beer and hops had been the two most significant exports to the United States from Bohemia.[11]

By 1922, Bat'a's company had lost three-quarters of its prewar export business, a problem exacerbated by the Czech crown's rising value. Tomáš Bat'a responded to this crisis with bold measures. He cut his workforce and the price of his shoes in half, decreased salaries and wages by 40 percent, and introduced profit sharing for the workers.[12] The strategy succeeded, and by 1925, Bat'a was expanding again. By 1928, the company had more than 13,000 employees.

Tomáš Bat'a was soon dubbed the "Henry Ford of Europe." This was not only because he was "the leader in the industrial Americanization of Europe" and admired Ford's production process. He also shared Ford's paternalist approach to labor, especially the development of company towns and corporate welfare.[13] What is striking about Bat'a's success, however, is the extent to which the culture of this globalizing firm—like that of the Ford Motor Company—resembled the culture of an antiglobal settlement.

During the 1920s and 1930s, Zlín expanded into a massive company town, infamous for its control over its workers' everyday lives. In 1923, Tomáš Bat'a was elected mayor. The company housed three-quarters of its employees, and it soon boasted its own newspaper, kindergarten, library, cinema, orchestra, sports clubs, and zoo, along with social and health departments and a "psycho-technical laboratory" charged with classifying, recruiting, and surveilling workers. Trade unions were banned (Bat'a described his goal as transforming workers into capitalists), but working conditions were considered good by European standards. The goal of this system was to create "Bat'amen," employees whose highest loyalties were to the company itself.

The ideal Bat'aman was, on the one hand, a globalist: indifferent to nationalism, willing to relocate to another part of the world, fluent in two to three languages. The company cultivated these attributes in Bat'a training programs and rewarded them with promotions and opportunities abroad. But the Bat'a *lifestyle* was entirely compatible with the ideals of anti-global settlement activists, down to the architecture of the housing, the role of women, and anxiety about uncontrolled mobility—especially that of so-called vagrants and Roma, who were chased out of town. Locally, the company relied on the mass migration of Moravian peasant youth from rural farms to the factory. But once these migrants arrived within the city limits, their lives and mobility were strictly controlled. Single men and women lived in company dormitories under the close watch of company supervisors, who recorded their progress toward achieving the Bat'a ideal as well as their flaws and transgressions. Married employees with children were rewarded with Bat'a townhomes, where the scrutiny was no less intense.

There was an extremely strict gendered division of labor in the Bat'a factories. Women were employed primarily as stitchers and fired if they got pregnant or married. Their only route out of closely guarded dormitories and into highly sought townhomes was through marriage to another Bat'a employee. For men within the company, meanwhile, promotion was contingent on adherence to strict norms of masculinity, including marriage, children, and a "clean-cut" appearance. The company also took a keen interest in the sex lives of employees and townspeople, using its control of the local police force to punish or expel women whose sexual morality was deemed questionable.[14]

The Bat'a company behaved like an autarkic state in other ways as well. It became more vertically integrated during the 1920s and 1930s, with the creation of new departments for advertising, research, rubber processing, textile production, leather processing, aviation, civil engineering, forestry, agriculture, rail, and transport.[15] In other words, like many states in the 1930s, the Bat'a company aspired to achieve self-sufficiency by controlling every aspect of its supply chain, its labor force, and the production and distribution of its products. Bat'a was to become a world unto itself.

The strategy was remarkably successful. Bat'a's growth during the mid to late 1920s was not entirely surprising—this was the interlude during which most of Europe enjoyed a brief respite from turmoil, with greater political stability and economic growth everywhere. Far more remarkable, however, was the fact that Bat'a continued to expand as the global economy collapsed in the 1930s. Between 1929 and 1938, the number of employees increased sixfold including 23,000 employees abroad. The firm's exports increased commensurably.[16]

The Great Depression was not without setbacks for the Bat'a company. At the time of Tomáš Bat'a's death, the firm was suffering under the impact of increasing tariffs and prohibitions on imports. Several factories were idle, and there were reportedly warehouses filled with an estimated 25,000,000 pairs of unsellable shoes.[17] The company fired more than 5,000 workers in 1932 alone and introduced a five-day workweek—bad news for a majority of workers who were paid by the piece. Resistance by workers to these measures only intensified Bat'a's culture of surveillance and control.[18]

Over time, however, global expansion offered new opportunities to workers at home. By the mid-1930s, the Bat'a company had recovered, and it even created 11,000 new jobs in Czechoslovakia between 1935 and 1937. This reflects a key difference between Bat'a's globalization and the postindustrial globalization of the late twentieth and twenty-first centuries. Bat'a did not shift to overseas production in order to find the cheapest sources of labor and then ship its shoes back to Europe (leaving Czech workers without their jobs). Rather, its factories abroad generally produced shoes for regional markets abroad. Factories in India did not produce cheap shoes for Czechs; they produced cheap shoes for Indians, while factories in Zlín produced shoes for Czechs and other Europeans.

In other words, the Bat'a company successfully countered economic nationalism and anti-globalism in the 1930s by globalizing differently. The airplane was more than just a symbol of this strategy. For a landlocked country, Tomáš Bat'a insisted, it was an advantage conferred by necessity. He believed that the airplane, rather than the steamship, represented the future of global trade. "It is our ocean!" he cried, speaking of the air. "We have no other. We must make use of the one we have."[19]

BAT'A'S GLOBALIZATION was not only a product of economic and technological innovation. In the context of intense economic nationalism, this also required a clever marketing strategy: advertising in each market that the firm employed local labor and used local materials. Bat'a thus responded to the backlash against globalization by attempting to convince consumers that Czechoslovak shoes were actually "local" products.[20]

The Bat'a company self-consciously represented itself as "local" everywhere it went. Executive Hugo Vavrecka explained that the company was recruiting men from around the world and training them in Zlín because it recognized how important it was to combat the image of the "foreign" firm: "We have young men in our factory from Yugoslavia, Bulgaria, Poland, France, England, Egypt, India, etc., to train them ... because everywhere there is a strong reaction against foreigners. It pays to know the details of your customers, to be able to know their local dialects, their various religious habits, especially in Egypt and India."[21] In Switzerland, where the company had a factory in Moehlin, Bat'a turned May Day into a celebration of Swiss nationalism, decorating the entire factory with Swiss flags and banners that proclaimed, "The Swiss galosh—our invention!" In Poland, the company newspaper emphasized that Czech workers intermarried with local Poles and that their children spoke perfect Polish.[22]

Bat'a was the most famous and successful firm in interwar Czechoslovakia to globalize, but other firms (and indeed the government) also looked outward. For example, the Pilsen-based weapon manufacturer Škoda Works shipped weapons to allies in Eastern Europe such as Yugoslavia and Romania, trading weapons for raw materials such as tobacco, copper, zinc, and lead. Škoda also sold its weapons worldwide, particularly in China, where the company invested heavily between the wars. In the 1930s, the firm even got into the sugar business in China, setting up sugar refineries in the province of Guangdong. This did not mean that the company got out of the arms business. As of 1935, Czechoslovakia was the world's largest weapons exporter, and in 1938, more than half of the company's business was in exports.[23]

There was still plenty of economic nationalism in Czechoslovakia. As in Austria, Germany, and Italy, this included efforts to increase national self-sufficiency in food supplies through internal colonization.

Intensified agricultural production was to balance out an economy that was highly concentrated in industry and exports. A massive land-reform project sought to redistribute up to one-quarter of the state's total land to small farmers, including Czech legionnaires and migrants returning to Czechoslovakia from Austria, Germany, the United States, the Soviet Union, and other parts of the world. The land was generally seized or purchased from large German and Hungarian landowners and given to Czechs or Slovaks. In particular, Czechoslovak authorities were keen to "colonize" the borderlands of Czechoslovakia, regions with large minority populations in Slovakia, the Sudeten region of Bohemia, and Subcarpathian Ruthenia. In 1920, Czechoslovak government officials even specified that return migrants should be "used as much as possible in their homeland as colonizing material, in particular to reinforce security in disloyal districts of the Republic."[24]

Yet popular Czech economic nationalism tended to target domestic minorities, especially German speakers, Hungarians, and Jews, more than foreign trade (given the state's powerful export industries). The Czechoslovak government continued to look outward more than other Habsburg successor states. Czech leaders even mounted a successful international public relations campaign to promote the image of Czechoslovakia abroad as the most Western, democratic, and modern country of the Habsburg successor states—and as a desirable business partner.[25]

Czechoslovakia was therefore the only Habsburg successor state with a global consular presence, opening fifty-three new consulates by 1938, from Latin America to the Middle East and Africa. Consuls were active partners in the efforts of firms such as Bat'a to set up shops and factories abroad, providing intelligence and information on markets and local conditions.[26] In 1929, the government even established an Oriental Institute in order to promote more economic exchange with Asia. The rationale was the possibility of opening future markets, one economist explained. "Against the West, the Orient is economically in its infancy . . . the economic possibilities here are, practically speaking, almost unlimited."[27] Tomáš Bat'a clearly agreed.

Czechoslovak leaders were also able to capitalize on their own recent "liberation" from imperial rule to expand the state's access to global markets. Czechoslovak consul Jozef Lusk gave a speech at the groundbreaking ceremony for the first Bat'a's factory in India in which he insisted that Bat'a and Czechoslovakia (in contrast to the British) had only peaceful intentions in India. "In founding foreign factories we do not want to conquer, we do not do politics, we just want to work and offer cooperation to all people of good will."[28] By producing shoes in India, hiring Indian labor, and using Indian raw materials, Bat'a could represent itself as a company that would build, rather than undermine, Indian self-sufficiency. Bat'a could be swadeshi.

SHOES AND cars provide very different modes of transport. But in terms of globalization, Ford may have been the American Bat'a. Both industrialists framed their firms' global expansion as a humanitarian mission to bring development and modernization to the world: to decrease, rather than increase, global inequality. Both appropriated populist and nationalist slogans. Both globalized while simultaneously claiming to promote individual and national self-sufficiency.

Ford's global expansion began before the First World War but accelerated in the 1920s as the auto company expanded its plants and operations from Detroit to locations in South America, Asia, South Africa, Australia, and across Europe.[29] Ford also vertically integrated production by sourcing its own raw materials, culminating in a doomed project to create two giant rubber plantations and company towns in the Brazilian Amazon. Fordlandia featured American homes, hospitals, roads, and even a golf course but failed miserably to produce rubber for a profit. It was sold to the Brazilian government at a loss of more than $7 million in 1945.[30]

At the same time that his firm manufactured and sold cars, trucks, and tractors abroad, Henry Ford loudly condemned "foreign exploiters" and insisted that he was facilitating the development and self-sufficiency of local or national automobile industries. "We ought to wish for every nation as large a degree of self-support as possible. Instead of wishing to keep them dependent on us for what we manufacture, we should wish them to learn to manufacture themselves and build up a solidly founded civilization," he argued.[31]

Until the late 1920s, foreign branches of Ford were tightly controlled by Detroit. By 1928, however, European governments were increasingly eager to nurture their own domestic automobile industries. In response, the company promised to promote greater national ownership and sovereignty for its foreign branches. Ford of America would hold 60 percent of the stock of a new English company called Ford of England, which in turn owned 60 percent of the stock of each national branch in Europe. Each firm was ordered to employ more local managers, source parts locally, and hire local workers. Ford hoped that this would counter the widespread feeling that Ford was an unwelcome foreign competitor.[32]

With the onset of the Great Depression, Ford, like Bat'a, leaned further into globalization by "nationalizing" its branches abroad. In 1929, the Ford Motor Company even signed a joint-venture agreement with the Soviet Union to assist in the construction of automobile plants in Russia that would produce Ford cars and trucks. Up to fifty Russians per year were to come to Detroit to study "methods and practices of manufacture and assembly," while Ford agreed to send its experts to Russia. In an interview with *Nation's Business*, Henry Ford defended his activities in Russia at a time of intense anti-Communism in the United States (and in spite of his own anti-Communism) in terms of an inevitable drive toward national self-sufficiency abroad. "I believe it is my duty to help any people who want to go back to work and become self-supporting," he explained. Ford represented himself as an enemy of the global division of labor, of imperialist economic practices everywhere. "This system of keeping certain nations dependent on others economically must disappear. . . . When Russia and China and India and South America come into consuming power, what are you going to do? . . . Surely you don't visualize Britain and America as nothing but vast factories to supply the world! A moment's thought will make clear why the future must see nation after nation taking over its own work of supply. And we ought to be glad to help the work along."[33]

And if European governments were willing to partner with Ford, it was largely because they agreed. They believed, as Stefan Link argues, that importing Ford's technology would enable them to stop importing its cars. This strategy was facilitated by Ford's own populist-inflected "open-source" policies. The company made no real effort to keep its methods or technologies secret, and actually welcomed streams of foreign visitors and trainees into its factories in the 1920s and 1930s.[34]

Things became more challenging for Ford during the 1930s, when states further tightened their grip on foreign enterprises and foreign exchange. In France, the government pressured Ford to merge with a domestic company, Mathis. In Italy, Ford tried and failed to negotiate mergers with Isotta Fraschini and Fiat and was ultimately forced to abandon plans to construct a new plant altogether. Benito Mussolini informed Ford officials that "it was not the desire of the Italian Government to permit any big volume of imported automobiles, but rather to foster a 100 per cent Italian manufacture thereof."[35] Revolutions in Latin and South America during the 1930s were also bad for Ford's global business. Plans for new assembly plants in Brazil and Argentina were canceled. In Chile, Peru, and Uruguay, the company virtually ceased operations because of nationalist economic policies in those countries. Ford was run out of Japan by nationalists. Already by 1933, only two of fourteen European and North African branches of Ford had managers from the United States. All of the factories employed local labor and used more local parts and materials to build their cars.[36]

Like Bat'a and Ford, other US firms also expanded operations abroad in response to high tariffs. American companies opened seventy-one new foreign factories in 1930, ninety-two in 1931, and ninety-four in 1932. Firestone globalized with new tire plants in South Africa, Brazil, and India in the 1930s, while Goodyear expanded to Java and Brazil. IBM began manufacturing in Japan in 1937.[37] GM likewise responded to high tariffs in the 1930s by establishing manufacturing plants in Western Europe, increasing national ownership, using more local parts and supplies, and merging with local firms.

In Germany, Ford agreed to the Nazi regime's demands to manufacture cars for domestic sale using only German parts and refitted truck designs to serve the military's needs. The Nazi government strictly controlled exports and prevented the repatriation of profits through controls on foreign exchange. This forced Ford and other foreign companies to reinvest their profits in Germany. It turned out to be a good deal for Ford: sales went up from about 10,000 vehicles in 1934 to more than 36,000 in 1938. Profits in the same period increased from $2,000 to $487,000.[38] Many American firms that did not want to cut their losses in Germany made the same choice to cooperate with the Nazi regime. American direct investment in Germany actually increased almost 50 percent between 1929 and 1940, because firms could not repatriate profits and instead ploughed them back into their plants and facilities there.[39]

Czechoslovakia meanwhile became a small state with a big footprint. A 1937 article in the *New York Times* noted that Zlín had the largest shoe factory in the world. That raised alarm bells everywhere shoes were made, including the United States. The firm's costs were so low and factories so mechanized, the article insisted, that Bat'a could easily undersell American manufacturers in spite of a 20 percent tariff on imports.[40] Alongside the article, the *Times* reprinted a cartoon from the *Massachusetts Fall River Herald* that featured a map of Czechoslovakia as a giant boot stomping on the Massachusetts shoe industry.

IN SPITE of the firm's efforts to "go local," Bat'a faced protests everywhere it made or sold shoes. Shoe manufacturers both in the United States and in Germany denounced the company for taking advantage of non-unionized labor costs in Zlín to undersell local producers. A representative of the German shoemakers association claimed, "There are conditions in Zlín that are unthinkable in the civilized world. Unions of any kind are hindered from the outset. . . . Never once has an independent organization of workers with influence been able to come into existence."[41] Bat'a was also targeted directly by the Nazi "Economic Intelligence Service," which in 1931 published a pamphlet that aimed to expose Bat'a for falsely labeling its shoes "German products." The pamphlet warned customers that only a small portion of Bat'a shoes were actually made in Germany and elaborated that "not only the product, but also the production methods cannot be designated 'German.'" Nazi newspapers also falsely denounced Bat'a as a "Jewish" firm, with headlines condemning "The Shoe Jew Bat'a in Dresden."[42]

Boycotts and protests, sometimes violent, accompanied the opening of new Bat'a stores and factories in Hungary, Bulgaria, Yugoslavia, and the Netherlands. In Poznan, Poland, rumors also circulated that Bat'a was a "Jewish firm." The Czechoslovak consul in Poland advised that Bat'a counter these rumors by inviting a local priest to bless the store on opening day. The firm accepted the suggestion. The consul reported that the priest's blessing had "left a very good impression on the large number of gathered citizens."[43]

In Damascus in 1932, the opening of a new Bat'a store provoked a boycott and a violent protest, in which both employees and customers were assaulted. The store had to be guarded day and night by twenty gendarmes and police officers. A year later, more violence erupted when the firm announced that it was opening a factory in Beirut. Protesters cried out "Bat'a, Bat'a the Jew" and threw stones at the windows and doors of the store. The Czechoslovak consul in Beirut advised the Bat'a firm to quickly "hire a native store manager" and to advertise the fact that Bat'a was not Jewish owned.[44]

In Palestine, meanwhile, anti-Bat'a agitation began before the first stores opened in Jerusalem and Tel Aviv. Arab and Jewish shoe manufacturers even launched a joint campaign to urge the population to "buy local." They also lobbied the government to increase tariffs on Bat'a. On the day the Bat'a store in Tel Aviv finally opened, protesters shattered the store's windows and assaulted a delivery boy. In Jerusalem, the opening proceeded without incident, but shortly afterward a group of "delegates of the local shoe producers" approached the store's manager, threatening that if he didn't increase prices "they could not guarantee his personal safety."[45]

When Bat'a began planning a factory in Maryland in 1939, American shoe manufacturers, unions, and members of Congress all mobilized against the planned immigration of one hundred Czechs to work as instructors. Protesters denounced the Czech workers as refugees in disguise and a threat to the American way of life. Powers Hapgood, national director of the United Shoe Workers of America, CIO, protested, "We have every sympathy for bona fide refugees, but these work-ers have been brought here to establish another 'Zlín,' a community in which life is not strictly 'free' and in which the workers' lives are con-trolled to the economic benefit of the Bat'a company."[46]

In fact, the workers chosen to go to America were not refugees—they were selected for their skills. Bat'a did transfer dozens of Jewish employees abroad at the beginning of the Second World War, effec-tively saving their lives. These included several Jewish doctors who were employed in Bat'a's hospital in Zlín, which was run by Dr. Bohuslav Albert. When Dr. Albert heard the news that the Nazis had invaded what remained of Czechoslovakia in March 1939, he immediately tried to arrange for the Jewish doctors under his supervision and their fami-lies to be transferred to Bat'a firms abroad. Yet there was no deliberate campaign to save Jewish workers. Out of the 1,100 Jews who worked for Bat'a in 1939–1940, only 70—all highly skilled and multilingual, like other Bat'a transfers—were transferred to safety.

Eugen Straussler was among the lucky ones. He was given the choice of Singapore or Kenya. He chose Singapore and left a month later with his wife, Marta, and two young sons, Petr (age four) and Tomáš (age two). When the Japanese invaded Singapore, Eugen volunteered with the British Army, and Marta and her sons fled the island. Thinking they were going to Australia, the family landed in India, where Marta briefly managed a Bat'a store in Darjeeling. Eugen volunteered to serve the Allied cause and was killed in the war in the Pacific. In India, Marta met and remarried a British Army major named Kenneth Stoppard, who promised to bring her and her sons to safety and a new life in England. The Czech-Jewish boy Tomáš Straussler became the English playwright Tom Stoppard. All four of Tom's grandparents died in the Holocaust. It would be many decades before he learned of his own origins.[47]

IN THE context of growing economic nationalism and anti-colonial-ism, Bat'a's advance into India also did not go unchallenged. Tomáš Bat'a took his first trip to India in 1925, intending primarily to search for raw materials. He did not immediately recognize the potential of the vast Indian market. While the first Bat'a shoes arrived in India in 1925, and the first stores were opened in Calcutta and Bombay in 1926, the stores served mostly European customers.[48]

Indeed, Tomáš Bat'a was no great proponent of Indian equality or self-sufficiency in his initial contact with India. After his return from his 1925 trip, he wrote an essay titled "Two Races." The "Nordic man," he claimed, had the duty to "produce for the sun-drenched man what he cannot himself, chiefly science, organized government and industrial goods, and in exchange takes from him the products of his mighty sun—crops and raw materials." Nor did Bat'a believe that India had the same right to sovereignty that Czechs had recently gained. "A nation has a right to sovereignty only as long as it can manage its land in such a way to best benefit humanity in general," he argued.[49]

By the time of his worldwide flight in 1931, however, Tomáš Bat'a's rhetoric had shifted considerably. It is difficult to say whether his ideas evolved or whether he simply recognized a good business opportunity. In 1932, a Moravian newspaper reported on the Indian movement to boycott British goods and presented this as a golden opportunity for Czechoslovakia. The newspaper claimed that "the first of Bat'a's planes was already well on its way to India. The moment Gandhi blows his political firecracker . . . the engines of Bat'a's Fokker will overtake Italy. The planes will bring trade organizers to India, perhaps soon factory builders, and certainly footwear, all from Bat'a, an industrialist from little Czechoslovakia."[50]

After his second trip to India in 1931, Tomáš Bat'a consistently stressed his firm's contribution to Indian self-sufficiency. In doing so, he contrasted Czechoslovakia's investment in India to the exploitative and colonialist British and Japanese. "By merely exporting our shoes to India as the Japanese are doing today, this service would be only one-sided, and as such destined sooner or later to vanish. But if our work serves the people and the country in the real meaning of the word, the foundation will be on a healthy basis and its future will be safeguarded. Because then the very people of India will be proud of it, will guard it and defend it."[51] Bat'a shoes were labeled "Made in India," and advertisements promoted the firm's contribution to Indian self-sufficiency.

One advertisement, titled "Keeping a Promise," assured readers, "India is rapidly becoming self-supporting. Bat'a has contributed to this development in no uncertain manner. Bat'a shoes are made in India, by Indians, from Indian materials. And they are worn by more people in the country than any other brand."[52]

But the Bat'a company's support for Indian "self-sufficiency" became a more complicated matter on the ground. Bat'a did not "nationalize" its operations in India by responding to the demands of Indian nationalists for self-determination. Rather, the firm often adapted to colonial racial and social hierarchies and norms. The salaries Bat'a paid to Indian workers (12–15 rupees a month) were, according to the Czechoslovak consul in India, "below the lowest income of a coolie or a local Haryana who sleeps on the street, wears rags, and feeds on garbage." Czech employees were paid more (35–40 rupees a month), but not enough to establish them on par with other Europeans in India. The consul urged Bat'a to reorganize the firm's labor according to more hierarchical colonial norms. Failure to do so would risk alienating the British, by threatening the racial and social divide between Europeans and Indians.[53] Bat'a accepted this advice. The new factory town built at Bat'anagar segregated Indian and Czech workers in housing and social facilities. Czech workers received substantially superior housing, and the typical Czech family in India soon employed two or three domestic servants. It was a lavish lifestyle compared to Depression-era standards in Czechoslovakia.

This did not go unnoticed by Bat'a's Indian workers. Some protesters attempted to expose as false Bat'a's claim that it was fostering Indian national self-sufficiency. In a letter to the newspaper the *Daily Liberty*, a reader criticized the way in which the Bat'a firm had taken advantage of the anti-colonial boycott of British goods, such that the firm "is now successful in controlling the whole shoe market of India by organizing 150 shops of its own and appointing hundreds of wholesale agents in every nook and corner of India." The writer claimed that Bat'a only manufactured children's canvas shoes in Indian factories but "other shoes which are imported from Czechoslovakia are being sold as Indian made and are purchased as Indian made shoes." In addition, the writer claimed that the Bat'a firm had initially promised the Indian government that all of the labor in its factories would be Indian, but that in fact, "all highly paid workers in the factory are imported."[54]

Discontent over these and other issues led to a major strike in 1939, when 3,000 Indian workers (out of an approximate workforce of 3,500) walked off the job. Workers demanded the right to unionize, higher wages, better job security, the reduction of rent in company housing, improvement in housing, free health care, the expansion of a Moslem mosque, and the construction of a new Hindu temple.[55]

The situation escalated when Bat'a decided to use police escorts to transport strikebreakers to the Bat'anagar factory. When the police truck was attacked by striking workers, officers fired on the crowd, wounding four people. At this point, the entire Czech colony was brought under police protection, and plans were made to potentially evacuate women and children. In Calcutta, the Indian Trade Congress denounced Bat'a and called for a boycott of all Bat'a products, calling out Czech exploitation of native workers and Indian resources. The strike lasted two weeks before the Bat'a company reached an agreement with the workers. After the strike, the company invested more money to improve the housing and working conditions of its Indian workers. The firm slowly began to replace Czech managers with Indians. But the last Czech manager didn't leave Bat'anagar until the mid 1960s.[56]

FIFTEEN

Local Foods

LITTORIA, 1932

ON DECEMBER 18, 1932, Benito Mussolini celebrated the conquest of a swamp. The occasion was the inauguration of the city of Littoria (renamed Latina after the war), a Fascist "new town" created in the Agro Pontino region of Italy. For centuries, the region had been plagued by malaria and was inhospitable to human habitation. "Comrades! Today is a great day for the black shirt revolution. It is a great day for the Agro Pontino. And it is a glorious day in the history of the nation. That which has been attempted in vain for the past 25 centuries, we have today transformed into a living reality," Mussolini proclaimed. The victory was not simply over pestilent mosquitoes, however. It was also a day to celebrate Italy's mastery over the forces of globalization. "I want to praise the workers who came from every part of Italy and the colonies . . . to work here. It is perhaps opportune to recall that not long ago, in order to find work, it was necessary to cross the Alps or traverse the ocean. . . . Today the land is here, only half an hour from Rome."[1]

Over the next five years, Mussolini would give versions of this speech countless times, at ribbon-cuttings for Fascist "New Cities" throughout Italy. "I want to tell you that we will no longer send the flowers of our race to faraway and barbaric lands if we are not sure that they will be

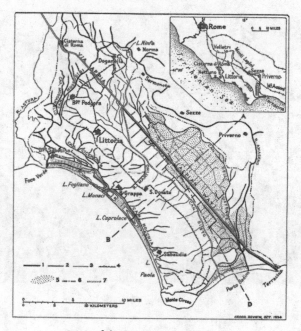

Map of the Pontine Marshes, 1934.

protected by the tricolor of the homeland," he announced at the inauguration of Pontinia one year later.[2] Instead, the "flowers of the race" were to become pioneers in places such as Pontinia. In the Agro Pontino region alone, Littoria and Pontinia were followed by Sabaudia (1934), Aprilia (1937), and Pomezia (1939). The Fascist government ultimately created up to 160 Fascist new towns or rural settlements between 1928 and 1940.[3]

These were Fascism's anti-global cities. The Fascist regime had begun its quest for national self-sufficiency well before the first settlers arrived in Littoria. As in Austria, the drive for autarky was closely linked to the upheaval of the First World War and its aftermath. Arrigo Serpieri, the Fascist minister of agriculture, reflected in 1938, "The last quarter of a century has opened everyone's eyes to reality." It had been a "tragic lesson—and marvelously efficacious." Through economic hardship, Italians now understood that "economic independence is a necessary condition for political independence." While autarky would require

Mussolini participating in the harvest.

short-term sacrifices, it would reap rich dividends. "A certain degree of economic autarky, even if it requires great sacrifice, is the necessary condition for political power . . . but at the same time, since political power is an instrument for achieving greater wealth and improving one's own quality of life, it is possible over time to compensate for the sacrifices necessitated by autarky."[4]

The first great Fascist initiative undertaken in the name of self-sufficiency was Mussolini's "Battle for Grain," inaugurated in 1925. The campaign was immortalized with photos of the bare-chested *Duce* working the harvest in sun-kissed fields of wheat. It was supported by an ambitious scientific effort to produce a new hyperproductive strain of wheat, *ardito,* which would feed the nation more efficiently from Italian soil. As of 1931, laws stipulated that bread and pasta had to be made from at least 95 percent Italian-grown wheat.[5]

Achieving full-blown autarky became an official goal of the Italian state after the League of Nations imposed economic sanctions on Italy in 1935–1936, in response to the Italian invasion of Abyssinia. The sanctions increased Italy's economic and political dependence on Germany and

Mussolini's determination to break free of its reliance on imports from the Allies (though these sanctions were lifted before the end of 1936).

Mussolini's iconic harvest porn was not the only propaganda generated by the campaign for self-sufficiency, however. Italian bookstores and libraries were flooded with tracts touting the benefits of self-sufficiency at the level of the nation and the individual, including books and pamphlets on "autarkic cooking," "linguistic autarky," "the radio as a tool for commercial advertising and autarky," "honey for food, medicine, and economic autarky," alongside guides to "empire, race, and autarky," "autarky and the schools," and "spiritual autarky."

Italians also received relentless instruction on the value of autarkic consumption and food preparation. Autarky, Fascist propaganda insisted, was more than an economic program. It was a mentality. A way of life. Elisabetta Randi's guidebook to autarkic cooking explained, "The word 'autarky,' as it currently circulates, and which dominates speeches, journalism, and research, is one of those words that encompasses, with its brief sound, a way of life, a world of ideas, of proposals, of actions." What she called "alimentary autarky" was essential to the future of the Italian nation. "A people cannot be strong and dominate when it is dependent on others for food: hence the importance of alimentary autarky, which is the foundation of economic wealth in times of peace, and an essential basis of military power, of resistance, and victory in a time of war."[6]

What all this meant for the Italian consumer was clear: "There is no doubt that the first duty of the consumer in the fascist regime is to choose national products, with the intent of defending Italian labor and the nation's financial stability," instructed Adelmo Cicogna in a popular guidebook. He and other lifestyle gurus also urged measures that we would today associate with environmentalism: limiting consumption, eliminating waste, and "recuperating all that is possible from every substance."[7] Randi's autarkic cookbook recommended chewing bread longer and more slowly to make it last and included recipes for stale bread (crostini for soup), minestrone flavored with parmesan rinds, and "autarkic desserts," like biscotti and cakes made from potatoes, rice, or ricotta cheese. These were, of course, recipes already favored by peasants and workers, who made use of whatever they had. Cicogna had no patience for consumers who were dazzled by foreign products. "It is simply a crime that foreign products are purchased out of stupid snobbery," he declared. Films, automobiles, textiles and manufactured goods, furs, shoes, sweets, perfumes, medicines, fruit, photographic equipment, jewels, pianos, cards, furniture, crystal, cutlery—these were "all products optimally made in Italy and also exported, and that have nothing to envy of their foreign counterparts."[8]

Fascist propagandists repeatedly drove home a gendered association between globalism, luxury, and female vanity. Autarky, by contrast, was linked to masculine self-discipline and sacrifice for the common good. The struggle for autarky also placed special burdens on women as housewives and consumers. In her pamphlet on the "Duties and Ideals of the Fascist Woman," Elsa Gross addressed herself to an imagined wealthy female consumer. "Fascism demands of our lovely ladies that they impose some limitations on their vanity . . . that, instead of spending thousands abroad each year for the purchase of thousands of useless things, they content themselves . . . with a dress or a hat made in Rome, Turin, or Florence instead of Paris," along with Italian perfumes and cosmetics. The average Italian woman had never had the means to purchase "thousands of useless things," let alone French perfume or Parisian fashions. But the frivolity of this imagined consumer's sacrifice no doubt made it easier for readers to identify with the larger cause.

The Fascist regime reinforced its campaign for autarkic eating with weeks designated to celebrate Italian products, such as the Festival of Bread, the Festival of the Grape, and the National Day of Rice. The regime even invented new autarkic foods, such as chinotto, made from bitter oranges and quinine, and marketed as an alternative to Coca-Cola.[9] Gradually, the quest for autarky extended from food and soft drinks to manufactured goods and energy. At a German-Italian Congress on autarky in 1942, under secretary in the Ministry of Corporations Ermanno Amicucci explained, "Autarky is expanding. Especially to primary materials of public interest—from coal to oil, from iron to textiles, from rubber to fats—in order to secure the independence of our country from the heavy weight of the monopolistic interests of the

Fascist propaganda poster: "National Competition for the Victory of Wheat," ca. 1926.

plutocracy." He detailed ambitious efforts to create synthetic substitutes for products including cotton, wool, copper, nickel, and tin. Lanital, a synthetic textile made from milk products, was promoted as a substitute for wool and cotton, but the regime had more success with rayon (not invented by Italians, but under Fascism, Italy was its largest European manufacturer).[10]

"NEW CITIES" such as Littoria were perhaps the most spectacular manifestations of Italian deglobalization between the wars. They were meant to solve several stubborn problems at once: poverty, unemployment, the inequality of land distribution, labor unrest, and agitation. Initially, Mussolini had supported land reform, but almost immediately after the March on Rome in October 1922, he ditched such radical ideas (along with his more radical allies) in favor of an alliance with large landowners. Policies that would have divided up large estates or limited landlords' power to raise rents and evict tenants were tabled or repealed. If the Fascist state wanted to increase the number of small landholders, it would have to find or make the land itself: either by "conquering" it from Italy's wetlands or invading territories abroad.[11]

The New Cities and the goal of "bonifica" (land reclamation) reflected other political goals of the Fascist state as well. New Cities were intended to embody rural ideals and to combat the alleged moral, political, and eugenic hazards of urbanization. The ideal settler's home in Italy (as in interwar Austria, Germany, and elsewhere) was a single-family dwelling with a garden, an ideal formulated in opposition to big-city tenement buildings and mass housing. Rural life had once been associated with backwardness, but these new settlements were to be emblems of modern and hygienic living.[12]

Fascist parliamentary representative Vittorno Vezzani explained that isolated rural homes better protected the population from pandemics, "while, from the moral and demographic perspective, they better conserve healthy family habits," meaning high birthrates.[13] These Fascist New Cities were intended to create Fascist "New Men," as the goal of bonifica extended from the land to the humans who occupied it. In Serpieri's words, "The country-dweller is a profoundly different type, in his physical and moral entirety, from the urban or industrial man . . . the country-dweller is the representative of discipline, sobriety, and simple customs."[14] Increasing the Italian birthrate was a key goal of the new Fascist settlements. The colonists arriving in Littoria were expected to produce many children. Italy, which had long seen itself as overpopulated, would soon have room to spare for all of these children, Mussolini assured followers. "In a reclaimed, cultivated, irrigated, disciplined and therefore fascist Italy, there is sufficient space and bread for another ten million men. Sixty million Italians will make the weight of their mass and their strength felt in world history."[15]

In addition to demographic and eugenic goals, settlements such as Littoria responded to the upheavals caused by global migration and trade before the First World War, restrictions on trade and migration since 1914, and the denial of Italy's imperial aspirations at the Paris Peace Conference. Since the late nineteenth century, Italy's most visible "globalists" had been the millions of peasants and workers who sought a living abroad, especially in Europe and North and South America. By the end of the century, the Italian government increasingly saw emigration as a substitute for formal empire: emigrants from Italy's diverse regions would literally "become" Italian overseas (rather than Sicilians, Abruzzi, or Venetians). They would spread Italian culture around the world, create global markets for Italian products, and enrich the homeland through their remittances. The government, for its part, encouraged Italians abroad to maintain political, economic, and cultural ties to their homeland through an expanding network of consuls, Italian schools and associations, welfare assistance, and laws that enabled emigrants and their children to retain their Italian citizenship long after they had left their homes. This model worked relatively well. About 16.6 million Italians emigrated between 1870 and 1921, but many returned home or made multiple round-trips. For example, between 1902 and 1914, Italian authorities estimated that for every one hundred emigrants to the United States, fifty-nine Italians returned home.[16] In the United States, many of the migrants who remained in the country, and their children, came to see themselves as "Italian Americans."[17]

The Italian government's efforts to retain the loyalties of citizens abroad initially intensified under Fascism. While Mussolini denounced US efforts to exclude Italian immigrants as a "condition of tyrants," his consuls mobilized to organize and rally Italian Americans for the Fascist cause. The government supported emigrants economically with loans or supplies for businesses, provided subsidies to private organizations that were loyal to the regime, and sought to carefully manage *fasci all'estero*, Fascist political units abroad, including the Fascist League of North America.

Italian consuls stationed in the United States sometimes resorted to intimidating tactics. In Yonkers and Newark, for example, consuls interrogated local Italian Americans about their political loyalties, and in Detroit, consul Giacomo Ungarelli, a staunch Fascist, made it his mission to convert the entire Italian American community into a disciplined Fascist colony. He attempted to infiltrate the Sons of Italy, the Dante Alighieri Society, the three Italian newspapers in town, the Italian Chamber of Commerce, and local churches, and did not hesitate to use threats of economic boycott or physical force to bring people in line. He also sponsored summer vacations at Fascist camps in Italy for Italian American schoolchildren and distributed Fascist textbooks to local schools. His activism proved highly divisive in the community. While there was considerable support for Fascism among Italian Americans (and, it should be said, among other Americans who were fascinated by *il Duce*), there was also a militant anti-Fascist resistance. After complaints to the US State Department, Ungarelli was recalled, but the Italian government's efforts to influence Italians abroad continued.[18]

After 1914, transatlantic migration was reduced to a trickle by both the war and US anti-immigrant legislation. While 13 million Italians applied for passports to leave Italy in the years leading up to the First World War, only 4 million would emigrate in the thirty years between 1914 and 1944. Between 1922 and 1942, 60 percent of Italian emigrants were destined for France or Argentina and only 15 percent (mainly family members of Italian Americans) to the United States. For the Italian government, there were simply more mouths to feed at home.[19]

Meanwhile, Fascist leaders increasingly began to see emigration as a badge of shame. Anti-emigration sentiments had circulated for a long time, but they were now reinforced by feelings of humiliation. Italians were being treated by the US government and its quota as racially inferior and undesirable, even as Italian Americans built up the US economy and military through their labor and service. Leaders of the Italian government's Commission for Migration and Colonization blamed the closing of borders in North America for "burdening the labor market and contributing to the expansion of unemployment" in Italy. But channeling emigration toward internal colonization in Italy—where "land waits to be vivified, valorized, improved, economically and demographically, by Italian labor and capital"—was a matter of national pride.

Internal colonization meant colonizing the south of Italy, as well as the newly acquired territory from Austria, including the Trentino, Trieste, Istria, Dalmatia, and Fiume (which Fascist Italy did finally acquire in 1924). "Internal colonization" also prepared the way for Italy's imperial expansion in the 1930s, when the same organizations and individuals charged with settling the Agro Pontino turned their attention to the colonization of Libya and Ethiopia. Indeed, even foreign journalists writing about the Italian colonization of Libya understood it as an extension of the Fascist project in the Agro Pontino. Martin Moore of the *Daily Telegraph* wrote: "The peasant who has seen farms won from the water needs no superhuman effort of faith to have confidence in farms won from the sand; migration to Libya is but one step further than migration to the one-time Pontine Marshes."[20]

Colonies in Africa extended the anti-global vision of the Pontine settlements. On the one hand, they were intended to defiantly fulfill the Italian imperial aspirations thwarted by the Paris Peace Treaties, "restoring" Italy to great power status. At the same time, however, Fascism's empire—like the British Empire for the British—was intended to render Italy more self-sufficient, as colonists extracted food and resources from conquered territories. In 1926, Arrigo Serpieri insisted on the "necessary expansion of Italy in the world—no longer an expansion of poor people wandering to build roads and canals, to pierce mountains or to excavate mines or till land for the benefit of others, but an organized and methodic expansion of a people that wants to use its own demographic power to create exclusively Italian power."[21]

Mussolini had first called for intensive internal colonization and colonial expansion to replace emigration in 1924. In 1927, the regime shifted decisively from a policy of accommodating emigration to repressing it. That year, all existing passports held by Italians in Italy were declared invalid, and Mussolini ordered local prefects to proceed with "utmost severity and restrictiveness" in issuing any new passports. This was not only a strategy to curb emigration, but also a way to smother anti-Fascist dissent around the world by preventing Socialists and other dissidents from emigrating. In 1930, legislation increased penalties for clandestine emigration, and new measures were introduced to encourage return migration.[22]

After 1927, both internal and external colonialism were vaunted by Fascists not simply as emergency solutions, but as politically preferable alternatives to emigration and global free trade. "Today, the real America for all Italians is Libya," preached one Fascist slogan.[23] Or Littoria, a short hop from Rome. The new towns in the Agro Pontino included reserved spots for migrants repatriated from abroad, and families whose applications for passports were rejected were redirected toward these new "Americas."[24]

The settlers themselves were not always enthusiastic colonizers, however. One woman who moved to the Agro Pontino as a child recalled that her father was unemployed and her family was in severe debt in the aftermath of the 1929 economic crisis. Emigration to America seemed like their best hope, but their request for passports was denied. Instead, they were shipped off to the Pontine Marshes with the promise of guaranteed housing and employment.[25] These settlers were often particularly disappointed with what they found there.

At the level of propaganda, Fascists never ceased to herald land reclamation and settlement efforts as an unmitigated success. In 1941, the president of the L'Opera Nazionale Combattenti (ONC; National Agency for Veterans) celebrated the Agro Pontino settlements as "a technical achievement that has no precedent in the history of civilization." As for the Agro Pontino, "It is no longer a forested and muddy land, a pestilential, stagnant swamp, where for two thousand years life has been primitive, nourished by a few shepherds and herders, plagued by malaria and death." It was now "a bright and productive agricultural land, dried out, deforested, with regimented waterways and lakes, intersected by a dense network of roads . . . dotted with thousands of farmhouses that crown five cities and eighteen villages, enticing and comfortable as centers of civic life."[26]

But upon closer examination, Italy's anti-global policies, including its settlements, had mixed results. In spite of passport restrictions, more Italians still emigrated each year than were ever settled in the Agro Pontino, which had an estimated population of 60,000 in 1935. Between 1930 and 1940, the Fascist regime organized the migration of more than 700,000 people, either resettling them internally, in Italian colonies abroad, or sending them to work in Germany. This was however only 60 percent of the number of Italians who moved spontaneously each year within or beyond Italian borders. Agriculture actually declined in significance for the Italian economy under Fascism.[27] And while Italy was 95 percent independent in food production by 1939, food autonomy came at the cost of increasing food prices and declining nutrition and caloric intake. Consumers paid more money for bread, and there were deficits in other food products such as meat. By the beginning of the Second World War, massive food shortages were contributing to the regime's growing unpopularity, especially in the south.[28]

At the level of human suffering, the balance sheet was even more negative. In 1933, close to 125,000 workers were employed on the land reclamation projects in the Agro Pontino. Mussolini saw these workers as disposable, and many died in abhorrent conditions. During the war, infections with malaria increased greatly, as the regime cut back expenditures on public health in order to fund the war effort. In Italy, the number of individuals infected with malaria more than tripled during the last three years of the war, reaching nearly half a million in 1945.

In keeping with the regime's focus on autarky, settlement workers who contracted malaria were sometimes treated with mercury, an ineffective and painful treatment that was used to replace treatment with imported quinine. The regime hid these illnesses and deaths from the public. An engineer who had worked in the Agro Pontino testified in 2003 that there were at least 3,000 deaths from malaria among workers in the region—all casualties in the "battle" for swampland.[29]

The colonists were extolled as models of Fascism's "New Men and Women": racially vigorous, fertile, self-sufficient, and devoted to the regime and its goals. But again, the reality was far removed from this propaganda. In the Agro Pontino in 1939, for example, 55 new families arrived to the New Cities—477 individuals. But in the same year, 488 individuals left—whether because they requested repatriation or were expelled for bad conduct. Many got sick with malaria or other illnesses, which the regime continued to cover up.[30] Similar situations emerged in other Fascist settlements across Italy.

Inspectors and officials often complained that the selection process for colonists was not rigorous enough. In part, this was because the local Fascist Party leaders and officials charged with choosing colonists saw it as an excellent opportunity to get rid of politically or socially troublesome families. Settlement authorities repeatedly sent directives emphasizing the importance of selecting colonists who were morally, psychologically, and racially fit—as well as politically reliable. In Sardinia, "The migratory currents to direct toward the island should represent vigorous elements who will contribute to the refinement of the local race," one inspector insisted. Clearly something needed to change: he reported in frustration that out of the fifteen families settled in the Sardinian colony of Pimpisu, seven were being repatriated because of either health problems or attitude problems. Likewise, in the "Villagio Mussolini" in Sardinia, an official conceded, "The results have hardly been encouraging." Even colonists who were suited to agricultural labor or fishing were not capable of producing enough to be self-sufficient. They needed to find salaried work in addition to cultivating their farms simply in order to secure the "necessities of life."[31]

Administrators everywhere constantly complained that settlers rarely lived up to the image of the Fascist new man or woman. As it turned out, whether in democratic or authoritarian contexts, transplanting and transforming workers (even those with farm experience) into self-sufficient farmers was a dubious enterprise. There were high levels of theft, slowdowns, alcohol abuse, and absenteeism. In 1938, 26,000 colonists threatened to strike if their demands for more state support were not met. Very few could actually support themselves.[32]

The Fascist dream of achieving autarky through colonization in the Agro Pontino ultimately ended where it began, in a malarial swamp. Littoria suffered the most. By 1943, Italy was facing military defeat. Mussolini was ousted on July 25, and Italy changed sides in the war less than two months later. Germany retaliated brutally for this betrayal, occupying most territory under Italian control and inflicting terror on the civilian population. As the German army retreated from the Agro Pontino region in 1944, the Nazis unleashed a form of biological warfare on the province, what historian Frank Snowden has called "the only known example of biological warfare in twentieth-century Europe." In order to prevent the Allied advance, the Wehrmacht deliberately reversed the pumps that had drained the Agro Pontino and flooded the region with seawater from the Tyrhennian Sea. At the same time, they purposefully created ideal conditions for the breeding of a particularly deadly species of mosquito, *Anopheles labranchiae*, which flourished in salt water. Aware of the German plan, Italian malariologist Alberto Missiroli predicted that it would result in "the greatest epidemic recorded by human history."

The Germans had meanwhile rounded up supplies of quinine, necessary to treat malaria, and hidden them in Viterbo, Tuscany. While neither the flooding nor the mosquitoes halted the advance of the Allies toward Rome, Littoria was decimated. The settlers' homes were systematically leveled, either by German and Allied troops or by flooding. Many families were forced to sleep in tents or stables, exposed to the elements—and the mosquitoes. The provincial health inspector in Littoria, Vincenzo Rossetti, estimated that more than 100,000 out of 245,000 people in the city were infected with malaria in 1944. Globalization may have been temporarily banished, but within a very short time, the swamp, and the mosquito, had reconquered Littoria.[33]

SIXTEEN

Economic Appeasement

LONDON AND GENEVA, 1933

ON JUNE 12, 1933, delegates from sixty-six states gathered at the Geological Museum in London in a last-ditch effort to save the global economy. The stakes were high both for globalization and for internationalism itself. Failure of this World Economic Conference, the preparatory committee warned, "threatens a world-wide adoption of ideals of national self-sufficiency which cuts unmistakably across the lines of economic development. Such a choice would shake the whole system of international finance to its foundations, standards of living would be lower, and the social system, as we know it, could hardly survive."[1]

King George V opened the conference. In an address broadcast around the world, he exhorted gathered delegates "to cooperate for the sake of the ultimate good of the whole world," praising "a new recognition of the interdependence of nations and of the value of collaboration between them." Attendees were urged to "honor this new consciousness of common interest to the service of mankind."[2]

But as most of the members of the audience already knew, this "consciousness of common interest" was more an expression of wishful thinking than political reality. Globally, imports had dropped by 66 percent since the collapse of the stock market in New York in 1929, while exports had declined by 68 percent. Liberal member of Parliament George Peel blamed politics. "This stupendous fall in the trade of the forty-nine principal countries of the earth is due not to deficiency in productive capacity but to that economic nationalism, war's parent and war's progeny, which has made more victims than war itself."[3]

The World Economic Conference took place against a background of economic despair and political turmoil. An estimated 30 million people were unemployed around the world. In January 1933, Adolf Hitler had been named Germany's chancellor. In March, he consolidated his power with the Enabling Act, ostensibly an "emergency" measure that allowed him to rule by decree. In the months that followed, the Gestapo began knocking on doors; the Nazis took over local governments, banned trade unions, and interned their leaders and other political opponents in Dachau, the first Nazi concentration camp.

Meanwhile, the United States had a new leader, Franklin Delano Roosevelt. No one quite knew what to expect from Roosevelt. In the months leading up to the conference, he made statements suggesting that he supported the goals of stabilizing currencies and reducing trade barriers. But on July 3, Roosevelt sent a very different message to the delegates in London: the United States would not pin the dollar to gold or sterling. This was a major blow to internationalists who saw a common system of currency valuation as the key to stabilizing the world economy.

Even before Roosevelt issued this "bombshell" message, there was widespread skepticism about the chances of a breakthrough in London. Six months before the delegates gathered, John Maynard Keynes wrote, "It is easy to predict the agenda of the Conference. A number of resolutions will be passed declaring that many things ought to be changed, but without a serious intention of changing them. The Conference will agree in its collective capacity that tariffs and quotas have reached a pitch of absurdity that are a menace to international trade, but there will be no offers by individual countries to reduce them."[4]

The royal fanfare that opened the World Economic Conference could not overcome "an atmosphere of gloom and almost despair." Foreign correspondents reinforced the impression of a "listless and hopeless spirit."⁵ In a dispatch entitled, "Why Conferences Fail," Harold J. Laski reported that none of the opening speeches outlined any specific plan or program. "The depth of the economic nationalisms here in conflict is obviously profound." The British position was that "everyone's tariff is open to question except their own." France repeatedly insisted on a return to the gold standard. The German delegate presented "a fantastic memorandum demanding colonies in Africa and territory in Russia," while Russia put forward "an excellent essay on the contradictions of capitalism."⁶

The World Economic Conference disbanded early. Campaigns to achieve national self-sufficiency only intensified in its aftermath. Leon Trotsky, writing from exile in Mexico City, observed a growing tendency toward autarky even in non-Fascist countries. "Not all of them have the courage to inscribe 'autarky' openly upon their banners. But everywhere policy is being directed toward as hermetic a segregation as possible of national life away from the world economy," he observed. "Only twenty years ago all the schoolbooks taught that the mightiest factor in producing wealth and culture is the worldwide division of labor, lodged in the natural and historic conditions of the development of mankind. Now it turns out that world exchange is the source of all misfortunes and all dangers. Homeward ho! Back to the national hearth!" Against this backdrop, he concluded, "The interminable series of political, economic, financial, tariff and monetary conferences only unfolded the panorama of the bankruptcy of the ruling classes."⁷

The League of Nations officials and experts who had planned and organized the World Economic Conference returned to Geneva deeply demoralized. League official William Martin Hill recalled, "In the years following the breakdown of the London Conference, years in which any form of world cooperation became increasingly difficult for political reasons, the Economic and Financial Organization continued its efforts to stem the drive towards autarky and improve certain aspects of commercial relationships." While there was limited progress, such as a shift away from protectionism in US tariff policies and a tripartite agreement on currency between Britain, France, and the United States, "So far as the state of Europe was the main preoccupation, it was disheartening work; and there can have been few members of the staff in Geneva who, in this period, were not oppressed with the sense of impending catastrophe and the ultimate futility of their efforts."[8]

While certainly not responsible for the breakdown of the global economy, the World Economic Conference would be remembered as one of the great failures of the League of Nations. Speculation abounded in its aftermath that the league—and internationalism itself—was in its death throes. That impression was consolidated by a string of other disappointments in the 1930s: a two-year-long World Disarmament Conference that disarmed no one, and the Japanese invasion of Manchuria and Italian invasion of Ethiopia, against which the league seemed powerless.[9] Headlines like "Can the League Be Saved?" and "Goodbye to the League" reflected the sentiment of skeptics as well as disillusioned believers.[10] Already in 1932, Dorothy Thompson concluded, "The history of Europe since Locarno is a history of defeated internationalism, and no one loves a loser."[11]

FRANK LIDGETT McDOUGALL was among the depressed delegates in London. McDougall, an economic and agricultural advisor to Australian prime minister Stanley Bruce, once described himself as a "working farmer with no knowledge of economics, politics, or anything." He had been a staunch supporter of Empire Free Trade throughout the 1920s. He worked for the Empire Marketing Board and even played a role in negotiating the 1932 Ottawa Agreement, which formalized the policy of Imperial Preference. But in the aftermath of Ottawa, he became disillusioned with the ideal of imperial self-sufficiency. In 1936, McDougall conceded that the agreement had not provided any tangible benefits to consumers or producers. "The economic policy of the British Empire cannot be on a self-sufficiency basis. . . . From a standpoint of economic welfare, isolation in 1936 would not be 'splendid'."[12]

The breakdown of the global economy, and the failure of efforts to revive it with traditional tools (such as cutting tariffs or returning to the gold standard), pushed experts such as McDougall to question their basic assumptions about the relationships between political internationalism, economic globalization, peace, and prosperity. There was still intense disagreement among experts, who argued from different political and geographic perspectives about how best to reconfigure the global economy. But no one believed that it was possible or desirable to return to 1913 or 1929.

Some liberal economists certainly continued to beat the drum of free trade. As Quinn Slobodian has argued, the lesson these economists took from the Great Depression and the rise of both Communism and Fascism was that markets had to be better insulated from democratic political pressures. In the preface to the 1933 edition of the *Theory of International Trade*, for example, Austrian economist Gottfried von Haberler defended free trade: "Some readers will doubtless be surprised that the policy of Free Trade, which is in glaring contrast to the policy actually adopted by nearly every country in the world, should be advocated in this book." He remained convinced that the benefits of free trade were a matter of scientific fact. "Nobody would dream of asking medical science to change its findings just because everybody followed some custom which it had pronounced injurious to health."[13] The ideas of these men were marginal at the time but would gain influence decades later under the rubric of "neoliberalism."[14]

Haberler's day would come. But the policies that McDougall and his colleagues advocated would come first, shaping reconstruction after the Second World War, decolonization, and Cold War economics. McDougall became a leader in the field that would come to be known as "development." He argued that lifting the standard of living among the poor, domestically and internationally, was the key to regenerating the global economy. In his 1937 essay, McDougall thus speculated, "If, as a part of the new approach to methods of international cooperation, means were found to bring about even slight improvements in the standards of living of the masses in India and China, the effects upon world trade would be very great."[15]

McDougall singled out India and China, but rather than distinguishing "developed" from "undeveloped" economies, his focus was on the poor in every country, industrialized or not. In a 1939 report on the activities of the International Labor Organization, director John G.

Winant maintained, "If in a country such as the United States there is a 'submerged tenth' or a submerged fifth even of families who are terribly poor, what can be said of the situation in countries where the average income is only a half or a quarter or a tenth of that in the United States? The great mass of mankind still live in a state of intolerable poverty.... There must be a levelling upwards of the lower incomes, both within each country and between the different countries."[16] A new consensus emerged that more widespread prosperity was not simply a (potential) consequence of globalization, but actually a *precondition* for revitalizing the global economy.

In order to address domestic and global inequality, experts first set out to measure and quantify it. That meant trying to compare how much people earned, how much they spent for basic necessities, and what, if anything, was left over. The International Labor Organization (ILO) undertook the first living standards survey in Europe in 1929. Sponsored by Henry Ford and the Twentieth Century Fund (department store magnate Edward Filene's foundation), the survey was partly motivated by Ford's desire to measure the cost of living so that he would know how much to pay workers in his European production plants. The project was met with suspicion by European auto manufacturers, who suspected (correctly) that Ford intended to poach their best workers by offering higher wages.

It was an ambitious statistical and sociological undertaking. ILO field agents spent months in places such as Detroit, Istanbul, Warsaw, and Cork, compiling data on family budgets, wages, and the costs of essential goods. Investigators in Detroit even shipped trunks containing sample commodity baskets around Europe for the purpose of comparison. While the store-bought wool suits, silk stockings, and household appliances that arrived from Detroit impressed European field officers, they did not make it easier to measure the cost of living (let alone compare "standards of living") internationally. The entire venture ultimately stumbled on the problem of culture: there was little agreement, across Europe or the Atlantic, about which goods were "essential" and which were luxuries, about what constituted "quality," let alone "quality of life."[17]

Warsaw-based economists and social scientists, among them Ludwik Landau, developed some of the first models for measuring inequality between nations. Landau and other Polish émigré economists advocated policies of intensive industrialization and industrial employment as the key to increasing the prosperity of predominantly agrarian Eastern European economies such as that of Poland, seeing them as models for developing countries outside of Europe.

This approach faced competition in the 1930s, not only from advocates of self-sufficiency and village industries such as Mahatma Gandhi. As historian Malgorzata Mazurek argues, it was also in direct competition throughout the 1930s with a model of "development" through emigration and population transfers promoted by experts in the International Labor Organization and within Poland. Instead of bringing jobs to people, through industrialization, people would emigrate to the jobs. This had been the dominant trend before 1918, when millions of Eastern and Southern Europeans emigrated to North America to make a living. At a 1938 conference sponsored by the ILO that brought together representatives from Eastern European and Latin American countries, attendees still agreed upon "the great economic and social importance of migration for settlement, both for countries of emigration and immigration and for the world as a whole. . . . For the world as a whole it has the advantage, by bringing labor and land in closer touch, of reducing that state of economic disequilibrium which is retarding or jeopardizing social progress and well-being in all countries."[18]

But this model was premised on open borders, and few countries were actually open to migrants in the 1930s. It was also deeply rooted in a colonialist imagination, in which there were "empty spaces" in the world waiting to be filled and productivized. In the late 1930s, such emigration schemes began to overlap with fantasies of ethnic cleansing, as Polish and Romanian government officials concluded that Eastern European "development" required the emigration of Eastern Europe's "excess" Jews.[19]

In the League of Nations, an alternative vision of development began to circulate, one centered on improving standards of living and increasing consumption. Experts in the league's Economic and Financial Organization, collaborating closely with colleagues in the social and health organizations and the International Labor Organization, turned explicitly toward addressing social issues in the late 1930s—issues once considered marginal to the mission of the Economic and Financial Organization. League experts led by Frank McDougall and Alexander Loveday focused particularly on increasing consumption through improved nutrition, rural development, better housing, and income redistribution. Historian Patricia Clavin argues that these policies represented a new and broader understanding of international "security" in the late 1930s that would shape the postwar world.[20] Crucially, this League of Nations ideal of development represented a new weapon against anti-globalism, premised on decreasing poverty and increasing consumer demand in order to revitalize the global economy.

THIS SHIFT in strategy was not simply the product of changing ideas. It was, as experts emphasized, largely driven from below by mass politics. Citizens were simply demanding more social rights and a higher standard of living—whatever that meant to them. Indeed, the very ambiguity of the concept of "standard of living" was crucial to its global appeal. In some parts of the world, improvement in "standards of living" entailed increasing access to basic necessities, such as food, housing, electricity, and medical care. But in other contexts, an "increase in the standard of living" might include more opportunities for leisure or vacation time, the acquisition of more "luxury" consumer goods, or greater social security through welfare benefits. The universalist appeal of increasing "standards of living" obscured the extent to which global inequality was a product of colonialism and of structural and material inequalities that divided wealthy and poor countries. But at the same time, the mission to improve people's "standard of living" brought together a broad range of governments, organizations, and citizens around the world.

In this new era, explained ILO director Howard Butler in 1937, "No state, whatever its ideological complexion or its political structure, affects to ignore the claims of the great mass of its citizens to a certain standard of life and a certain security of employment. Both are now regarded as almost statutory rights, which it is the duty of Government to ensure."[21] But how were governments to fulfill these new obligations? The answer, Butler claimed, was "Planning." This term had new significance and appeal in democracies and dictatorships alike in the wake of the Great Depression. Inspired in part by envy or fear of the Soviet Union's Five-Year Plan, there was a global romance with the idea that states could plan and control the development of the economy, infrastructure, housing, and cities, as well as the size and health of the population.

In the economic realm, "Planning" was not only a strategy for maximizing profit or efficiency, Butler explained. "Its primary objective is social, to guarantee not only greater wealth but its better distribution."[22] "Planning" was typically seen as a method for reducing domestic inequality but could also be implemented on an international scale. "If social justice is to form a basis for universal peace, there must be some approach to greater economic equality between nations. So long as there is such extreme poverty as still predominates in a large number of countries, there can be no question of justice, and in the end no possibility of peace," he argued.

But in the 1930s, most government "Planning" was not directed toward reviving global trade. It was instead focused on achieving greater independence from the global economy. "The most outstanding feature of the times is perhaps the drive for greater self-sufficiency, which is almost everywhere apparent," Butler observed. Here too the Soviet example was inspirational. In spite of the rhetoric of "Socialism in one country," the Soviet Union had actually not intended to achieve autarky with its Five-Year Plan. A decline in foreign trade was an unanticipated consequence of the plan. But this was not clear to outsiders. To Western eyes, it appeared that the USSR had deliberately and successfully planned its way toward greater self-sufficiency through rapid industrialization. Official Soviet statistics and propaganda overstated economic growth—reporting massive growth in output between 1928 and 1937, while other global economies were stagnating or collapsing.[23] Soviet reporting also occluded the catastrophic consequences of the Five-Year Plan, including the famine that killed millions of people in Ukraine in 1931–1932. To the outside world, "Planning" appeared to pay off.

European efforts to achieve self-sufficiency had tangible and, to some extent, positive results, Butler argued. "No nation can fairly be blamed for attempting to develop its production of foodstuffs or raw materials to the highest economic point or to find substitutes for those which it cannot produce." And yet he was equally convinced, like most of his colleagues in the League of Nations, that there was a profound trade-off *between* self-sufficiency and standards of living, arguing in 1935, "Any considerable advance in self-sufficiency is likely to be purchased at some sacrifice in the standard of living."[24]

The challenge was to convince the public. It was not simply that free trade had a public relations problem. Increasingly, League of Nations experts recognized that reopening the global economy required *first* increasing global levels of consumption and standards of living, in order to create new markets and demand. "The best hope of finding a way out of the present troubles," Butler argued in 1935, "is to raise the standards of the millions who are now underfed, underclothed and under-equipped. The cares of the American, Argentine, Australian, Canadian or Eastern European farmer would be conjured away if the urban populations of Europe and America could eat even a little more bread, butter and meat per head. There would be little talk of overproduction in industry or agriculture if the millions of China and India could be brought up even a short distance in the scale of consumption."[25]

FRANK MCDOUGALL would become an important architect of this strategy, which he gave the (unfortunate) name "economic appeasement." Globalism had no chance against economic nationalism unless it appealed to the masses. Tariff deals and currency stabilization were not sufficient. "Proposals for the sweeping away of trade barriers completely fail to arouse the enthusiasm of the general mass of the people of the United Kingdom, France, the United States of America, or indeed of any other country."[26]

"Economic appeasement," by contrast, entailed "something more than an international agreement to promote the revival of trade." Rather, he envisioned "a direct attack upon low standards of living conducted both on the national and international plane," which would in turn "lead to increases both of consumption and production and thus provide a new approach to the problem of reducing barriers to trade."

McDougall's first concern was to improve the lives of workers and peasants. This was a moral obligation, but recent elections had demonstrated that it was also a political necessity. The election of the Popular Front government in France, with its wide-ranging promises to improve workers' quality of life, the New Deal in the United States, and other initiatives to expand social services and consumption worldwide demonstrated "that the people are demanding Government action to improve the lot of the less fortunate classes."[27]

McDougall advocated social policies that would improve nutrition, housing, and access to clean water and electricity. He outlined three methods to increase workers' purchasing power: international agreements to improve the conditions of labor and increase wages; investments in social services; and lowering retail prices of food and other basic necessities. These measures, he conceded, would benefit mostly urban populations. For rural populations, particularly the "peasant population of Eastern and South-Eastern Europe," other strategies were necessary, such as improving agricultural methods and distribution. This would in turn increase peasants' purchasing power and result in "the redistribution of population between industry and agriculture at higher standards of living."[28]

The European Conference on Rural Life, planned for 1939, aimed to address "standards of living" in all of its aspects. In preparation for the conference (which never took place because of the war), dozens of national monographs were prepared by individual countries. These monographs, illustrated with idealized images of peasants in folk costumes and laced with nationalist tributes to peasant values, also contained extensive information about nutrition, education, housing, leisure, culture, public hygiene, and infrastructure in rural areas.

While his vision for "economic appeasement" was broad, food was at the heart of McDougall's concerns. One of the League of Nations' most successful and influential campaigns in the late 1930s focused on promoting better nutrition in Europe and beyond. In 1935 the League's General Assembly created a Mixed Committee on the Problems of Nutrition. The approach was holistic, considering the physiological, social, cultural, agricultural, and economic aspects of nutrition. Eastern Europe was well represented by delegates from Poland, Czechoslovakia, and Yugoslavia.[29]

The report claimed that the expansion of global trade in food products in the late nineteenth and early twentieth centuries had substantially improved nutrition worldwide and, in particular, increased the consumption of wheat, meat, butter, and fruit. But the rise of agricultural protection in the 1930s represented a serious setback. As prices on imported foods increased, people tended to substitute less nutritious foods—margarine for butter, for example—and to rely more on staples such as bread.[30] These forms of protection had a real impact on people's diets: Germans were eating 45 percent less imported food in 1935 than in 1929, and Italians imported 40 percent less food in 1934 than in 1929.[31] Subsistence farmers in Central and Eastern Europe generally ate what they grew, which consisted primarily of one or two cereals and potatoes, cabbage, or beans. The consumption of meat, eggs, milk, butter, fruit, and vegetables was pitiably low.[32]

Even in wealthy countries, inequality meant that widespread malnourishment remained a fact of life, although not caused by a reduction of trade. Records of food consumption compiled by the US Bureau of Labor Statistics suggested that 90 percent of the African American population and 70 percent of the white population had substandard diets.[33]

The committee concluded that the "malnutrition which exists in all countries is at once a challenge and an opportunity: a challenge to men's consciences and an opportunity to eradicate a social evil by methods which will increase economic prosperity."[34] Fears of hunger had been one of the major forces behind the post–First World War campaign for national self-sufficiency in Europe. Ironically, by the end of the 1930s, nutrition seemed to point the way out. By convincing people that the benefits of global trade would reach their dinner tables, experts hoped to usher in a new era of economic internationalism.

And perhaps, League of Nations officials hoped, "economic appeasement" could save the league itself. Pietro Stoppani of the league's Economic and Financial Organization noted that it was an approach that "strikes a new note . . . offers a new slogan; it is inspired by optimism; its aims are humanitarian."[35] In a personal letter to J. Avenol, the league's secretary-general, Australian prime minister Stanley Bruce insisted that "economic appeasement" represented the last best hope for the league to "restore its prestige which has been so badly shaken by recent happenings in the political sphere."[36]

THE SLOGAN of "appeasement" lost luster in September 1939 when Hitler invaded Poland and Britain and France finally declared war on Germany. But McDougall's ideas caught on and enjoyed a second life under a different name: "Freedom from Want." In his State of the Union Address in 1941, Franklin D. Roosevelt elaborated on "Four Freedoms" that people "everywhere in the world" should enjoy. In October 1942, McDougall would pen a memorandum entitled *Draft Memorandum on a Programme for Freedom of Want of Food*. That memo caught the attention of Eleanor Roosevelt, who invited McDougall for dinner at the White House during the process of planning the new United Nations. Over dinner, "when the President momentarily became absorbed in the contents of his plate," McDougall recalled, "I hurriedly said that it was necessary to give them (UN) something to do, something perhaps not too controversial, like an international agency for food and agriculture."[37]

The first conference of the United Nations, held in Hot Springs, Virginia, in the spring of 1943, took up this proposal. The Final Act of the Conference explicitly linked the eradication of hunger to the reconstruction of the global economy. It was a Keynesian, demand-driven model. Full employment would produce greater wealth, which would in turn enable people to purchase more food, which would in turn create more demand for food products and more economic growth. "The first cause of hunger and malnutrition is poverty. It is useless to produce more food unless men and nations provide the markets to absorb it. There must be an expansion of the whole world economy to provide the purchasing power sufficient to maintain an adequate diet for all."[38] That conference created the basis for the Food and Agriculture Organization (FAO) of the United Nations, founded in October 1945. McDougall remained behind the scenes at the FAO, as a technical advisor. But in his own path from "Empire Free Trade" to "Freedom from Want," he had charted a path toward the ideals of development, the welfare state, and full employment that would shape the reconstruction of Europe and the world after the Second World War.

SEVENTEEN

Space to Breathe

GOSLAR, 1936

ON NOVEMBER 25, 1936, the town of Goslar, Saxony, was crowded with cheering Nazi peasants. The occasion was the Fourth Annual *Reichsbauerntag* (Reich Peasant/Farmer's Day), the Nazis' annual celebration of their farmers. Reich Farmer's Day had become an annual event since the Nazi seizure of power, but this was a special Farmer's Day, during which Goslar was designated the official *Reichsbauernstadt* (the Reich Peasant/Farmer's City). It was also an occasion to promote the recently announced Four-Year Plan, intended to put the Nazi economy on autarkic footing.

The first Reich Farmer's Day had taken place in Weimar in 1934. But Weimar, a city associated with German enlightenment figures such as Goethe and Schiller, never quite fit the bill as a headquarters for the Nazi peasant movement. Goslar, by contrast, seemed to match the ideals promoted by the regime's Blood and Soil (*Blut und Boden*) propaganda. With a population of less than 30,000, it was surrounded by rural farmland and populated mostly by Protestant farmers who were strong supporters of the Nazi movement.

The festivities opened on a Wednesday night in the town's City Hall, filled to capacity with spectators eager to catch a glimpse of the gathered dignitaries. There was a Wehrmacht concert, followed by performances of the horn and music corps and 200 singers from the local Jaeger battalion. To tumultuous applause, the *Reichsbauernführer* (Reich Farmers' Leader) rose to the stage, limping slightly from a recent sports injury.

Richard Walther Darré was an unlikely candidate for *führer* of the Nazi peasant movement. Born in Argentina in 1895, he passed his childhood comfortably in Belgrano, a suburban neighborhood in Buenos Aires. His family was urban, cosmopolitan, and prosperous; his father had relocated from Germany to Argentina in 1888 as a partner in a German import-export business, an agent of Germany's expanding global economic power. His Swedish German mother was born in Argentina. As a child, Darré received a private education and learned to speak four languages fluently (German, Spanish, English, and French). When he was nine years old, his parents sent him to Heidelberg to be educated, and at the age of sixteen he attended King's College School in Wimbledon, England, as an exchange student. It was only on the eve of the First World War that Darré even developed an interest in land and agriculture, as a student at the German Colonial School in Witzenhausen. Even then, his primary interest was in furthering Germandom abroad. He imagined a future far from Germany, perhaps managing a colonial estate in Argentina.

Darré's trajectory was transformed—and radically deglobalized— by the First World War. He served in the German army, was lightly wounded, and considered returning to Argentina afterward to pursue his colonial career. But he was discouraged by high land costs. His family's fortune was soon lost in Germany's hyperinflation. Eventually he studied animal breeding at the University of Halle and received a PhD there. He also spent time working on farms in East Prussia, Finland, and the Baltic, experiences that affirmed his belief in the superiority of the "Nordic" race. In his first published political essay, Darré opposed internal colonization in Germany because he feared that settling urban workers on farms would introduce a "dubious racial element" to the noble German peasant stock, encouraging "the specter of racial death that threatens us."[1]

Darré joined the Nazi Party in 1930. He quickly established himself as a gifted political organizer and campaigner, mobilizing count-less rural Germans into the party. The Nazi Party performed especially well in rural regions in the 1932 elections.[2] Darré was rewarded with an appointment as chief of the *Schutzstaffel* (SS) Race and Settlement Main Office, responsible for monitoring the racial quality of the SS and planning future conquests in the east.

Not long after the Nazi seizure of power, Darré was appointed min-ister for food and agriculture and began his tenure as Reichsbauern-führer. For Darré, the Nazi project of cultivating the Aryan race began with protecting German agriculture and German "blood" from the forces of globalization. One of his most significant initiatives was the controversial Hereditary Farm Law (*Erbhofgesetz*), passed in September 1933 to both preserve family farms and protect the racial lineage of farm-ers. Selected farms, owned by model "Aryan" farmers and designated as "Hereditary Farms," could be passed only from father to a single son and could not be mortgaged, sold, or repossessed by banks; they were perma-nently insulated from both the global economy and from the alleged threat of racial "contamination" through sale to non-Aryan owners.

Darré's speech at the festivities in Goslar reflected his fixation on the menace of racial death through globalization. He invoked the "danger of an onslaught from Asia, an onslaught that could extinguish all of the culture and life of a thousand-year-old culture." That Asian danger was specifically Jewish: Darré believed that Jews incarnated the threat of the global economy, of Bolshevism, and of racial contamination all at once. In Goslar in 1936, he declared that "the Germanic peasant and the Jewish nomad are binary opposites," and that the Jew was therefore the "mortal enemy of the peasantry, especially of Germanic blood." The German peasantry had to either "become conscious of the deadly threat of Jewish parasitism, or it will sooner or later be destroyed by this Jewish parasitism."[3]

Herbert Backe, Darré's first deputy (and eventual replacement), was also a keynote speaker at the 1936 Reichsbauerntag. Like his boss, he had grown up far from German *Boden* and surrounded by non-German *Blut*. Not coincidentally, Backe was also part of the German diaspora unmade by the First World War. Born the son of a Prussian trader in

Batumi, Georgia, in the Russian Empire in 1896, he attended mostly Russian schools. While the Backe family had a beloved dacha in the countryside, they were a generation removed from the land. The First World War put a sudden end to Herbert Backe's idyllic childhood, as the Russian government interned the German-speaking community in Russia as enemy nationals. Backe found himself imprisoned in the Urals in harsh conditions until he escaped by foot and train to St. Petersburg. With the help of the Swedish Red Cross, he eventually fled Russia and set foot on German soil for the first time in June 1918, at the age of twenty-two. Although he had been interned by Russian nationalists during the war (and not by Bolsheviks), the experience left him seething with rage toward Russia and Communism. He would get his revenge twenty years later, devising and implementing a "Hunger Plan" to starve millions of Russians during the Second World War.[4]

And yet Backe's first feeling upon landing on German soil was not one of joyful homecoming, but bitter disappointment. "In 1918 I was deeply let down by the attitude of the German people, which was not prepared to invest itself in a great idea as a result of the collapse [of the Wilhelmine Empire]." He finally found the "idealistic" community he was seeking in National Socialism. He became a party member in 1925. "The ideas represented here corresponded to my outlook: national community; common good over individual interest; the understanding that an individual life is only secure in a healthy national body and state; a commitment to idealism over materialism." The Nazi Party, he recalled, was the only party that understood the "liberal epoch" was over.[5]

Backe developed an interest in agriculture while working as a farmhand near Hanover and then studied agronomy at the University of Göttingen in the 1920s. He worked on a large estate in Pomerania and eventually purchased his own run-down farm. The Great Depression convinced him that the global economy was incompatible with the survival of the German peasantry and propelled him into politics. It was not long ago, he wrote in 1938, that Germans had not only "fed ourselves from our own land, but also clothed ourselves with German wool and linen." But in the last decades of the nineteenth century, "The relationship between the Volk and its territory was blown up by the transnational global economy. Individuals no longer felt bound to the Volk to which they belonged by blood, did not feel rooted in their native soil, but instead belonged above all to a global economic community." Under National Socialism, these ruptured links between the nation, blood, and soil would be restored.[6]

A major message of the Reichsbauerntag in 1936 was that farmers needed to increase output in a battle for production (*Erzeugungsschlacht*) that would eliminate the need to import foods and make Germany independent of the global economy. As in Italy, however, it was not merely a matter of producing more, but also of consuming differently. "The entire nation must and can participate, whether farmer or distributor, miller or baker, housewife or cook—everyone must make an effort to make complete use of and value the foodstuffs that are so precious to our nation." This meant learning to eat seasonally again, reducing waste, ceasing to demand "the most beautiful spring vegetables from abroad in March." Germans were instructed to reduce their fat consumption by 25 percent and return to a local diet that was based on products "brought forth by the German land." This new "nationally bound" diet and economy, Backe claimed, was the opposite of the "Jewish economy." "Judaism knows no nationally bound economy, because while it [Judaism] constitutes a nation and a race, it has no space (*Raum*), because it has never been rooted in any land, and never can be rooted in any land," he argued.[7]

The "Jew" became a symbol of the terrible fate of all humans in the globalized twentieth century. In a 1931 memo entitled "Blut und Boden," German noble and Nazi supporter Max August de la Vigne von Erkmannsdorf insisted that since the First World War, "Man has become deracinated, has no more homeland, no land under his feet, has become a restless wanderer in the world doomed to ruin. He is the same as the eternal Jew who wanders throughout every land without rest or repose . . . always faster and faster, without any destination or meaning, the mad rush itself alone is the final goal of this twentieth century madness."[8]

There was no simple link between anti-global politics and the rise of Nazism, however. Throughout the turbulent years of the Weimar

Republic, as Germans struggled to cope with the Versailles settlement, the loss of Germany's colonies, hyperinflation, and the Great Depression, Germans on both the right and the left sought insulation from what were seen as globalization's battering forces, including migration and global trade. Nor was there a teleological turn away from internationalism and globalization from 1918 onward. For a short time, many of Germany's leaders actively sought Germany's reintegration in international political and economic institutions, beginning with the Dawes Plan of 1924, which put the German economy back on a stable footing, and culminating in Germany's entry into the League of Nations in 1926. While the First World War had delivered a hard blow to the forces behind globalization and internationalism, it was the Great Depression that convinced many Germans and Europeans that the age of global capitalism was definitively over, bringing the Nazis to power on a surge of anti-global rhetoric and activism.

In the July 1932 election campaign, Hitler proclaimed, "There's so much international, so much world conscience . . . there's the League of Nations, the Disarmament Conference, Moscow, the Second International, the Third International—and what did all that produce for Germany?"[9] The Nazi state was to be sovereign, self-sufficient, bound by neither the norms of international law nor the dictates of international organizations and treaties. "The global economy is broken and will never again exist in its past form," proclaimed Johann Wilhelm Ludowici, who was charged with implementing the Third Reich's domestic settlement policies. "We have developed our economy from the hearth to the world, increasing our estrangement from the German land, and now we must find our way back from the world to the hearth, in the name of healthy rootedness [*Bodenständigkeit*]."[10]

FARMERS WERE not the only constituency that rallied to the Nazis' anti-global platform. Small shopkeepers and artisans constituted another core constituency of the Nazi movement. They were lured by the Nazi promise to take action against another powerful symbol of globalism and globalization in the interwar era: the department store.

Nazi propaganda
poster advertising
Reichsbauerntag, 1936.

Since the first "temples of consumption" appeared in German provincial cities in the 1890s, the stores had been magnets for controversy.
This was not only because they appeared to threaten local businesses,
but because they were synonymous with globalism. As historian Paul
Lerner has shown, department store owners in Germany deliberately
marketed their stores as globalist venues for commerce and entertainment. Many German department stores even adopted the world itself
as an emblem. Like flags, globes beckoned customers from department
store rooftops or at their entryways. Customers could indulge fantasies
of travel and escape as they took in spectacular displays of international
goods, purchased luggage and travel accessories, and even booked voyages abroad at in-house travel agencies.[11]

The German public also closely associated the department store
with Jews. Most of Germany's major department store chains had been
founded in German provincial towns and cities by Jews, including
Wertheim, Hermann Tietz, Leonhard Tietz, Schocken, Nathan Israel,

Jandorf, and others. Of the five largest department store chains in Germany before 1933, only one, Karstadt, was not a Jewish firm.[12]

Although department stores accounted for only 4–5 percent of retail sales as of 1930, they had proliferated in German cities and towns big and small, growing faster than anywhere else in the world except the United States. Their success was linked to several innovations that distinguished the department and chain store from traditional small retailers. Department stores and chain stores sold their wares at high volumes and low prices, making products more accessible than they were at small shops. They offered sales and discounts, but published standard prices (rather than requiring customers to negotiate prices individually). Department stores also spectacularly advertised and displayed their goods and allowed customers to browse, inspect, and touch them without pressure to buy (whereas in small shops, products were typically kept behind counters or in locked showcases). Goods could be exchanged or returned, and they were usually available immediately (whereas in specialty shops, they often had to be ordered and delivered weeks later). Finally, department stores became destinations for leisure as well as shopping. They increasingly staged exhibitions, demonstrations, and musical performances and offered services such as restaurants, banks, and salons.[13]

The rise of the department store was undeniable, but not always celebrated. As symbols of modern mass consumption, they featured prominently in novels, plays, and parliamentary and public debate. Already in the 1890s, small shopkeepers and retailers feared that they would be destroyed by the department stores' cutthroat pricing. Social critics worried about the "seductive" nature of department store displays and advertising, against which women in particular were considered defenseless. Fears about department stores were channeled into negative stereotypes of Jews as hucksters, speculators, and "foreign" capitalists who preyed upon innocent German women, an image that built on a stereotype of Jews as sexual predators. Hans Buchner, the economics editor of the *Völkischer Beobachter*, published two tracts expounding on the evils of the department store before 1933. The department store, he insisted, was inherently international. "That the 'German branch'...

works today with London, tomorrow with New York, and the day after tomorrow with Paris is entirely in line with the system."[14] Well before the Nazis came to power, therefore, the department store had become a lightning rod for social and cultural anxieties about modern consumerism, Jewish economic power, and globalization.

Nazi anti-globalists channeled these anxieties into their movement. Point 16 of the 1920 Nazi Party platform declared: "We demand the creation of a healthy middle class and its preservation; immediate communalization of large department stores and their rental at low prices to small retailers." Expectations were therefore high when the Nazis came to power. Small-business owners and craftspeople anticipated immediate relief from competition from chain and department stores. Before seizing control of the government, the Nazis nourished these hopes with a steady stream of virulently anti-Semitic propaganda targeting the stores. "As is well known, the Jewish 'business spirit' and Galician commercialism do not stop at border posts," wrote Hans Mertel in the *Völkischer Beobachter* in 1930. "These two specific Hebrew characteristics are equally active in all countries where there is something to gain. Just like bank and stock market capital, department store capital, which is known to be in the same kosher hands as the former, has a pronounced international character."[15]

Beginning in 1928, when the first Nazi delegates were elected to the Reichstag, local Nazis celebrated their victory by shattering department store windows in Berlin, an event captured on film. In the summer of 1932, there were at least ten attacks on department stores, including acts of terror in which *Sturmabteilung* (SA) members used tear gas and set off explosives in Leonhard Tietz and Woolworth stores in Krefeld, Wuppertal, and Düsseldorf.[16]

These efforts were supported by the Defense League of the Commercial Middle Class, a pressure group representing the interests of small retailers. The organization regularly stationed its members outside the doors of department stores, where they intimidated shoppers and distributed menacing flyers. One warned, "You are being watched, Madam! Why are you addicted to doing your shopping where goods are cleverly displayed in order to tempt you to buy? If you don't want to

Anti-Jewish sign posted in shop window.

jeopardize your husband's income, stay away from consumer cooperatives and large chain stores and buy only from your local retailer."

In some towns, local government officials found more coercive ways to support the "buy local" campaign. In Friedberg and Neckargmünd, state employees were fired after being spotted shopping at chain stores. In Hersfeld, anyone receiving public assistance was required to sign a formal declaration promising that they would spend the public funds only in "local small businesses." The declaration specified that shopping in "Jewish businesses, consumer cooperatives or chain stores" was forbidden. In Butzbach, all government purchases had to be made from "native German retailers of Aryan origins." And in Warburg, the Defense League of the Commercial Middle Class posted notices and staged protests outside department stores, demanding the "elimination of the destructive Jewish influence from the economic, political, and cultural life of the German people." Pamphlets and posters warned that the group would not shy away from publicly naming and shaming "saboteurs."[17]

* * *

WHILE SOME Nazis stood watch for "national traitors" outside department stores, others stormed the nation's gardens. Weimar-era settlement offices and urban gardening associations were all Nazified in the process known as *Gleichschaltung*, or "coordination." In this case, "coordination" was facilitated by the fact that both settlement and allotment gardening had always been such a politically malleable ideal. Georg Bonne, who began promoting the idea of nutritional autarky in the late nineteenth century, first published his book *How Can We Make Germany's Food Supply Independent from Foreign Countries?* in 1921. His book was republished in 1935. In the preface to the second edition, Bonne boasted that the National Socialist state had finally embraced his vision of de-urbanization and deglobalization. Germany needed to decentralize its large cities and give plots of land to workers so that they could make their own food, not only "for reasons of simple humanity and justice, but because in the case of a defensive war, when it comes down to the existence or non-existence of our nation," Germany would be forced to feed itself.

In a familiar refrain, Bonne argued that achieving autarky would require Germans to sacrifice consumption. He advocated a total ban on alcohol and tobacco, substances he denounced as "primary sources of human inferiority [*Minderwertigkeit*] and the increase in inferior people [*Minderwertigen*]." Meat consumption was to be reduced, and Germans were to exchange the empty calories of white bread for nutritious and authentically German black bread. Promoting this new autarkic lifestyle would naturally fall to housewives, and particularly to settler women, as it was "the duty of German women in the National Socialist state to make Germany's nutrition independent of foreign countries."[18]

Nazi settlement schemes built on existing programs and movements but also transformed them and infused them with their own ideology. With respect to allotment gardening, traditionally promoted on the left, the regime insisted that unlike the Weimar allotment garden, which served as a form of leisure for workers, the Nazis would use allotment gardens to help "preserve the healthy German blood" of peasants displaced to the city.[19] Allotment gardening under Nazism was intended to be a way of preventing a "spiritual flight from the land" and of preventing racial degeneration in the cities.[20]

It was even easier for the Nazis to co-opt the rural settlement movement, which was already largely a right-wing project by the early 1930s. In Prussia, a right-wing settlement movement had already developed out of pre–First World War efforts to "Germanize" and colonize the eastern borderlands. By the time the Nazis came to power, the settlement movement in Weimar Germany had created 57,288 settlements, mostly in the east. These settlements were typically small in size and struggled to survive. The situation of settlers in Pomerania was disastrous in the early 1930s.[21] The Evangelical Settlement Service, which relocated 218 families from "impoverished industrial regions" in the west to settlements in the east between 1929 and 1931, reported that the only families succeeding were those willing "to renounce all of the achievements of civilization (including electricity) and who had the single-minded determination to reintegrate into their eastern German homeland through hard agricultural labor."[22]

These challenges did not discourage Nazi experts from promoting the dream of autarky and rural resettlement. As with all areas of Nazi policy, responsibility for internal colonization was divided between several (often competing and conflicting) agencies. In addition to the Nazi Party itself, there was the *Reichsnährstand* (Reich Nutritional Agency) under Darré and Backe, responsible for agricultural and food policies; the *Reichsheimstättenamt* (Reich Homestead Office), charged with implementing housing and settlement policies; and the *Rasse und Siedlungs Hauptamt* (Race and Settlement Main Office), one of several agencies responsible for Nazi colonization in the east. Other agencies with a say on matters of international trade and economics included the Reichsbank, the Economics Ministry, and academic institutions such as the Kaiser Wilhelm Society in Berlin, where scientists conducted research with the goal of increasing nutritional autarky and producing synthetic substitutes for raw materials.[23]

One of the more influential Nazi advocates of autarkic economic policies was the journalist and propagandist Ferdinand Zimmermann, who published under the name Ferdinand Fried. Fried studied political economy and philosophy at Friedrich Wilhelms University in Berlin in the 1920s, where his teachers included Max Sering and Werner

Sombart. Their influence is evident in his writings on autarky and on Jews, which were in turn widely read by Nazi policy makers including Heinrich Himmler, Darré, and Backe. Beginning in 1933, he worked in the Reichsnährstand under Darré and Backe and became a member of the SS in 1934. In his 1931 book, titled *Autarky*, he linked individual and national self-sufficiency to "true" spiritual freedom. Autarky for Fried was "not only a purely economic or political question, but a world-view, a radical change in thinking," he claimed.[24] In practical terms, Fried's plan included all the usual elements. "Autarky means conscious disentanglement from the global economy," he explained. The ability of German consumers to renounce foreign goods was their greatest weapon. "Every orange or banana that we forgo, every ball of cotton or bag of coffee that we don't buy, is a hard and effective blow against the outside world."[25]

As in Weimar Germany, the settlement movement was intended to help Germany achieve independence from global forces. Johann Wilhelm Ludowici elaborated the major goals of Nazi settlement projects in a 1935 book. He envisioned settlement as a means of fighting unemployment and weathering economic crisis, but also for creating and reinforcing the Nazi *Volksgemeinschaft*, mixing together people from different social classes and geographic backgrounds. In the past, he claimed, there had been "two Germanies," the Germany of the city— and of globalization—and the Germany of the countryside. To the city resident, he claimed, "a coffee plantation in South America, a cotton or grain farm in North America, or a rubber plantation in Dutch India was much closer spiritually and materially than a German farmhouse that was perhaps located only an hour from his city villa or rented apartment." These city Germans had "in reality emigrated abroad, because their subsistence and their livelihood was very largely based on foreign raw materials, foreign food and foreign markets." Now, under the Nazi regime, Ludowici claimed that a massive "reverse migration" was under way as city dwellers remigrated "home" to the German nation. "Millions of Germans today are immigrating back to Germany, in their world-view, politically, economically, and spatially. This immigration movement must however be managed and observed by Reich planners from a racial, social, and economic perspective."[26]

Like Darré, Ludowici touted "Blood and Soil" as the basis of the settlement project and the renewal of the German nation, insisting that attachment to the land was an essential German trait. "The German has never been a nomad . . . but has always fought for land on which he could become sedentary." Settlement was a defensive mechanism against foreign influences as well. By settling Germany's borderlands with "strong German settlers," the regime would protect its borders "against the infiltration of a foreign race, the influence of a foreign culture, and the encroachment of foreign economy."[27]

Nazi settlement programs departed from earlier settlement schemes in their focus on racial selection. Previously, settlement organizers had screened prospective colonists for their farming experience. Their goal was to increase the number of Germans in contested eastern border regions, but they rarely insisted on any particular racial or eugenic criteria.[28] The settlers Backe sought, by contrast, were to be model Germans from a racial perspective: "Settlers must be truly valuable, racially flawless, hereditarily-genetically and medically tested as well as people of proven character."[29] Interior Ministry guidelines for selection of settlers instructed that prospective settlers should be rejected if they had been married for a significant amount of time without producing children or if their wives were older than thirty and never been pregnant. Jews, mixed-race individuals, anyone in a mixed marriage, those with hereditary diseases, and childless couples need not apply.[30]

As the Nazi regime prepared to go to war, settlement became a new kind of weapon, a pretext to expel Jews from the community. For example, in November 1938, Paul W., a prospective settler in Leipzig, wrote to the settlement division of the Agriculture Ministry, requesting that the ministry force "the Jew Ernst de Taube" to sell him his land. "My wish is that the Jew be informed by the Ministry that if he doesn't come to an agreement to sell his land to me, his property will be taken from him by force, since he is not intensively farming it." The ministry also compiled lists of property in Jewish hands that could be appropriated for settlement purposes, estimating that in the Rhineland alone, there were 1,595 Jews occupying 507 hectares of land suitable for the "regeneration of the German peasantry or new settlement."[31]

As in interwar Austria, another aspect of the Nazi ideology of settlement was the fetishization of the single-family home, represented as the antithesis of the modern city apartment building. Surprisingly, for a regime that claimed to be steeped in the collectivist values of the Volksgemeinschaft, Nazi propaganda appealed precisely to individualist fantasies of ownership and privacy, and to a vision of masculinity based on these ideals. Throughout the 1930s, the German Workers' Front published glossy magazines and books that promoted a Nazi fantasy of the single-family home. "A home on a homestead is the highest level of lifestyle that can be achieved for the working masses. One's own home on one's own land creates a sense of ownership, mature men full of character, to whom Heimat and fatherland are no longer empty words."[32] Another settlement advocate wrote in 1938 that next to economic advantages, the "major attraction" of settlement "is actually the deep desire to have one's own land and above all one's own house, where 'no one can interfere.' This drive for personal independence is the best and true core of the settlement efforts in Eastern Prussia."[33]

Nazi settlement plans—including those framed in terms of a "return" to Blood and Soil, were not anti-modern, however. Like settlement activists and anti-globalists elsewhere in interwar Europe, Nazi ideologists were convinced that more self-sufficient national economies represented the way of the future. Nazi political economist Johannes Stoye explained in 1937, "The turn away from the liberal division of labor in trade from country to country, the exaggerated and therefore unhealthy specialization that accompanied it, is being superseded by a spirit of self-reliance, connection with one's own values."[34]

The Nazi quest for greater autarky was also deeply reliant on science. As Susanne Heim has shown, the Third Reich's quest for autarky led to a boom in agricultural research. Agricultural science received more government money than all other branches of science throughout the years of Nazi rule.[35] Scientists linked to the Kaiser Wilhelm Institutes devoted themselves to research in animal and plant breeding with the goals of making land more productive and decreasing reliance on imports. Particular attention was devoted to the cultivation of what were called *bodenständig* or "homegrown" pigs, animals that fed entirely from German crops rather than imported fodder. In practice that meant potatoes, a crop that flourished on German soil. Increasing potato yields—and encouraging Germans (as well as pigs) to eat more potatoes was another goal of Reich scientists and propagandists. Potatoes already composed 12 percent of the average German's diet, but that number had to increase in order to decrease reliance on imported foods.

Potatoes were also seen as the key ingredient to closing what was called the "fat deficit." As of 1936, Germany still relied on imports for 60 percent of the fats its population consumed. By raising what historian Tiago Saraiva calls "fascist pigs"—fatter pigs raised on German potatoes, agronomists and policy makers hoped that Germany could come nearer to food independence. In order to close the fat deficit, researchers also focused on breeding plants high in oil or protein content, such as soy, sunflowers, and pumpkins. Research in hydrobiology meanwhile aimed to increase the production of fish and the amount of protein Germans got from eating fish rather than meat. Finally, and most ominously, Nazi researchers such as Heinrich Kraut performed experiments on Soviet prisoners of war and forced laborers from Eastern Europe in order to determine how little foreign workers could be fed without affecting their work performance. The goal was not only to increase the production of food but also to decrease the amount of food consumed by foreign workers and forced laborers in order to reserve more for Germans.[36]

The drive for autarky went well beyond the realm of food, of course. As in Fascist Italy, there were also scientific campaigns to find alternatives to imported cotton and wool. And there were other critical natural resources, such as rubber, that were in short supply. The rise of the automobile—not only as a vehicle for leisure travel but also as a crucial instrument of war—meant that demand for rubber to make tires increased exponentially from the 1930s onward. German imports of natural rubber increased from 34,000 tons in 1925 to 100,000 tons in 1937. More than half of this rubber was needed for tires. The war—and the expansion of the Third Reich through conquest—only exacerbated the problem. Nazi authorities estimated that they would need 300,000 tons of rubber in 1940 and set a goal of being "independent" in rubber production by 1943.[37]

Rubber was however a tropical agricultural product and particularly vulnerable to shortage in the event of a wartime blockade. The Nazi regime therefore invested considerable energy and money in the production of synthetic rubber, called Buna. Infamously, I. G. Farben's Buna plant was located in the larger Auschwitz concentration camp complex and used slave labor from the camp. These workers included the young chemist Primo Levi, whose life was saved only because he was seen as potentially useful to the Buna production effort.

Buna supplies were however infamously inadequate. The quality was poor—it had to actually be enhanced with small amounts of real rubber in order to be serviceable—and the quantity produced was never sufficient. As of January 1941, the Wehrmacht warned that its rubber reserves would last only one more month.[38] Nazi scientists therefore invested more in a second solution, growing rubber on European soil. This effort had gained steam with the conquest of Eastern Europe and the plunder of Soviet laboratories. Since the 1930s, Soviet scientists had been attempting to produce rubber from a plant called *kok-sagyz*. With the benefit of stolen Soviet samples, German authorities and scientists began to grow kok-sagyz in occupied territories. This included a plant-breeding station in Auschwitz that was staffed primarily by imprisoned female scientists.[39]

Finally, going "back to the land" did not mean retreat to a romantic utopia "off the grid." Nazi settlers were also supposed to harness new forms of technology to achieve the regime's goals. In a 1936 meeting of the Nazi Council of Ministers, Hermann Göring thus insisted that the "German economy, including agriculture, must increase its capacity to the extent that all materials are produced in Germany that can be produced, based on the existing level of science and technology. In this effort we must push the outermost limits of our technical capabilities."[40]

Propaganda generally depicted the settler's single-family home as the foundation of the modern good life. Instead of dark and stuffy "rental barracks" with their dismal back courtyards, settlers enjoyed "clean, fresh, airy homesteads. With barns and gardens, large parcels of land and healthy children." The settlers' standard of living was supposed to be equivalent to or higher than that of workers living in city apartments, because settlers allegedly had more disposable income thanks to the savings they achieved by growing their own food.[41]

Even as they promoted a good life of consumption and advanced technology in single-family homes, however, Nazi organizations created schools to inculcate settler women with the values (and skills) of home production, saving, and sacrifice. Once again, a huge amount of unpaid female and child labor supported the fantasy of the settler's "self-sufficiency." Work outside the home "stands in open contradiction to the life of a settler woman," explained one Nazi settlement advisor. That was because the success of any homestead relied on the nonstop labor of women on the farm. The Nazi regime's "settlement advisors" taught settler women "the value of self-production in the garden and barn, including storage, conservation, and stockpiling; the uses of Angora and sheep's wool," and many other methods of home production, which "gives the accomplishments of the settler woman in home economics a much greater national-economic weight than that of a city woman in a pure consumer household."[42]

As in many realms of Nazi policy, there were large gaps between the promises made on the campaign trail and actions once the Nazi hold on power was secure. Many factors explained the slow pace of development, including deference to large estate owners, who produced the bulk of German potatoes and cereals.[43] As the Nazi regime began to rearm in preparation for war in 1936, moreover, the building of single-family homes in rural settlements fell down the priority list. It was now more important to build mass housing for workers near armaments plants. Rearmament also caused a shortage of building materials and workers to build rural settlements.

In the end, German settlement projects were characterized by the same gaps between rhetoric and reality that plagued other settlement projects in Europe and the United States. While self-sufficiency in food production increased by about 10 percent in the 1930s, this was in part because of a decline in German exports. Many settlements both in Germany and in the occupied east failed to become economically viable (let alone provide completely for a settler's family).[44] Finally, even as settlement advocates insisted that settlements would become a bulwark against foreign migration and invasion, the Nazi regime imported more foreign workers than ever onto German soil during the Second World War, as the wartime labor shortage intensified. By the time Germany was defeated, there would be more than 7 million foreign workers, primarily from Eastern Europe, toiling in German factories and on German farms.

THE REGIME'S fantasy of economic independence was nearly impossible to achieve, even for individual farmers, let alone for the entire Reich. Food shortages were already stalking the German economy by 1937, in part because so many resources had been diverted toward rearmament. Darré noted in his diary on January 22, 1937, "The food situation is not looking good, you cannot cover your body with a washcloth," and blamed the Four-Year Plan. A few months later he worried about a "catastrophic shortage of labor in agriculture" and noted, "I will try to get agriculture workers with German blood from abroad."[45] Other shortages were also emerging from Germany's autarkic efforts, particularly in textiles. As of August 1935, there was enough cotton in Germany for two and a half weeks, and there were shortages of wool as well.[46]

Personality conflicts and power struggles between ambitious leaders also stymied Nazi efforts. Tensions between Darré and Backe emerged early on. Backe described his boss in a letter to his wife as a "loser" who was "weak" and "insecure." A year later, Darré wrote in his diary that Backe demonstrated "a total lack of talent for political questions, a particular Russian weakness for making decisions linked to vanity and an ambitious wife."[47]

Backe was the clear victor in this struggle. But the conflict was actually far less about ideology than about personality, skills, and the regime's changing needs. Darré had been a highly successful political mobilizer, propagandist, and campaigner, skills essential to the regime's rise to power. But Backe was the more effective policy maker and administrator. And especially during wartime, Backe's ability to manage a massive rationing system proved more important than Darré's charisma. He was charged with managing food policy in the Four-Year Plan and consulted early on about plans to invade Russia. Most infamously, he developed and implemented a plan to feed Germans by starving Soviet civilians. When Germany invaded the Soviet Union, the Wehrmacht and German collaborators ate entirely from local reserves, requisitioning 9 million tons of grain. The result was the death of 4–7 million Soviet civilians from hunger. Backe's "success" in starving Russians and managing the German food supply during the war accelerated Darré's downfall. In 1942, Darré was forced aside with a medical pretext, and Backe replaced him at the helm of the Ministry of Food and Agriculture.[48]

The conflict between Darré and Backe was typical of broader tensions within the Nazi regime. First there was Hitler's tendency to play subordinates against one another and to create overlapping competencies that guaranteed conflict and competition. Second, there were endemic conflicts between prewar goals and ideology and wartime exigencies. Finally, there was internal conflict around political and economic goals, including autarky itself. Nazi leaders disagreed among themselves both about the extent to which autarky was realistic or desirable for Germany and how best to achieve it.

There was widespread consensus among Nazi leaders that Germany needed *Lebensraum*—living space—both to compensate for lands taken from Germany by the Treaty of Versailles and to achieve the goal of economic self-sufficiency. But it was a more open question whether Germany's quest for Lebensraum could be satisfied through internal colonization. As late as 1939, Nazi settlement expert Ernst Knoll claimed that Germany had plenty of Lebensraum available within its existing borders—it just needed to be settled and cultivated. Germany had enough land to create 469 million small settlements, he insisted; with an average family of five per settlement, this was sufficient to settle every person on Earth within German borders.[49]

But most Nazi geopolitical experts disagreed, insisting behind closed doors that autarky was both unrealistic and undesirable for Germany. The chief economic strategist for the Wehrmacht, Gen. Georg Thomas, argued that it would be a mistake to completely withdraw from the global economy. In spite of the Four-Year Plan, Germany still imported 20 percent of its foodstuffs from abroad, especially fats, and was now facing a shortage of labor. And there were downsides to autarky, including the higher cost of many products and the labor needed to produce substitutes. In light of these realities, Thomas advocated a return to global trade for Germany, particularly as "the most highly civilized lands are those most interlaced with the world abroad." Rudolf Eicke, another economic expert in the regime, agreed with this perspective, insisting that as "a people without space ... and not least as a political Great Power, we have the highest interest in strengthening global trade."[30]

Other prominent Nazis shared the view that autarky would lead to a decline in German living and cultural standards—to the detriment, perhaps, of the regime's popular legitimacy. In 1936, Robert Ley, the leader of the German Workers' Front (which was, not coincidentally, composed largely of consumers), posed the question, "Was foreign trade discovered by God or by the Devil? Is it actually itself an idol or a demon?" His own answer was clear. He mocked Germans who would ostracize a German housewife "who buys Brazilian coffee or a few Spanish lemons as a traitor to the Volk" at the same time that they burst with pride "when somewhere in South America a German bathtub is installed." For Ley, autarky meant backwardness. "Cutting ourselves off from the global economy ... over the long run means not only renouncing conveniences of daily life that are provided by foreign goods, it means renouncing participation in the cultural and technological advancement of the world."[31] Other experts disputed that autarky was even possible. Behind the scenes, an economic expert confessed, "Even if we had 20 million sheep, we would only be able to produce 20 percent of the wool we consume domestically."[32]

In spite of such disagreements, Nazi propaganda and trade publications continually published articles promoting autarky as the only means for Germany's survival. German consumers—particularly women— were flooded with propaganda urging them to shop, cook, and eat autarkically. As in Fascist Italy, consumer guides and cookbooks emphasized a need to limit consumption of fats, buy and eat only seasonal "products of the German soil," and prevent waste. At the same time, Nazi propaganda insisted that dietary needs were themselves racially specific, the ultimate manifestation of the link between Blood and Soil. Humans thrived on soil native to their "race." German soil produced the foods

Nazi propaganda poster, date unknown: "Hitler is building. Help along. Buy German Goods."

that best nourished German "blood." Foods eaten by "eskimos or bush Africans" were not appropriate for Germans, nor could Germans survive on the "extremely parsimonious and makeshift fare that fuels the often hard labor of a Chinese coolie."[53]

When they were not pickling vegetables and preparing autarkic recipes, German women were urged to extend the do-it-yourself spirit beyond the kitchen, by making their own furniture and taking to the spinning wheel to produce their own linens and clothing (ideally, traditional German dirndls). In support of this campaign, weaving schools and spinning evenings were established across Germany.[54] The *Kreuzzeitung* reported, "The rural population should once again be in a position to create their own wool and textile goods, from raw material to finished product."[55] All of this propaganda intensified during the war.

German women's magazines were now filled with articles exhorting women to "Make it Yourself!"—with instructions on how to produce clothing, linens, toys, shoes, and bags at home.[56] Settlers' associations also rallied for the war effort, urging settlers and gardeners to contribute even more to the German economy. The outbreak of war meant that everyone "who farms a piece of German land" had the "undeniable duty to restlessly exploit all of the resources still at hand."[57]

THE NAZI regime finally resolved the tensions between its anti-global ideology and the realities of the German economy through imperial conquest. Already in the 1920s and 1930s, German academics, institutions, and businessmen had turned toward the Balkans to replace other economic relationships. They built an informal empire that provided Germany with both raw materials and political influence. When the war began, Nazi policy makers and experts shifted explicitly from seeking autarky for the German nation toward achieving autarky for continental Europe—dominated by Germany. They called their vision of the Nazi empire *Grossraumwirtschaft*, a deceptively (and deliberately) benign-sounding term that can be roughly translated as a "large regional economy." In practice, this "large regional economy" looked a lot like an empire in which colonies (in this case Eastern European states) provided raw materials in exchange for German industrial goods.[58]

In pursuing a "large regional economy," Germany, like Fascist Italy, claimed to simply be following the lead of other imperial powers. Britain and France had both already created protectionist bubbles around their empires. Japan, meanwhile, strove to create an anti-colonial autarkic empire in East Asia. The Greater East Asia Co-Prosperity Sphere was intended to be a self-sufficient regional bloc that was free of white, Western domination and led by Japan.[59] German geopolitical experts such as Karl Haushofer saw the Japanese empire (along with the United States and Russia) as a model for what Germany would achieve in Central Europe.[60] Nazi leaders promoted the fiction of a "peaceful" economic alliance with continental neighbors while admitting behind closed doors that neighbors already saw through the rhetoric of

"Grossraumwirtschaft"—they recognized that it was a euphemism for Nazi domination. "The problem of *Grossraumwirtschaft* can only be discussed in public with the utmost caution, so that the affected countries don't become nervous," warned Gustav Schlotterer, leader of the "Eastern Section" of the Reich's Economics Ministry.[61]

Darré and Backe were both long-term proponents of Grossraumwirtschaft. In his diary, Darré enthusiastically recorded Hitler's discussions of his plans for imperial expansion within Europe. In October 1936, after dinner with Hitler, he noted that Hitler found "Mussolini's Abyssinian adventure incomprehensible. Germany has no colonial desires. The Baltic is the future German sea." In September 1937, two years before the invasion of Poland, Darré reported gleefully that Hitler agreed with his view that, "Our future is in the Baltic and the Russian realm. Better to sacrifice two million men in wars again and finally have space to breathe."[62]

Backe contrasted the Nazi ideal of the Grossraumwirtschaft favorably to the pre–First World War global economy and underscored the hypocrisy of the British Empire. "Only in a Germany united by National Socialism" could there be "enough strength to free ourselves from the chains of the global economy and to become increasingly independent." Meanwhile, he claimed, "The world watched the charade put on by the English imperialists, whose creed is free trade and the global division of labor, and who elevated the fight against autarky to a dogma at the same time that they practically realized the autarky of a *Grossraum* in their own empire." Germany had now found its own way to empire and to self-sufficiency. "In the place of the international global economy there is the large regional economy, characterized by the union of peoples of the same or related race and same space." Backe portrayed this European Grossraumwirtschaft as a peaceful union that would guarantee Europe's food supply, even as millions of Soviet citizens were enslaved or starved in order to provide Germans with "nutritional freedom."[63]

TENSIONS BETWEEN the Nazi Party's anti-global propaganda, pressure from local supporters, and policies also characterized the campaign against department stores. Much to the chagrin of many of the party's grassroots supporters, the Nazi seizure of power did not immediately bring about the expected crackdown on department stores. Provincial governments were empowered to double taxes on department stores in March 1933, but not a single store was actually seized or closed and rented out to a small shopkeeper.[64] Hermann Tietz, on the brink of bankruptcy, was even bailed out with a generous loan in June 1933. The Nazi regime could not entirely do without these symbols of global commerce.

There were several reasons for the reversal, chief among them that nearly one-third of Germans were unemployed in 1933, and department stores employed tens of thousands of non-Jewish employees. When local Nazis took matters into their own hands, Nazi authorities in Berlin actually intervened to stop them. Rudolf Hess issued a statement in July 1933 declaring that "actions against department stores and similar businesses are prohibited," in the interest of preserving the jobs of the "large number of German employees and workers." Boycotts, blacklists, advertising bans, and the harassment of customers (not to mention bombs and tear gas) were also banned soon after the Nazi regime consolidated its power.[65] The regime instead took mostly symbolic measures against the stores, forbidding members of the party from shopping in uniform and banning the stores from selling Nazi merchandise, such as swastika flags, photos of Hitler, SA dolls, and Hitler Youth uniforms.[66]

Small-business owners who supported the regime did not hesitate to express their feelings of betrayal. One outraged writer protested, "We trusted Adolf Hitler's word, immediate help for small and medium-sized businesses and the economy. We are desperate! The economy is shrinking every day, nothing is being done for us. . . . Can you simply break your word like that?"[67] Lorenz Sieberg in Bonn wrote directly to the Economics Ministry: "During the time of the national awakening the middle class alone made the largest sacrifices . . . The middle class was laughed at, but the party could count on us in all elections. As shopkeepers we were denounced as Nazi dogs and our business declined and the department stores gained the advantage." When the Nazis came to power, supporters expected relief. But it had been more than a year, and "these large chain stores are not only tolerated but are actually supported by the state." Sieberg protested, "Didn't we sacrifice everything for our leader Adolf Hitler? Are we now therefore a stepchild? Absolutely nothing has been done for us."[68] Another disillusioned shopkeeper from Magdeburg complained that "not a single department store or nickel-and-dime has been closed." To the contrary, "Jewish businesses are growing again with disguised names and Jews behind the scenes. That is the worst! Instead of hanging these exploiters . . . they are now breathing morning air and mocking our new Germany."[69]

But if the regime was not aggressively targeting department stores, it was far from business as usual for Jewish owners. Instead, the threat of popular violence helped the regime pressure department store owners to cooperate with the Nazi state. Even before the Nazi seizure of power, department store owners attempted to defend themselves and their role in the German economy. In 1931, several department store owners, including members of the Tietz and Schocken families, published an editorial in the *Berliner Tagblatt* to counter the accusation that their stores were putting small retailers out of business or were selling mostly foreign goods. They pointed out that only 4.5 percent of total retail sales took place at department stores and claimed that only 2 percent of the business they did was in foreign goods, countering the image of the global emporium. They also reminded readers that the stores distributed German goods to department stores around the world.[70]

A publication celebrating the fiftieth anniversary of the Hermann Tietz chain depicted the Tietz firm as a family concern that had started out as a "progressive small business."[71] Schocken put out a memo defending the company from accusations of deliberately cutting prices in order to force small retailers out of business.[72] In October 1933, Schocken executives also met with representatives of the Economics Ministry, where they emphasized their efforts to create and maintain employment. The Schocken chain had 5,435 employees and had not fired anyone (except for 150–200 women, who were replaced with more expensive male employees) in spite of flagging sales during the economic crisis.[73]

The department store survived the Nazi regime, but many of their Jewish owners, managers, and employees did not. Jewish department store owners and employees were harassed, arrested, fired. Their businesses and homes were confiscated and sold to non-Jewish investors at fire-sale prices. On April 1, 1933, the Nazis staged an official blockade of Jewish businesses, allegedly in reprisal for "Jewish" propaganda that sullied the image of the Nazis abroad. The so-called boycott was heavily promoted by Nazi women's groups. Henry Max Adler, an employee at the Israel Department Store in Berlin, recalled "the Stormtroopers standing outside the shops and screaming . . . they were just screaming their heads off 'Juden Raus!,'" "Down with the Jude!" and they were painting these terrible things on these windows." The next day, he recalls, "the people they just cleaned it up and then business as usual."[74] Although the boycott was supposed to be "orderly," it escalated into violence against people and property. Adler's father-in-law had a butcher shop in Charlottenburg in West Berlin where the windows were shattered; his business never recovered. While many Germans ignored the boycott, it sent clear signals of exclusion and intimidation to both the public and German Jews, and also marked "Jewish" businesses for the public.[75]

Georg Manasse, the general manager of the Schocken firm, was first taken into custody "for his own protection" in March 1934 and forced to resign his position in June of that year, along with Jewish employees in many stores around Germany. Before he left his office, he wrote a memo to his successors. "I have given more than half my life to this company. I have served it with body and soul. I walk out the door with a heavy heart. Out of solidarity, which will continue into the future, I stand ready to provide advice from the sidelines, to whatever extent possible."[76] Manasse fled Germany to Sweden (and then on to the United States) with his wife and four children a year later, and his boss, Salman Schocken, emigrated to Palestine and then to the United States.

On November 9, 1938, during the so-called Night of Broken Glass, at least twenty-nine department stores were destroyed in an officially sanctioned pogrom targeted at Jewish businesses and people. The Jewish manager of a department store in Chemnitz was beaten to death in the cellar of the store. The remaining Jewish-owned department stores were soon completely "Aryanized." Georg Wertheim transferred the firm to the name of his wife, Ursula, considered an Aryan under Nazi law. The couple even divorced in an attempt to retain control of the company, but she was also forced out in 1939. The stores' names were also Aryanized: Tietz became Kaufhof, Wertheim became AWAG, Schocken became Merkur.[77] The German department store was "deglobalized," even as their owners scattered around the world.

THE WAR ended in 1945 with fantasies of Grossraumwirtschaft in shambles. Darré was arrested by the Allies and tried at Nuremberg. His lawyers (and later apologists) used the fact that he was pushed aside by the regime as evidence of his innocence. Blaming everything on Backe, his defense claimed that he had been sidelined because of his ideological differences with the regime, noting that "anti-Semitism is in itself no crime against humanity." In particular, Darré had nothing to do with "nihilistic views that lead to mass murder."[78] He was charged with eight crimes but convicted of only two: "atrocities and offenses committed against civilian populations between 1938 and 1945" (the starvation of 6–7 million) and "membership of criminal organizations" (the Nazi Party). These convictions earned him a seven-year prison sentence. He was nonetheless released in 1950 and died of liver cancer in 1955.

Herbert Backe, by contrast, made no excuses. Indeed, he was surprised to be arrested by the Allies, expecting that his expertise on food policy (and perhaps his commitment to fighting Communism) would be valued by the Americans and British. Writing his testimony in prison in 1946, he remained convinced that historians would one day appreciate the extent to which "National Socialist policies served peaceful development" in Europe. "I am convinced that historians will one day correctly appreciate Hitler and his behavior," he continued. "They will understand that he was placed in a time in which one ideology—that of liberalism— was at its end, because its time was up." Backe's time was also up. Fearing that the Allies planned to deliver him to the Soviet Union, the land of his birth, he committed suicide in his prison cell on April 6, 1947.[79]

CONCLUSION

A NEW ERA OF WORLD COOPERATION:
NEW YORK, 1939

THE CROWD THAT gathered in the lobby of the Great Northern Hotel in New York City was agitated. Thousands of men and women pushed and shoved their way toward the entrance of the ballroom, where a rally was about to begin. Some journalists tried to document the scene and were assaulted by the crowd, to the shouts of "keep the newspapers out!" In the packed ballroom, a man repeatedly yelled, "Is there a Jew in the House?" A neighbor shushed him and was himself accused of being a Jew and nearly attacked, until he protested that he was Italian.

It was May 24, 1939, and the "Great Pro-American Mass Meeting in Behalf of Free Speech and Americanism" had begun. The meeting had initially been scheduled to take place in Carnegie Hall, but at the last minute Carnegie Hall thought better of the idea and refused to let the crowd in.

There were at least two Jews in the house: Rosika Schwimmer and her personal secretary, Edith Wynner, both undercover. The rally was co-sponsored by the American Federation Against Communism, the American Patriots, and the Christian Front. A previous "Pro-American" rally had been held in Madison Square Garden on February 20 of that year, attended by 20,000 people. Film footage shows attendees giving the Hitler salute; a young protester who breaches the stage is beaten up by uniformed guards and then carried away by police while the crowd shouts its approval. Fritz Kuhn, leader of the German-American Bund, mocks the "Jewish-controlled press" and promises the crowd that he will fight for a "socially just, white Gentile ruled United States."[1]

One of the most popular speakers at the May rally was Joe McWilliams of the American Nationalist Party. He promised that "what Hitler had done in Germany, and Mussolini, in Italy was wonderful, but what they (the American Nationalists) would do in the United States will be the best of all." Greeted with wild cheers, he pledged that if Roosevelt brought America into the war, he would "stand on Sixth Avenue with a machine gun, shooting at some target." Schwimmer, aged sixty-two, remained in the lobby. Wynner became anxious for her safety and emerged from the ballroom. She was relieved to find Schwimmer seated in a comfortable chair next to the literature table. One of the attendees had asked her to guard the table, to make sure that no one took the swag for sale without paying for it.[2]

BY THE late 1930s, it was clear to Rosika Schwimmer that the League of Nations had failed. As Europe lurched toward another war, she and her colleagues began planning for the next postwar reconstruction, for the new world order. In a 1939 speech, Schwimmer argued that the league had been doomed from the start. "Versailles dictators" had been "panting for punishment of the defeated nations" instead of striving for world peace. "Manchuria, Ethiopia, China, Austria, Czechoslovakia, Spain, Memel, world rearmament on astronomical scales, millions of stateless men, women, and children roaming the world in search of shelter and food are the mile-stones on the death march of the League of Nations."[3]

In a 1937 pamphlet, Schwimmer and her colleague Lola Maverick Lloyd laid out a vision for a more democratic form of world government. It would begin with a World Constitutional Convention, to which no government and military leaders would be invited. Rather, delegates would be elected directly from the general population in each country. Their idea was to create a form of world government

Poster for "Great
Pro-American Mass
Meeting," 1939.

Great Pro-American
MASS MEETING

In behalf of

FREE SPEECH
and
AMERICANISM

WEDNESDAY, MAY 24, AT 8:30 P. M.

AT CARNEGIE HALL
57th ST. AND 7th AVE., NEW YORK CITY

SPEAKERS
BOAKE CARTER
Radio's Fearless News Editor, on the timely subject
"FREE SPEECH AND THE NEWS"
and others.

Presiding—GEORGE U. HARVEY
Dynamic, Capable Borough President of Queens
President of "WE AMERICANS"

This meeting is under the sponsorship of:
American Federation Against Communism
American Patriots
The Christian Front
American Nationalist Party.

Tickets may be purchased from:
CARNEGIE HALL, 57th St. and 7th Ave., New York, N. Y.
IROQUOIS HOTEL, 149 West 44th Street, New York, N. Y.
WALTER OGDEN, 413 West 59th Street, New York, N. Y.

General Admission 25c   Reserved 50c   Special Reserved 99c

that would represent the people's interests, rather than those of the world leaders that had brought the world to the brink of war for a second time in thirty years.

The primary goal of this imagined World Organization was to preserve peace. But Schwimmer and Lloyd saw the reconstitution of the global economy as central to this broader mission. They called for a commission "to plan the regulation of the world's production of raw materials and the control of its distribution according to the needs of all nations, thus removing the excuse for forcible conquest of territory and for continued existence of empires, colonies, mandates," as well as a "commission to plan the abolition of all tariffs and customs and the establishment of free trade between all nations."[4]

*   *   *

NINE BLOOD-SOAKED years later, the League of Nations met in Geneva to dissolve itself. Carl Joachim Hambro of Norway presided. Since the General Assembly had last gathered, "A world order has gone to pieces and a new, and we trust a better, one is slowly and painfully emerging from the debris and disaster," he began. Hambro did not shirk from responsibility for the league's failures. "We know that we were reluctant to shoulder responsibility for the great decisions, where greatness was needed, and we know that we cannot escape history." But if the league had "failed to achieve its greatest immediate objective," he hoped that "our disappointments and deceptions may be turned to use in cementing the structure of a new world security."[5]

The years between 1939 and 1946, years of death and destruction on an unprecedented scale, were also years of planning. As Europe's deck was cleared of the rubble of fascism, state leaders, experts, and planners around the world mapped out the foundation of what they hoped would be a more robust form of globalism and a more stable and equitable global economy. They disagreed about how to accomplish their goals, however, depending on how they understood the origins of the catastrophe that the world had just survived.

There were as many visions for the postwar reconstruction of the global economy as there were diagnoses of what had gone wrong in the 1930s. Fantasies of achieving national autarky or self-sufficiency had been largely discredited, as they were now associated with Italian, German, and Japanese militarism. But that didn't mean a return to Stefan Zweig's World of Yesterday. The goal of many postwar planners, thinkers, and economists was to make the revival of globalization compatible with policies that provided greater economic and political stability and equity, both domestically and internationally.

During the war, Franklin Delano Roosevelt had committed to bring the ideals and policies of the New Deal to the rest of the world, including an expansive notion of economic rights as "human rights."[6] After Roosevelt named "Freedom from Want" among the four essential freedoms, the principle was projected internationally and enshrined in the Atlantic Charter issued by Roosevelt and Churchill in 1941. In addition to the far-reaching goal of assuring "that all the men in all the lands may live out their lives in freedom from fear and want," the charter promised that the Allies would "further the enjoyment by all states, great or small, victor or vanquished, of access, on equal terms, to the trade and to the raw materials of the world which are needed for their economic prosperity" and "bring about the fullest collaboration between all nations in the economic field with the object of securing, for all, improved labor standards, economic advancement, and social security."

These measures were explicitly framed as insurance against the rise of a new Hitler or Mussolini. A key question remained unresolved, however: the extent to which national sovereignty should be compromised in pursuit of reviving globalism (and whose sovereignty, specifically). There were also ongoing tensions between the goal of creating more democratic multilateral institutions to regulate the global economy and the rise of the United States and the USSR as hegemons in a bipolar, Cold War world.

The global economy was so fundamental to postwar planning because during the war, thinkers and planners across the Atlantic linked the rise of fascism directly to globalization's collapse. Writing in 1944, Karl Polanyi insisted that the rise of fascism was not a consequence of the Great War, the Treaty of Versailles, "Junker militarism," or "Italian temperament." It was rather a response to the indignities imposed by economic liberalism and globalization. Fascism was "an ever-given political possibility, an almost instantaneous emotional reaction in every industrial community since the 1930s." He explained, "The idea of a self-adjusting market implied a stark Utopia. Such an institution could not exist for any length of time without annihilating the human and natural substance of society; it would have physically destroyed man and transformed his surroundings into a wilderness. Inevitably, society took measures to protect itself, but whatever measures it took impaired the self-regulation of the market, disorganized industrial life, and thus endangered society in yet another way." Making the world safe for globalization *and* democracy at the same time would require new measures to protect human dignity from the indignities imposed by the market.[7]

When leaders and policy makers gathered during and after the Second World War to reinvent the global economic system, many agreed with Polanyi's diagnosis. In its final publication, called *Economic Stability in the Post-War World*, economists in the League of Nations' Economic and Financial Organization (which had relocated to Princeton, New Jersey) reaffirmed the ideal of greater economic equality between states. The report cited a fundamental shift "in public opinion on economic questions." It was now widely believed that "wide differences in the standards of living of different peoples are a menace to social order and international understanding, the growing sense of world unity." Postwar economic policy would have to address inequality. It would shift in focus from production to consumption, toward the goal of securing "a minimum standard of living for all," a phrase that echoed Frank McDougall's ideas from the 1930s.[8]

On the domestic front (in both Eastern and Western Europe), postwar planners designed policies intended to maintain full employment and to create a safety net in the event of inevitable downturns. Social benefits were both a right and essential to the functioning of a stable global economy. "All measures of social insurance, but especially unemployment insurance, contribute to the stability of consumers' demand, and hence to the stability of the whole economy," the league's economists advised.[9]

In Britain in 1942, William Beveridge authored his famous report, titled *Social Insurance and Allied Services*, outlining plans for a postwar welfare state in Britain, including universal health care. Beveridge's *Full Employment in a Free Society*, published two years later, argued that it was the responsibility of the state to maintain a low unemployment rate. Both reports were based on the principles of Keynesian economics, which stipulated that governments should spend more, rather than less, during an economic depression in order to stimulate the economy and fight unemployment.

On the international side there was also greater attention to global inequality and economic development after the Second World War.[10] Historians typically see the Bretton Woods Agreement of 1944 as the key moment in the foundation of a postwar global monetary system. The conference resulted in a plan that replaced the gold standard with a system based on the US dollar (a reflection of American power at the time), which was in turn pegged to gold at a fixed rate of $35 an ounce.

Delegates to the Bretton Woods Conference inaugurated the International Monetary Fund as a central bank to lend money to governments in the case of an imbalance of payments. Governments that took part in the system could inflate or deflate their currency by up to 10 percent without the approval of the International Monetary Fund, giving them more flexibility to use fiscal and monetary policy to manage their domestic economies. At the same time, the delegates to Bretton Woods created the International Bank for Reconstruction and Development to provide loans for postwar reconstruction and economic development. The agreement was supposed to make the revitalization of a global economy compatible with expanding welfare states, full employment, and development goals. It was a "Third Way" between the hyper-globalized nineteenth century and the protectionist 1930s.

Latin American policy makers, along with officials and experts from China, India, and Eastern Europe, pushed hard for the Bretton Woods Agreement to prioritize development, both by supporting state-led development policies and providing international loans and support.[11] One of the last reports published by the League of Nations addressed this issue head-on. It explicitly aimed to reassure so-called developed countries that they had nothing to fear from the industrialization of poor countries. Having studied the previous seventy years of trade and industrialization, the league concluded that with a country's industrialization, demand for foreign manufactured goods actually increased overall, at least until the 1930s when international trade relations broke down.[12]

Paul Rosenstein-Rodan, a Polish economist (widely seen as a founder of development economics), was a leading advocate of international support for developing economies. Writing from exile in Britain during the war, he observed that while welfare states and progressive taxation could redistribute the wealth produced by globalization domestically, there was no such system internationally. "In effect, today, the United States, Great Britain, France and Germany, representing 13 per cent of the world's population, own almost 50 per cent of the world's goods, and more than two-thirds of the world's income are reserved for less than one-third of the world's population."[13] The result was widespread anger and disillusionment with globalization. "It is no wonder that many nations, many peoples, have become impatient. They have been told that if only order and peace obtained for a sufficiently long period, wealth would increase and at least the opportunities of all nations and all peoples would be equal; and yet in a hundred years, which is a sufficiently long period, they have seen that these promises have not been fulfilled." He called for international efforts to provide greater "equality of opportunity" between different nations. According to Rosenstein-Rodan, there were two choices for countries such as Poland that had large-scale underemployment and poverty: emigration or industrialization. Because "large-scale resettlement and emigration are not feasible," he argued, "international capital must be made available to the poorer countries to help them to reach a level from which onwards they can grow richer 'on their own.' The development of the economically backward areas of the world is ... the most important task facing us in the making of the peace."[14]

Notably, however, Rosenstein-Rodan was not willing to condemn colonialism—perhaps in concession to his British hosts. In response to a question about whether his call for foreign investment in colonized countries veered "dangerously" toward calling for "the exploitation of those areas," Rosenstein-Rodan replied, "If a great Colonial Power, such as Great Britain, were to retire from the task of bringing the colonial peoples towards the goal she had set before them, it would be far worse than continuing her work. 'Exploitation' of this type would be more beneficial than complete indifference."[15]

This ambiguity about colonialism and sovereignty was baked into the foundation of new postwar organizations and ideals. The Atlantic Charter had declared that the Allies "respect the right of all peoples to choose the form of government under which they will live; and they wish to see sovereign rights and self-government restored to those who have been forcibly deprived of them." Such universalist language naturally raised hopes and expectations among subjects of colonial empires worldwide. European leaders, however, did not necessarily share this assumption.[16]

The United Nations was also characterized by tensions between universalist rhetoric and the persistence of racial, gender, economic, and political hierarchies. The United Nations was formally inaugurated in San Francisco in October 1945 with a membership of 51 states (in

2021 it had 193 members). The preamble of the Charter of the United Nations proclaimed that its purpose was "to reaffirm faith in fundamental human rights, in the dignity and worth of the human person, in the equal rights of men and women and of nations large and small." The United Nations was intended to address and compensate for the weaknesses of the League of Nations and to represent a more democratic and inclusive form of global governance. Schwimmer and her colleagues should have been pleased.[17]

But while proclaiming the equality of nations, some nations (namely the United States, Great Britain, France, the USSR, and China, which had permanent seats on the United Nations Security Council) were clearly more equal than others. While declaring that the United Nations was based on the "principle of the sovereign equality of all members," the charter was also hazy about the persistence of empire and racial discrimination. As historian Mark Mazower has argued, many British leaders hoped that the United Nations would help sustain the authority of a "civilizing" British Empire.[18] In the United States, Jim Crow remained the law throughout the South, and de facto discrimination continued in the North. If women now had more formal political rights in many countries, they were generally expected to leave the war factories behind and return home to their "traditional" roles when the men came home. Americans meanwhile imagined that the abuse of "human rights" was something that occurred in distant lands, not right in their own backyards, in spite of the protests of civil rights leaders to the contrary.[19]

But even if the universalist ideals expressed in the founding document of the United Nations were aspirational, they inspired action. Anticolonial leaders immediately began to lobby the United Nations to make demands for national sovereignty. By 1946, the United Nations General Assembly had already become a powerful forum for anti-imperial agitation. It would take time, but women also made growing demands for their own human rights. It would not be business as usual after 1945.[20]

With respect to the global economy, anti-colonial leaders continued to insist (as they had in the interwar years) that decolonization was a necessary precondition to any form of internationalism or globalization that was not exploitative. During the Second World War, Jawaharlal

Nehru, the future prime minister of India, had further developed this argument. "Internationalism can indeed only develop in a free country," he declared. "When we talked of the independence of India it was not in terms of isolation. We realized, perhaps more than many other countries, that the old type of complete national independence was doomed, and there must be a new era of world cooperation." But this was not to be the "globalism" of the British Empire or Empire Free Trade. Instead, India would seek an alliance that "should preferably cover the world or as large a part of it as possible, or be regional. . . . The British Commonwealth did not fit in with either of these conceptions."[21]

These were the core ideals of what would become the nonaligned movement. That movement blossomed after the Second World War in the crossfire of decolonization and the Cold War. It was intended to represent a new global alliance of states that were neither "aligned with" nor dependent on any imperial power, including the United States and the Soviet Union.[22] When delegates from twenty-four Asian and African countries met in Bandung, Indonesia, in April 1955, the first resolution they agreed upon was "the urgency of promoting economic development in the Asian-African region . . . on the basis of mutual interest and respect for national sovereignty."[23]

DECOLONIZATION AND the efforts of the nonaligned movement did produce a more inclusive form of internationalism than had existed before 1945. But the goals of promoting a more equitable and democratic model of globalization remained contested. Neoliberal economists such as Ludwig von Mises did not believe that globalization had produced fascism, but rather that fascists and socialists had interfered with the workings of the liberal global economy. As historian Quinn Slobodian argues, after the war these economists sought to make global markets safe *from* democracy rather than *for* democracy by encasing them in international institutions that would, if necessary, infringe on national sovereignty and counter economic nationalism. In 1944, von Mises argued explicitly that postwar international institutions would need to "include a rigid limitation of sovereign rights of every country. Measures which affect debts, the money systems, taxations, and other important matters have to be administered by international tribunals, and without an international police force such a plan could not be carried out. Force must be used to make debtors pay."[24]

The neoliberal economists were, in a sense, correct in their diagnosis. As long as globalization exacerbated inequality and compromised sovereignty, people would organize to contest it in a democratic system, using mass politics or nationalism as their weapon. The Bretton Woods system provided a technocratic fix, but without substantial popular participation. And in several ways, Bretton Woods institutions and postwar welfare states disappointed hopes for more equitable domestic and global economies.

Racial and gender inequality were anchored in new postwar welfare states that reinforced the ideal of families with a sole (white) male breadwinner.[25] Beveridge himself argued, "In the national interest it is important that the interruption [of paid employment] by childbirth should be as complete as possible." Policies that reinforced the ideal of the white male breadwinner were essential to the continuation of the "British race" and empire, Beveridge argued. "In the next thirty years housewives as mothers have vital work to do in ensuring the adequate continuance of the British race and of British ideals in the world."[26]

British and US representatives to the conference meanwhile disagreed about the extent to which International Monetary Fund (IMF) loans would be conditional on external audits and interventions in domestic finances—including demands to slash government budgets for social programs and development. In practice, harsh conditions were almost immediately attached to IMF loans offered to countries in the Global South. This made the loans unattractive to all but the most desperate and chipped away at the promise of a rapprochement between globalization, equality, and social security.[27]

Many of the more idealistic and ambitious development goals of the Bretton Woods Agreement were also abandoned beginning in the late 1940s, with the transition to the Truman administration in the United States, which was more inclined than Roosevelt to accommodate Wall Street. When Truman launched the Marshall Plan it was another signal that the United States would act unilaterally in the reconstruction of the global economy after the Second World War, rather than through multilateral institutions such as the IMF and World Bank. The Cold War stimulated interest in preventing dominoes from falling, but Cold War ideology simultaneously undermined US government support for the growth of welfare states and for state-led development, now tarnished as "Communist."[28]

Regionalism offered another Third Way between globalization and protectionism. On the brink of the Second World War, Ludwig von Mises was still dreaming of a world economy modeled on the Habsburg Empire. In 1938, he proposed an Eastern Democratic Union composed of former Habsburg and Ottoman territories. The union would have a unitary economic policy, along with free trade and unrestricted mobility within its borders, while allowing national autonomy in cultural policies. While he later renounced the idea, regional trade blocs often took over where "autarkic empires" left off after the Second World War.

Federations such as the European Economic Community were polarizing for neoliberal thinkers: some denounced them as a protectionist throwback to the 1930s, while others supported them as models of (and stepping-stones toward) global integration. The European Common Market, founded in 1957 by the Treaty of Rome, initially included the remaining colonial possessions of France, Belgium, and the Netherlands, maintaining a system of imperial preference. Unlike the Nazi *Grossraumwirtschaft* and the Greater East Asian Co-Prosperity Sphere, however, these regional blocs were intended to serve the interests of the entire region, not a single dominant power.[29] In the postwar years, the model of a regional economic community, characterized by greater freedom of mobility and goods within its borders, represented a middle ground between hyper-globalization and the self-contained 1930s. Yet greater integration into these regional blocs constrained the ability of governments to adopt trade and monetary policies in response to both local economic conditions and democratic will.

*   *   *

IN ONE very significant way, postwar leaders and experts did not attempt to reglobalize the world. There was never any intention to facilitate the free mobility of people after the Second World War. This was true even as millions had been displaced by the war and postwar ethnic cleansing, and millions more migrated for both economic and political reasons in the decades that followed. While the United Nations Declaration of Human Rights insisted on the human right to "exit" one's country, no expert or leader of any influence argued for a return to the imagined "free market" in migration associated with the years before the First World War.

The massive post–Second World War displacement of people was considered a humanitarian crisis of epic proportions, one that required careful management and control by international institutions and states. Allied governments estimated that there would be 20–30 million homeless or displaced people in Europe alone after the war.[30] These former forced laborers, prisoners of war, concentration camp inmates, refugees, and internally displaced persons crowded European trains, refugee camps, and cities after the Second World War. But rather than let the human chips fall, governments and new international organizations sought to carefully channel migration according to the dictates of postwar diplomacy, Cold War politics, and the economic needs of Allied countries.

Commissions from Allied countries saw displaced persons camps as giant reserves of manual labor for the reconstruction of their postwar economies. They scoured the camps for the young and the fit, for farmers, miners, and domestic servants, and for children who could be easily "assimilated" to suit pronatalist goals. The disabled, the elderly, the sick, and the traumatized need not apply.[31] The United States ultimately admitted several hundred thousand refugees after the Second World War under the Displaced Persons Act, but did not repeal the racist quota system instituted by the Johnson-Reed Act of 1924 until 1965. The gates of Ellis Island and Angel Island did not reopen. Instead, the postwar years saw a massive rise in deportations from US soil, particularly of migrants from Mexico. Many of these deportations were carried out under the euphemistic rubric of "voluntary departure." Tens of millions of migrants were bribed, tricked, or coerced into signing their own deportation agreements.[32]

Meanwhile, multiple new international organizations aimed to provide relief to the displaced, including the United Nations Relief and Rehabilitation Administration (1944), the International Refugee Organization (1946), the United Nations High Commissioner for Refugees (1950), and the International Organization for Migration (1951). None of these organizations espoused a doctrine of "free mobility." Rather, they served to coordinate, control, and care for refugees and migrant workers. Just as economists sought to reorganize the global economy, some experts still imagined that the organized "transfer" of people from overpopulated regions of the world to those that were supposedly "empty" would create demographic equilibrium, serving the goals of peace and development. This vision was applied not only to Jewish refugees but also to Germans. European demographers believed that Germany was experiencing a major and threatening crisis of overpopulation after the Second World War. A 1946 report by the International Committee for the Study of European Questions concluded that while the Nazis had successfully devastated the populations of occupied countries, Germany's own population had actually grown by 7.5 percent since 1939, with menacing implications. "*The danger resulting from this state of affairs is extremely grave.* It is all the greater since while the German population has grown from 67 to 72 million, German territory has been reduced by about one-fourth since 1945, due to the loss of Eastern Prussia and Silesia."[33]

In 1951, J. Donald Kingsley, director-general of the International Refugee Organization, blamed European overpopulation for the rise of fascism in Europe. "One of the foremost threats to the maintenance of a democratic system and of peace is the existence for any extended time of large pools of human misery in the midst of plenty," he claimed. "Mussolini and Hitler were, to a very large degree, the products of such misery."[34] That same year, the International Organization for Migration was created to concern itself with the "organized transfer of refugees, displaced persons and other individuals in need of international migration services." The use of the phrase "organized transfer" set up an implicit contrast with the "disorderly" migrations of the previous era.[35]

In Europe, decolonization offered a pretext to shut down long-standing migration networks across the Mediterranean, between metropoles and former colonies, in favor of "free" mobility within Europe.[36] When Western European economies began to boom in the 1950s and 1960s, there was a huge demand for migrant labor. Germany, Belgium, Switzerland, and other European countries imported hundreds of thousands of guest workers from Southern Europe, Turkey, Yugoslavia, and North Africa. But they did so with the (false) understanding that these workers would ultimately return home—and therefore didn't need the kinds of social and political rights guaranteed to citizens.[37]

In the Cold War West, policy makers proclaimed that mobility was a "human right" linked to democracy and freedom, in order to contrast the capitalist West with the "enslaved" Socialist Bloc, where states kept their own citizens captive.[38] But in practice, the demise of "free" mobility was another compromise intended to reconcile globalization, equity, and democracy. States provided more social security and welfare benefits to citizens than ever, but made the barriers to entry and exit higher. Anti-migrant rhetoric focused on the ways in which migrants allegedly fed parasitically or opportunistically on increasingly generous welfare benefits. In Eastern Europe, governments justified restrictions on emigration in terms of the growing investments the state was making in citizens' education and welfare, investments that would be lost if workers left the country. Decolonization enabled European governments to wash their hands of responsibility for former colonies and restrict migration from those countries, even though the economic legacies of colonialism long outlasted formal political rule. Meanwhile, experts promised Western leaders that funding "development" would prevent the world's unwanted poor from knocking on their doors; instead of people migrating to jobs, the jobs would come to the people.

THIS BOOK has attempted to reframe the period between the two world wars as one in which individuals and states attempted to pause, reverse, or reorganize the globalization of their economies and societies, from the workings of international finance to the contents of their cupboards. Fascists, in particular, capitalized on and accelerated anti-global politics. Fascism was not only an extreme form of nationalism. It was a response to the perception that the global economy was rigged; to fears of exclusion from global and imperial power in the aftermath of the war; to the perception that the liberal internationalists who created the new world order at Versailles were hypocrites. It built on and nourished a conviction that survival would require greater self-sufficiency at the level of the individual and the nation.

But it was never only Fascists who indulged fantasies of greater autonomy from the global economy. Progressive Socialists, anti-colonial nationalists, and New Deal Democrats also launched powerful critiques of the global economy in the 1920s and 1930s. They sought ways to achieve more independence from global commerce or to reform it, to make the global economy more fair and more stable. These efforts, across the political spectrum, remind us that globalization is never an unstoppable process.

Anti-global movements typically began at the grassroots level, with popular demands for land, food, or relief from the instability and inequality associated with the global economy. But by the 1930s, these demands had been taken up by powerful states in Europe and North America. From Mussolini's efforts to drain Italy's swamplands; to New Deal homesteading projects; to state-led campaigns to persuade consumers to buy "Empire products," cook only "Italian foods," or boycott Jewish-owned stores, anti-globalism became state policy. Some of these policies were popular; others failed abjectly.

Across geographic and ideological divides, internal colonization and settlement projects were particularly difficult to realize. Supposedly fertile land turned out not to be so fertile. The urban workers or farmers transported to these settlements did not have the skills to farm successfully in unfamiliar environments. The start-up and labor costs of home production were underestimated. The aspiration for autarky was unrealistic.

It was also notoriously challenging to change consumer behavior. Even when movements for self-sufficiency had tremendous moral and political appeal (such as Gandhi's *swadeshi* movement), consumers sometimes revolted; in the case of swadeshi, they complained about the expense, discomfort, or inconvenience of making their own clothing. The same went for campaigns for Empire Free Trade and for demands that consumers buy, cook, and eat only local foods.

These "failures" should not be taken to indicate that either popular or state-led anti-global movements were inconsequential, however. Popular demands and pressures for insulation from the global economy profoundly shaped government policies between the two world wars. Rogue settlers demanded and received land in interwar Austria. Unemployed workers in the United States petitioned the government for homesteads and received them. In Nazi Germany, small-business owners staged violent protests outside Jewish businesses and department stores, pressuring the government to take more severe action against Jews. Governments increased tariffs, closed borders to migrants and refugees, and withdrew from international organizations and agreements. When efforts to achieve autarky domestically failed, states went to war to gain more land, more food, and more self-sufficiency through conquest. And finally, the architecture of globalization and internationalism itself transformed, as internationalists dusted their pants, regrouped, and attempted to design new institutions to reform and reconstruct the global economy and international governance.

However much politicians and experts might have wished to "insulate" the global economy or globalism from democracy, moreover, they never succeeded in banishing mass politics from the scene. As long as people did not have a true voice in shaping globalization, they used mass politics to mobilize against it. In the decades to come, bitterness and disappointment about the failures of postwar leaders to make the global economy more fair would resurface in popular political movements on the left and right. So would dreams of autarky and self-sufficiency—both at the level of the state, in places such as Spain, Turkey, North Korea, and Cuba, and at the level of the family, in homesteading, survivalist, and back-to-the-land movements of the 1960s and 1970s and beyond.

Idealistic visions for the reform of the global economy would persistently challenge the orthodoxies of economic liberalism and globalization. In the halls of the United Nations General Assembly, a group of developing countries presented the Charter of Economic Rights and Duties of States for ratification in 1974. That charter affirmed the United Nations' commitment to "the promotion by the entire international community of the economic and social progress of all countries, especially developing countries," and called for reforms including reparations for colonialism, along with more foreign aid, greater respect for sovereignty over economic policies and resources in developing countries, and "promoting increased net flows of real resources to the developing countries from all sources." These goals are far from realization, but they remain vital as aspirations for millions.[39]

Discontent with globalization would continue to erupt globally, in movements of small-businesspeople and farmers against global corporations; in xenophobic violence and new restrictions on immigration and emigration. Challenges would also come in the form of street protests by migrants; in wars for decolonization and the struggle for racial justice; in movements that urged consumers to "buy local" in order to protect the environment.

Later, as neoliberals began to dismantle the postwar welfare state, discontent would resurface in strikes by miners in Margaret Thatcher's Britain and in protests on the streets of Seattle during the 1999 World Trade Organization meeting; in calls to boycott shoes and clothing produced by child labor; in attention to the effects of globalization on women of color, who are disproportionately recruited to do the low-wage care work that is outsourced to migrants.[40] At the end of the Cold War, capitalist "victors" and neoliberal economists insisted that economic liberalism was a precondition for democracy, and that opening borders to capital and goods would inevitably produce democratization. But it would become clear in the decades that followed that tensions between globalization, equality, and democracy remained painfully unresolved.

EPILOGUE

In 1946, Hitler Youth leader Baldur von Schirach testified at Nuremberg that Henry Ford's book *The International Jew* was the "decisive anti-Semitic book" that inspired him and his Nazi friends in the 1920s. "I read it and became an anti-Semite." Hitler famously singled out Ford for praise in *Mein Kampf.* In America, he argued, "It is Jews who govern the stock exchange.... Every year makes them more and more the controlling masters of the producers in a nation of one hundred and twenty million; only a single great man, Ford, to their fury, still maintains full independence." In 1938, Ford accepted the Grand Cross of the German Eagle from the Nazi government. He eventually became a member of the anti-Semitic America First Committee, which pressured the US government to stay out of the Second World War.

In Germany during the Second World War, the Cologne factory of the Ford Motor Company churned out military vehicles by use of slave labor from Eastern Europe. The shoe factories of the so-called Ford of Europe also served the German war effort. During and after the Second World War, the Bat'a Shoe Company would split three ways. The Nazis seized the company's factories in Eastern Europe and employed slave labor from concentration camps. After the war, that branch was seized again and nationalized by the Communists. Jan Bat'a barely escaped Europe and tried to shift operations to Belcamp, Maryland. In the process, however, he alienated President Franklin Delano Roosevelt by supporting a primary challenger in 1940 and refused to unambiguously condemn the Nazis or support the Czechoslovak government-in-exile.

Bat'a also promoted a far-fetched scheme to move the entire population of Czechoslovakia to Patagonia. None of this won him the favor of the Allies or Czechs at home. He was blacklisted by the American government, convicted in absentia in postwar Czechoslovakia for collaboration, and narrowly escaped to Brazil, where he died in 1965.

Thomas Bat'a, the son of Tomáš, was far more successful. He emigrated to Canada and set up another Bat'a outpost there. The Canadian Bat'a immediately entered into the service of the Allies, fulfilling military contracts throughout the war. Thomas denounced the Nazis. He identified himself as a Canadian. He was rewarded for his efforts on behalf of the Allies with control of the vast majority of the Bat'a firm's branches and wealth outside the Socialist Bloc. By 1962, Bat'a was producing and selling shoes in 79 countries and employed 80,000 people. As of 2022, many Indians would be surprised to learn that Bat'a is not an Indian firm; it remains the largest footwear retailer in India.[1]

Ralph Borsodi continued to operate his School of Living until the death of his wife in 1948. He then embarked on a tour of Asia, inspired by Gandhi's ideals of self-sufficiency and village industries, in search of what he called "Asianism." He was disappointed. "Today Asia has abandoned what Asia really has to offer the world," he lamented. Borsodi argued that the only real hope for Asia and the rest of the world was to adopt the "neglected values" of "Old Asia"; namely, the value of the family and village life.[2] He moved to another homesteading community in Florida, where he fought desegregation, and then on to Exeter, New Hampshire, where he attempted to invent and circulate an "inflation-proof" village currency in the 1970s.

Shortly before Borsodi's death in 1977, a reporter from the *New York Times* revisited the homesteading communities of Rockland County, New York. They had become affluent suburbs. "They originally set out for the 'frontier'; with dreams of establishing truly open communities, living off the land, attaining self-sufficiency, and blazing a trail for others to follow. Most of these dreams have been left behind. 'Living off the land' inevitably came to nothing more than an occasional goat or chicken and a few abortive vegetable gardens." Resident Evelyn McGregor recalled, "Borsodi had all sorts of plans on how we were going to make our own clothes and grow our own food. . . . But as soon as we got our house built, we kicked him out."[3]

Borsodi's role model, Gandhi, was nominated for the Nobel Peace Prize (for the fifth time) in 1948. After helping to lead India to independence, Gandhi protested the partition of India and Pakistan and the eruption of religious violence, undertaking several hunger strikes. He was assassinated in January 1948 by a Hindu nationalist before the prize was awarded.

The Indian national flag is still woven from khadi, which has enjoyed a renaissance among ethically conscious fashion designers and consumers in India. *Vogue* magazine reported in 2019, "Once the stereotypical uniform of somber politicians and a symbol of self-reliance in India's independence struggle, khadi is now the darling textile of India's fashion houses, and is frequently spotted at pop-up shops, art biennales, and on runaways across the country." One designer explained, "Khadi gave India economic freedom during the independence struggle, but today it gives environmental freedom. It is the call of the hour considering the ill effects of the synthetic textile industry." Ethics still come at a cost, however. This new generation of fashionable khadi is clearly aimed at a luxury market, as designers aim to transform a "poor-man's cloth into glamorous ensembles."[4]

The US Supreme Court decision that rendered Rosika Schwimmer stateless in 1929 was finally overturned in 1946. Alongside Gandhi, Schwimmer was also nominated for the Nobel Peace Prize in 1948. But she died, still stateless, before learning that no prize was awarded.

ACKNOWLEDGMENTS

I BEGAN THIS book in 2016. Donald Trump had been elected president, and British voters had opted for Brexit. There was a refugee crisis, and populist, right-wing parties were winning elections across Europe with anti-migrant platforms. I could not have predicted that in the years that followed, a global pandemic would "deglobalize" the world with unprecedented restrictions on travel and obstacles to trade, even as the virus defied all efforts to barricade it. Nor could I have predicted a war in Ukraine—ongoing as I write this—that would prompt the withdrawal from Russia of more than 400 firms. Companies that once represented powerful symbols of globalization and westernization, such as McDonald's, Coca-Cola, Ikea, Apple, and Uniqlo, have, as of this writing, ceased operations in Russia. Many countries are trying to achieve independence from Russian oil. The future of globalization seems very uncertain.

The past is supposed to help us better understand the present. But in this case, I have been more surprised by the ways in which the present has altered the way I see the past. I have spent many years teaching and studying the history of nationalism, internationalism, migration, and fascism. Current events have altered my understanding of those subjects. I hope that this book will shed some light on both the past and the present, and that its insights will transcend the moment in which it is so clearly embedded.

Telling this story required me to recklessly write about places and events outside my own geographic areas of expertise. I could not have done so without the advice and wisdom of many generous colleagues and friends, though the book's weaknesses are mine alone. I am grateful in particular to Dominique Reill, Pamela Ballinger, and Lucy Riall for their insight on Italian and Adriatic histories and for reading and commenting on draft chapters; Jonathan Levy for reading chapters and discussing the history of capitalism and the United States, for co-teaching a seminar with me on the history of globalization that shaped my thinking, and for joining me in Italian conversation classes; and to Seth Koven for helping me refine my arguments about anti-colonialism and the British Empire. This book was also improved by more than a year of discussion and writing with my colleague Peter Becker at the University of Vienna, and by every one of the wonderful participants in the Zoom seminar and Gösing workshop on Deglobalization and Anti-Globalism in Central Europe.

Deborah Cohen and Leora Auslander spent many evenings reading, discussing, and providing critical feedback and support on every aspect of this project. Those evenings were precious to me. Alison Frank Johnson read and commented on several chapters and drafts, cheered me on when I was feeling demoralized, and was the ideal hiking and schnitzel-eating companion. Everything I write is inspired and improved by my conversations, friendship, and collaboration with Pieter Judson: I'm grateful for his patience with too many emails and for his company on working holidays and pandemic detours.

Particularly in the context of the COVID-19 pandemic, I was extremely fortunate to have the assistance of several amazing research assistants. Thank you to Jakub Vrba in Prague; Stephanie Reitzig, Nikolina Zenovic, and Naama Maor in Chicago; Isaac Bershady in New Jersey; and especially to Eric Phillips. He deserves tremendous credit for his assistance locating images, securing permissions, and preparing the manuscript for publication. Mo Crist at Norton has also been extremely helpful in the publication process.

I have been generously supported in my research and writing by multiple institutions. These include the University of Chicago, the Guggenheim Foundation, and the Macarthur Foundation. I also could not have written this book without the assistance of many archivists who helped me in my research, both on-site and remotely. Finally, I am greatly indebted to my agent, Don Fehr, and my editor, Alane Mason, who have been so enthusiastic about this project from the beginning.

The world and my life have changed tremendously since I started writing this book. But I first owe thanks to the people who have been there all along, my parents, Debbie and Marc Zahra. They encouraged me to believe I could do and be anything. I also want to thank my new family members, Mark Irvine, Marion Cadman, and Lucy Irvine, for their company in Chicago and in L'Aquila. One of the few lucky by-products of the pandemic has been the opportunity to spend more time together. William Irvine, my husband, has been my best friend and greatest supporter. I'm grateful for his curiosity, humor, kindness, and love, and for listening to me talk about globalization for so many years.

I am also grateful to William for my daughter, Eloisa, who arrived in 2018. She was born with her eyes wide open, ready to see the world, and she has opened my own eyes to see the world differently. As I complete this book she is a lively, imaginative preschooler who brings joy and discovery into every day of my life. This book is dedicated to her.

LIST OF ARCHIVES

Archivio Centrale dello Stato, Rome (ACS)

    Ministero dell'Interno, Direzione generale di pubblica sicurezza, 1919–1921

    Direzione Generale Bonifica e Colonizazzione

    Commissariato Generale per le Migrazioni e la Colonizzazione Interna

    Opera Nazionale Combattenti, Agro Pontino

Archiv ministerstva zahraničních věcí (AMZV), Prague, Czech Republic

    IV. Sekce Národohospodáská

Austrian State Archive, Vienna (Österreichisches Staatsarchiv; OestA)

    Allgemeines Verwaltungsarchiv (AVA), Ministry of the Interior

    Archiv der Republik (AdR), Auswärtige Angelegenheiten, St. Germain

    Archiv der Republik (AdR), Bundesministrerium für Land und Forstwirtschaft, Siedlungswesen

    Großdeutsche Volkspartei

Reichskommissar für die Wiedervereinigung Österreichs mit dem Deutschen Reich

Bat'a Information Center, Zlín, Czech Republic

Biblioteca Agraria Universita di Firenze, Florence, Italy

Fondo Serpieri

Biblioteca Nazionale Centrale di Firenze, Florence, Italy

Bundesarchiv, Berlin

Reichsgesundheitsamt, R 86

Deutsche Arbeitsfront, Zentralbüro, Arbeitswissenschaftliches Institut, NS 5-VI

Reichsministerium für Ernährung und Landwirtschaft, R 3601

Deutsche Reichsbank, R 2501

Reichswirtschaftsministerium, R 310

Reichslandbund, R 8034-II

Reichsstelle für Raumordnung, R 113

Bundesarchiv, Koblenz

Nachlass Herbert Backe

Nachlass Walther Darré

Center for Jewish History, New York

American Jewish History Society, Family Location Service Collection

American Jewish History Society, Cecilia Razovsky Papers

Leo Baeck Institute, George Manasse Collection

Geheimes Staatsarchiv Prueßischer Kulturbesitz (GstA), Berlin

Nachlass Erich Bollert

American Joint Distribution Committee (JDC) Archive, New York Collection

Národní archiv, Prague, Czech Republic

   Předsednictvo ministerské rady

National Archives and Records Administration, College Park, Maryland

   Department of Subsistence Homesteads, RG 96

National Archives of Ireland

National Library of Ireland

New York Public Library (NYPL)

   Gino Speranza Papers

   Rosika Schwimmer Papers

   Lillian Wald Papers

Politisches Archiv des Auswärtigen Amts, Berlin

   RZ 214 Sonderreferat Deutschland, 1920–1934

   RZ 511 Aus und Rückwanderung

Rutgers University, Special Collections

   Roosevelt, NJ Collection

United Nations Archive and Library, Geneva

   League of Nations Secretariat

      Economic and Financial Section

      Health and Social Questions Section

      Communications and Transit Section

   League of Nations External Funds

      Financial Reconstruction of Austria

   Women's International League for Peace and Freedom

NOTES

Introduction

1. Dorothy Thompson, "The Gray Squirrel," *Saturday Evening Post*, February 20, 1932, 7.
2. Mary Sheepshanks, "Is Internationalism Dead?" *Jus Suffragii, Monthly Organ of the International Woman* 10, no. 9 (June 1, 1916): 1.
3. Stefan Zweig, *The World of Yesterday* (London, 1943), 308–10.
4. John Maynard Keynes, *The Economic Consequences of the Peace* (1919; repr., New York, 1971), 10–11.
5. Jeffrey G. Williamson, *Trade and Poverty: When the Third World Fell Behind* (Cambridge, MA, 2013).
6. Keynes, *Economic Consequences*, 21–22.
7. Keynes, *Economic Consequences*, 243–45, 50–51.
8. Thompson, "Gray Squirrel," 7.
9. For the economic history of interwar deglobalization, see especially Harold James, *The End of Globalization: Lessons from the Great Depression* (Cambridge, MA, 2001); Robert Boyce, *The Great Interwar Crisis and the Collapse of Globalization* (New York, 2009); Kevin H. O'Rourke and Jeffrey G. Williamson, *Globalization and History: The Evolution of a Nineteenth-Century Atlantic Economy* (Cambridge, MA, 1999).
10. Adam Tooze and Ted Fertik, "The World Economy and the Great War," *Geschichte und Gesellschaft* 40, no. 2 (April–June 2014): 214–38.
11. Ronald Finlay and Kevin H. O'Rourke, *Power and Plenty: Trade, War, and the World Economy in the Second Millennium* (Princeton, NJ, 2007), 432–43.
12. Giovanni Federico and Antonio Tena-Junguito, "World Trade, 1800-1938: A New Data Set." EHES Working Papers in Economic History, no. 93, European Historical Economics Society, January 2016, http://www.ehes.org/EHES_93.pdf; Giovanni Federico and Antonio Tena-Junguito, "World Trade, 1800-2015," Vox EU, February 7, 2016, https://voxeu.org/article/world-trade-1800-2015.
13. Adam Mckeown, "Global Migration, 1846-1940," *Journal of World History* 15, no.

2 (2004): 167; Christopher A. Casey, "Deglobalization and the Disintegration of the European News System, 1918-34," *Journal of Contemporary History* 53 no. 2 (2018): 267–91; Dani Rodrik, *The Globalization Paradox. Democracy and the Future of the World Economy* (New York, 2011), 34–46.

14. On this history, see especially James, *End of Globalization*; Boyce, *Great Interwar Crisis*; Adam Tooze, *The Deluge: The Great War, America, and the Remaking of the Global Order, 1916-31* (New York, 2015); Adam Tooze, *Wages of Destruction: The Making and Breaking of the Nazi Economy* (New York, 2006); Christoph Kreutzmüller, Michael Wildt, and Moshe Zimmermann, *Volkswirtschaft, Racism and Economy in Europe Between the Wars (1918-1939/45)* (Newcastle, UK, 2015); Rodrik, *Globalization Paradox*, 24–46.

15. Douglas Irwin, *Against the Tide: An Intellectual History of Free Trade* (Princeton, NJ, 1996).

16. Stefan Link, "How Might 21st-Century De-Globalization Unfold? Some Historical Reflections," *New Global Studies* 12, no. 3 (2018): 347. On "free trade" as a political doctrine in Britain, see Frank Trentmann, *Free Trade Nation: Commerce, Consumption, and Civil Society in Modern Britain* (Oxford, 2009). On British imperial power and free trade, see Bernard Semmel, *The Rise of Free Trade Imperialism: Classical Political Economy, the Empire of Free Trade, and Imperialism, 1750-1850* (Cambridge, UK, 1970), 152–54; Anthony Howe, *Free Trade and Liberal England, 1846-1946* (Oxford, 1997); Sven Beckert, *Empire of Cotton: A Global History* (New York, 2014); Rodrik, *Globalization Paradox*, 32–33.

17. Rodrik, *Globalization Paradox*, 29.

18. Jürgen Osterhammel, *Globalization. A Short History*, trans. Niels P. Petersson (Princeton, NJ, 2005), 81. On globalization/internationalism and nationalism, see also Sebastian Conrad, *Globalization and the Nation in Imperial Germany*, trans. Sorcha O'Hagen (Cambridge, UK, 2010); Glenda Sluga, *Internationalism in the Age of Nationalism* (Philadelphia, 2015); Vanessa Ogle, *The Global Transformation of Time* (Cambridge, MA, 2015); Erik Grimmer-Solem, *Learning Empire: Globalization and the German Quest for World Status, 1875-1919* (Cambridge, UK, 2019).

19. For a critique of the "pendulum" theory, see Link, "How Might 21st-Century De-Globalization Unfold?," 343–65. See also Charles Bright and Michael Geyer, "World History in a Global Age," *American Historical Review* 100, no. 4 (October 1995): 1034–60.

20. Thompson, "Gray Squirrel," 7.

21. See among others Erez Manela, *The Wilsonian Moment: Self-Determination and International Origins of Anticolonial Nationalism* (Oxford, 2009); Eric Weitz, "From the Vienna to the Paris System: International Politics and the Entangled Histories of Human Rights, Forced Deportations, and Civilizing Missions," *American Historical Review* 113 (December 2008): 1313–43.

22. On anti-colonial "worldmaking," see Adom Getachew, *Worldmaking After Empire: The Rise and Fall of Self-Determination* (Princeton, NJ, 2019).

23. John Maynard Keynes, "National Self-Sufficiency," *Yale Review* 22, no. 4 (1933): 178.

24. Zweig, *World of Yesterday*, 310.

25. Link, "How Might 21st-Century De-Globalization Unfold?," 348; see also Beckert, *Empire of Cotton*; Osterhammel, *Globalization*; Finlay and O'Rourke, *Power and Plenty*.

26. Chris Otter, *Diet for a Large Planet: Industrial Britain, Food Systems, and World Ecology* (Chicago, 2020), 11.

27. Kevin O'Rourke, "Economic History and Contemporary Challenges to Globalization," *Journal of Economic History* 79, no. 2 (June 2019): 356–82.

28. Tooze, *The Deluge*; Barry Eichengreen and Peter Temin, "The Gold Standard and the Great Depression," National Bureau of Economic Research, Working Paper 6060, June 1997; Jonathan Levy, *Ages of Capitalism: A History of the United States* (New York, 2021), 397-435.

29. On international financial governance between the two world wars, see especially Jamie Martin, *The Meddlers: Sovereignty, Empire, and the Birth of Global Economic Governance* (Cambridge, MA, 2022); Patricia Clavin, *Securing the World Economy: The Reinvention of the League of Nations 1920-1946* (Oxford, 2013); Nathan Marcus, *Austrian Reconstruction and the Collapse of Global Finance, 1921–1931* (Cambridge, MA, 2018); Quinn Slobodian, *Globalists: The End of Empire and the Birth of Neoliberalism* (Cambridge, MA, 2018).

30. Leora Auslander, "Negotiating Embodied Difference: Veils, Minarets, Kippas and Sukkot in Contemporary Europe. An Essay," *Archiv für Sozialgeschichte* 51 (2011): 401–18.

31. Carl Schorske, *Fin-de-Siecle Vienna: Politics and Culture* (New York, 1979).

32. Alice Weinreb, *Modern Hungers: Food and Power in Twentieth-Century Germany* (New York, 2017), chaps. 1–2; Isabel Hull, *A Scrap of Paper: Breaking and Making International Law During the Great War* (Ithaca, NY, 2014), 141–82.

33. On political mobilization in the losing states, see Robert Gerwarth, *The Vanquished: Why the First World War Failed to End, 1917-23* (New York, 2016).

34. Andrea Komlosy, *Grenze und ungleiche regionale Entwicklung. Binnenmarkt und Migration in der Habsburgermonarchie* (Vienna, 2003).

35. Natasha Wheatley, "Central Europe as Ground Zero of the New International Order," *Slavic Review* 78, no. 4 (Winter 2019): 900–911.

36. Peter Becker and Natasha Wheatley, eds., *Remaking Central Europe: The League of Nations and the Former Habsburg Lands* (Oxford, 2021); Slobodian, *Globalists*; Katherine Sorrels, *Cosmopolitan Outsiders: Imperial Inclusion, National Exclusion, and the Pan-European Idea* (New York, 2016); Sluga, *Internationalism in the Age of Nationalism*.

37. Susan Pedersen, "Back to the League of Nations: Review Essay," *American Historical Review* 112, no. 4 (2007): 1091–1117. On the mandate system, see Susan Pedersen, *The Guardians: The League of Nations and the Crisis of Empire* (Oxford, 2015). On interwar humanitarianism and internationalism, see Bruno Cabanes, *The Great War and the Origins of Humanitarianism, 1918-1924* (Cambridge, UK, 2014); Clavin, *Securing the World Economy*.

38. Thompson, "Gray Squirrel," 7.
39. Thompson, "Gray Squirrel," 97.
40. Lynn Hunt, *Writing History in the Global Era* (New York, 2015).
41. Tiago Saraiva, *Fascist Pigs: Technoscientific Organisms and the History of Fascism* (Cambridge, MA, 2016); see also Susanne Heim, Carola Sachse, and Mark Walker, eds., *The Kaiser Wilhelm Society under National Socialism* (Cambridge, UK, 2009).
42. Johann Wilhelm Ludowici, *Das Deutsche Siedlungswerk* (Heidelberg, 1935), 26.
43. Thompson, "Gray Squirrel," 100.
44. Gesine Gerhard, *Nazi Hunger Politics: A History of Food in the Third Reich* (Lanham, MD, 2015); see also Sven Beckert, "American Danger: US Empire, Eurafrica, and the Territorialization of Industrial Capitalism, 1870–1950," *American Historical Review* 122, no. 4 (2017): 1137–70.

Chapter 1

1. "Editorial Notes," *Jus Suffragii, Monthly Organ of the International Woman* 7, no. 10 (July 15, 1913): 2.
2. Michelle Rief, "Thinking Locally, Acting Globally: The International Agenda of African American Clubwomen, 1880-1940," *Journal of African American History* 89, no. 3 (Summer 2004): 203–22; Sheleina M. Downey, "Precursor to Women of Color Feminism: The International Council of Women of the Darker Races and their Internationalist Orientation," *Meridians: Feminism, Race, Transnationalism* 19, no. 2 (October 2020): 271–77.
3. All quotations are from Elizabeth Cady Stanton et al., *History of Woman Suffrage*, vol. VI, 1900-1920 (New York, 1922), 847–59. Program details are from International Women's Suffrage Alliance, 7th Congress, Budapest, 1913, Folder 8, Charlotte Gilman Perkins Papers, Radcliffe Institute for Advanced Study, Harvard University.
4. Vanessa Ogle, *The Global Transformation of Time* (Cambridge, MA, 2015).
5. "A nők a választójogáért," *Népszava* (Budapest, Hungary), June 22, 1913, 3.
6. "A proletárnők gyülése – Popp Adél és Keir Hardie beszédei," *Népszava* (Budapest, Hungary), June 20, 1913, 7–8.
7. On the mandate system, see Susan Pedersen, *The Guardians: The League of Nations and the Crisis of Empire* (Oxford, 2015).

Chapter 2

1. All quotations are from Rose Pesotta, *Days of Our Lives* (Boston, 1958); see also Elaine J. Leeder, *The Gentle General: Rose Pesotta, Anarchist and Labor Organizer* (Albany, NY, 1993).
2. Walter F. Willcox, "Immigration into the United States," in *The International Migrations, Volume II: Interpretations*, ed. Walter F. Willcox (New York, 1931),

83–122; Donna R Gabaccia, *Italy's Many Diasporas* (Seattle, 2000), 67; Annemarie Steidl et al., *From a Multiethnic Empire to a Nation of Nations: Austro-Hungarian Migrants to the US, 1867-1940* (Vienna, 2017).

3. Arthur Livingston, "Gino Speranza. The Evolution of an American," in *The Diary of Gino Speranza. Italy, 1915-1919*, vol. 1, ed. Florence Colgate Speranza (New York, 1966).

4. Gino Speranza, "The Newer Spirit of Immigration," n.d. [ca. 1914], Box 35, Gino Speranza Papers, New York Public Library (henceforth Speranza Papers).

5. Remarks of Mr. Gino C. Speranza before a congressional committee on the subject of the restriction of Italian immigration. Delivered between March 1911 and March 1919, Box 35, Speranza Papers.

6. Remarks of Mr. Gino C. Speranza, Box 35, Speranza Papers.

7. Gino Speranza, *Race or Nation: A Conflict of Divided Loyalties* (Indianapolis, 1923), 103.

8. Gino Speranza, "Some aspects of the immigration problem," n.d., Box 35, Speranza Papers.

9. Werner Sombart and Mordecai Epstein, *The Jews and Modern Capitalism* (London, 1913), 21, 25, 170–71.

10. For a contemporary reappraisal of Sombart, see Adam Sutcliffe, "Anxieties of Distinctiveness: Werner Sombart's The Jews in Modern Capitalism and the Politics of Jewish Economic History," in *Purchasing Power: The Economics of Modern Jewish History*, ed. Rebecca Kobrin and Adam Teller (Philadelphia, 2015), 238–59. On contemporary reception of Sombart, see Derek Penslar, *Shylock's Children: Economics and Jewish Identity in Modern Europe* (Berkeley, 2001), 165–73.

11. Werner Sombart, *A New Social Philosophy*, trans. Karl Frederick Geiser (Princeton, NJ, 1937), 187.

12. For a discussion of the Russian-French circle in which the text likely originated, see Faith Hillis, "The 'Franco-Russian Marseillaise': International Exchange and the Making of Antiliberal Politics in Fin de Siècle France," *Journal of Modern History* 89, no. 1 (2017): 39–78.

13. On Jews as agents of globalization, see Sarah Abrevaya Stein, *Plumes: Ostrich Feathers, Jews, and a Lost World of Global Commerce* (New Haven, CT, 2008). For histories of Jews and capitalism, see Penslar, *Shylock's Children*; Rebecca Kobrin and Adam Teller, eds., *Purchasing Power: The Economics of Modern Jewish History* (Philadelphia, 2015).

14. Eric Lohr, *Russian Citizenship: From Empire to Soviet Union* (Cambridge, MA, 2012).

15. Broughton Brandenburg, *Imported Americans: The Story of the Experiences of a Disguised American and His Wife Studying the Immigration Question* (New York, 1904), 40.

16. On sex trafficking from Eastern Europe, see Keely Stauter-Halsted, *The Devil's Chain: Prostitution and Social Control in Partitioned Poland* (Ithaca, NY, 2015);

Nancy M. Wingfield, *The World of Prostitution in Late Imperial Austria* (Oxford, 2017).

17. United States Immigration Commission (1907-1910) and William Paul Dillingham, *Steerage Conditions: Partial Report, on Behalf of the Immigration Commission, on Steerage Conditions* (Washington, DC, 1909), AVA, MdI, Allgemein 8, Carton 138, Österreichisches Staatsarchiv (OestA).

18. Pesotta, *Days of Our Lives*, 242.

19. Cited in Jennifer Guglielmo, *Living the Revolution: Italian Women's Resistance and Radicalism in New York City, 1880-1945* (Chapel Hill, NC, 2010), 41.

20. "Hungarian Adamless Eden," *New York Times*, July 25, 1907, 3.

21. William Thomas and Florian Znaniecki, *The Polish Peasant in Europe and America*, vol. 1, (New York., 1958), 827–28; Ladislaus Schneider, *Die ungarische Auswanderung. Studie über die Ursachen und den Umfang der ungarischen Auswanderung* (Pozsony, 1915), 129; Linda Reeder, *Widows in White: Migration and the Transformation of Rural Italian Women, Sicily, 1880-1920* (Toronto, 2003).

22. Rose Laub Coser, *Women of Courage: Jewish and Italian Immigrant Women in New York* (Westport, CT, 1999), 86.

23. Louis Adamic, *The Native's Return: An American Immigrant Visits Yugoslavia and Discovers His Old Country* (New York, 1934), 39; Pauline Parnes Reimer, interview by Janet Levine, August 1, 1994, Series EI, no. 512, 41, Ellis Island Oral History Project.

24. Brandenburg, *Imported Americans*, 196.

25. Eddy Portnoy, "Man Steals Family Photos So Not to Appear Forverts' 'Missing Husbands' Gallery," *Forward Association*, July 27, 2013, http://forward .com/culture/looking-back/181213/man-steals-family-photos-so-not-to-appear -forverts/; Charles Zunser, *The National Desertion Bureau, Its Functions, New Problems and Relations with Local Agencies* (New York, 1924), I-360, Family Location Service Collection, American Jewish Historical Society.

26. Anna R. Igra, *Wives Without Husbands: Marriage, Desertion, and Welfare in New York, 1900-1935* (Chapel Hill, NC, 2007), 59; *Service to the Broken Family. 1953 Annual Report of the National Desertion Bureau, Inc.*, I-360, Family Location Service Collection, American Jewish Historical Society.

27. For more on migrant disillusionment, see Tara Zahra, *The Great Departure: Mass Migration from Eastern Europe and the Making of the Free World* (New York, 2016).

28. Marie Ganz, *Rebels: Into Anarchy and Out Again* (New York, 1919), 4.

29. Louise Odencrantz, *Italian Women in Industry: A Study of Conditions in New York City* (New York, 1919), 286.

30. Cited in Guglielmo, *Living the Revolution*, 142.

31. Guglielmo, *Living the Revolution*, 139–98; Daniel Soyer, "Introduction," in Daniel Soyer, ed., *A Coat of Many Colors: Immigration, Globalization, and Reform in New York City's Garment Industry* (New York, 2005); Hadassa Kosak, "Tailors and Troublemakers. Jewish Militancy in the New York City Garment Industry,

1889-1910," in Daniel Soyer, ed., *A Coat of Many Colors: Immigration, Globalization, and Reform in New York City's Garment Industry* (New York, 2005), 115–39.

32. Ganz, *Rebels*, 79, 73.

33. "Women in Bread Riot at Doors of City Hall," *New York Times*, February 21, 1917, 7.

34. Pesotta, *Days of Our Lives*, 250–51.

35. Rose Schneiderman, *All for One* (New York, 1967), 100–101.

36. Schneiderman, *All for One*, 98–99.

37. Tony Michels, *A Fire in Their Hearts: Yiddish Socialists in New York* (Cambridge, MA, 2005).

38. David Lloyd George, *War Memoirs of David Lloyd George, 1914-1915* (Boston, 1933), 50.

Chapter 3

1. "Ford Voyage Starts Amid Wild Scenes," *Chicago Daily Tribune*, December 5, 1915, 1.

2. Barbara Kraft, *The Peace Ship: Henry Ford's Pacifist Adventure in the First World War* (New York, 1978), 11.

3. "Says Week's Halt Would End the War: Mrs. Schwimmer, Peace Advocate, Says Only U.S. Can Bring About an Armistice. Men Are Ready to Stop. Thousand of Women Suicides in Warring Countries, She Tells Reform Rabbis," *New York Times*, December 8, 1914, 3.

4. Ingrid Sharp, "'A foolish dream of Sisterhood': Anti-Pacifist Debates in the German Women's Movement, 1914-1919," in *Gender and the First World War*, ed. Christa Hämmerle et al. (London, 2014), 195–213.

5. Cited by Sharp, "'A foolish dream of Sisterhood'," 205.

6. Adam Tooze and Ted Fertik, "The World Economy and the Great War," *Geschichte und Gesellschaft* 40, no. 2 (April–June 2014): 214–38.

7. Anton Retzbach, *Der Boykott, eine sozial-ethische Untersuchung* (Freiburg im Bresgau, 1916), 51.

8. For a comparative history of the boycott, see David Feldman, ed., *Boycotts Past and Present: From the American Revolution to the Campaign to Boycott Israel* (New York, 2019).

9. Display advertisement, *The Times* (London, England), August 26, 1915, 8.

10. Display advertisement, *The Times*.

11. R. D. De Maratray, "Economy and Boycott," *The Times* (London, England), December 16, 1915, 8.

12. Mary Chamberlain, "The Women at the Hague," Survey, June 5, 1915, in *Social Justice Feminists in the United States and Germany. A Dialogue in Documents, 1885-1933* (Ithaca, NY, 1998), 202–12, quotation 207.

13. Gertrud Bäumer, "Der Bund deutscher Frauenvereine und der Haager Frauenkongress," *Die Frauenfrage* 17 (1915–16): 82–85, cited in Kathryn Kish Sklar et al.,

eds., *Social Justice Feminists in the United States and Germany. A Dialogue in Documents, 1885-1913* (Ithaca, NY, 1998), 196, 198.

14. Jane Addams, "Women and Internationalism," in *Women at The Hague: The International Conference of Women and Its Results*, ed. Jane Addams et al. (New York, 1972), 124–25, 129.

15. Jane Addams, "Factors in Continuing the War," in *Women at The Hague: The International Conference of Women and Its Results*, ed. Jane Addams et al. (New York, 1972), 94–95.

16. Louis Lochner, *America's Don Quixote: Henry Ford's Attempt to Save Europe* (London, 1924), 9–10.

17. Kraft, *Peace Ship*, 43–44.

18. Edward Marshall, "Commercialism Made This War: Henry Ford Argues for Peace Abroad," *New York Times*, April 11, 1915, 14.

19. Theodore Delavigne, "Henry Ford to Push World-Wide Campaign for Universal Peace: Will Devote Life and Fortune to Combat Spirit of Militarism Now Rampant," *Detroit Free Press*, August 22, 1915.

20. Telegram to Feministenverein in Budapest, November 1915, Box 65, Rosika Schwimmer Papers, New York Public Library (henceforth Schwimmer Papers).

21. Outline of the Plan of the Henry Ford Peace Expedition, December 1915, Box 485, Schwimmer Papers.

22. Henry Ford's letter to Congress and Senate, December 1, 1915; Rodger W. Babson to Louis Lochner, December 2, 1915; Box 67, Schwimmer Papers.

23. Jane Addams, *Peace and Bread in Time of War* (New York, 1922), 35, 40.

24. Henry La Fontaine to Louis Lochner, November 25, 1915, Box 65, Schwimmer Papers.

25. "Ford Asks Bryan to Be First Mate on His Peace Ship," *New York Times*, November 26, 1915, 1.

26. Karl H. von Wiegend, "Germany Is Cool to Ford's Scheme," *The World* (New York, NY), November 29, 1915.

27. Rosika Schwimmer to Mrs. Ford, December 4, 1915, Box 67, Schwimmer Papers.

28. Addams, *Peace and Bread*, 39.

29. Lochner, *America's Don Quixote*, 32–33, 63.

30. Burnet Hershey, *The Odyssey of Henry Ford and the Great Peace Ship* (New York, 1967), 115.

31. Statement of Events Connected with Mr. Henry Ford's Leaving the Ford Expedition, Box 67, Schwimmer Papers; Lochner, *America's Don Quixote*, 89.

32. Committee of Administration to H.F., January 10, 1916, Box 67, Schwimmer Papers.

33. "Autocratic Leader Split Ford's Party: Mme Schwimmer Blamed for Disrupting Delegation and Stirring Discord," *New York Times*, January 31, 1916, 2, republished dispatch article by William C. Bullitt, *Philadelphia Public Ledger*, January 30, 1916.

34. Lochner, *America's Don Quixote*, 137.

35. Lochner, *America's Don Quixote*, 148–49
36. Kraft, *Peace Ship*, 279.
37. "Copenhagen Checks Ford's Propaganda," *Detroit Free Press*, January 1, 1916, 3.
38. Mrs. Ford to Madame Schwimmer, August 16, 2016, Box 80, RS Collection, Schwimmer Papers..

Chapter 4

1. On the volume of global trade, see Kevin H. O'Rourke and Jeffrey G. Williamson, *Globalization and History: The Evolution of a Nineteenth-Century Atlantic Economy* (Cambridge, UK, 1999), 29–35.
2. Chris Otter, *Diet for a Large Planet: Industrial Britain, Food Systems, and World Ecology* (Chicago, 2020), 2, 6, 12.
3. David Blackbourn, *The Long Nineteenth Century: A History of Germany, 1780-1918* (New York, 1998), 330–31.
4. Alice Weinreb, *Modern Hungers: Food and Power in Twentieth-Century Germany* (Oxford, 2016), 16; Corinna Treitel, *Eating Nature in Modern Germany: Food, Agriculture, and Environment, 1870-2000* (Cambridge, UK, 2017), 161.
5. Weinreb, *Modern Hungers*, 16; Treitel, *Eating Nature*, 161. On the challenges to the free-trade movement, see Frank Trentmann, *Free Trade Nation: Commerce, Consumption, and Civil Society in Modern Britain* (Oxford, 2008).
6. Treitel, *Eating Nature*, 121–28; David Blackbourn, *The Conquest of Nature: Water, Landscape, and the Making of Modern Germany* (New York, 2007), 274.
7. Max Sering, *Die innere Kolonisation im östlichen Deutschland* (Leipzig, 1893), 14. There is a large literature on agronomy and the settlement movement in imperial and Weimar Germany. See Carolyn D. Taratko, "Feeding Germany: Food, Science, and the Problem of Scarcity, 1871-1923" (PhD diss., Vanderbilt University, 2019); Georg Stöcker, *Agrarideologie und Sozialreform im Deutschen Kaiserreich: Heinrich Sohnrey und der Deutsche Verein für ländliche Wohlfahrts- und Heimatpflege, 1896–1914* (Göttingen, 2011). On Sering, see also Erik Grimmer-Solem, *Learning Empire: Globalization and the German Quest for World Status 1875-1919* (Cambridge, UK, 2019), 227–32.
8. Max Sering, *Verhandlung des Landes-Ökonomie-Kollegiums am 9.Februar 1912 über die Politik der Grundbesitzverteilung in den Grossen Reichen* (Berlin, 1912), 3–4.
9. Isabel Hull, *A Scrap of Paper: Breaking and Making International Law During the Great War* (Ithaca, NY, 2014), 141–82.
10. Belinda Davis, *Home Fires Burning: Food, Politics, and Everyday Life in World War I Berlin*, (Chapel Hill, NC, 2000), 22, 25; Reichsgesundheitamt, *Schädigung der deutschen Volkskraft durch die feindliche Blockade. Denkschrift des Reichsgesundheitsministeriums* (Berlin, 1919), 6–7; Lance E. Davis and Stanley L. Engerman, *Naval Blockades in Peace and War: An Economic History since 1750* (Cambridge, UK, 2006), 201.
11. Maureen Healy, *Vienna and the Fall of the Habsburg Empire: Total War and*

Everyday Life in World War I (Cambridge, UK, 2004), quotation 47; on food 31–86; Alice Hamilton, "At the War Capitals," in *Women at The Hague: The International Congress of Women and Its Results*, ed. Jane Addams et al. (New York, 1916), 41.

12. Anna Eisenmenger, *Blockade: The Diary of an Austrian Middle-Class Woman, 1914-1924*, trans. Winifred Ray (New York, 1932), 18.

13. Davis, *Home Fires Burning*, 114–24, 129–30.

14. Healy, *Vienna and the Fall*, 38; Rudolf Kučera, *Rationed Life: Science, Everyday Life, and Working-Class Politics in the Bohemian Lands, 1914-1918* (New York, 2016), 25–28; Davis, *Home Fires Burning*, 31.

15. Kučera, *Rationed Life*, 14–15; Davis, *Home Fires Burning*, 181–82.

16. Manès Sperber, *God's Water Carriers*, trans. Joachim Neugroschel (New York, 1987), 133.

17. Cited in Kučera, *Rationed Life*, 29; Healy, *Vienna and the Fall*, 31, 43–45, 54–56; quotation, 55.

18. Healy, *Vienna and the Fall*, 75–85; Davis, *Home Fires Burning*, 81, 222–23.

19. Reichsgesundheitsamt, *Schädigung der deutschen*, 52–53.

20. Hull, *A Scrap of Paper*, 170. For the 1918 report, see Reichsgesundheitsamt, *Schädigung der deutschen*, 14; Healy, *Vienna and the Fall*, 41–42.

21. Friedrich Lützow, *Unterseebootskrieg und Hungerblockade* (Berlin, 1921), 26.

22. Max Sering, *Das ländliche Siedlung als Quelle gesunden Volkstums* (Berlin, 1915), quotations, 1, 6–8, 11.

23. Taratko, "Feeding Germany," chap. 5

24. Rundfunkrede des Ministers für Ernährung und Landwirtschaft Freiherr von Braun, 23 July 1932, 19 uhr, Landwirtschaftliche Siedlung, R118221, Sonderreferat Deutschland, 1920-1934, Politisches Archiv Auswärtigen Amt, Berlin.

25. Mark Hobbs, "'Farmers on notice': The Threat Faced by Weimar Berlin's Garden Colonies in the Face of the City's Neues Bauen Housing Programme," *Urban History* 39 (May 2012): 263–84.

26. See, for example, Paul-André Rosental, *A Human Garden: French Policy and the Transatlantic Legacies of Eugenic Experimentation*, trans. Carolyn Avery (New York, 2020); Liora Bigon and Yossi Katz, *Garden Cities and Colonial Planning: Transnationality and Urban Ideas in Palestine and Africa* (New York, 2014); Susan Currell, "Breeding Better Babies in the Eugenic Garden City: 'Municipal Darwinism' and the (Anti)Cosmopolitan Utopia in the Early Twentieth Century," *Modernist Cultures* 5, no. 2 (2010): 267–90.

27. Davis, *Home Fires Burning*, 118.

28. Francesca M. Wilson, *In the Margins of Chaos: Recollections of Relief Work in and Between Three Wars* (New York, 1945), 130.

29. Wilson, *In the Margins of Chaos*, 272.

30. Taratko, "Feeding Germany," 203–6. See also Elisabeth Jones, "Internal Colonization in Weimar Germany. Transnational and Local Approaches to Rural Governance in the 1920s," in *Governing the Rural in Interwar Europe*, ed. Liesbeth van

der Grifft and Amalia Ribi Forclaz (New York, 2018), 24–44; and Liesbeth van de Grift, "Cultivating Land and People: Internal Colonization in Interwar Europe," in *Governing the Rural in Interwar Europe*, ed. Liesbeth van der Grifft and Amalia Ribi Forclaz (New York, 2018), 68–92.

31. Franz Oppenheimer, *Die Siedlungsgenossenschaft: Versuch einer positive Überwindung des Kommunismus durch Lösung des Genossenschaftsproblems und der Agrarfrage* (Leipzig, 1896).

32. Taratko, "Feeding Germany," 183–95

33. Taratko, "Feeding Germany," 206–12.

34. David Haney, *When Modern Was Green: Life and Work of Landscape Architect Leberecht Migge* (London, 2010), 93–112. On Oppenheimer, see Taratko, "Feeding Germany."

35. Leberecht Migge, *Garden Culture of the Twentieth Century*, ed. and trans. David Haney (Washington, 2013), 196–97. On the allotment garden movement, see Micheline Nilsen, *The Working Man's Green Space: Allotment Gardens in England, France, and Germany, 1870-1919* (Charlottesville, VA, 2014).

36. Leberecht Migge, *Laubenkolonien und Kleingärten* (Munich, 1917), 1, 12, 15.

37. Haney, *When Modern Was Green*, 131.

38. Leberecht Migge, *Jedermann Selbstversorger! Eine Lösung der Siedlungsfrage durch neuen Gartenbau* (Jena, 1918), 39–40; Haney, *When Modern Was Green*, 114–21.

39. Leberecht Migge, *"Der Soziale Garten": Das Grüne Manifest* (Berlin, 1926), 11–14.

Chapter 5

1. Cyrus Edson, "The Microbe as Social Leveller," *North American Review* 161, no. 467 (October 1895): 422, 425.

2. K. David Patterson and Gerald F. Pyle, "The Geography and Mortality of the 1918 Influenza Pandemic," *Bulletin of the History of Medicine* 65, no. 1 (Spring 1991): 13–14; Carol R. Byerly, "The U.S. Military and the Influenza Pandemic of 1918-19," *Public Health Reports* 125, suppl. 3 (2010): 82–91.

3. Sergio Correia, Stephan Luck, and Emil Verner, "Pandemics Depress the Economy, Public Health Interventions Do Not: Evidence from the 1918 Flu," March 26, 2020. Available at SSRN: https://dx.doi.org/10.2139/ssrn.3561560.

4. "Influenza Slashes Railroad Receipts," *Minneapolis Morning Tribune*, December 21, 1918, 19; "Epidemic Effects Cloth Output," *Fall River Evening Herald*, October 19, 1918, 1; "Epidemic Cuts Coal Output," *Washington Post*, October 14, 1918, 6.

5. Homer Folks, "War, Best Friend of Disease," *Harper's Magazine*, December 1, 1919, 456.

6. Howard Phillips, "Influenza Pandemic," in *International Encyclopedia of the First World War*, ed. Ute Daniel et al. (Berlin, 2014), doi 10.15463/ie1418.10148.

7. R. Bruce Low, "The Incidence of Epidemic Influenza During 1918-19 in Europe

and in the Western Hemisphere," in *Report on the Pandemic of Influenza, 1918-19*, Her Majesty's Stationery Office (London, 1920), 203.

8. Early Manifestations of Influenza from Transatlantic Vessels Arriving at New York, March 20, 1919, 20, RG 90, Records of the United States Public Health Service.

9. *Report on the Pandemic of Influenza, 1918-19*, xix.

10. Frank G. Boudreau, *Ancient Disease–Modern Defence: The Work of the Health Organization of the League of Nations* (New York, 1939), 8.

11. Heidi Tworek points to the ways that information about epidemics "globalized" during the interwar period even as the movement of people and goods slowed down. Heidi J. S. Tworek, "Communicable Disease: Information, Health, and Globalization in the Interwar Period," *American Historical Review* 124, no. 3 (June 2019): 813–42.

12. "Get 'Flu' and Be Happy," *Kansas City Star*, July 28, 1918.

13. Nurses Emergency Council, 1918, Number of Cases and Influenza and Pneumonia Cared for in Homes by Various Agencies Cooperating Through the Nurses Emergency Council During October 1918, Lillian Wald Papers; Lillian Wald, "The Work of the Nurses' Emergency Council," *Public Health Nurse Quarterly* 10, 305. Lillian D. Wald, *Windows on Henry Street* (Boston, 1934), 98.

14. Lillian D. Wald, *The House on Henry Street* (New York, 1915), 4–6.

15. On relationships between German Jews and Eastern European Jews in the United States and Europe, see Steven E. Aschheim, *Brothers and Strangers: The East European Jew in German and German Jewish Consciousness, 1800–1923* (Madison, WI, 1982); Jack Wertheimer, *Unwelcome Strangers: East European Jews in Imperial Germany* (New York, 1987).

16. Wald, *House on Henry Street*, 290, 306.

17. Nayan Shah, *Contagious Divides: Epidemics and Race in San Francisco's Chinatown* (Berkeley, 2001), quotations from page 1.

18. Howard Markel and Alexandra Minna Stern, "The Foreignness of Germs: The Persistent Association of Immigrants and Disease in American Society," *Millbank Quarterly* 80, no. 4 (2002): 764.

19. Alan Kraut, *Silent Travelers: Germs, Genes, and the Immigrant Menace* (Baltimore, 1994), 84–93; Shah, *Contagious Divides*, 120–57.

20. Howard Markel, *Quarantine! East European Jewish Immigrants and the New York City Epidemics of 1892* (Baltimore, 1999), 31.

21. "No Way to Stop Immigration. Quarantine the Only Safeguard Against the Cholera," *New York Times*, August 29, 1892, 1, 5, cited in Markel, *Quarantine!*, 88.

22. Jacob A. Riis, *How the Other Half Lives: Studies Among the Tenements of New York* (New York, 1890), 109.

23. Vejas G. Liulevicius, *War Land on the Eastern Front: Culture, National Identity, and German Occupation in World War I* (Cambridge, UK, 2000), 80–81; Paul Weindling, *Epidemics and Genocide in Eastern Europe* (Oxford, 2000), chap. 4.

24. "Ein neuer Schritt zum Frieden," *Neues Wiener Tagblatt*, September 15, 1918, 1.
25. Beschwerde über Mangel auf dem Gebiete der Seuchenabwehr und Nährungsmittelfürsorge, Reichsgesundheitsamts, February 20, 1919, R86/4539, bd. 4 Ansteckende Krankheiten/Generalia, BA.
26. "Orient und Mittelmeer," *Wiener Morgenzeitung*, August 4, 1921, 1.
27. Weindling, *Epidemics and Genocide*, 112, on the use of Zyklon, 128–37; Niederschrift über die am 2. Juni 1922 im Reichsministeriums des Innern abgehaltene kommissarische Beratung, betreffend die zur Abwehr der Seuchengefahr aus dem Osten erforderlichen Massnahmen, July 3, 1922, R86/4541, Bundesarchiv, Berlin; Gesundheitliche Massnahmen in Durchwandererverkehr, August 3, 1922, R86/4541, Bundesarchiv, Berlin; Durchschlag, Berlin, February 26, 1921, R86/2402, Bundesarchiv, Berlin.
28. Weindling, *Epidemics and Genocide*, 117; *Second Annual Report of the Epidemic Commission of the League of Nations*, August 1, 1922, United Nations Archive, Geneva, League of Nations, Section(s) Sociale, de la Santé et de l'Opium, 12B Health, 15002 Epidemic Commission of the League, 823 (R823-12B-15002-22506).
29. Weindling, *Epidemics and Genocide*, 6.
30. Letter from Lutiant Van Wert to "Louise," National Archives Identifier 2641556, Department of the Interior. Office of Indian Affairs, Haskell Institute; "Prayer Sunday's Influenza Remedy," *Providence Daily Journal*, October 5, 1918, 2.
31. "Influenza Toll 27 at Pueblo. Renewed Activity of Disease Prompts Talk of Continuing Ban in Denver," *Rocky Mountain News*, November 6, 1918, 3.
32. "Epidemic Continues to Rage Through Italian Section of Denver," *Denver Post*, November 17, 1918, 4.
33. Work of the Sisters During the Epidemic of Influenza, October 1918. Records of the American Catholic Historical Society of Philadelphia 30, no. 2 (June 1919): 149–51.
34. Work of the Sisters, 141, 171.
35. "'Contagious Disease' Placards Proposed for Houses in Which There Are Influenza Patients," *Democrat and Chronicle* (Rochester, NY), October 27, 1918, 7.
36. "Fighting Influenza," *Lowell Sun* (Lowell, MA), October 3, 1918, 6.
37. "Influenza Traced to Chinese Plague," *Albany Evening Journal*, October 16, 1918, 4.
38. "Checking the Epidemic," *The Oregonian*, October 11, 1918, 10.
39. "Magazine Section," *San Francisco Chronicle*, November 17, 1918, 5.
40. American Red Cross, *The Mobilisation of the American National Red Cross During the Influenza Pandemic, 1918–1919* (Geneva, 1920), 23.
41. Wald to Warburg, October 31, 1918, Lillian Wald Correspondence, July–December 1918, Lillian D. Wald Papers, New York Public Library.
42. Wald, *Windows on Henry Street*, 337.

Chapter 6

1. Quoted by Robert Lekachman, "Introduction," in John Maynard Keynes, *The Economic Consequences of the Peace* (New York, 1971), x–xi.
2. *What the League Has Done for Austria* (London, 1924).
3. Walther Vogel, "Die territorialen und bevölkerungspolitischen Veränderungen Deutschlands durch den Friedensvertrag," in *Der Friedensvertrag und Deutschlands Stellung in der Weltwirtschaft* (Berlin, 1921), 19–38; Heinrich Dade, "Der Friedensvertrag und die Versorgung Deutschlands mit landwirtschaftlichen Erzeugnissen," in *Der Friedensvertrag und Deutschlands Stellung in der Weltwirtschaft* (Berlin, 1921), 39–40, quotation 40.
4. For a summary, see Margaret Macmillan, *Paris 1919: Six Months That Changed the World* (New York, 2003), 157–206.
5. Kurt Lersner, ed., *Versailles! Volkskommentar des friedensdiktats* (Berlin, 1921), citation 4.
6. Max Sering, *Das Friedensdiktat Von Versailles und Deutschlands Wirtschaftliche Lage* (Berlin, 1920), 1, 24, 36; Lersner, *Versailles!*, 44, 58–60, 67–68.
7. "Comments by the German Delegation on the Conditions of the Peace," in *International Conciliation: Documents of the American Association for International Conciliation*, vol. 2 (New York, 1919), 1920, 1221.
8. "Die wirtschaftliche Lage. Nach der Rede des Abg. Dr. Renner beim Metallarbeiter-Verbandstag in Linz am 13 Juli 1921," *Tagblatt* (Linz), July 22, 1921, 2.
9. Kundgebung in Graz gegen den Friedensvertragsentwurf, June 14, 1919; Tirol, An die Tiroler Landesregierung Innsbruck, June 20, 1919, Karton 6, Archiv der Republik (AdR), Auswärtige Angelegenheiten (AAng), Bundeskanzleramt Auswärtige Angelegenheiten (BKA-AA), St. Germain, Österreichisches Staatsarchiv (Oesta).
10. Count Albert Apponyi, *The Peace-Treaty Proposed to Hungary* (London, 1920), 4.
11. "Proteste und Petitionen an die Reichsregierung und die Nationalversammlung," in *Die Kolonialfrage im Frieden von Versailles; Dokumente zu ihrer Behandlung*, ed. Hans Poeschel (Berlin, 1920), 111–12.
12. "Unterschriftensammlung des Reichsverbands der Kolonialdeutschen. Für die Wiedererlangung von Kolonialbesitz," in *Die Kolonialfrage im Frieden von Versailles; Dokumente zu ihrer Behandlung*, ed. Hans Poeschel (Berlin, 1920), 112.
13. Johannes Bell, Minister für die Kolonien, "Funkspruch an das amerikanische Volk im Mai 1919," in *Die Kolonialfrage im Frieden von Versailles; Dokumente zu ihrer Behandlung*, ed. Hans Poeschel (Berlin, 1920), 118–21; General von Lettow-Vorbeck, "Funkspruch an das englische Volk von General von Lettow-Vorbeck im Mai 1919," in *Die Kolonialfrage im Frieden von Versailles; Dokumente zu ihrer Behandlung*, ed. Hans Poeschel (Berlin, 1920), 122–23.
14. Protestkundgebung des Niederösterreichischen Gewerbevereines in Wien gegen den Gewaltfrieden, June 6, 1919, Karton 6, AdR, AAng, BKA-AA, St. Germain, OestA.

15. Protest der Vertrauensmänner des Böhmerwaldes gegen den Friedensvertragentwurf, June 4, 1919, Karton 6, AdR, AAng, BKA-AA, St. Germain, OestA.
16. Larry Wolff, *Woodrow Wilson and the Reimagining of Eastern Europe* (Stanford, 2020), 56–114.
17. "Ein neuer Schritt zum Frieden," *Neues Wiener Tagblatt,* September 15, 1918, 1.
18. Tara Zahra, "The Minority Problem: National Classification in the French and Czechoslovak Borderlands," *Contemporary European History* 17 (May 2008): 138.
19. Quoted in Macmillan, *Paris 1919,* 99.
20. Stephen Miles Bouton, *And the Kaiser Abdicates: The German Revolution, November, 1918–August, 1919* (New Haven, CT, 1921), 269–71.
21. John Maynard Keynes, *Economic Consequences,* 4.
22. Keynes, *Economic Consequences,* 227–28.
23. Mate Rigo, "Imperial Elites After the Fall of Empires: Business Elites and States in Europe's East and West, 1867-1928" (PhD diss., Cornell University, 2016); Andreas Weigl, "Beggar-thy-Neighbor vs. Danube Basin Strategy: Habsburg Economic Networks in Interwar Europe," *Religions* 7, no. 16 (November 2016): 129.
24. Count Harry Kessler, *Germany and Europe* (New Haven, CT, 1923), 5, 129.

Chapter 7

1. H. James Burgwyn, *The Legend of the Mutilated Victory: Italy, the Great War, and the Paris Peace Conference, 1915-1919* (Westport, CT, 1993), 270.
2. Francesco Nitti, *The Decadence of Europe* (New York, 1923), viii.
3. Cited in René Albrecht-Carrié, *Italy at the Paris Peace Conference* (New York, 1938), 146–47.
4. Cited in Dominique Kirchner Reill, *The Fiume Crisis: Life in the Wake of the Habsburg Empire* (Cambridge, MA, 2020), 23–73. I am extremely grateful to Reill for her generous reading of and assistance with this chapter, which is heavily indebted to her work. Gabriele D'Annunzio, "Lettera ai Dalmati," *Il Popolo d'Italia,* January 15, 1919.
5. Gabriele D'Annunzio, *The Fiume Question,* trans. Henry Furst (Fiume, 1919), 9.
6. Reill, *Fiume Crisis,* 1–6.
7. Citation from J. N. Macdonald, *A Political Escapade: The Story of Fiume and D'Annunzio,* (London, 1921), 131.
8. Reill, *Fiume Crisis.*
9. On Fiume as a global port city, see Tyler James Callaway, "Hungary at the Helm: Austria-Hungary's Global Integration During the Age of Empire" (PhD diss., New York University, 2019), esp. chap. one; Reill, *Fiume Crisis,* 24–25.
10. I thank Dominique Reill for providing me with this source. Andrea Ossinack, Letter to editor of the *Westminster Gazette,* May 22, 1919, Cass. 241-1919: Prot. 3641, Vittoriale-Archivio Fiumano (AFV).
11. Reill, *Fiume Crisis,* 81. See also Krešimir Sučević Međeral, "Businessman – The

Case of Ossinack Family and Fiume," *Collegium Antropologicum* 41, no. 4 (2017): 351–60.

12. Glenda Sluga, *The Problem of Trieste and the Italo-Yugoslav Border: Difference, Identity and Sovereignty in Twentieth-Century Europe* (Albany, NY, 2001); Maura Hametz, *Making Trieste Italian, 1918–1954* (Rochester, NY, 2005).

13. "Cronaca della città. Stato d'animo," *Il Piccolo*, April 4, 1920, cited in Marco Bresciani, "Multi-national Towns/Ports Between Imperial Legacies and Postwar Disorders: The Case of the Habsburg Upper Adriatic" (unpublished manuscript). On elites in Trieste, see Hametz, *Making Trieste Italian*, 25, 47, 58; Giorgio Negrelli, *Al di qua del mito: diritto storico e difesa nazionale nell'autonomismo della Trieste asburgica* (Udine, 1979).

14. Marco Cuzzi, *Cibo di guerra: Sofferenze e privazioni nell'Italia dei conflitti mondiali* (Milan, 2015); Fabio Degli Esposti, "L'economia di Guerra italiana," in *La società italiana e la Grande Guerra*, ed. Giovanna Procacci (Annali della Fondazione Ugo la Mafia, 2013), 187–213; Maria Concetta Dentoni, "Food and Nutrition (Italy)," trans. Noor Giovanni Mazhar, in *International Encyclopedia of the First World War*, ed. Ute Daniel et al. (Berlin, 2014), https://encyclopedia.1914-1918 -online.net/article/food_and_nutrition_italy; Francesco L. Galassi and Mark Harrison, "Italy at War, 1915-1918," in *The Economics of World War I*, ed. Stephen Broadberry and Mark Harrison (Cambridge, UK, 2005), 276–309.

15. Cuzzi, *Cibo di Guerra*, 70–75.

16. Galassi and Harrison, "Italy at War, 1915-18," 276–309; Giovanna Procacci, "La protesta delle donne delle campagne in tempo di guerra," *Annali dell'Istituto Alcide Cervi* 13 (1991): 57–87; Roberto Bianchi, "Quelle che protestavano, 1914-1918," in *La Grande Guerra delle italiane: Mobilizzazioni, diritti, transformazioni*, ed. Stefania Bartoloni (Rome, 2016), 202–3.

17. Agitazione agraria, 12 Aprile 1919, PS 1920, Busta 77, Archivio Centrale dello State, Rome (henceforth ACS). On peasant protests and land occupations in 1919, see Roberto Bianchi, *Pace, Pane, Terra: il 1919 in Italia* (Rome, 2006), 41–64.

18. Prefettura della provincia di Roma, Invasioni di terreni, 28 Agosto 1919, PS 1920, Busta 77, ACS.

19. Giuseppe Tassinari, *Ten Years of Integral Land-Reclamation Under the Mussolini Act* (Faenza, 1939), 11.

20. "Italy," *Commerce Reports* 1, no. 8 (February 20, 1922): 442.

21. Arrigo Serpieri, *La Guerra e le classi rurali italiane* (New Haven, CT, 1930), 209–13.

22. Invasione delle terre nella provincia di Roma, October 2, 1920, PS 1920, Busta 77, ACS.

23. Luigi Einaudi, "I tumulti populari e il dovere del governo," *Corriere della Serra*, July 6, 1919, in Luigi Einaudi, *Cronache economiche e politiche di un trentennio (1893-1925)*, vol. 5 (1919–20) (Torino, 1959), 273.

24. Copia dal rapporto inviata 27 Dicembre 1921, sottoprefetto di Albenga, PS 1921, Busta 67, ACS.

25. Civitella di Romagna, Manifestazioni per mancanza di allogi, 15 Febraio 1921, PS 1921, Busta 67, ACS.
26. Oggeto – per la bonifica della Donzella, Rovigo 29 Maggio 1921, PS 1921, Busta 74, ACS.
27. On the "children's crusade," see Emiliano Loria, "On Piracy," accessed August 3, 2020, https://loccidentale.it/quando-la-pirateria-era-made-in-italy/.
28. D'Annunzio, *Fiume Question*, 19.
29. Daniela Rossini, *Woodrow Wilson and the American Myth in Italy: Culture, Diplomacy and War Propaganda*, trans. Antony Sugaar (Cambridge, MA, 2008), 184–87.
30. "D'Annunzio and His War," *New York Times*, December 3, 1920, 14.
31. "D'Annunzio Leaves Fiume in Airplane," *New York Times*, December 31, 1920, 1.

Chapter 8

1. On Schwimmer's tenure in Switzerland, see Tibor Glant, "Against All Odds: Vira B. Whitehouse and Rosika Schwimmer in Switzerland, 1918," *American Studies International* 40, no. 1 (2002): 343–51.
2. Though, as Oscar Sanchez-Sibony argues, the USSR never really achieved anything like autarky. Oscar Sanchez-Sibony, *Red Globalization: The Political Economy of the Soviet Cold War from Stalin to Khrushchev* (Cambridge, UK, 2014).
3. Rosika Schwimmer to Mien Palthe, August 19, 1919, Box 118, Rosika Schwimmer Papers, New York Public Library (henceforth Schwimmer Papers).
4. Letter of December 12, 1919, from Budapest, Box 120, Schwimmer Papers.
5. On revolutionary and counterrevolutionary violence in Central Europe, see Robert Gerwarth, *The Vanquished: Why the First World War Failed to End, 1917-23* (New York, 2017). On Judeo-Bolshevism, see Paul Hanebrink, *A Specter Haunting Europe: The Myth of Judeo-Bolshevism* (Cambridge, MA, 2018); Eliza Ablovatski, "The Central European Revolutions of 1919 and the Myth of Judeo-Bolshevism," *European Review of History* 17, no. 3 (Cosmopolitanism, Nationalism and the Jews of East Central Europe) (2010): 473–89.
6. On Freikorps violence in the east, see Vejas Liulevicius, *War Land on the Eastern Front: National Identity and German Occupation in World War I* (Cambridge, UK, 2000); Annemarie Sammartino, *The Impossible Border: Germany and the East* (Ithaca, NY, 2010).
7. Gerwarth, *The Vanquished*, 118–32.
8. Victor Klemperer, *Munich 1919. Diary of a Revolution* (Malden, MA, 2017), 75, 85, 100.
9. Stephen Miles Bouton, *And the Kaiser Abdicates: The German Revolution, November, 1918–August, 1919* (New Haven, CT, 1921), 254.
10. *Foodstuffs and Supplies for Europe, 1919: Hearings Before the United States Senate Committee on Appropriations*, 65th Congress, 3rd sess. (January 15, 1919), 5.
11. Quoted in N. P. Howard, "The Social and Political Consequences of the Allied Food Blockade of Germany, 1918-19," *German History* 11, no. 2 (1993): 183.

12. On this about-face and US food aid to Germany after World War I, see Alice Weinreb, *Modern Hungers: Food and Power in Twentieth-Century Germany* (New York, 2017), 33–39.

13. Joseph Marcus, "Is There White Terror in Hungary?" June 5, 1921, NY AR1921_011915, American Joint Distribution Committee (JDC) Archives (henceforth JDC Archives).

14. Claire Morelon, "Street Fronts: War, State Legitimacy and Urban Space, Prague 1914-1920" (PhD diss., University of Birmingham, 2015), 197.

15. Cited in Rebekah Klein-Pejšová, *Mapping Jewish Loyalties in Interwar Slovakia* (Bloomington, IN, 2015), 38.

16. Jeffrey Veidlinger, *In the Midst of Civilized Europe: The Pogroms of 1918-1921 and the Onset of the Holocaust* (New York, 2021), 5, 24–25. See also William Hagen, *Anti-Jewish Violence in Poland, 1914-1920* (Cambridge, UK, 2018).

17. Veidlinger, *In the Midst of Civilized Europe*, 83–88; Hagen, *Anti-Jewish Violence*, 156. On Jewish self-defense, see especially Jan Rybak, *Everyday Zionism in East-Central Europe: Nation-Building in War and Revolution, 1914-20* (Oxford, 2021).

18. Mission of the United States to Poland, 1919-1921 New York Collection, Poland, Discrimination and Persecution, 1919-21, JDC Archives.

19. *Report by Sir Stuart Samuel on his Mission to Poland*, Her Majesty's Stationery Office (London, 1929), 22–24.

20. On arrests, see Hagen, *Anti-Jewish Violence*, 512.

21. "Fellow Citizens!" NY_AR1921_01045, JDC Archives.

22. Rosika Schwimmer to Frau Lesser, March 16, 1920, Box 121, Schwimmer Papers.

23. United States v. Schwimmer, 279 U.S. 644 (1929); Rosika Schwimmer to Justice Oliver Wendell Holmes, January 28, 1930, Box 494, Schwimmer Papers.

Chapter 9

1. Stefan Zweig, *The World of Yesterday* (London, 1943), 215.

2. Zweig, *World of Yesterday*, 29.

3. On the Austrian Idea and climate, see Deborah Coen, *Climate in Motion: Science, Empire and the Problem of Scale* (Chicago, 2018), pt. 1.

4. Robert Musil, *The Man Without Qualities*, vol. 1, trans. Sophie Wilkins (New York, 1995), 185.

5. Andrea Komlosy, *Grenze und ungleiche regionale Entwicklung: Binnenmarkt und Migration in der Habsburgermonarchie* (Vienna, 2003), 22–27.

6. Ernst von Schwarzer, *Gelt und Gut in Neu-Österreich* (Vienna, 1857), 14; Friedrich List, *National System of Political Economy*, trans. G. A. Matile (Philadelphia, 1856), 72.

7. See Alison Frank Johnson's forthcoming book on Austria's global empire.

8. Joseph Roth, *The Emperor's Tomb*, trans. Michael Hoffman (New York, 2013), 146.

9. H. R. Fleischmann, "Die Wiedereinstellung des reisenden Kaufmannes in den Wirtschaftdienst," *Der Reisende Kaufmann* 33, no. 1088 (Vienna, October 1919): 1.

10. On economic policies in interwar East-Central Europe, see Iván T. Berend and György Ránki, *Economic Development in East-Central Europe in the 19th and 20th Centuries* (New York, 1974); Jan Kofman, *Economic Nationalism and Development: Central and Eastern Europe Between the Two World Wars* (Boulder, CO, 1997); Christoph Kreutzmüller, Michael Wildt, and Moshe Zimmermann, eds., *National Economies: Volks-Wirtschaft, Racism and Economy in Europe Between the Wars, 1918-1939/45* (Newcastle upon Tyne, 2015).

11. Sir Arthur Salter, "The Reconstruction of Austria," *Foreign Affairs* 2, no. 4 (June 15, 1924): 630.

12. Zweig, *World of Yesterday*, 215.

13. František Palacký, "Letter to Frankfurt," April 11, 1848, published in Balázs Trencsényi and Michal Kopeček, eds., *National Romanticism: The Formation of National Movements*. Discourses of Collective Identity in Central and Southeast Europe 1770–1945, vol. 11 (Budapest, 2007), 322–29.

14. Natasha Wheatley, "Central Europe as Ground Zero of the New International Order," *Slavic Review* 78, no. 4 (Winter 2019): 900–11.

15. On interwar internationalism, see especially Peter Becker and Natasha Wheatley, eds., *Remaking Central Europe: The League of Nations and the Former Habsburg Lands* (Oxford, 2021); Glenda Sluga, *Internationalism in the Age of Nationalism* (Philadelphia, 2013); Glenda Sluga and Patricia Clavin, *Internationalisms: A Twentieth-Century History* (Cambridge, UK, 2016); Daniel Laqua, ed., *Internationalism Reconfigured: Transnational Ideas and Movements Between the Wars* (London, 2011); Bruno Cabanes, *The Great War and the Origins of Humanitarianism, 1918-1924* (Cambridge, UK, 2014).

16. Hans Schober, "The Austrian Problem," *Advocate of Peace*, November 1922, 377.

17. Oszkar Jászi, and Stefan von Hartenstein, *Der Zusammenbruch des Dualismus und die Zukunft der Donaustaaten* (Vienna, 1918), 46, 49, 96. For an overview of federative ideas in East-Central Europe, see Holly Case, "The Strange Politics of Federative Ideas in East-Central Europe," *Journal of Modern History* 85, no. 4 (2013): 833–66.

18. *Denkschrift aus Deutsch-Österreich* (Hirzel, 1915), 71, cited in Madeline Dungy, "International Commerce in the Wake of Empire: Central European Economic Integration Between National and Imperial Sovereignty," in Becker and Wheatley, *Remaking Central Europe*, 220.

19. *Collective Treaties Facilitating International Commerce in Europe: Report of the Austrian National Committee to the Committee on Trade Barriers* (Vernay, 1926), 3, cited in Dungy, "International Commerce in the Wake of Empire," 225.

20. Richard Coudenhove-Kalergi, "Das Paneuropäische Manifest," in *Kampf um Paneuropa, aus dem 1. Jahrgang von Paneuropa* (Vienna, 1925), 9. On pan-Europe, see Sven Beckert, "American Danger: US Empire, Eurafrica, and the Territorialization of Industrial Capitalism, 1870–1950," *American Historical Review* 122, no. 4 (2017): 1162; Katherine Sorrels, *Cosmopolitan Outsiders: Imperial Inclusion, National Exclusion, and the Pan-European Idea, 1900-1930* (New York, 2016).

21. István Bethlen, *The Treaty of Trianon and European Peace: Four Lectures Delivered in London in November 1933* (London, 1934), 152, 177–82.
22. Andreas Weigl, "Beggar-thy-Neighbor vs. Danube Basin Strategy: Habsburg Economic Networks in Interwar Europe," *Religions* 7, no. 16 (November 2016): 129.
23. Quinn Slobodian, *Globalists: The End of Empire and the Birth of Neoliberalism* (Cambridge, MA, 2018).
24. Zweig, *World of Yesterday*, 226.
25. Cited by John Deak, in "Dismantling Empire: Ignaz Seipel and Austria's Financial Crisis," in Günther Bischof and Fritz Plasser, eds., *From Empire to Republic: Post-World War I Austria* (New Orleans, 2010), 123–41, here 135.
26. On League of Nations reconstruction of Austria, see Nathan Marcus, *Austrian Reconstruction and the Collapse of Global Finance, 1921-1931* (Cambridge, MA, 2018); Patricia Clavin, *Securing the World Economy: The Reinvention of the League of Nations: 1920-1946* (Oxford, 2013); Patricia Clavin, "The Austrian Hunger Crisis and the Genesis of International Organization After the First World War," *International Affairs* 90, no. 2 (March 2014): 265–78; Jamie Martin, *The Meddlers: Sovereignty, Empire, and the Birth of Global Economic Governance* (Cambridge, MA, 2022), chap. 2. On the ways that the financial reconstruction affected the bureaucracy, see Deak, "Dismantling Empire," 135–38.
27. "Der Genfer Vertrag und die Intelligenzberufe," *Tagblatt,* October 19, 1922, 1.
28. "An das Arbeitende Volk in Stadt und Land!" *Arbeiter-Zeitung,* August 31, 1923, 1.
29. Martin, *The Meddlers,* chap. 2.
30. European Self-help in Relief, Folder 9, Box 632, American Relief Administration (ARA), Hoover Archive (HA), Stanford University.
31. On orientalism and Eastern Europe, see Larry Wolff, *Inventing Eastern Europe: The Map of Civilization on the Mind of the Enlightenment* (Stanford, 1994); Maria Todorova, *Imagining the Balkans* (Oxford, 1997).
32. "Czecho-Slovakia," *The Record of the Save the Children Fund* 1, no. 1 (October 1, 1920): 4.
33. Susan Pedersen, *The Guardians: The League of Nations and the Crisis of Empire* (Oxford, 2015); Mark Mazower, *Governing the World: The History of an Idea* (New York, 2013); Mark Mazower, *No Enchanted Palace: The End of Empire and the Ideological Origins of the United Nations* (Princeton, NJ, 2009).
34. Sara Silverstein, "Reinventing International Health in East Central Europe: The League of Nations, State Sovereignty, and Universal Health," in Becker and Wheatley, *Remaking Central Europe,* 71–98.
35. Peter Becker, "Remaking Mobility: International Conferences and the Emergence of the Modern Passport System," in Becker and Wheatley, *Remaking Central Europe,* 193–213; League of Nations, Organization for Communication and Transit, *Transport Problems Which Arose from the War of 1914-1918 and the Work of Restoration Undertaken in This Field by the League of Nations* (Geneva, 1945), 34–35.

36. Dungy, "International Commerce in the Wake of Empire," 213–40; League of Nations Economic Committee, *The Treatment of Foreign Nationals*, September 8, 1924, League of Nations Archive.

37. Report of the Economic Committee to the Council on Its Fifteenth Session, Geneva, June 3, 1925, League of Nations Archive.

38. David Petrucelli, "Fighting the Scourge of International Crime: The Internationalization of Policing and Criminal Law in Interwar Europe," in Becker and Wheatley, *Remaking Central Europe*, 241–58.

39. Zweig, *World of Yesterday*, 221.

40. Zweig, *World of Yesterday*, 219.

41. Zweig, *World of Yesterday*, 232.

42. Michael Steinberg, *Austria as Theater and Ideology: The Meaning of the Salzburg Festival* (Ithaca, NY, 2000).

43. Zweig, *World of Yesterday*, 263, 249.

Chapter 10

1. "Swimmer Saves 2 Fleeing Ellis Island," *New York Times*, September 15, 1924, 1.

2. On the creation of the "illegal" immigrant in the United States, see Mae Ngai, *Impossible Subjects: Illegal Aliens and the Making of Modern America* (Princeton, NJ, 2014).

3. "Renovating Ellis Island," *New York Times*, January 24, 1924, 16; "Conditions on Ellis Island," *New York Times*, July 13, 1924, 18; "A Decent Ellis Island," *New York Times*, December 24, 1923, 10.

4. Dorothee Schneider, "The United States Government and the Investigation of European Emigration in the Open Door Era," in *Citizenship and Those Who Leave: The Politics of Emigration and Expatriation*, ed. Nancy Green and François Weil (Champaign, IL, 2007), 198.

5. *L'émigration polonaise, son importance et son organisation* (Warsaw, 1922), 10; Donna R. Gabbaccia, *Italy's Many Diasporas* (Seattle, 2000), 130–31; US Department of Commerce, Bureau of the Census, *A Statistical Abstract Supplement. Historical Statistics of the U.S. Colonial Times to 1957*, 56–57.

6. Joseph Roth, *The Wandering Jews*, trans. Michael Hoffmann (New York, 2001), 102–103.

7. Adam Tooze, *The Deluge: The Great War, America, and the Remaking of the Global Order, 1916–31* (New York, 2015), 302.

8. Tooze, *The Deluge*, 348.

9. Lisa McGirr, *The War on Alcohol: Prohibition and the Rise of the American State* (New York, 2016).

10. Kathleen M. Blee, *Women of the Klan: Racism and Gender in the 1920s* (Berkeley, 1991), 17; Linda Gordon, *The Second Coming of the KKK: The Ku Klux Klan of the 1920s and the American Political Tradition* (New York, 2017), 26–30, 194–95. On the economics of the Klan, see Roland G. Fryer and Steven D. Levitt, "Hatred and

Profits: Under the Hood of the KKK," *Quarterly Journal of Economics* 127, no. 4 (2012): 1883–925.

11. On Dubois's pan-African thought, see especially Brandon Kendhammer, "Dubois the Pan-Africanist and the Development of African Nationalism," *Ethnic and Racial Studies* 30, no. 1 (2007): 51–71.

12. Adam Ewing, *The Age of Garvey: How a Jamaican Activist Created a Mass Movement and Changed Black Politics* (Princeton, NJ, 2014), 80–81.

13. "Opening of UNIA Convention," *The Marcus Garvey and Universal Negro Improvement Association Papers, Volume II: August 1919–August 1920*, ed. Robert A. Hill (Berkeley, 1983), 478. On Garveyism, see Ronald J. Stephens and Adam Ewing, eds., *Global Garveyism* (Gainesville, FL, 2019); Ewing, *Age of Garvey*.

14. "Hon. Marcus Garvey Tells of Interview with the Ku Klux Klan," originally published in *Negro World*, July 15, 1922, reprinted in Marcus Garvey and Bob Blaisdell, *Selected Writings and Speeches of Marcus Garvey* (Mineola, NY, 2012).

15. "Bramble Bush Government," *Kourier Magazine*, December 1, 1924, 10–14.

16. H. W. Evans, "The Klan's Next Duty: Send Home Every Unfit Alien," *Kourier Magazine*, 2, no. 3 (February 1926): 1–2.

17. US Department of Labor, Bureau of Immigration, *Annual Reports of the Commissioner General of Immigration for the Fiscal Year Ended June 30, 1930*.

18. Francisco E. Balderrama, *Decade of Betrayal: Mexican Repatriation in the 1930s* (Albuquerque, 2006). On the history of deportation in the United States, see especially Adam Goodman, *The Deportation Machine: America's Long History of Expelling Immigrants* (Princeton, NJ, 2020).

19. Cecilia Razovsky, *America's Present Immigration Policy: The Visa and Quota Laws as They Affect the Clients of Social Agencies*, 4, Box 1, Cecilia Razovsky Papers, American Jewish Historical Society (henceforth Razovsky Papers).

20. Kenneth Rich and Mary Brant, *Maintenance Orders in Separated Families as Seen by the Immigrants Protective League in Chicago*, 1927, Folder 3, Maintenance and Support, Non-Support, Preliminary Study 1923-29 no. 1, SW109, International Social Service, University of Minnesota Social Welfare Archive.

21. Razovsky, *America's Present Immigration Policy*.

22. Razovsky, *Humanitarian Effects of the Immigration Law*, May 12, 1927, Box 1, Razovsky Papers; Razovsky, *America's Present Immigration Policy*.

23. Bruno Cabanes, *The Great War and the Origins of Humanitarianism, 1918-1924* (Cambridge, UK, 2014), chap. 3.

24. On statelessness and the collapse of empire, see Mira Siegelberg, *Statelessness: A Modern History* (Cambridge, MA, 2020).

25. Emma Cadbury and Anna Aszkanazy, "The Problem of the 'Staatenlosen' from the Humanitarian Side," in *The Problem of Statelessness (People Deprived of Nationality): Some Facts, Arguments and Proposals Presented to an International Conference Called by the Women's International League for Peace and Freedom* (Geneva, 1930), 12–22, quotation 21.

26. "For the First Time in Days," May 22, 1919, NY_AR1921_02528, 1919–21, American Joint Distribution Committee Archives (henceforth JDC Archives).

27. Roth, *Wandering Jews*, 67.

28. Roth, *Wandering Jews*, 66.

29. R586/11/9557/10481, West Galician refugees in Vienna - Jewish Delegations Committee - Transmitted a memorandum on the right of option of these refugees, requesting the League of Nations to intervene on this subject with the Austrian government, December 20, 1920, United Nations Archives Geneva.

30. R586/11/9557/11344, Expulsions of Galician Jews from Austrian territory - M. Elchof, delegate to the League of Nations - Memorandum on this question, entitled "Repatriation of Polish subjects whose stay becomes prejudicial to the Austrian people," United Nations Archives Geneva.

31. Gerald Stourzh, "Ethnic Attribution in Late Imperial Austria: Good Intentions, Evil Consequences," in *From Vienna to Chicago and Back* (Chicago, 2007), 175, footnote 33, my translation. For the entire text of the court's decision, see Erkenntnis z. 2973 ex 1921, Verwaltungsgerichtshof, June 9, 1921, reprinted in Oskar Besenböck, "Die Frage der jüdischen Option in Österreich, 1918-1923" (PhD diss., University of Vienna, 1992), 166–75.

32. *Austria - Issues concerning minorities in Austria*, report by Mr. Balfour, adapted by the Council on March 3, 1921, S363/28/5, Minorities Section, Archive of the League of Nations.

33. Joseph Marcus, "Is There White Terror in Hungary?" June 5, 1921, 87–88, AR1921_011915, JDC Archives. See also Paul Hanebrink, "Transnational Culture War: Christianity, Nation, and the Judeo-Bolshevik Myth in Hungary, 1890-1920," *Journal of Modern History* 80, no. 1 (March 2008): 55–80.

34. *Emigration and Immigration: Legislation and Treaties* (Geneva, 1922), xiv.

35. Leopold Caro, *Ku nowej Polsce* (Lwow, 1923), 13.

36. Jan Žilka, "Několik myšlenek o naší vystěhovalecké politice," *Československé emigrace* 3, no. 6 (June 1928): 1.

37. International Labor Organization, *The International Emigration Commission* (Geneva, 1922), 89.

38. Tara Zahra, *The Great Departure: Mass Migration from Eastern Europe and the Making of the Free World* (New York, 2016).

Chapter 11

1. Versammlung des Reichsverbandes Kolonien in der Heimat, October 7, 1926, Carton 517, Bundesministerium für Land und Forstwirtschaft, Siedlungswesen, Archiv der Republik (AdR), Österreichisches Staatsarchiv (OestA).

2. "Die Siedlungsfrage im Parlament," *Arbeiter-Zeitung*, September 24, 1926, 2.

3. Verein Kolonien in der Heimat, Besetzung der Oberau, September 27, 1926, Carton 517, Bundesministerium für Land und Forstwirtschaft, Siedlungswesen, AdR, OestA.

4. Innenkolonisationsprojekt Hübscher-Freisinger, March 14, 1927, Carton 517, Bundesministerium für Land und Forstwirtschaft, Siedlungswesen, AdR, OestA.

5. Ausserung zu Innenkolonisationsvorschlägen, 1931, Carton 519, Bundesministerium für Land und Forstwirtschaft, AdR, OestA.

6. Hans Kampffmeyer, *Siedlung und Kleingarten* (Vienna, 1926), 108.

7. Internationales Büro der Kleingärtner; Entwicklung der Einrichtungen für Kleinwirtschaftsiedlung und Arbeitergärten, July 11, 1932, Carton 518, Bundesministerium für Land und Forstwirtschaft, Siedlungswesen, AdR, OestA.

8. Francesca M. Wilson, *In the Margins of Chaos: Recollections of Relief Work in and Between Three Wars* (New York, 1945), 131.

9. Eine grosse Siedlerkundgebung in Wien, March 12, 1922, Carton 39, Großdeutsche Volkspartei, OestA.

10. Adolf Loos, "Wohnen lernen!" 1921, reprinted in Adolf Loos, *Gesammelte Schriften*, ed. Adolf Opel (Vienna, 2010), 557–60.

11. Inge Podbrecky, "Das Andere für Alle. Adolf Loos und die Siedlerbewegung," in *Leben mit Loos*, ed. Inge Podbrecky und Rainald Franz (Vienna, 2008), 131–48.

12. Max Ermers, Österreichs *Wirtschaftsverfall und Wiedergeburt. Ein Wirtschaftsprogramm zur Selbstrettung* (Vienna, 1922); Heinrich Jungbauer, *Unabhängigkeit durch Landwirtschaft* (Vienna, 1920), 32–35.

13. Klaus Novy, "Selbsthilfe als Reformbewegung. Der Kampf der Wiener Siedler nach dem Ersten Weltkrieg," in *Hands on Urbanism 1850–2012. Vom Recht auf Grün*, ed. Elke Krasny (Vienna, 1981), 126–60; Otto Krapfinger, "The Art of Urban Architecture from Below. Josef Frank's Positions at the Turning Point from the Viennese Settlement Movement to Monumental Community Housing Projects," in *Josef Frank: Against Design: Das Anti-formalistische Werk Des Architekten*, ed. Christoph Thun-Hohenstein et al. (Vienna, 2016), 89.

14. Wilson, *In the Margins of Chaos*, 130.

15. Roderich Müller Guttenbrunn, "Siedler," *Der Baustein* 1, no. 5 (1930): 1.

16. Josef Frank, "The Peoples' Apartment Palace," originally published in *Der Aufbau* 1, no. 7 (1926): 107–11, trans. and reproduced in *Josef Frank. Writings*, vol. 1, ed. Tano Bojankin et al. (Vienna, 2013).

17. L. Berthold und J. H. Tuschnig, "Warum wünsche ich mir ein Eigenheim," *Der Baustein. Monatsschrift für Wohnbau und Siedlungswesen, Heimkultur und Gartenpflege* 1, no. 4 (April 1930): 4–5.

18. Albert Gessmann, *Wie werden wir uns ernähren? Innenkolonisation, Agrarfrage, Ernährungsproblem* (Vienna, 1932), 14.

19. Leo Tartakower, *Selbstversorgung* (Vienna, 1934), 3.

20. Franz Egert, *Autarkie* (Innsbruck, 1934), 6, 51, 59, 100.

21. Ernst Streeruwitz, *Der Aufbau des Österreichischen Siedlungswerkes: Bericht des Ökw-Arbeitsausschusses Innenkolonisation* (Vienna, 1933), 3, 18.

22. Julius Wilhelm, "Abbau der Großstadt und innere Kolonisation," *Gegen den Strom! Flugschriften in zwölfter Stunde*, Heft 4 (Vienna, 1935), 8–34.

23. Kauft österreichischer Waren! Wirtschaftlicher Leitfaden für Lehrpersonen (Vienna, 1934), 19, 64–65.

24. Hermann Neubacher, "Stadtrandsiedlung," *Sonderheft: Stadtrandsiedlung. Sonderabdruck aus der Österreichischen Gemeindezeitung* 10, no. 4 (February 15, 1933): 2–4.

25. Die Stadtrandsiedlung Leopoldau, *Bericht der Gemeinwirtschaftlichen Siedlungs und Baustoffanstalt* (Vienna, 1932), 7–18.

26. Cited in Robert Hoffmann, *"Nimm Hack und Spaten": Siedlung und Siedlerbewegung in Österreich, 1918-1938* (Vienna, 1987), 179; "Der Bundeskanzler und der Präsident des Nationalrates über die Eigenheimbewegung," in *Die Baugenossenschaft* 4 (1931): 98, 101.

27. Franz Bachinger, "Siedlung und Arbeitsdienst als Staatsnotwendigkeit," *Arbeit und Boden: Zeitschrift für die Siedlungsbewegung und den Arbeitsdienst* 1, no. 1 (April 15, 1933): 2.

28. "Aus der Woche," *Der österreichische Volkswirt*, August 13, 1932, 1103.

29. Ludwig Mises, "Autarkie bedeutet Untergang der Kultur!" *Berliner Tagblatt*, March 31, 1932, NS/5/VI/14140, Bundesarchiv, Berlin.

30. Ludwig von Mises, *Liberalism: The Classical Tradition*, trans. Bettina Bien Greaves (Indianapolis, 2005), 28, 30.

31. Robert Hoffmann, "Zwischen Wohnreform und Agrarromantik. Siedlungswesen und Siedlungsideologie in Österreich von der Jahrhundertwende bis zur Weltwirtschaftskrise," in *Die Zukunft liegt in der Vergangenheit: Studien zum Siedlungswesen der Zwischenkriegszeit*, ed. Margit Altfahrt et al. (Vienna, 1983), 21–22, 36; Robert Hoffmann, *Nimm Hack' und Spaten: Siedlung und Siedlerbewegung in Oesterreich, 1918-1938* (Vienna, 1987), 57.

32. Albert Gessmann, *Wie werden wir uns ernähren?* (Vienna, 1932), 24; Österreichisches Kuratorium für Wirtschaftlichkeit, *Der Aufbau des österreichischen Siedlungswerkes* (Vienna, 1933), 32–33.

33. Margit Altfahrt, "Anspruch und Wirklichkeit. Realität einer Arbeitslosensiedlung am Beispiel Leopoldau," in *Die Zukunft liegt in der Vergangenheit*, 77–100.

34. "Frauenarbeit in Siedlungsdörfern," *Arbeiterinnen Zeitung*, June 1, 1933, 8.

35. Klara Friedländer, "Die neue Frauenfrage," *Das Wort der Frau*, December 18, 1932, 3.

36. Emil Magschiß, "Was ist Innenkolonisation?" *Mein Stückchen Land, Wochenbeilage der Illustrierten Kronen-Zeitung für Gartenbau, Kleintierzucht und Tierliebhaberei*, December 2, 1932, 5.

37. Wilhelm Bolek, "Das End der Siedlernot," *Der Siedler* 18, no. 4 (April 1938): 3; "An unsere Mitglieder!" *Der Siedler* 18, no. 4 (April 1938): 2.

38. Entwicklung der Wohnbautätigkeit, March 1, 1939, Carton 151, Reichskommissar für die Wiedervereinigung Österreichs mit dem Deutschen Reich, AdR, OestA.

39. Merkblatt für die Anztagstellung auf Zulassung und Förderung von Wohn und Siedlungsanlagen, Carton 150, Reichskommissar für die Wiedervereinigung Österreichs mit dem Deutschen Reich, AdR, OestA.

40. Die Arbeitsgebiete der Heimstätten in der Ostmark; Auszug aus der Denkschrift über Judenumsiedlung und Wohnungsbedarf in Wien, October 11, 1939, Carton 152, Reichskommissar für die Wiedervereinigung Österreichs mit dem Deutschen Reich, AdR, OestA.

41. Ministerialdirektor Dr. Knoll, Die Bedeutung der Heimstätte für den Bestand und für die Zukunft des deutschen Volkes, November 1938, Carton 152, Reichskommissar für die Wiedervereinigung Österreichs mit dem Deutschen Reich, AdR, OestA.

42. Margarete Schütte-Lihotzky, *Warum ich Architektin wurde* (Salzburg, 2004), 98.

Chapter 12

1. "Stirred up by Henry Ford's Shotgun Gardens," *Literary Digest*, September 12, 1931, 10.
2. Paul K. Conkin, *Tomorrow a New World: The New Deal Community Program* (Ithaca, NY, 1959), 29.
3. Glenn F. Jenkins, "Ford's New Design for Economic Life: A View of His 'Empire' Near Dearborn, Where He Is Uniting Farm and Industry," *New York Times*, October 22, 1933, 22.
4. Cited in Conklin, *Tomorrow a New World*, 28.
5. Henry I. Harriman, "Factory and Farm in Double Harness," *New York Times*, October 15, 1933, 6.
6. For a profile of an ideal Ford farmer-factory worker, see John Bird, "One Foot on the Land," *Saturday Evening Post*, March 18, 1944, 12, cited in Howard P. Segal, *Recasting the Machine Age: Henry Ford's Village Industries* (Amherst, 2005), 15–16.
7. Robert Cohen, *Dear Mrs. Roosevelt: Letters from Children of the Great Depression* (Chapel Hill, NC, 2002), 5.
8. Letter to Eleanor Roosevelt from Miss Helen Bell, February 19, 1934, Box 3, RG 96, Records of the Farmers Home Administration, Correspondence with the General Public to Which Individual Replies Were Made, 1933-35, Box 3, National Archives and Records Administration, College Park, MD (henceforth NARA).
9. "Temporary Idleness for 75,000 Ford Men," *New York Times*, July 30, 1931, 2; Alex Baskin, "The Ford Hunger March," *Labor History* 13 (June 1972): 331–60.
10. Henry Ford and Samuel Crowther, *Today and Tomorrow* (Garden City, NY, 1926), 34. On Ford's globalization and his "open-source" policy toward technology, see especially Stefan Link, *Forging Global Fordism: Nazi Germany, Soviet Russia, and the Contest over the Industrial Order* (Princeton, NJ, 2020).
11. Kiran Patel, *The New Deal: A Global History* (Princeton, NJ, 2016), 13.
12. Ford and Crowther, *Moving Forward*, 242, 245
13. Ford and Crowther, *Moving Forward*, 254.
14. Georgios Paris Loizides, "'Making Men' at Ford: Ethnicity, Race, and Americanization During the Progressive Period," *Michigan Sociological Review* 21 (Fall

2007): 116, quotation 127; Greg Grandin, *Fordlandia: The Rise and Fall of Henry Ford's Forgotten Jungle City* (New York, 2010), 39.

15. Ford and Crowther, *Today and Tomorrow*, chap. 3.
16. Link, *Forging Global Fordism*.
17. Grandin, *Fordlandia*.
18. Link, *Forging Global Fordism*, chap. 1.
19. Cited in Segal, *Recasting the Machine Age*, 3.
20. Henry Ford, "Farming: The Food Raising Industry," in *Ford Ideals: Being a Selection from 'Mr. Ford's Page' in the Dearborn Independent* (Dearborn, MI, 1922), 87.
21. Samuel Crowther, *America Self-Contained* (Garden City, NY, 1933), 1, 5, 14, 338.
22. On the decentralists, see especially Steven Conn, *Americans Against the City: Anti-Urbanism in the Twentieth Century* (Oxford, 2014), 59–61.
23. Paul Johnston, "The Back-to-the-Land Movement," in *A Place on Earth: A Critical Appraisal of Subsistence Homesteads*, ed. Russell Lord and Paul Johnston (Washington, DC, 1942), 14.
24. Thomas Jefferson, *Notes on the State of Virginia* (Paris, 1781).
25. John Crowe Ransom, "Reconstructed but Unregenerate," in *I'll Take My Stand: The South and the Agrarian Tradition*, ed. Twelve Southerners (New York, 1930), 6, 14.
26. Twelve Southerners, eds., *I'll Take My Stand* (New York, 1930); Harriman, "Factory and Farm"; Ralph Borsodi, *Flight from the City: An Experiment in Creative Living on the Land* (New York, 1933).
27. Ralph Borsodi, "A Civilization of Factories, or a Civilization of Homes?" *New Republic*, July 31, 1929, 281–83. On Borsodi, see especially Conn, *Americans Against the City*, 76–85.
28. Borsodi, *Flight from the City*, 5, 20, 112.
29. *Ford News*, April 1937, inside front cover.
30. "Ford Asserts New Deal Allied to Financiers," *Los Angeles Times*, November 2, 1936, 6.
31. Rexford Tugwell, "Is Ford Economic Messiah?" *Maclean's* magazine (September 15, 1926), 37. On the anti-urban aspects of the New Deal, see Conn, *Americans Against the City*, 94–113.
32. Franklin Delano Roosevelt, "Address Before the American Country Live Conference on the Better Distribution of Population Away from Cities," August 19, 1931, in *The Public Papers and Addresses of FDR*, vol. 1 (New York, 1938–50), 1, 511.
33. Franklin Delano Roosevelt, "The Annual Message to the Legislature," January 6, 1932, in *The Public Papers and Addresses of FDR*, vol. 1 (New York, 1938–50), 116–17.
34. Department of the Interior, Memorandum for the Press, Thursday October 12, 1933.
35. Russell Lord, "Back to the Farm?" *Forum and Century* LXXXIX, no. 2 (February 1933): 97.
36. Quoted in Johnston, "The Back-to-the-Land Movement," 34.

37. Phares Horstman to Mrs. Roosevelt, May 10, 1934, Box 16, RG 96, Correspondence with the General Public to Which Individual Replies Were Made, 1933-35, NARA.

38. Department of Subsistence Homesteads. Memorandum for the Press, September 16, 1934; Russell Lord and Paul Johnston, eds., *A Place on Earth: A Critical Appraisal of Subsistence Homesteads* (Washington, DC, 1942), 14, 37.

39. Edgar J. Adams to Department of Subsistence Homesteads, February 13, 1934, Box 1, RG 96, Correspondence with the General Public to Which Individual Replies Were Made, 1933-35, NARA.

40. Edith Atkinson to Department of Subsistence Homesteads, February 4, 1935, Box 1, RG 96, Correspondence with the General Public to Which Individual Replies Were Made, 1933-35, NARA.

41. W. F. Berry to Franklin D. Roosevelt, Received May 20, 1934, Box 3, RG 96, Correspondence with the General Public to Which Individual Replies Were Made, 1933-35, NARA.

42. Blanche Hooey, Austin, Texas, to Mrs. Roosevelt, February 3, 1934, Box 16, RG 96, Correspondence with the General Public to Which Individual Replies Were Made, 1933-35, NARA.

43. Anonymous to Mrs. Franklin D. Roosevelt, Arkansas City, May 6, 1935. Box 1, RG 96, Correspondence with the General Public to Which Individual Replies Were Made, 1933-35, NARA.

44. Conkin, *Tomorrow a New World*, 202.

45. Douglas A. Irwin, *Peddling Protectionism: Smoot-Hawley and the Great Depression* (Princeton, NJ, 2011), 219.

46. Economic historians have increasingly come to a consensus that neither Smoot-Hawley nor the Reciprocal Trade Agreements Act had a large effect on the Great Depression, however. See Douglas A. Irwin, "From Smoot-Hawley to Reciprocal Trade Agreements: Changing the Course of U.S. Trade Policy in the 1930s," in *The Defining Moment: The Great Depression and the American Economy in the Twentieth Century*, ed. Michael D. Bordo et al. (Chicago, 1998), 325–52.

47. On transnational connections, see especially Diane Ghirardo, *Building New Communities: New Deal America and Fascist Italy* (Princeton, NJ, 1989).

48. A Believer in Subsistence Farms to F.D.R., Chicago, September 22, 1934, Box 1, RG 96, Correspondence with the General Public to Which Individual Replies Were Made, 1933-35, NARA.

49. Department of Subsistence Homesteads, Memorandum for the Press, September 16, 1934, 3.

50. Myrtle Mae Borsodi, "The New Woman Goes Home," *Scribner's Magazine*, February 1937, 52–55.

51. Dorothy Van Doren, "Breadwinner or Breadmaker?" *Scribner's Magazine*, May 1937, 33–34.

52. Catherine Bauer, "The Swiss Family Borsodi," *The Nation*, October 25, 1933, 489–90.

53. On the fate of the greenbelt towns, see especially Conn, *Americans Against the City,* 99–108.

54. Michael Shally-Jensen, "New Deal, New Life: Culture and History of a Jewish Cooperative Colony in New Jersey, 1933-39" (PhD diss., Princeton University, 1992), 114–15.

55. "Jewish Community Farm to Be Run on New Basis," *New York Times,* January 7, 1934, 12.

56. Hickman Powell, "New Deal Town, Now 30 Months Abuilding, Awaits 35 Families," *New York Herald Tribune,* May 7, 1936, 1.

57. Shally-Jensen, "New Deal, New Life," 173–78.

58. John Hayes of New Brunswick, New Jersey, to Charles Pynchon, Department of Interior, September 24, 1934, Box 15, Department of the Interior, Division of Subsistence Homesteads, Information on Subsistence Homesteads, NARA.

59. Shally-Jensen, "New Deal, New Life," 278–79.

60. "Workers Families Begin Rural Life," *New York Times,* July 11, 1936, 17.

61. Leo Libove, interview by Peter Berlinrut, n.d., Box 16, Folder 7, Roosevelt, New Jersey, Collection, Rutgers University, cited in Sora H. Friedman, "No Place Like Home: The Founding and Transformation of the New Deal Town of Jersey Homesteads, New Jersey" (PhD diss., George Mason University, 2005), 142.

62. Shally-Jensen, "New Deal, New Life," 352–53.

63. Shally-Jensen, "New Deal, New Life," 367.

64. Shally-Jensen, "New Deal, New Life," 446.

65. Shally-Jensen, "New Deal, New Life," 430.

66. Jacob H. Dorn, "Subsistence Homesteading in Dayton, Ohio, 1933-35," *Ohio History Journal* 78, no. 2 (1969): 75–93, quotation 86.

67. On the Dayton colony, see William H. Issel, "Ralph Borsodi and the Agrarian Response to Modern America," *Agricultural History* 41, no. 2 (April 1967): 155–66; see also Conn, *Americans Against the City,* 76–85.

68. Borsodi, *Flight from the City,* xiii, xv.

Chapter 13

1. "If Gandhi Comes Here," *Lancashire Daily Post,* July 1, 1931, 1. I am grateful to Seth Koven for pointing me to this incident.

2. "Discussions with Mr. Gandhi," *Lancashire Daily Post,* September 26, 1931, 6.

3. Mahatma Gandhi, "Interview to Unemployed Workers' Deputation," in *The Collected Works of Mahatma Gandhi,* 98 vols. [e-book] (New Delhi, 1999), vol. 53, 419–20.

4. "Speech in Lancashire," September 26/27, 1931, Gandhi, *Collected Works,* vol. 53, 415.

5. Mahatma Gandhi, *The Wheel of Fortune* (Madras, 1922), 8.

6. "Speech on Swadeshi," Bombay, July 31, 1921, in Gandhi, *Collected Works,* vol. 24, 35; Asha Sharma, *An American in Gandhi's India: The Biography of Satyanand Stokes* (Bloomington, IN, 2008), 132.

7. Gandhi, *Wheel of Fortune*, 8, 12; Lisa Trivedi, *Clothing Gandhi's Nation: Homespun in Modern India* (Bloomington, IN, 2007), quotation 1.

8. Mahatma Gandhi, "What Comprises Foreign Goods?" in Gandhi, *Collected Works*, vol. 43, 1–2.

9. Trivedi, *Clothing Gandhi's Nation*, 9.

10. Mahatma Gandhi, "An Appeal to the Nation," *Young India*, July 17, 1924, 236.

11. Mahatma Gandhi, "Question of Safeguards," *Young India*, April 16, 1931, 79.

12. Anna Varki, *One Woman's India: From the Gandhian Era to the Cyber Age* (Chennai, 2018), chap. 1.

13. Indian National Congress, *Report of the Civil Disobedience Enquiry Committee Appointed by the All-India Congress Committee, 1922* (Allahabad, 1922), 51.

14. Trivedi, *Clothing Gandhi's Nation*, 70–71.

15. M. K. Gandhi, "Myself, My Spinning-Wheel, and Women," *Daily Herald* (London), September 28, 1931, 8.

16. M. K. Gandhi, "A Village Experiment," *Young India*, September 10, 1925, 312.

17. M. K. Gandhi, "Too Costly," *Young India*, July 30, 1925, 262.

18. M. K. Gandhi, "Luxury and Laziness," *Young India*, June 5, 1924, 190–91.

19. "Presidential Address at Punjab Provincial Conference," April 11, 1928, in Jawaharlal Nehru Memorial Fund et al., *Selected Works of Jawaharlal Nehru*, ed. S. Gopal (New Delhi, 1972–1982), vol. 3, 244.

20. Jawaharlal Nehru, *The Discovery of India* (Oxford, 2004), 407–8.

21. Mahatma Gandhi, "My Conception of Patriotism," *Young India*, April 4, 1929, 107.

22. Eamon de Valera, *India and Ireland* (New York, 1920), 18.

23. Mike Cronin, "Golden Dreams, Harsh Realities: Economics and Informal Empire in the Irish Free State," in *Ireland: The Politics of Independence, 1922-1949*, ed. Mike Cronin and John M. Regan (London, 2000), 148–51.

24. Eamon de Valera, "A Constructive Policy," August 22, 1927, *Speeches and Statements by Eamon de Valera, 1917-73*, ed. Maurice Moynihan (New York, 1980), 153.

25. Eamon de Valera, "Economic Policy," July 12 and 13, 1928, in *Speeches and Statements by Eamon de Valera, 1917-73*, ed. Maurice Moynihan (New York, 1980), 154–55.

26. Keith Hutchinson, "Eire's Search for Self-Sufficiency," *The Nation*, January 31, 1942, 145.

27. Advertisement, *Ballymena Observer*, November 25, 1938, 5. Emphasis in original.

28. Letter from Mrs. Bridget Loftus, April 25, 1938, s 9264B, National Archives of Ireland, Dublin.

29. "Exchange Is Robbery" [handbill in the form of a dialogue advocating economic self-sufficiency], Grace Gifford Plunkett (1888–1955), artist, n.d. [ca. 1932-35?, National Library of Ireland.

30. Cronin, "Golden Dreams, Harsh Realities," 144–63; Gerard McCann, "Protectionism and the 'Economic War' in Interwar Ireland," *Journal of European Economic History* 3 (2014): 39–68.

31. Mary E. Daly, *Industrial Development and Irish National Identity, 1922-1939* (Syracuse, NY, 1992), 60–66.

32. Hutchinson, "Eire's Search for Self-Sufficiency," 145.

33. On the evolution of British ideas about free trade, see Frank Trentmann, *Free Trade Nation: Commerce, Consumption, and Civil Society in Modern Britain* (Oxford, 2008).

34. Jim Tomlinson, *Dundee and the Empire: 'Juteopolis,' 1850-1939* (Edinburgh, 2014), chap. 7.

35. Walter Elliot, "The Work of the Empire Marketing Board," *Journal of the Royal Society of Arts* 79, no. 4101 (June 26, 1931): 736–74.

36. "Empire Shopping Week," *Birmingham Daily Gazette*, April 29, 1924, 7.

37. "Empire Shopping Week," *Somerset and West of England Advertiser*, May 25, 1923, 4.

38. Stefan Goebel, "Cities," in *Cambridge History of the First World War*, vol II, ed. Jay Winter (Cambridge, UK, 2013), 365; Suchetana Chattopadhyay, "War, Migration and Alienation in Colonial Calcutta: The Remaking of Muzaffar Ahmad," *History Workshop Journal* 64 (2007): 214–16.

39. On anti-colonial protests in response to food shortages and inflation at the end of the war in the British Empire, see Jamie Martin, "Strained Interdependence: Inflation, Uprisings, and the Crisis of the British Empire after the First World War" (unpublished manuscript).

40. David Thackeray, *Forging a British World of Trade: Culture, Ethnicity, and Market in the Empire Commonwealth, 1880-1975* (Oxford, 2019), 85; Felicity Barnes and David M. Higgins, "Brand Image, Cultural Association and Marketing: 'New Zealand' Butter and Lamb Exports to Britain, c. 1920–1938," *Business History* 62, no. 1 (Winter 2020): 70–97; Felicity Barnes, "Lancashire's 'War' with Australia: Rethinking Anglo-Australian Trade and the Cultural Economy of Empire, 1934–36," *Journal of Imperial and Commonwealth History* 46, no. 4 (Autumn 2018): 707–30; Erika Rappaport, *A Thirst for Empire: How Tea Shaped the Modern World* (Princeton, NJ, 2019), chap. 7.

41. D. R. Gadgil, *Imperial Preference for India: The Ottawa Agreement Examined* (Poona City, 1932), 4.

42. Empire Marketing Board, *May 1930 to May 1931* (London, 1931).

43. Empire Marketing Board, *May 1931 to May 1932* (London, 1932).

44. Thackeray, *Forging a British World of Trade*, 85–86.

45. L. S. Amery, *A Plan of Action: Embodying a Series of Reports Issued by the Research Committee of the Empire Economic Union and Other Papers* (London, 1932).

Chapter 14

1. "Seeks New Shoe Markets by Plane," *New York Times*, December 11, 1931, 8; "Uses Plane to Sell Shoes," *New York Times*, December 27, 1931, 45. For a comprehensive history of the Bat'a firm in relationship to globalization and welfare capitalism,

see Zachary Austin Doleshal, *In the Kingdom of Shoes: Baťa, Zlín, Globalization, 1894-1945* (Toronto, 2022). I would like to thank Doleshal, Milan Balaban, and Julia Mead for assistance with research for this chapter.

2. Tomáš Baťa, *O svém letu do Indie* (Zlín, 1932), 3–4.

3. Zdeněk Pokluda, Jan Herman, and Milan Balaban, eds. *Baťa na všech kontinentech* (Zlín, 2020), 130–32.

4. Pokluda, Herman, and Balaban, *Baťa na všech kontinentech*, 14, 41, 28, 137; Doleshal, *In the Kingdom of Shoes*, 162–63.

5. Jan Baros, *The First Decade of Baťangar* (Baťangar, 1945), 6.

6. Eugen Erdely, *Baťa: Ein Schuster Erobert die Welt* (Leipzig, 1932), 172.

7. Doleshal, *In the Kingdom of Shoes*, chap. 5.

8. Tomáš J. Baťa, *Baťa: Shoemaker to the World* (Toronto, 1990), 4; Doleshal, *In the Kingdom of Shoes*, 34–36.

9. Baťa Information Center, accessed June 6, 2021, http://en.tomasBaťa.org/biography/; Lukas Perutka, Milan Balaban, and Jan Herman, "The Presence of the Baťa Shoe Company in Central America and the Caribbean in the Interwar Period (1920-1930)," *America Latina en la Historia Economica* 25, no. 2 (May–August 2018): 42–76; Doleshal, *In the Kingdom of Shoes*, 53.

10. Doleshal, *In the Kingdom of Shoes*, 54.

11. J. F. Smetanka, "American Commerce with the Czechoslovak Nation," in Vojta Beneš and J. F. Smetanka, *Economic Strength of the Czechoslovak Lands* (Chicago, 1919), 25, 27–28.

12. Anthony Cekota, "Tomáš Baťa—Pioneer of Self-Government in Industry," in Miloslav Rechigl Jr., ed., *The Czechoslovak Contribution to World Culture* (London, 1964), 342–49.

13. Norman Hapgood, "Europe's Henry Ford—Shoemaker Baťa," *New York Times*, March 8, 1931, section *New York Times Magazine*, 83.

14. Doleshal, *In the Kingdom of Shoes*, 80–82, 100–104, 143–49.

15. Baťa Information Center, accessed June 6, 2021, http://en.tomasBaťa.org/biography/.

16. Perutka, Balaban, and Herman, "Presence of the Baťa Shoe Company in Central America," 49–50.

17. "Bata, Shoe Magnate, Dies in Plane Crash," *New York Times*, July 13, 1932, 8.

18. Doleshal, *In the Kingdom of Shoes*, 133.

19. Norman Hapgood, "Europe's Henry Ford—Shoemaker Baťa."

20. Doleshal, *In the Kingdom of Shoes*, 162.

21. Cited by Doleshal, *In the Kingdom of Shoes*, 127.

22. Doleshal, *In the Kingdom of Shoes*, 126.

23. Aleš Skřivan, "Škodovy závody a výstavba cukrovarů v Číně před druhou světovou válkou," *Listy cukrovarnické a řepařské* 127, no. 11 (2011): 361–65; Aleš Skřivan, "Arms Production in Interwar Czechoslovakia," *Journal of Slavic Military Studies* 23 (2010): 630–40; Jonathan Grant, *Between Depression and Disarmament: The International Armaments Business, 1919-39* (Cambridge, UK, 2018).

24. Zásady pro repatriaci československých příslušníků prováděnou ministerstva sociální péče, 15 července 1920, Předsednictva Ministerské Rady, Carton 2825, Národní Archiv, Prague. On internal colonization, see also Daniel Miller, "Colonizing the Hungarian and German Border Areas During the Czechoslovak Land Reform, 1918-1938," *Austrian History Yearbook* 34 (2003): 303–17.

25. Andrea Orzoff, *Battle for the Castle: The Myth of Czechoslovakia in Interwar Europe* (Oxford, 2009). On Czech economic nationalism in the domestic context, see Catherine Albrecht, "Economic Nationalism in the Sudetenland, 1918-1938," in *Czechoslovakia in a Nationalist and Fascist Europe, 1914-1950*, ed. Mark Cornwall and R. J. W. Evans, Proceedings of the British Academy (New York, 2007), 89–108. On Czechoslovak foreign trade, see Alice Teichova, *An Economic Background to Munich: International Business and Czechoslovakia, 1918-1938* (Cambridge, UK, 1974).

26. This is clear from the files in the Archiv MZV ČR, IV. Sekce Národohospodáská, Karton 1080, 1081, 1082.

27. "Ustavení Orientálního Ústavu," *Československá republika*, Praha, Státní tiskárna v Praze, 1.3.1928, 249(52) (1928), 1.

28. "Budujeme Batangar. Zvláštní zpráva našeho indického dopisovatele," *Sdělení zaměstnanců firmy Baťa* 17, no. 45 (November 16, 1934): 4.

29. Mira Wilkins and Frank Ernest Hill, *American Business Abroad: Ford on Six Continents* (Cambridge, UK, 2011), 203.

30. On Ford in the Amazon, see Greg Grandin, *Fordlandia: The Rise and Fall of Ford's Jungle City* (New York, 2010).

31. Wilkins and Hill, *American Business Abroad*, 153.

32. Wilkins and Hill, *American Business Abroad*, 194.

33. Cited in Wilkins and Hill, *American Business Abroad*, 226.

34. Stefan Link, *Forging Global Fordism: Nazi Germany, Soviet Russia, and the Contest over the Industrial Order* (Princeton, NJ, 2020), 10–11, 127.

35. Cited in Wilkins and Hill, *American Business Abroad*, 230.

36. Wilkins and Hill, *American Business Abroad*, 251.

37. Mira Wilkins, *The Maturing of Multinational Enterprise: American Business Abroad from 1914-1970* (Cambridge, MA, 1974), 172, 190.

38. Wilkins and Hill, *American Business Abroad*, 283–84.

39. Wilkins, *Maturing of Multinational Enterprise*, 185.

40. F. Lauriston Bullard, "Shoe Industry Fears Czech Inroads," *New York Times*, November 14, 1937, section Review, 74.

41. "Kampf gegen das soziale Dumping," *Fränkische Tagespost*, February 14, 1929, Archiv MZV, IV. Sekce Národohospodářská, Karton 1080.

42. Sigurd Paulsen, "Ein Sonderfall, 'Deutsche' Bata-Schuhe," in *Der Entscheidende Augenblick: Deutsche Ware–oder Auslandsware*, ed. Sigurd Paulsen and Mathilde Freiin von Beigeleben, Schriftenreihe der Volkswirtschaftlichen Aufklärungsdienstes, Heft 3, 1931; Agitace proti Bátově proddejš v Drážďanech, 2 dubna 1931, Archiv MZV ČR, IV. Sekce Národohospodáská, Karton 1081.

43. Otevření prodejny fmy T.a A. Baťa v Poznani, March 31, 1930, Archiv MZV, IV. Sekce Národohospodářská, Karton 1080.

44. Bata akc. spol. boykot v Damašku, 9 července 1932, Archiv MZV, IV. Sekce Národohospodářská, Karton 1081; Memo from Baťa manager in Damascus to Czechoslovak consul in Beirut, November 3, 1933, Archiv MZV, IV. Sekce Národohospodářská, Karton 1082.

45. Fa. T.a A. Báta ve Zlíně, otevření prodejen v palestině, Jerusalem, November 27, 1930, Archiv MZV, IV. Sekce Národohospodářská, Karton 1081.

46. Louis Stark, "Policy Shift Puts Immigration Ban on Baťa Shoe Men," *New York Times*, December 29, 1939, 1.

47. Hermione Lee, *Tom Stoppard: A Life* (New York, 2021), 8–12, 17, 23.

48. See, for example, Statisická data o počtu Evropanů v Indii a o vyrobě obuvi v Indii, Bombay, 18 června 1930, Archiv MZV, IV. Sekce Národohospodářská, Karton 1080.

49. Tomáš Baťa, "Dvě rasy," *Sdělení zaměstnanců firmy Baťa*, May 30, 1925, 1–2.

50. "Baťa a Gandhi," *Lidové noviny*, Brno, January 4, 1932, 3.

51. Baros, *First Decade of Bat'angar*, 24.

52. Image from *Architektur aus de Schuhbox: Bat'as Internationale Fabrikstädte* (Leipzig, 1976), 79.

53. Memo from Consul Dr. J. Lusk in Calcutta to Baťa, "jen k vlastním rukám před. Čipery neb Meisla," 30 srpna 1933, Archiv MZV ČR, IV. Sekce Národohospodáská, Karton 1082.

54. Letter to the Editor of the *Daily Liberty* from N. K. Chopra, June 21, 1933, Calcutta, Archiv MZV ČR, IV. Sekce Národohospodáská, Karton 1082.

55. "About 2,500 Workers on Strike," *Times of India*, January 6, 1939; Police Firing at Bat'anagar," *Times of India*, January 10, 1939; "Demand of Baťa Shoe Workers: Strike Continues," *Times of India*, January 7, 1939.

56. Nepokoje dělnictva v Baťově továrně v Batangaru, January 8, 1939, Archiv MZV ČR, IV. Sekce Národohospodářská, Karton 1082; Milan Balaban, Jan Herman, and Dalibor Savič, "The Early Decades of the Baťa Shoe Company in India," *Indian Economic and Social History Review* 58, no. 3 (2021): 16–22.

Chapter 15

1. "I discorsi del Duce. Per l'inaugurazione di Littoria, December 18, 1932," L'Agro Pontino. Anno XVIII (Rome, 1939), 7.

2. "L'Inaugurazione di Pontinia. Il Discorso del Duce," L'Agro Pontino al 18 dicembre Anno XIV (Rome, 1935), iii.

3. Antonio Pennacchi, *Fascio e martello: Viaggio per le città del duce* (Rome, 2010), 287–97.

4. Arrigo Serpieri, "L'autarchia economica della Nazione." Estratto dalla Rivista "Lo Stato," April 1938, 4–5, 10. Fondo Serpieri, Biblioteca Agraria Universita di Firenze.

5. On the role of science in the Fascist campaign for autarky, see especially Tiago Saraiva, *Fascist Pigs: Technoscientific Organisms and the History of Fascism* (Cambridge, MA, 2016).

6. Elisabetta Randi, *La cucina autarchia: Nozioni theoriche e pratiche di autarchia alimentare* (Florence, 1942), 11, 17.

7. Adelmo Cicogna, *Per l'autarchia: Manuale del consumatore Italiano* (Rome, 1939), 3.

8. Randi, *La cucina autarchia*, 54, 325; Cicogna, *Per L'autarchia*, 3, 10–11.

9. Carol Helstosky, "Fascist Food Politics: Mussolini's Policy of Alimentary Sovereignty," *Journal of Modern Italian Studies* 9, no. 1 (2004): 6.

10. Ermanno Amicucci, "L'Autarchia e le nuove materie prime," *Atti del 1° Convegno tecnico Italo-Germanico dell'autarchia* (Torino, 1942), 9, 11–13. On autarchic fabrics, see Eugenia Paulicelli, *Fashion Under Fascism: Beyond the Black Shirt* (London, 2004); Jeffrey T. Schnapp, "The Fabric of Modern Times," *Critical Inquiry* 24, no. 1 (Autumn, 1997), 191–245.

11. Carl T. Schmidt, *The Plough and the Sword: Labor, Land and Property in Fascist Italy* (New York, 1938), 34–41.

12. Mia Fuller, "Tradition as a Means to the End of Tradition: Farmers' Houses in Italy's Fascist-Era New Towns," in *The End of Tradition?*, ed. Nezar Alsayyad (New York, 2004), 171–80.

13. Vittorno Vezzani, *La casa rurale: Discorso pronunciato alla camera dei deputi 9 Marzo 1937* (Rome, 1937), 9.

14. Arrigo Serpieri, *La bonifica integrale* (Padova, 1937), 14.

15. Cited in Federico Caprotti, *Mussolini's Cities: Internal Colonialism in Italy, 1930-1939* (Youngstown, NY, 2007), 71.

16. Anna Maria Rath, "Italian Migration Movements, 1876-1926" in *International Migrations. Volume II: Interpretations*, ed. Walther F. Willcox (New York, 1931), 463.

17. Mark Choate, *Emigrant Nation: The Making of Italy Abroad* (Cambridge, MA, 2008); Donna R. Gabaccia, *Italy's Many Diasporas* (Seattle, 2000); Simone Cinotto, *Making Italian America: Consumer Culture and the Production of Ethnic Identities* (New York, 2014).

18. Philip Cannistraro and Gianfausto Rosoli, "Fascist Emigration Policy in the 1920s: An Interpretive Framework," *International Migration Review* 13, no. 4 (1979): 673–92; Philip V. Cannistraro, "Fascism and Italian-Americans in Detroit, 1933-1935," *International Migration Review* 9 no. 1 (1975): 29–40.

19. Gabbaccia, *Italy's Many Diasporas*, 130–131; US Department of Commerce, Bureau of the Census, *A Statistical Abstract Supplement. Historical Statistics of the U.S. Colonial Times to 1957* (Washington, DC, 1960), 56–57; Carl Ipsen, *Dictating Demography: The Problem of Population in Fascist Italy* (Cambridge, UK, 2009), 55–56.

20. Cited in Roberta Pergher, *Mussolini's Nation-Empire: Sovereignty and Settlement in Italy's Borderlands, 1922-1943* (Cambridge, UK, 2017), 83. Pergher also specifies

important differences between the Pontine projects and those in Libya and the Alto Adige; namely, the focus on asserting Italian sovereignty in those regions. On links between the internal and external colonization, see also Mia Fuller, *Moderns Abroad: Architecture, Cities, and Italian Imperialism* (New York, 2007); Ipsen, *Dictating Demography*, 120–35.

21. Arrigo Serpieri, *Il valore delle nostre colonie* (Capodistria, 1926), 19.

22. Ipsen, *Dictating Demography*, 51–65, Mussolini quotation 61.

23. Cited in Gabaccia, *Italy's Many Diasporas*, 144.

24. Pamela Ballinger, "Colonial Twilight: Italian Settlers and the Long Decolonization of Italy," *Journal of Contemporary History* 51, no. 4 (2016): 813–38.

25. Caprotti, *Mussolini's Cities*, 173–74; Ipsen, *Dictating Demography*, 112, 143.

26. Araldo di Crollalanza, "L'epilogo vittorioso della bonifica pontina," November 1941, Busta 1, Ministero dell'agricoltura e delle foreste, Direzione Generale Bonifica e Colonizazzione, Opere di bonifica in Lazio, Maremma toscana, Umbria, 1900-1962, Archivio Centrale dello State, Rome (henceforth ACS).

27. Frank Snowden, *The Conquest of Malaria: Italy, 1900-1962* (New Haven, CT, 2006), 144–45; Ipsen, *Dictating Demography*, 143; Diane Ghirardo, *Building New Communities: New Deal America and Fascist Italy* (Princeton, NJ, 1989), 46–47; Perry Willson, *Peasant Women and Politics in Fascist Italy: The Massaie Rurali* (London, 2002), 15.

28. Helstosky, "Fascist Food Politics," 1–26; Saraiva, *Fascist Pigs*, 22–23.

29. Snowden, *Conquest of Malaria*, 156–58.

30. Relazione sull'attività della Delegazione di Littoria in Agro Pontino, nell'Anno 1939, Busta 35G, Commissariato Generale per Le Migrazioni e la colonizzazione Interna, ACS.

31. Bonifica di Pimpisu Cagliari (Sardinia). Relazione Sanitaria, December 17, 1930; Vincenzo Nardi, La colonizzazione in provincia di Cagliari, Terralba–Villagio Mussolini, Commissariato Generale per Le Migrazioni e la colonizzazione Interna, Busta 48G, ACS.

32. ACS, Opera Nazionale Combattenti Agro Pontino, Busta 46, Malcontento fra i nuovi coloni rimpatriati dall'Estero, October 26, 1940; Ghirardo, *Building New Communities*, 53–56.

33. All from Snowden, *Conquest of Malaria*, chap. 7 (including quotations).

Chapter 16

1. George Peel, "The World Economic Conference: The Result," *Contemporary Review* (July 1, 1933): 129.

2. Tom Gjelten, "For G-20 Leaders, 1933 Summit Holds Lessons," NPR, March 31, 2009, https://www.npr.org/templates/story/story.php?storyId=102562499.

3. Gjelten, "For G-20 Leaders."

4. John Maynard Keynes, "The World Economic Conference 1933," *New Statesman and Nation* (December 24, 1932): 825–26.

5. Oswald Garrison Villard, "The World Conference at Work," *The Nation,* July 5, 1933.
6. Harold J. Laski, "Why Conferences Fail," *The Nation,* July 19, 1933, 65.
7. Leon Trotsky, "Nationalism and Economic Life," *Foreign Affairs* (April 1934): 395–97.
8. William Martin Hill, *The Economic and Financial Organization of the League of Nations* (Washington, DC, 1946), 70–71.
9. The memory of these failures dominated scholarship on the League of Nations until very recently, when Susan Pedersen and others began to reevaluate its legacies, particularly the accomplishments of the league's technical agencies. Susan Pedersen, "Back to the League of Nations," *American Historical Review* 112, no. 4 (October 2007): 1091–117.
10. Robert Dell, "Can the League Be Saved?" *The Nation,* February 21, 1934; Almeric Hugh Paget, "Good-by to the League," *Saturday Evening Post,* August 15, 1936, 1.
11. Dorothy Thompson, "The Gray Squirrel," *Saturday Evening Post,* February 20, 1932.
12. John O'Brien, "F.L. McDougall and the Origins of the FAO," *Australian Journal of Politics and History* 46, no. 2 (June 2000): 166–74, quotation 167.
13. Gottfried von Haberler, *The Theory of International Trade: With Its Applications to Commercial Policy* (London, 1937), viii.
14. Quinn Slobodian, "A World of Walls," in *Globalists: The End of Empire and the Birth of Neoliberalism* (Cambridge, MA, 2018), 27–54.
15. F. L. McDougall, "Annex: Economic Appeasement," *Economic Committee: Remarks on the Present Phase of Economic Relations,* September 1937, 28, C-352-M-242-1937-II-B, Archive of the League of Nations.
16. John G. Winant, *International Labor Organization: Report of the Director, 1939* (Geneva, 1939), 73.
17. Patricia Clavin, *Securing the World Economy: The Reinvention of the League of Nations, 1920-1946* (Oxford, 2013), 174; Victoria de Grazia, "A Decent Standard of Living: How Europeans Were Measured by the American Way of Life," in *Irresistible Empire: America's Advance through Twentieth-Century Europe* (Cambridge, MA, 2006), 75–129.
18. International Labor Organization, *Conference of Experts on International, Technical and Financial Co-Operation with Regard to Migration for Settlement,* Geneva, February–March 1938, R4440-10A-26525-26525-Jacket 1, League of Nations, United Nations Archive, Geneva.
19. Malgorzata Mazurek, *Economics of Hereness: The Polish Origins of Global Developmentalism 1918-1968* (forthcoming), chap. 4; Tara Zahra, *The Great Departure: Mass Migration from Eastern Europe and the Making of the Free World* (New York, 2016), chap. 4.
20. Clavin, *Securing the World Economy,* chap. 5.
21. Harold Butler, *International Labor Organization: Report of the Director, 1937* (Geneva, 1937), 58. On the ILO and the emergence of "social rights" in the inter-

war era, see Sandrine Kott et al., *Globalizing Social Rights: The International Labor Organization and Beyond* (London, 2013).

22. Harold Butler, *International Labor Organization. Report of the Director, 1935* (Geneva, 1935), 10.

23. On the Soviet Union as a model for rural planning, see Kiran K. Patel, "The Green Heart of Governance: Rural Europe During the Interwar Years in a Global Perspective," in *Governing the Rural in Interwar Europe*, ed. Liesbeth van der Grifft and Amalia Ribi Forclaz (New York, 2018), 5–7. On autarky in the USSR, see Michael R. Dohan, "The Economic Origins of Soviet Autarky, 1927/28-1934," *Slavic Review* 35, no. 4 (December 1976): 603–35; Paul R. Gregory and Joel Sailors, "The Soviet Union During the Great Depression: The Autarky Model," in *The World Economy and National Economies in the Interwar Slump* (New York, 2003), 191–210; Oscar Sanchez-Sibony, *Red Globalization: The Political Economy of the Soviet Cold War from Stalin to Khrushchev* (Cambridge, UK, 2014).

24. Butler, *International Labor Organization. Report of the Director, 1935,* 60.

25. Butler, *International Labor Organization. Report of the Director, 1935,* 85.

26. F. L. McDougall, *Economic Appeasement,* Geneva, August 30, 1937, 4, R440-10A-28167-28167, League of Nations, United Nations Archive, Geneva.

27. McDougall, *Economic Appeasement,* 1–2.

28. McDougall, *Economic Appeasement,* 7.

29. *Final Report of the Mixed Committee of the League of Nations on the Relation of Nutrition to Agriculture, Health and Economic Policy* (Geneva, 1937), 12.

30. *Final Report of the Mixed Committee,* 207.

31. *Final Report of the Mixed Committee,* 214.

32. *Final Report of the Mixed Committee,* 320–21.

33. *Final Report of the Mixed Committee,* 310.

34. *Final Report of the Mixed Committee,* 53.

35. Pietro Stoppani, *Mr. McDougall's Memorandum on 'Economic Appeasement,'* March 23, 1937, 1–2, R440-10A-28167-28167, League of Nations, United Nations Archive, Geneva.

36. *Letter from Stanley Bruce to Secretary General J. Avenol,* March 1, 1937, 1–2, R440-10A-28167-28167, League of Nations, United Nations Archive, Geneva.

37. O'Brien, "F.L. McDougall and the Origins of the FAO," 174.

38. United Nations Conference on Food and Agriculture: Hot Springs, Virginia, May 18–June 3, 1943. Text of the Final Act, 11.

Chapter 17

1. Richard Walther Darré, "Zu dem Artikel 'Innere Kolonisation,'" *Deutschlands Erneuerung* 10, no. 4 (April 1926): 155.

2. The party received 51 percent of the vote in Schleswig-Holstein, 48 percent in Frankfurt an der Oder, Pomerania, and Liegnitz, and 47 percent in East Prussia.

Gustavo Corni, *Hitler and the Peasants: Agrarian Policy of the Third Reich, 1930–1939*, trans. David Kerr (New York: 1990), 32.

3. Rede auf dem vierten Reichsbauerntag in Goslar am 29 November 1936, in R. Walther Darré, *Aufbruch des Bauerntums: Reichsbauerntagsreden 1933 bis 1938* (Berlin, 1942), 68, 72.

4. Gesine Gerhard, *Nazi Hunger Politics: A History of Food in the Third Reich* (Lanham, MD, 2015), 67–68.

5. Herbert Backe, Grosser Bericht Ziegenhain 1946, Nachlass Backe, N1075/3, Bundesarchiv, Koblenz.

6. Herbert Backe, *Das Ende des Liberalismus in der Wirtschaft* (Berlin, 1938), 29.

7. Backe, *Das Ende des Liberalismus*, 46

8. Blut und Boden, December 7, 1931, Memo by Max August de la Vigne von Erkmannsdorf, R2501-6608, Bundesarchiv, Berlin.

9. Klaus A. Langweit, ed., *Hitler: Reden, Schriften, Anordnungen*, vol. 5, pt. 1: Februar 1925 bis Januar 1933 (Munich, 1996), 284.

10. Johann Wilhelm Ludowici, *Das Deutsche Siedlungswerk* (Heidelberg, 1935), 26.

11. Paul Lerner, *The Consuming Temple: Jews, Department Stores, and the Consumer Revolution in Germany, 1880-1940* (Ithaca, NY, 2015), 57–58.

12. Lerner, *Consuming Temple*, 5.

13. Lerner, *Consuming Temple*, 29–33, 40–41. On the rise of department stores in interwar Europe, see also Victoria de Grazia, *Irresistible Empire: America's Advance through Twentieth-Century Europe* (Cambridge, MA, 2005), 160–70.

14. Hans Buchner, *Dämonen der Wirtschaft: Gestalten und Dunkle Gewalten aus dem Leben unsere Tage* (Munich, 1928), 144–46. See also Hans Buchner, *Warenhauspolitik und Nationalsozialismus* (Munich, 1929).

15. Hans Richard Mertel, "Die internationale Verfilzung der Warenhäuser," *Völkischer Beobachter*, December 23, 1930.

16. Lerner, *Consuming Temple*, 207–8.

17. Anhaltende Boykottierung und Diffamierung der Nahrungsmittel-Filialbetriebe, July 5, 1933, R117916, Politisches Archiv des Auswärtigen Amts, Berlin.

18. Georg Bonne, *Wie können wir Deutschlands Ernährung vom Auslande unabhängig machen?* (Dresden, 1935), 9, 6, 39, 12, 28.

19. Gert Gröning and Joachim Wolschke-Bulmahn, *Von Ackermann bis Ziegelhütte: Ein Jahrhundert Kleingartenkultur in Frankfurt am Main* (Frankfurt, 1995), 69.

20. "Das Reich gibt neue Mittel für die Kleingärtner," *Völkischer Beobachter*, July 7, 1939, 2; "Jeder vierten Familie einen Garten!," *Völkischer Beobachter*, June 20, 1939, 1.

21. Corni, *Hitler and the Peasants*, 119; Denkschrift über die Lage der landwirtschaftlichen Siedler in der Provinz Pommern, January 1933, Nachlass Backe 1094III/2, Bundesarchiv, Koblenz.

22. Evangelischer Siedlungsdienst, Zur Rücksiedlung von ostdeutschen Industriearbeitern, 17 Februar 1933, Nachlass Backe 1094III/2, Bundesarchiv, Koblenz. On

reasons for the failure of settlements, see also Elisabeth Jones, "Internal Colonization in Weimar Germany. Transnational and Local Approaches to Rural Governance in the 1920s," in *Governing the Rural in Interwar Europe*, ed. Liesbeth van der Grifft and Amalia Ribi Forclaz (New York, 2018), 24–29.

23. On the Reichsheimstättenamt, see Ulrike Haerendel, *Kommunale Wohnungspolitik im Dritten Reich: Siedlungsideologie, Kleinhausbau und "Wohnraumisierung" am Beispiel Münchens* (Munich, 1999). On the Kaiser Wilhelm Society, see Susanne Heim, Carole Sachse, and Mark Walker, eds., *The Kaiser Wilhelm Society under National Socialism* (Cambridge, UK, 2009).

24. Ferdinand Fried, *Autarkie* (Jena, 1932), 42. On Fried, see also Joshua Derman, "The Prophet of a Partitioned World: Ferdinand Fried, 'Great Spaces,' and the Dialectics of Deglobalization, 1929–1950," *Modern Intellectual History* 18, no. 3 (2021): 757–81.

25. Fried, *Autarkie*, 46, 50.

26. Ludowici, *Das deutsche Siedlungswerk*, 28–29.

27. Ludowici, *Das deutsche Siedlungswerk*, 1, 10, 18.

28. Beurteilung der Erbgesundheit. Richtlinien für Neubauern und Anligersiedler, 16 August 1940, Zeitungsdient des Reichsnährstandes, NS/5/VI, 5260, Bundesarchiv, Berlin.

29. Herbert Backe, *Agrar und Siedlungspolitik* (Berlin, 1935), 2–3, 13.

30. Ernst Knoll, *Grundsätzliches zur deutschen Wohnungs und Siedlungspolitik* (Berlin, 1939), 122, 132.

31. Letter from Paul W. Leipzig, November 22, 1938; Aufstellung des Gesamtbesitzes in Hand von Juden deutscher Staatsangehörigkeit, R3601/3158, Bundesarchiv, Berlin.

32. *Die deutsche Heimstätten-Siedlung* (Berlin, 1935), 5–6.

33. F. Lochner, Königsberg, "Die Siedlerheimstätte in Ostpreußen," *Bauen, Siedeln, Wohnen*, Jg. 18 (February 1938): 56, 63.

34. Johannes Stoye, *Die Geschlossene deutsche Volkswirtschaft: Geopolitik, Autarkie, Vierjahresplan* (Leipzig and Berlin, 1937), 1, 36.

35. Susanne Heim, *Plant Breeding and Agrarian Research in Kaiser Wilhelm Institutes, 1933-1945: Calories, Caoutchouc, Careers*, trans. Sorcha O'Hagan (New York, 2008), 8.

36. Heim, *Plant Breeding*, 27–35; Tiago Saraiva, *Fascist Pigs: Technoscientific Organisms and the History of Fascism* (Cambridge, MA, 2016), chaps. 3–4, esp. pp. 71–72, 123.

37. Heim, *Plant Breeding*, 97–101.

38. Heim, *Plant Breeding*, 101-103

39. Heim, *Plant Breeding*, 125–49.

40. Sitzung des kleinen Ministerrats am 21 Oktober 1936 12 Uhr mittags, R3601/3423, Bundesarchiv, Berlin.

41. "So sollst do wohnen!" *Der Angriff*, March 6, 1937, R113/3102, Bundesarchiv, Berlin.

42. Frau Dr. Vorwerck, Die Frau in der Siedlung, 27 October 1938, Vortrag der Sondertagung Siedlerbetreuung der Reichsarbeitstagung d. Reichsheimstättenamtes der DAF, NS/5/VI, 5260, Bundesarchiv, Berlin. On the role of women in Nazi settlement in the east, see Elizabeth Harvey, *Women in the Nazi East: Agents and Witnesses of Germanization* (New Haven, CT, 2003). On "autarkic housekeeping" in Nazi Germany, see Nancy R. Reagin, "Marktordnung and Autarkic Housekeeping: Housewives and Private Consumption Under the Four-Year Plan, 1936–1939," *German History*, 19, no. 2 (April 2001): 162–84. On autarky as it pertained to clothing, see Irena Guenther, *Nazi Chic? Fashioning Women in the Third Reich* (London, 2004), 232–42.

43. Corni, *Hitler and the Peasants*, 129, 134, 164–65.

44. Haerendel, *Kommunale Wohnungspolitik*, 146; "Vorschau auf die Wohnungsbau und Siedlungsleistung 1938," *Bauen, Siedeln, Wohnen*, Jg. 18 (June 1938): 368.

45. Diary entries, January 22, 1937, March 17, 1937, August 2, 1939, *Die Tagebücher R. Walther Darres, 1930-1945*, ed. Hanns Deetjen in 1972, NL Backe 1094I/78, Bundesarchiv, Koblenz.

46. Die Deutsche Rohstoffversorgung, August 14, 1935, R2501/6608, Bundesarchiv, Berlin.

47. Diary entry, March 2, 1936, *Die Tagebücher R. Walther Darres, 1930-1945*, NL Backe 1094I/78, Bundesarchiv, Koblenz; Gerhard, *Nazi Hunger Politics*, 80.

48. Gerhard, *Nazi Hunger Politics*, 82–86.

49. Knoll, *Grundsätzliches zur deutschen Wohnungs*, 132.

50. Weltwirtschaft oder Autarkie als Betrachtung von seiten der Landesverteidigung, June 21, 1938, R2501/6581; Deutschlands Kampf in der Weltwirtschaft, October 7, 1936, Rudolf Eicke, Volkswirtschaftlichen und statistischen Abteilung der Reichsbank, R2501/6608, Bundesarchiv, Berlin.

51. Robert Ley, "Autarkie oder Exportförderung? Der Außenhandel als Werkzeug der Wirtschafts und Sozialpolitik," Berlin, 1936, R2501/6608, Bundesarchiv, Berlin.

52. Die Reichsbeauftragten über die Rohstofflage, August 12, 1936, R2501/6608, Bundesarchiv, Berlin.

53. Reichsausschuß für volkswirtschaftliche Aufklärung, *Ernährungspolitik und Schule* (Berlin: 1938), quotations 34–35. See also Margarete Nothnagel, *Harmonische Ernährung für wenig Geld durch gesunde Kost mit der "Deutschen Ernährungsuhr"* (Dresden, 1939). For more on the links between food, blood, and soil in Nazi ideology and policy, see Alice Weinreb, *Modern Hungers: Food and Power in Twentieth-Century Germany* (Oxford, 2017), chap. 2.

54. "Spinnrad kommt wieder zu Ehren," *Die Zeit: Sudetendeutsches Tagblatt*, January 16, 1941; Friedrich Rehm, "Die Landfrau in ihrem Heim: Erneuerung der bäuerlichen Wohnkultur," *Die deutsche Landfrau*, August 2, 1936; "Weben, die Handarbeit der modernen Frau," *Völkische Frauenzeitung*, February 3, 1935; "Das Spinnrad lebt wieder auf," *Völkischer Beobachter*, February 14, 1935; D. Ohlsen, "Spinnräder surren wieder," *Der Angriff*, February 14, 1935. On links between autarky and fashion in Nazi Germany, see Irene Guenther, *Nazi Chic?*, 112–113.

55. "Handweberei zum eigenen Gebrauch," *Kreuzzeitung*, March 15, 1935.
56. See *Deutsche Hauswirtschaft. Zeitschrift der Reichsfrauenführung*, no. 6 (June 1942), 84–94; no. 9 (September 1942), 132; no. 10 (October 1942), 147.
57. R. Kaltenbrach, "Die Kleinsiedlung in der Ernährungssicherung," *Deutsche Hauswirtschaft* 19 (December 1939): 1087.
58. Wei Li, *Deutsche Pläne zur Europäischen wirtschaftlichen Neuordnung, 1939-1945* (Hamburg, 2007).
59. Jeremy Yellen, *The Greater East-Asian Co-Prosperity Sphere* (Ithaca, NY, 2019).
60. Stefan Zweig, *The World of Yesterday* (London, 1943), 145–46.
61. Wirtschafts-Pressekonferenz, 24 Juli 1940, Nachlass Darre 1075/9, Bundesarchiv, Koblenz.
62. Diary entries, October 24, 1936, September 30, 1937, January 6, 1938, *Die Tagebücher R. Walther Darres, 1930-1945*, Nachlass Backe 1094I/78, Bundesarchiv, Koblenz.
63. Herbert Backe, *Um die Nahrungsfreiheit Europas. Weltwirtschaft oder Grossraum* (Leipzig, 1942), 95, 216.
64. "Warenhaussteuer und Filialsteuer für 1933," *Völkischer Beobachter*, July 25, 1933, R2501-2421, Bundesarchiv, Berlin.
65. "Eine letzte Warnung. Keine Boykottmassnahmen gegen Warenhäuser," October 6, 1933, R8034II/6461, Bundesarchiv, Berlin.
66. "N.S.D.A.P. und Warenhaus," N.S. Parteikorrespond. February 13, 1934, R8034II/6461, Bundesarchiv, Berlin.
67. Anonymous, 21.9.1933, R2501-2421, Bundesarchiv, Berlin.
68. Lorenz Sieberg Jr., Bonn, to Wirtschaftsministerium, 16.12.1934, R3101/13587, Bundesarchiv, Berlin.
69. Letter to Herr Doktor Ley, Magdeburg, 15.2.1934, R3101-13586, Bundesarchiv, Berlin.
70. Warenhausverband in Abwehr. Referate von Bernhard, Georg Tietz, A.L. Tietz und Schocken, *Berliner Tagblatt*, November 12, 1931, R8034II/6461, Bundesarchiv, Berlin.
71. "50 Jahre Hermann Tietz," April 1932, R8034II/6461, Bundesarchiv, Berlin.
72. "Gibt es bei uns "Unterbietung?" 8.1.1934, George Manasse Collection, AR 6379, Leo Baeck Institute.
73. Sitzung im Arbeits und Wohlfahrtsministerium Dresden im Beisein des Vertreters des Wirtschaftsministerium, 10 October 1933, Arbeitsbeschaffung, Programm des Schocken-Konzerne, George Manasse Collection, AR 6379, Leo Baeck Institute.
74. Henry Max Adler, Oral History Interview, August 19, 1981, United States Holocaust Memorial, Museum, and Archive.
75. Christoph Kreutzmüller, *Final Sale in Berlin: The Destruction of Jewish Commercial Activity, 1930-1945* (New York, 2015), 106–10.
76. An die Polizei-Direktion Zwickau-Sachsen, March 27, 1934; Memorandum des

Herrn Georg Manasse niedergelegt zum Zeitpunkt seines Ausscheidens als Generaldirektor aus die Schocken-Konzern. Über wichtige Grundsätze des Geschäftspolitik des Schocken-Konzern. June 15, 1934, George Manasse Collection, AR 6379, Leo Baeck Institute.

77. Lerner, *Consuming Temple*, 201.
78. Plaidoyer Darre, Nachlass Darre 10941/1, Bundesarchiv, Koblenz.
79. Grosser Bericht Ziegenhain 1946, 17, 50, Nachlass Backe N1075/3, Bundesarchiv, Koblenz.

Conclusion

1. "A Night at the Garden," dir. Marshall Curry, 2017. Available at https://www .youtube.com/watch?v=MxxxlutsKuI.
2. Report of the Great Pro-American Mass Meeting in Behalf of Free Speech and Americanism, Wednesday, May 24, 1939, Box 489, Rosika Schwimmer Papers, New York Public Library (henceforth Schwimmer Papers).
3. Rosika Schwimmer, "Constructive World Organization Against World Chaos," radio speech March 31, 1939, WEVD, New York City, Box 479, Schwimmer Papers. This was a common view at the time, which historians have recently reassessed. Susan Pedersen, "Back to the League of Nations," *American Historical Review* 112, no. 4 (October 2007): 1091–117.
4. Lola Maverick Lloyd and Rosika Schwimmer, *Chaos, War, or a New World Order* (Chicago, 1937). On the history of visions of "World Order," see Mark Mazower, *Governing the World: The History of an Idea* (New York, 2012).
5. 21st Session of the Assembly, Geneva, April 1946 - Opening speech by the President, R5256/15/43780/40199, United Nations Archive of Geneva (UNOG). In fact, League of Nations experts participated extensively in discussions of how to rebuild the global economy after the Second World War. On economic planning for the postwar era within the league, see Patricia Clavin, *Securing the World Economy: The Reinvention of the League of Nations, 1920-1946* (Oxford, 2013), chaps. 8–9.
6. Elizabeth Borgwardt, *A New Deal for the World: America's Vision for Human Rights* (Cambridge, MA, 2005), 14–45 on the Atlantic Charter.
7. Borgwardt, *A New Deal for the World*, 3, 247.
8. League of Nations, *Economic Stability in the Post-War World: The Conditions of Prosperity After the Transition from War to Peace* (Princeton, NJ, 1945), 21; League of Nations, *The Transition from War to Peace Economy* (Princeton, NJ, 1943), 11–12. For more on the league's work during the war, see Clavin, *Securing the World Economy*, chap. 9.
9. League of Nations, *Economic Stability*, 293.
10. Jamie Martin, *The Meddlers: Sovereignty, Empire, and the Birth of Global Economic Governance* (Cambridge, MA, 2022), chap. 4. On the history of develop-

ment, see David Ekbladh, *The Great American Mission: Modernization and the Construction of an American World Order* (Princeton, NJ, 2010); Corinna Unger, *International Development: A Postwar History* (London, 2018).

11. Eric Helleiner, *Forgotten Foundations of Bretton Woods. International Development and the Making of the Postwar Order* (Ithaca, NY, 2014). See also Giles Scott-Smith and J. Simon Rofe, eds., *Global Perspectives on the Bretton Woods Conference and the Postwar World Order* (London, 2017).

12. Economic, Financial, and Transit Department, *Industrialization and Foreign Trade* (League of Nations, 1946), 5.

13. P. N. Rosenstein-Rodan, "The International Development of Economically Backward Areas," *International Affairs* 20, no. 2 (April 1944): 158.

14. Rosenstein-Rodan, "International Development of Economically Backward Areas," 159. On the role of Polish social scientists in the emergence of development economics (and the trade-off between industrialization and emigration), see Malgorzata Mazurek, *The Economics of Hereness: The Polish Origins of Global Developmentalism, 1918-1968* (forthcoming).

15. Rosenstein-Rodan, "International Development of Economically Backward Areas," 165.

16. Borgwardt, *New Deal for the World,* esp. 34–36.

17. Charter of the United Nations, accessed August 25, 2021, https://www.un.org/en/about-us/un-charter.

18. For this point, see Mark Mazower, *No Enchanted Palace: The End of Empire and the Ideological Origins of the United Nations* (Princeton, NJ, 2009).

19. On the displacement of "human rights" abroad, see Mark Phillip Bradley, *The World Reimagined: Americans and Human Rights in the Twentieth Century* (Cambridge, UK, 2016).

20. Mark Mazower, *Governing the World: The History of an Idea, 1815-Present* (New York, 2012).

21. Jawaharlal Nehru, *The Discovery of India* (1946; repr. New York, 2008), 472. On India's role at the Bretton Woods Conference, see Aditya Balasubramanian and Srinath Raghavan, "Present at the Creation: India, the Global Economy, and the Bretton Woods Conference," *Journal of World History* 28, no. 1 (2018): 65–94.

22. On Bandung, see Christopher J. Lee, ed., *Making a World After Empire: The Bandung Moment and Its Political Afterlives* (Athens, OH, 2019).

23. Homer Alexander Jack, *Bandung: An-on-the-Spot Description of the Asian-African Conference, Bandung, Indonesia, April, 1955* (Chicago, 1955), 18.

24. Cited in Quinn Slobodian, *Globalists: The End of Empire and the Birth of Neoliberalism* (Cambridge, MA, 2018), 111.

25. On gender, race, and the postwar welfare state in Britain, see Susan Pedersen, *Family, Dependence, and the Origins of the Welfare State: Britain and France, 1914-45* (Cambridge, UK, 1995); Denise Noble, "Decolonizing Britain and Domesticating Women: Race, Gender, and Women's Work in Post-1945 British Decolonial and

Metropolitan Liberal Reform Discourses," *Meridians: Feminism, Race, Transnationalism* 13, no. 1 (2015), 53–77.

26. William Beveridge, *Social Insurance and Allied Services* (London, 1942), 50–51.
27. Martin, *The Meddlers*, chap. 6.
28. Helleiner, *Forgotten Foundations*, 259–60.
29. On the conflict among neoliberals about European integration, see Slobodian, *Globalists*, chap. 6.
30. United Nations Information Organization, *Helping the People to Help Themselves: UNRRA. The Story of the United Nations Relief and Rehabilitation Administration* (London, 1944), 11.
31. See, among others, G. Daniel Cohen, *In War's Wake: Europe's Displaced Persons in the Postwar Order* (New York, 2012); Atina Grossman, *Jews, Germans, and Allies: Close Encounters in Occupied Europe* (Princeton, NJ, 2007); Pamela Ballinger, *The World Refugees Made: Decolonization and the Foundation of Postwar Italy* (Ithaca, NY, 2020); Anna Holian, *Between National Socialism and Soviet Communism: Displaced Persons in Postwar Germany* (Ann Arbor, MI, 2011); Peter Gattrell, *The Unsettling of Europe: How Migration Remade a Continent* (New York, 2019).
32. Adam Goodman, *The Deportation Machine: America's Long History of Expelling Immigrants* (Princeton, NJ, 2020).
33. Tara Zahra, *The Lost Children: Reconstructing Europe's Families After World War II* (Cambridge, MA, 2011), 152.
34. J. Donald Kingsley, *Migration from Europe: A Report of Experience* (Geneva, 1951), v, 2; "Cost of Resettling D.P.'s Seen as Low," *New York Times*, April 13, 1951, 6.
35. Constitution of the International Organization for Migration, accessed March 30, 2022, https://www.iom.int/constitution.
36. On the relationship between decolonization, migration, and European integration, see, among others, Todd Shepard, *The Invention of Decolonization: The Algerian War and the Remaking of France* (Ithaca, NY, 2006); Naomi Davidson, *Only Muslim: Embodying Islam in Twentieth Century France* (Ithaca, NY, 2012); Udi Greenberg, "Protestants, Decolonization, and European Integration, 1885–1961," *Journal of Modern History* 89, no. 2 (June 2017): 314–54; Pamela Ballinger, *The World Refugees Made: Decolonization and the Foundation of Postwar Italy* (Ithaca, NY, 2020); Jordanna Bailkin, *The Afterlife of Empire* (Berkeley, 2012).
37. On guest workers, see especially Rita Chin, *The Guest Workers Question in Postwar Germany* (New York, 2009); Lauren Stokes, *Fear of the Family: Guest Workers and Family Migration in the Federal Republic of Germany* (Oxford, 2022).
38. Susan L. Carruthers, *Cold War Captives: Imprisonment, Escape, and Brainwashing* (Berkeley, 2009); Tara Zahra, *The Great Departure: Mass Migration from Eastern Europe and the Making of the Free World* (New York, 2016).
39. Charter of Economic Rights and Duties of States, accessed August 25, 2021, https://www.aaas.org/sites/default/files/SRHRL/PDF/IHRDArticle15/Charter_of_Economic_Rights_and_Duties_of_States_Eng.pdf.

40. See, for example, Tehila Sasson, "Milking the Third World: Humanitarianism, Capitalism, and the Moral Economy of the Nestlé Boycott," *American Historical Review* 121, no. 4 (October 2016): 1196–224.

Epilogue

1. "Bata Is Not Indian. So How Did This Brand Become as 'Desi' as One Can Get?" Accessed March 30, 2022, https://www.thebetterindia.com/244022/bata-shoe -history-indian-foreign-which-country-organisation-indian-ceo-international -brand-batanagar-kolkata-ros174/.

2. Ralph Borsodi, *The Challenge of Asia: A Study of Conflicting Ideas and Ideals* (Melbourne, FL, 1956), 14–15.

3. William Tucker, "Out in Suburbia, the Frontier Spirit Isn't What It Was," *New York Times*, March 6, 1977, 311; Steven Conn, *Americans Against the City: Anti-Urbanism in the Twentieth Century* (Oxford, 2014), 90–92.

4. Jarseen Mayal Khanna, "Why All Eyes in the Fashion Industry Are Currently on Khadi," *Vogue*, April 11, 2019, https://www.vogue.in/content/vogue-investigates -how-khadi-is-making-waves-in-indias-fashion-industry.

INDEX

Page numbers in *italics* indicate photographs or illustrations; page numbers followed by *m* indicate maps.

AGAINST THE WORLD

Tara Zahra

READING GROUP GUIDE

AGAINST THE WORLD
Tara Zahra

DISCUSSION QUESTIONS

1. In *Against the World*, how does Tara Zahra describe the ideal of globalism between the war years? When the terms "globalism" and "globalist" are used today, do you feel they are describing the same concept? Why or why not? If the terms describe a different ideal, what do they describe today?

2. Zahra introduces the reader to the Peace Ship, a collection of self-appointed civilian ambassadors—including Henry Ford and Rosika Schwimmer—who hoped to bring about the end of World War I. The mission failed spectacularly. Was the Peace Ship's mission doomed from the start? Why or why not?

3. From 1918 to 1919, the flu pandemic ravaged the globe, ultimately killing millions. How did the pandemic shape both globalism and anti-globalism? Despite its devastating scope, the flu pandemic is often forgotten today. Textbooks and fictional depictions of the time give far more space to World War I. Why do you think the flu pandemic has largely faded from the public memory?

4. Many of the examples of anti-globalism and nationalism in *Against the World* come from autocratic, right-wing, sometimes even literally fascist countries, such as pre–World War II Germany. Were you surprised to see Gandhi, an iconic figure of peaceful protest, appear in the role call of nationalistic and anti-globalist leaders? In what way did Gandhi's campaign of nonviolent resistance against British rule fit the descriptions of nationalism and anti-globalism? Can you think of other peaceful, left-leaning example of nationalism or anti-globalism, either in Zahra's history or from other sources?

5. One of the odder episodes Zahra discusses is the quixotic occupation of the city of Fiume by poet and eccentric protofascist Gabriele D'Annunzio. One of the details in D'Annunzio's story, as well as several other stories of rise of extreme nationalism, is the fact that many people who were middle-of-the-road, respectable citizens—many of them with globalist aims—supported these movements. Why would people in the political center throw in their lot with nationalist anti-globalists? Is this a dynamic that is still common today?

6. Henry Ford, the industrialist and creator of the Model T, remains one of the most famous, if controversial, American historical figures to this day. In the chapter "The Air Is Our Ocean," Zahra introduces the Czech shoe tycoon Tomáš Bat'a. Compare and contrast Ford's relationship to globalism and anti-globalism with that of Bat'a. Which traits did this these two titans of industry share? In which ways did these men drastically differ?

7. Zahra explains how a movement toward self-sufficient local food production, back-to-the-land programs, and the development of intentional settlement communities were reactions to the perceived failures of globalism. Such ideas still circulate our culture today. How do the various ideas and movements Zahra describes differ from the modern concepts? What common threads run through both eras?

8. Though rarely the specific focus of Zahra's book, technological innovation is woven throughout the conflict between globalism and anti-globalism. The explosion of car culture and innovations in aviation transformed transportation. Developments in production reshaped work and factory floors. Even design experiments in living spaces played into globalist and anti-globalists ideas. How does technology shape the historical narrative Zahra tells? What new technologies fuel today's globalist and anti-globalist tendencies?

9. It is common to say that America is a "nation of immigrants," but Zahra details the interwar era's aggressively restrictive immigration

policies. Which concerns and influences drove the development of the era's immigration policies? How do those policies and the conflicts around them reflect our own contentious political conflicts regarding immigration?

10. Zahra introduces the reader to a massive cast of historical figures, some famous and some obscure. Were there any figures you specifically admired or sympathized with? Why did this person appeal to you? Were there any figures—admirable or not—who particularly brought this era to life for you? What was it about these people that especially represented the interwar years for you?

Meghan Kenny	*The Driest Season*
Nicole Krauss	*The History of Love*
Don Lee	*The Collective*
Amy Liptrot	*The Outrun: A Memoir*
Donna M. Lucey	*Sargent's Women*
Bernard MacLaverty	*Midwinter Break*
Maaza Mengiste	*Beneath the Lion's Gaze*
Claire Messud	*The Burning Girl*
	When the World Was Steady
Liz Moore	*Heft*
	The Unseen World
Neel Mukherjee	*The Lives of Others*
	A State of Freedom
Janice P. Nimura	*Daughters of the Samurai*
Rachel Pearson	*No Apparent Distress*
Richard Powers	*Orfeo*
Kirstin Valdez Quade	*Night at the Fiestas*
Jean Rhys	*Wide Sargasso Sea*
Mary Roach	*Packing for Mars*
Somini Sengupta	*The End of Karma*
Akhil Sharma	*Family Life*
	A Life of Adventure and Delight
Joan Silber	*Fools*
Johanna Skibsrud	*Quartet for the End of Time*
Mark Slouka	*Brewster*
Kate Southwood	*Evensong*
Manil Suri	*The City of Devi*
	The Age of Shiva
Madeleine Thien	*Do Not Say We Have Nothing*
	Dogs at the Perimeter
Vu Tran	*Dragonfish*
Rose Tremain	*The American Lover*
	The Gustav Sonata
Brady Udall	*The Lonely Polygamist*
Brad Watson	*Miss Jane*
Constance Fenimore Woolson	*Miss Grief and Other Stories*

Available only on the Norton website